SLAVERY'S EXILES

RY'S
EXILES

THE STORY OF THE AMERICAN MAROONS

Sylviane A. Diouf

NEW YORK UNIVERSITY PRESS

New York and London

NEW YORK UNIVERSITY PRESS
New York and London
www.nyupress.org

Book designed and typeset by Charles B. Hames

References to Internet websites (URLs) were accurate at the time of writing.
Neither the author nor New York University Press is responsible for URLs that
may have expired or changed since the manuscript was prepared.

Library of Congress Cataloging-in-Publication Data
Diouf, Sylviane A. (Sylviane Anna), 1952–
Slavery's exiles : the story of the American Maroons / Sylviane A. Diouf.
pages cm   Includes bibliographical references and index.
ISBN 978-0-8147-2437-8 (hardback)
1. Maroons—Southern States—History.
2. Fugitive slaves—Southern States—History.
3. Southern States—Race relations—History.   I. Title.
E450.D56   2014
305.800975—dc23   2013029821

New York University Press books are printed on acid-free paper, and their binding materials are
chosen for strength and durability. We strive to use environmentally responsible suppliers
and materials to the greatest extent possible in publishing our books.

Manufactured in the United States of America

10 9 8 7 6 5 4 3 2 1

Also available as an ebook

To Sény and Maya

CONTENTS

The photographs appear as a group following page 185.

ACKNOWLEDGMENTS

Everything starts with research and the people I am particularly indebted to for the existence of this book are the numerous archivists who have contributed their knowledge of the materials I was looking for and those I did not know existed.

I got wonderful assistance at the North Carolina State Archives from a great, dedicated staff. My sincere thanks go in particular to Christopher Meekins who enthusiastically opened up a whole treasure trove of documents and even looked for others on his lunch break. I am also very grateful to Vann Evans for his gracious and generous help. The archivists at the Library of Virginia, the South Carolina Department of Archives and History, the Georgia Historical Society, the Georgia Department of Archives and History, the Hargrett Library at the University of Georgia, and the New Orleans Public Library have been splendid.

Many thanks go to Diana Lachatanere at the Schomburg Center for Research in Black Culture, The New York Public Library; James D. Wilson, Jr., at the Center for Louisiana Studies of the University of Louisiana at Lafayette; and Melissa Stein at the Louisiana State Museum.

Debbie Gershenowitz, then senior editor at NYU Press, was an enthusiastic supporter from the start and I am so immensely grateful to her for her wonderful work on this book. My deepest appreciation goes to my editor, Clara Platter, who skillfully made this project a reality.

As always, my family has been actively supportive. My mother, Martine, Alain, and Mariam always my cheerleaders: they listened to me with patience, understanding, and encouraged me every step of the way. Maya, smart well beyond her years, has been pure joy. Last on this page, but always first on my mind, Sény has been my accomplice, my supporter-in-chief, and my confidante; always caring and thoughtful. He has enriched my life in so many ways; I am proud of his accomplishments and prouder yet of being his mother.

INTRODUCTION

"Lord, Lord! Yes indeed, plenty of slaves uster run away. Why dem woods was full o' 'em chile," recalled Arthur Greene of Virginia.[1] He knew that some stayed there for a few days only but he also knew that his friend Pattin and his family had lived in the woods for fifteen years until "Lee's surrender." Like them, over more than two centuries men, women, and children made the Southern wilderness their home. They hid in the mountains of Virginia and the low swamps of South Carolina; they stayed in the neighborhood or paddled their way to secluded places; they buried themselves underground or erected "snug little habitations."[2] They were Africans two days off the slave ship and people who intimately knew the geographic and social environment, its constraints, and the way to navigate it. They were not "truants" who had absconded for a short while, to rest, avoid a beating or recover from one, take a break, or visit relatives and friends on neighboring plantations. They were not runaways making their way through the wilds to reach a Southern city or a free state or to cross international borders to find freedom under a foreign power. The people whose stories are the subject of this book went to the Southern woods to *stay*.

Although it is based on scores of cases, *Slavery's Exiles* neither attempts to relate all documented instances of marronage nor is it about all maroons. The individuals and groups studied here shared three key characteristics: they settled in the wilderness, lived there in secret, and were not under any form of direct control by outsiders.[3] These criteria, which seem to encompass all maroons, do not. The well-known maroons of Spanish Florida, for example, are absent from these pages because they were officially recognized as free—even if in a limited way—by Spain who offered sanctuary to runaways from the British colonies and later the United States. People who settled among American Indians in their territories are not covered either for the same reason. They lived in villages and towns and not the wilderness, where their hosts openly accepted them and controlled them to various degrees.

This book also excludes individuals and communities that some scholars define as maroons, based on a broad definition of marronage as the act of fleeing enslavement. In this vein historian Steven Hahn notes that black enclaves in the North, which attracted new runaways and gave rise to autonomous leadership, social structures, institutions, and cultural practices are "historically specific variants of the broad phenomenon of maroons."[4] But by lumping together divergent experiences, we run the risk of flattening each group's specificities and of obscuring the maroon experience (as defined here) in favor of better-known forms of resistance. Moreover, this approach hides key differences between maroons and runaways who lived in black enclaves. The latter refused enslavement but not the larger society, which they wanted to be a part of even if they knew it could only be at its periphery. Although they organized to challenge them, runaways and free blacks continued to live under the discriminatory laws of white society, still subservient and controlled.

The experience of the people hidden in the wilds—the maroons examined in this book—could not have been more different. Autonomy was at the heart of their project and exile the means to realize it. The need for foolproof concealment, the exploitation of their natural environment, and their stealth raids on farms and plantations were at the very core of their lives. Secrecy and the particular ecology of their refuges forced them to devise specific ways to occupy the land and to hide within it. Negotiating and manipulating their landscape dictated the types of dwellings they could erect, when they could walk outside, or light a fire. They determined if, where, and how much land they could cultivate, what kinds of animals they could keep, how they got weapons and clothes, and what types of interaction they could have with the world they had left behind.

While numerous books have been devoted to the maroons of South and Central America and the Caribbean, none focus on the Thirteen Colonies and the United States. The first historian to seriously tackle the issue was Herbert Aptheker who published the classic article, "Maroons within the Present Limits of the United States" in 1939, and "Additional Data on American Maroons"—which relates to one case—in 1947.[5] Aptheker's research was groundbreaking because it established the existence of maroons, but it did not describe or analyze their experience.

At the other end of the spectrum, some post-Aptheker historians have denied the reality of marronage in the United States. For Michael Mullin, "The absence of a maroon dimension in the South, a serious loss for Southern slaves, is symbolized by the emphasis in studies of resistance on such individuals as Harriet Tubman."[6] Writing about the Southern maroons—with the exception of those in Florida, whom he recognized as genuine—Eugene Genovese affirmed, they "typically huddled in small units and may be called 'maroons' only as a courtesy." Many, he claimed, "degenerated into wild desperadoes who preyed on anyone, black, white or red, in their path." Southerners, who reserved the terminology maroons for the people of Jamaica and Suriname, were precursors in the denial of the American maroons' existence. They called the people in their midst outliers, or simply and much more often, runaways and banditti; and in the same spirit never called maroon settlements by their names or gave them any, thus negating their very existence.[7]

In the 1990s Gilbert C. Din and Gwendolyn Midlo Hall each devoted one chapter in works on larger issues to the community led by St. Malo in 1780s Louisiana, and John Hope Franklin and Loren Schweninger covered the maroon dimension in *Runaway Slaves: Rebels on the Plantation* in a short section titled "Collective Resistance." More recently, Timothy Lockley has compiled a well-researched sourcebook of records and newspaper articles on the maroons of South Carolina, and American maroons have also appeared in swamp, environmental, and literary studies that focus on the interaction of wilderness dwellers and nature, and connections between the representation of swamps and maroons in literature. Alvin O. Thompson's *Flight to Freedom: African Runaways and Maroons in the Americas* is a review, synthesis, and analysis of recent works "on the main Maroon states and colonies," which explains why it centers on Brazil, Jamaica, and Suriname and why the United States appear only very briefly.[8]

The absence of large colonies and the lack of "maroon wars," both thought of as characteristics of marronage, may explain why American maroons have for the most part remained under the radar. It is telling that only those of Florida, who lived in large communities and fought in the Seminole Wars, have generated attention and come to mind whenever one mentions maroons in the United States.[9] The overall invisibility of the American maroons thus seems to be due to restrictive definitions of marronage that do not correspond to the reality, whether in North America or in the rest of the hemisphere.

BEYOND PETIT AND GRAND

For the past few decades, when and wherever marronage has been studied, it has generally fallen into two neat categories: petit and grand. Gabriel Debien created and popularized these concepts in his 1966 article, "Le marronage aux Antilles françaises au XVIIIe siècle."[10] "Planters distinguished two types of marronage," he asserted, "Grand marronage was, in the true sense, flight from the plantation with no intention of ever returning," while absences of a few days were called petit marronage. Debien's categories have been tweaked over the years. To grand marronage have been appended notions of guerilla activity, high numbers, and long distance and the terminology has become synonymous with large, long-lived, warring communities in the Caribbean and South America despite the fact that, as anthropologist and historian Richard Price has remarked, "Known variously as palenques, quilombos, mocambos, cumbes, ladeiras, or mambises, these new societies ranged from tiny bands that survived less than a year to powerful states encompassing thousands of members and surviving for generations or even centuries."[11] Alvin Thompson notes that since most slaves escaped individually and collective flight was rare, it is perhaps more useful to speak of individual and collective marronage in order to recognize the lonely deserters.[12]

The study of marronage in the United States has led me to reconsider the various definitions and classifications used so far, and to develop a more expansive vision to better reflect what happened on the ground. It is clear that neither numbers, distance, longevity, nor guerilla-type activities are the most significant factors that define marronage, yet these criteria are often applied collectively or singularly as researchers see fit. Such practices prevent one from noticing, let alone understanding, the experiences of a large number of maroons: those who lived, individually and collectively, not far away but on the periphery of farms, plantations, and cities. Contemporary documents refer to these people as runaways or outliers, but neither term takes their specificity into account. Some of the men and women who lived behind the plantations were not technically "runaways" because they settled right where they were or went back to their homeplace, still on owners' or former owners' property. Their particular experience needs to be described by a new terminology. I call them "borderland maroons." As is manifest here, borderlands is taken in its most basic sense: it means the wild land that bordered the farms and plantations and the cities and towns.

The other terminology used in this book is "hinterland maroons," which refers mostly to communities—whatever their size—that settled in areas further away than the borderlands. Their main characteristic was that they were secluded and hard to reach, not primarily because of distance but because of the difficulty of the terrain. Thus, within the larger definition of the maroons who are the focus of this study—using wilderness, secrecy, and self-determination as parameters—geography helps bring to light the whole range of maroon life that evolved in what I call the "maroon landscape."

THE MAROON LANDSCAPE

Maroons are commonly imagined as occupying small perimeters deeply hidden in swamps and woods, and as detached from the surrounding slave territory as possible. But marronage is better apprehended, explained, and understood as being anchored in and making use of interconnected areas within the larger landscape. Only when viewed from that geographical perspective can its true scope and importance be uncovered.

When applied to the study of slavery, geography has been an enlightening device that has revealed the existence of a slavery landscape, slave landscape, plantations landscape, and swamp landscape.[13] The various studies geography has inspired have offered new ways of understanding the world of the men and women whose lives were constrained by it and whose work transformed it. They have also brought to light the manner in which they appropriated the land, creating in it their own spaces of culture and resistance. But absent from this geography, although it was well trodden and of singular importance in resistance, is the "maroon landscape" that simultaneously touched on others, overlapped with some, and was to some degree separated from all the others.

Studies have shown that while there were variations due to different owners' wealth, as well as the terrain and type of crops grown, the general landscape of the plantations was made up of three main sections. The most tightly controlled consisted of the so-called Big House, built on high and dry ground, close to the river landing or the main road. Adjacent were its dependences: the kitchen, dairy, carriage house, stable, smokehouse, laundry, and the domestics' quarters. It was a world of stringent social and racial boundaries, under lock and key, where everything and everybody had to be in their assigned place. Below and behind, as an overt symbol of their supposed inferiority and expected submission, lay the sphere of the enslaved, the "quarters": the cabins, the family gardens, hog pens and chicken coops, when allowed, and on larger estates, the mess hall and the "hospital." Cabins were usually placed in neat rows along a street—they were occasionally scattered in clusters in the fields on very large estates—an imposed arrangement that reflected a European sense of control and order.[14] Their close proximity one to the other was not conducive to concealment, not even to privacy. Rundown and cramped, the quarters were the centers of African and African American life, the places where culture was maintained and created, where knowledge, hope, love, and despair were shared. They were of course completely open to overseers, planters, patrollers, and militia who could—and by law had to—search them at will.

Beyond was the work ground: the blacksmith and the carpenter shops, the mule barn, the cow house, the fields, and the pastures. On large holdings, quarters and work areas could be located far from the Main House. A 1742 map of John Carter's *Shirley* plantation in Virginia shows that the distance between these two sections was about a mile. On the sugar estate *Laura* in Louisiana, the last of sixty-nine cabins stood four miles from the mansion. As anthropologist John M. Vlach has observed, enslaved men and women "were under control but they were not totally coerced by that control because, while they were being held down, they were also being held out and away from the center of authority."[15]

Behind the Big House, the cabins and the fields were woods, bayous, marshes, swamps, pocosins (palustrine wetlands), and creeks, some of which belonged to the farms and plantations; land still undeveloped that provided game, firewood, and timber and that could be cleared, dried, and exploited. To planters and overseers, these marginal lands were untamed, out of control, savage, dark, and mysterious, just like the "negroes and other slaves," whom the preamble of the 1712 South Carolina slave code described as having "barbarous, wild, savage natures."[16] It is, for example, in one of these areas that a group of men dubbed "daring banditti" had established their "*sculking [sic] quarters*." Two had been seen in the summer of 1808 and hotly pursued, but they had made their escape "into a thick and almost impenetrable underwood." It may seem that they lived deep in the forest, but their camp was located between "Rich Will's mansion house, and Mr. Strider's mill" near Leetown, West Virginia.[17]

To the men and women in the quarters, the borderlands were concurrently wild and social. At night and on Sundays, or whenever they had finished their daily assignments, men could exert their talents as hunters of raccoons, opossums, squirrels, birds, ducks, alligators, and rabbits. With their traps, snares, fire, wooden boxes, blowguns, and occasionally dogs, some became providers for their families of perhaps as much as half the meat they consumed.[18]

From the shore, or the dugout canoes they made with the tree trunks they felled in the backwoods, families gathered oysters, turtles, terrapins, and crabs, and fished with poles, nets, weirs, and traps.[19] Depending on farmers' and planters' acquiescence, they kept pigs, sheep, and occasionally cattle there and they could also have their own gardens. In Georgia, Charles Ball worked in a plot a mile and a half away from the quarters.[20] In the borderlands, men and women gathered the herbs, barks, and roots that formed the basis of their medicinal remedies. They collected black moss to fill mattresses, and sea grass and bark to make baskets for their own use and for sale. Some ventured quite far, like Ball, who had "become well acquainted with the woods and swamps for several miles round [his] plantation."[21] The secret paths men used to circulate without a pass, as they illicitly visited potential mates or their wives and children, crisscrossed the borderlands up or down to neighbors' plantations. Natural clearings were gathering places to pray and listen to liberating sermons, or barbecue hogs and cows. Borderlands were spaces of freedom that provided what enslaved people were denied elsewhere: autonomy, mobility, enterprise, a sense of physical security, freedom from scrutiny, control over their time and movement, and access to varied foods. As historian S. Max Edelson stresses, "Planters tried to impose a hard line of separation between plantations and wilderness, but slaves opened and inhabited the spaces in between."[22]

It was behind the farms and plantations that people recuperated after a beating or escaped the most debilitating cadences of the crop cycles. But it was also where others settled, determined to stay. The maroons inhabited the fluid landscape of the borderlands that shifted with the tides and was remodeled by the floods and the droughts, and the clearing and drying of lands for cultivation. The men and women who made it their home can be called "borderland maroons." They stood at the intersection of three worlds. One was their refuge, another the white-controlled territory of the fields, the Big House outbuildings, and sometimes the Big House itself. The third was the physical and social terrain carved out by the enslaved community, from the quarters to the neighboring plantations and farms. To be successful, maroons needed to build and maintain a symbiotic relation with these three geographical and social nodes. Hidden during the day, they cautiously appropriated the plantation grounds at night, walking from the borderlands to the quarters; and up to the dairy, the smokehouse and the kitchen on whose supplies they largely depended for survival. They intimately knew, and night after night, year after year traversed the entire map that they transformed into a space of interdependence, networks, and exchange.

* * *

With time, cities, farms, and plantations superimposed their ever-increasing geography of cleared grounds and fields upon part of the Southern land. As South Carolina Lt. Governor William Bull remarked in 1770, many large swamps that offered "inaccessible shelter for deserting slaves and wild beasts" had been drained and planted with rice.[23] Yet this manmade environment was still surrounded by dense forests and/or wetlands and the sight of vast swathes of wild land was often surprising to Northerners. One traveler describing the region in the 1850s wrote, "it abounds with interminable swamps, impenetrable cane brakes, and inaccessible everglades. The safe and secure hiding place, for Indians, run away slaves; . . . there is a most luxurious growth of canes, shrubs, vines, creepers, briars . . . forming a dense brake or jungle."[24] Lewis W. Paine, a white man who spent six years in jail for trying to help a maroon escape from Georgia, noted that maroons often stayed in the woods "for years" thanks to the natural cover offered by the thick vegetation. "There are large tracts of land," he wrote, "covered with heavy timber, containing not only deep and almost impenetrable swamps, but caves, holes, shelving rocks and banks. In these they secrete themselves during the daytime, venturing abroad only by night."[25]

Past the borderlands, further away from the seat of white power, maroon communities, sometimes of several dozen individuals, settled in the secluded zones of the hinterland. They chose spaces whose topography offered good cover, vantage points for sentries, closeness to a source of clean water, and adequate soil to grow crops. Not only did these places have to be hard to reach, but they also had to provide easy access to the plantations and towns where some items continued to be traded or stolen. Therefore, seclusion, not distance, was in most cases the determining factor in the establishment of a settlement in the hinterland.

Borderlands and hinterlands formed the "maroon landscape," a vast area whose several parts were connected by secret paths, discreet trails, and waterways navigated under cover of night and whose outer, intangible limits reached, dangerously, into the plantations and cities. Situated miles apart, borderlands and hinterlands were not exclusive. Some maroons settled in the borderlands and did not venture elsewhere; but others migrated to the hinterland, and then returned to the borderlands. Hinterland maroons sometimes moved to the borderlands before going back to their secluded settlements. These maroon migrations were complex, especially for large groups. At the point of departure, the migrants had to collect enough food for the journey and the days ahead. They had to establish a safe itinerary that would take them through the woods, and sometimes across rivers and creeks. Their travel had to be done at night and they had to find secure spots where a dozen or more people could safely rest during the day. At the point of destination, they needed to locate a space with adequate hunting and gathering prospects, and easy access to farms and plantations; and they had to build a new network of complicity. Each relocation, whether at the borderlands or in the hinterland, was a jump into the unknown. Some maroon groups succeeded in establishing camps in several counties, not a small achievement.

The maroon landscape as a whole encompassed the slaves' landscape, what historian Rhys Isaac has termed their "alternative territorial system" comprised of personal gardens, paths, trails, meeting spots, granaries, and storehouses clandestinely "visited."[26] Maroons used these trails, searched the same outbuildings for food and supplies, and went up to the quarters to get their share of their relatives' vegetables. But whereas their landscape covered the whole map of slave territory—official and secret—parts of the maroons' own land—especially the hinterland—remained unknown to most people on the plantations. Africans added another dimension to this secret landscape. As some attempted to return to their homelands, they embarked on clandestine journeys through the wilds in order to get to the ultimate place of autonomy, outside white control and power. The most remote border of the maroon landscape was Africa.

The maroons' landscape was a place of exile whose settlers sought not only freedom but also self-determination. It was a dynamic site of empowerment, migrations, encounters, communication, exchange, solidarity, resistance, and entangled stories. It was also, of course, a contested terrain that slaveholders, overseers, drivers, slave hunters, dogs, militias, and patrollers strove to control and frequently invaded. Still, it was a space of movement, independence, and reinvention where new types of lives were created and evolved; where networks were built and solidified, and where solidarity expressed itself in concrete ways that rendered the maroons' alternative way of life possible.

METHODOLOGY AND SOURCES

This social history of the maroons has a wide span; it focuses on Virginia, the Carolinas, Georgia, and Louisiana, with occasional forays into other colonies and states. This regional approach can vividly retrace the maroons' experience because it conforms to the reality on the ground: maroons moved around the South; the maroon landscape was not contained by county, colony, state, and international lines and borders. On the contrary, maroons used them to their advantage, crossing and recrossing them as needed. This very "appropriation" of various spaces was an intrinsic part of their experience.

Slavery's Exiles also has a long temporal scope—the entire slavery period—and is organized thematically rather than chronologically because its focus is on the maroons' individual and communal experience. Their world is at the center and the rest of Southern society—black and white—at its periphery. Viewed from that perspective, outside events were not overwhelmingly significant because the inescapable reality that superseded everything else and made many external factors almost inconsequential was that the maroons' experience rested on their remaining invisible no matter what the circumstances were. This was true in the 1600s, continued to be true during the Revolutionary War and remained so in 1862. It was the case in Georgia as it was in Virginia. The eighteenth-century laws that governed runaways and maroons were essentially current in the 1800s. The punishments the maroons risked were also consistent. Although extreme sentences like dismemberment were no longer practised by the nineteenth century, the most common—severe whippings, sale, outlawry, and death if not compliant when captured—hung over the heads of all maroons, whether they lived in 1772 Virginia or 1856 North Carolina. Variations in time and space are noted if relevant but, as will become clear, the diversity of circumstances did not supersede the basic consistency of the larger experience.

While secrecy surrounded their lives, the experiences of the maroons are far from being unknowable, even if they have not been as well documented, in firsthand accounts, as those of the runaways who settled in the North and Canada and gave oral and written accounts of their adventures to promote abolitionism. For the maroons, the alternative to bondage was a clandestine life outside white-controlled space and abolitionists had no use for them, except to paint them as lost souls living among and like wild beasts, so as to underscore the cruelty of slavery. Still, maroons could have shared their stories after Emancipation; but as was true for the majority of runaways—those who remained in the South—they lacked the high drama of the escape to the North. There was little sensationalism to be found in the maroons' daily lives, and their narrative of autonomous survival without benevolent white involvement would likely have had little mass appeal.

To complicate matters, nothing in the United States approaches the kind of resources on maroons available for some countries. There were no Captain Stedman or Moravian missionaries to the Southern maroons as in Suriname.[27] There are no twenty-eight slave hunters' diaries to be explored, as in Cuba. No maps of settlements are to be found, as they have been for some communities in Brazil, Suriname, Hispaniola, or Cuba.[28] Moreover, descendants of maroons still live in some of the communities their ancestors founded in Brazil, Jamaica, Colombia, Suriname, or French Guiana, for instance, where oral history, memories, myths, religious practices, languages, crafts, material culture, and farming techniques have been passed on over several centuries and are still alive today. No such rich reservoir of information exists in the South, where most settlements disappeared within a few years or even less.

That being said, a variety of primary sources inform this study. For the seventeenth century, most of them consist of legal documents such as Acts passed by the legislatures and court minutes. Although they do not address the maroon experience, they provide, in filigree, valuable evidence about the profile of the maroons, where they established themselves, and what activities they engaged in. For the eighteenth and nineteenth centuries, white society's perspective can be found in petitions, letters, county books, parish records, official correspondence, travelers' accounts, and plantation records. An abundance of runaway slave advertisements and jail notices map maroon geography, detail individual stories, and go to the heart of some of the very reasons for their existence. Newspapers also related their activities, the killings of white men who tracked them down, the destruction of settlements, and the capture of individuals and groups.

Fortunately, a number of other sources help reconstruct the maroons' stories in their own voices and the voices of their relatives and friends. Trial records are an important source of first-person accounts. To be sure, any such document must be handled with caution as defendants and prosecutors can distort, lie, and minimize or overstate facts and claims. The threat of and actual use of torture, sometimes bluntly acknowledged, must add a layer of circumspection to the person's account. But valuable information can be gathered by comparing testimonies and paying attention to details that were not central to the trials. That people planted rice, fished, or pounded China-smilax (a bushy plant with small fruit) did not matter to the prosecution, but these bits of evidence illuminate the maroons' daily life.

Memoirs and autobiographies of former runaways and freedpeople are a surprisingly rich source of information. Some lived in the woods and swamps for extended periods of time and when unable to continue, decided to migrate North; while others marooned as they waited for an opportunity to leave the South. They and others had relatives or friends who settled in the wilds and relayed what they knew of their particular experience.

Additionally, in the 1930s the Works Progress Administration (WPA) interviewed over two thousand formerly enslaved men and women, and these records reveal a wealth of details about numerous aspects of the maroons' lives, how their community perceived them, and how kin and friends supported them. Numerous interviews offer unique insights into their experience—from building a shelter to getting food—and provide invaluable information about the support they enjoyed on the plantations, what they looked like when they emerged from the woods, how they were treated when captured, and other details.

* * *

Who the maroons were, what led them to choose this way of life over alternatives, what forms of marronage they created and how they differed from one another, what their individual and collective lives were like, how they organized themselves to survive, and how their particular story fits into the larger narrative of slave resistance are questions that this study seeks to answer. To uncover, re-create, and analyze the world of slavery's exiles, this book is built around one chronological and subsequent thematic chapters.

Chapter 1 looks chronologically and geographically at marronage in Southern history; its development, the legal measures taken to try to prevent it, and the efforts launched to capture or kill individuals and destroy their communities.

Studies throughout the Americas show that Africans ran away disproportionately and were also represented in maroon communities in excess of their percentage in the larger population.[29] Chapter 2 examines the characteristics of African marronage and the specific experience of newly arrived Africans.

The chapters that follow focus on the experience of American-born maroons.

Chapter 3 explores the main reason why some people chose to settle in the borderlands and how they related to the slave world that stretched beyond their "doorsteps." A detailed description and analysis of the various aspects of their lives is the subject of chapter 4.

Past the borderlands, hinterland maroon communities were born, lived, and disappeared. Chapter 5 investigates the ways they formed and tried to ensure their survival through diversified economic and protective strategies. Chapter 6 delves into the complexity and fluidity of the maroon experience. It follows an eighteenth-century Louisiana community that straddled the whole breadth of the maroon landscape as it migrated and lived alternatively on the borderlands and in the hinterland. Chapter 7 explores the tribulations of a Georgia/South Carolina colony under siege, re-creating the personal and collective lives, activities, and defensive strategies of this large community retrenched in a fortified camp.

The exiles of the Great Dismal Swamp are the subject of chapter 8. The area—between Virginia and North Carolina—is believed to have held the largest number of maroons in the country. From the borderlands to the hinterland, they pursued contrasting social and economic strategies, from living in isolation to working for enslaved men.

Maroons have sometimes been portrayed as bandits by their contemporaries and by modern historians. But as chapter 9 shows, bandits were rather a maroon subgroup. The most ubiquitous types of banditry and the personalities and activities of a number of bandits are examined in order to assess their impact on the enslaved community and society at large. Chapter 10 focuses on the role maroons played or are supposed to have played in slave conspiracies and insurrections in the Carolinas and Virginia. Marronage only vanished with the demise of slavery, but as the last chapter shows, death, raids, sickness, and imprudence were the immediate causes that ended most maroons' lives in the woods and swamps.

Yet despite all odds, in generation after generation, with apprehension doubtless, and self-confidence unquestionably, countless men and women, determined to carve out of the wilderness a better life for themselves and their children, continued to embark on hopeful freedom quests.

THE DEVELOPMENT OF MARRONAGE
IN THE SOUTH

MAROONS made their entry early in the annals of Southern history. They appeared in all colonies where slavery was introduced and the struggle against them has been particularly well chronicled. Evidence of their activities can be found in treaties with Indian nations, official correspondence, petitions, and in innumerable statutes and Acts. Laws, of course, are not to be taken at face value; they are not an indication of what really transpires in any given society. Some anticipate potential situations while others are a response to actual events. The thousands of slave statutes enacted, revised, annulled, and extended from the early 1600s to the 1860s are only one indicator of a larger reality that was also made up of customs, slaveholders' private practices, ignorance, lax enforcement and enforcement even after the Acts had been repealed, interpretation, accommodation, municipal regulations, and other idiosyncrasies. While the statutes examined here do not cover the entire spectrum of maroon activities and antimaroon legislation, implicitly and with the above caveats, they and other documents help uncover what marronage was like in the early days and how it grew. From a longer time perspective, the development of antimaroon measures maps the geographic locations of the maroons, the evolving—real, potential, rumored, and fabricated—threat they posed and, concurrently, white anxiety.

THE UPPER SOUTH

There is little doubt that many Africans ran away to the woods as soon as they arrived in the colonies, but perhaps the earliest reference to their escapes in Virginia dates back to 1640. On June 30, the General Court granted a commission to two men to raise a party in what became York County "to go in p[ur]suit of certain runaway negroes and to bring them to the governor."[1] A month later, John Punch, an African indentured servant and two of his European colleagues were brought back from Maryland where they had run off. They were all condemned to receive thirty lashes but whereas the Scot and the Dutchman had to serve four additional years, the court stressed that "the third being a negro," he had to become a slave for life.[2] This ruling is considered the first legal evidence of the gradual establishment of slavery in Virginia where most blacks at the time were still indentured servants. In January 1639, however, a distinction had already been made between all whites—indentured and free—and all blacks, with the following statute: "ALL persons except negroes to be provided with arms and amunition [*sic*] or be fined at pleasure of the Governor and Council."[3] By 1660 the enslaved status of blacks was firmly in place and a new Act passed in March 1661 to discourage interracial escapes stressed that if an English servant ran away with "negroes," since time could not be added to servitude, the servant had to work for the black runaway's owner for as long as the latter was absent.[4]

As noted in the Introduction, British settlers never referred to maroons in the American mainland as maroons, but instead as runaways or outliers, and in the statutes the difference between both groups has to be inferred from the context. One case in point is the September 1672 Act entitled "An Act for the Apprehension and Suppression of Runawayes, Negroes, and Slaves." It made reference to "many negroes [who] have lately beene, and now are out in rebellion in sundry parts of this country."[5] They had not been found and it was feared that "other negroes, Indians or servants" might decide to join them, which might result in "many mischeifes" and have "very dangerous consequences." These feared "runaways" could not be short-term truants, nor could they be escapees hidden in towns. They had to be groups of people who settled independently and could attract a following of exploited people and provide them with a refuge. Through raids for food and ammunition and direct harassment, they could represent a threat to the development of the colony. To guard against that potential peril it was enacted that any "such negroe, molatto, Indian slave, or servant for life" who would join the "many negroes" could be wounded or killed on the spot if he resisted.

If some "runaways" had settled on their own, others had found their way to the Indian nations; therefore the Act also required Native Americans to apprehend those who would come to them and to bring them to a justice of the peace. For their services they were to receive "twenty armes length of Roanoake or the value thereof in goods." This cooptation of Native Americans was one of the cornerstones of the early struggle against maroons.

On June 8, 1680 the colony added "An act for preventing Negroes Insurrections" to its corpus of laws.[6] While the first part addressed the rebellious behavior of slaves, the second dealt directly with "any negroe or other slave [who] shall absent himselfe from his masters service and lye hid and lurking in obscure places, committing injuries to the inhabitants." In a reaffirmation of the 1672 law, they could lawfully be killed if they resisted arrest. The phraseology "obscure places," to which is often added "swamps and woods," came up again and again in legal documents throughout the South, including in the nineteenth century.[7] It was meant to cover—and at the same time define—the maroon landscape: the obscure places close to farms and plantations, and the hinterland of marshland and forests.

The earliest Act to deal nominally with maroons, "An act for suppressing outlying Slaves," appeared on the books on April 16, 1691.[8] Justices of the peace were asked to issue warrants against them and sheriffs to raise adequate forces to capture them. The Act gave one detail about their activities: they "hid and lurk[ed] in obscure places killing hoggs and committing other injuries." Killing hogs, as well as cows, sheep, and poultry, was a typical maroon occupation for survival which continued to be a major point of contention until the end of marronage.

A few months after the Act was passed, two maroons went on trial. Mingo (also spelled Mingoe) "a Mullatto Slave," Lawrence, and the English servant Richard Wilkins were "a considerable time run away & laid out."[9] Mingo and Lawrence had escaped from Rosegill, the large estate of Ralph Wormeley, who held in servitude close to 20 percent of the county's black men, women, and children.[10] The three men caused "great disturbance and Terror." Like a number of maroons, they were on the move and were disturbing "the good Subjects" of Virginia close and far: between the one hundred and fifty miles that separated Middlesex and Rappahannock, where they were active, lay four counties.

Lawrence was accused of kicking open the door of James Douglas's room at Wormeley's Hog House and grabbing two shirts, a pair of breeches, and a gun still in his possession when he was arrested. In Rappahannock, Mingo raided the overseer John Powell's quarters, taking two guns, a carbine, and other items. Mingo, Lawrence, and Wilkins, well-armed, killed hogs and other livestock that belonged to a variety of people in Rappahannock County. But on or just before October 26, Mingo surrendered to John Powell. The circumstances are not documented, but if he had resisted or fled, he could legitimately have been killed. Thus by giving himself up, Mingo was saving his life. He was brought to the court in Middlesex and confessed to stealing the firearms. Because no offense could be proved to have been committed in that county, he was transported to Rappahannock where he was sentenced to receive thirty lashes and to be whipped in the same manner by one constable after another until he reached his owner's estate. Lawrence was captured too. Tried on December 7 in Middlesex, he confessed to the theft of Douglas's gun. No documentation about his fate has surfaced. Severe whippings were the "mildest" punishments maroons received; over the years more brutal rules were enacted.

In August 1701, "Billy" became the first notorious maroon whose personal depredations were denounced in a piece of legislation when Virginia passed "An act for the more effectuall apprehending [of] an outlying negro who hath commited divers robberyes and offences."[11] Billy had already had three owners, and by then he had been living in the woods for several years. He was known to be "lying out and lurking in obscure places suposed within the countys of James City, York, and New-Kent." He was "devouring and destroying the stocks and crops, robing the houses of and committing and threatening other injuryes to severall of his majestyes good and leige people within this his colony and dominion of Virginia." Mindful of the potential help he could receive, the Act stressed that anyone who "witingly and wilingly entertaine, assist, harbour, conceale, truck or trade with the said negroe Billy," would be committing a felony and be punished accordingly. A reflection of the extent of his "depradations" and the increasing severity of antimaroon measures, Billy was condemned to death in absentia. In his actions one can see the characteristics that marked generations of maroons after him. Like some isolated individuals and small groups, Billy was itinerant: he roamed along an arc of fifty miles. As practically all maroons did, he appropriated stock and crops, and traded with and received assistance from enslaved men and women. And like the bandits, he burglarized houses and threatened his victims.

* * *

By the beginning of the eighteenth century there were enough "new Negroes," that is, recently arrived Africans who ran away and, by default, could only find refuge in the woods, that the Virginia legislature felt compelled to add a statute in October 1705 that addressed their particular circumstances.[12] It concerned runaways who did "not speak English, and cannot, or through obstinacy will not declare the name of his or her master or owner." The offenders were to be kept in the public goal until claimed by their rightful owner or hirer. The article was one of forty-one of "An act concerning Servants and Slaves" passed within a comprehensive law that addressed many other issues.[13] It strongly reinforced the arsenal of brutal antimaroon regulations. In article thirty-seven, the Act introduced the concept of outlawry against men and women who hid in the "swamps, woods, and other obscure places," killed hogs, and committed other injuries. A quorum of two justices of the peace was required to issue a proclamation ordering them to surrender. The statement had to be placed on a Sunday at the door of every church and chapel, immediately following service. If maroons still refused to come out after being thus exhorted through written words posted in the middle of sacred white territory, they could lawfully be killed, their owner being reimbursed their assessed value on public funds. The sentence reserved to the men and women who did not resist arrest had to be severe enough "for the reclaiming any such incorrigible slave, and terrifying others from the like practices." They could be punished "either by dismembering, or any other way, not touching" their lives, which included the cutting off of toes, ears, and penises (castration remained legal until 1769).

In early March 1710, maronnage came to the forefront once again, this time linked to a conspiracy. It was exposed by Will, who revealed that a dangerous plot had been hatched in James City by "great numbers of the said Negroes and Indian Slaves for making their escape by force from the services of their Masters and for Destroying and cutting off Such of her Majesty's Subjects as should oppose their Design."[14]

Several men were questioned about the conspiracy, which counted Africans, native-born men, and at least one Native American. On March 24, it was determined that Scipio, Jackman, Salvadore (a Native American), Tom, and Shawn were the "principal contrivers." Their behavior had been recently "very rude and insolent."[15] Peter, also a principal leader, had escaped and was "Lurking in or about the said County or the County's of James City Prince George or Isle of Wight."[16] In the end, Scipio and Salvadore were condemned to a gruesome death. They were to be hanged, decapitated, and quartered. As a deterrent to potential conspirators, each man's head and body parts were to be displayed in different counties.[17] By the first decade of the eighteenth century, then, increasingly barbaric sentences reflected the colonists' growing fear. While the informer Will's identity was held secret, it was discovered and so intense was the resentment that "Several Negro's Laid Wait for his Life." He was therefore sent away to the Northern Neck. To encourage others to betray conspiracies, he received his freedom in October 1710 in exchange for 40 pounds to his owner.[18]

What makes this episode particularly noteworthy is that it was a premeditated mass desertion of armed men intent on settling outside white-controlled territory. It seems to be the first and so far the only recorded case of a large-scale simultaneous movement of people whose objective was to reach some secluded area to form a maroon community. In contrast, throughout American maroon history, with few, limited exceptions, people escaped individually or in small groups before regrouping.

In April 1733, for example, six men ran away from two Middlesex estates, banded together in the swamps, and broke into a store in Gloucester County, stealing goods valued at thirty pounds.[19] As a posse pursued them, they successfully defended themselves with firearms and other weapons. The potential peril that armed raiders could represent was taken so seriously that the sheriffs of Gloucester, Middlesex, King and Queen, Richmond, Lancaster and Essex counties were given orders to raise forces to search their respective areas. If they discovered that the band had moved to another location, they had to inform the sheriff of that county to start his own hunt for the "runaways and felons," who were to be caught dead or alive. The search was to focus most particularly on Dragon Swamp, located in Middlesex County.

Possible dismembering, outlawry, and accrued vigilance did little to prevent or even reduce marronage. On August 10, 1721 Governor Alexander Spotswood informed the Executive Council that "diverse Negro's as well as his own" who lived on the frontier of Rappahannock County, ran away and were believed to be gone to the Blue Ridge Mountains of western Virginia. He feared that it would be difficult to apprehend them and should their number increase, it would prove detrimental to the frontier settlers and of ill consequence to the peace of the colony as a whole.[20] By then the representation of enslaved men and women in the total population had increased to 30 percent.[21] As Virginia developed its tobacco production, Africans were brought in in ever-larger numbers: between 1710 and 1720, 7,200 had disembarked from fifty-one ships.[22] From a high of 52 percent in 1710, they still represented 45 percent of the enslaved population.[23] Newcomers were the most likely to escape and settle into the wilderness, and with more Africans entering the Upper South, colonists were increasingly worried about having to share space with maroon communities, in addition to Native Americans.

Virginians were also well aware that maroon colonies were entrenched in the mountains of Jamaica. Hoping to avoid a similar situation, they sought the assistance of the Indian nations. On September 11, 1722 Governor Spotswood told the Chiefs of the Five Nations,

> You sent me last year a Belt of Wampum as a Testimony of your Promise, that you would seize and carry to Virginia some Runaway Negroes, belonging to that Colony, whenever you did discover and meet with them in the woods. Now I make a general Proposition to you on account of Runnaways & Slaves belonging to Virginia viz that if any such Negroe or Slave shall hereafter fall into your hands you shall straigtway conduct them to Coll: George Masons House on Potowmack River & I do in behalf of that Colony engage that you shall there receive immediately upon the delivery of every such Runaway one good Gun & two Blankets, or the value thereof, & in Token of this Proposition and Engagement *I lay down 5 Guns & 500 flints.*[24]

The Chiefs, however, were not overly enthusiastic about helping. Acknowledging their previous failure at rounding up Virginia's maroons, they replied to Spotswood's plea for collaboration:

> As to the Proposition you made relating to Negroes We promise that if any Runaway Negroes or slaves shall happen to fall into our hands we will carry them to Coll: Masons on Potowmack River for ye reward you proposed: But as to those Negroes which you said we promised last year to send home we hope you will excuse us because they lye very much out of our way & may be had more easily by other Indians Yet if we can serve Virginia in any other thing we shall be glad of an opportunity of doing it.[25]

Native Americans' cooperation was also sought in Maryland. The Council accused the Shawnees in 1722 of entertaining "our Runaway Negro Slaves" at their "Towns upon Potomack River." To entice them to give the maroons up, the Council proposed to offer two leaders "a Stroud Match Coat and a pair of Silk Stockings" as a preliminary gesture of friendship; and any Shawnee would receive two coats and one gun for every runaway he would return.[26] In 1725, the General Assembly passed "An Act to encourage the Takers up of run-away Slaves, that shall be taken up by any Person and brought in from the Back-Woods," which established a reward of five pounds to anyone who would bring maroons from the hinterland, north-west of the Monocacy River. Mountains around the river reached almost two thousand feet and were as good a refuge as any. The Act also specified that the runaways would have one ear cut off for the first offence; the other for the second offense in addition to the letter R branded on the chin. A year later, on July 19, 1726, the Upper House of the Assembly, deploring that "Sundry negroes . . . [made] their Escape to the Shuano [Shawnee] town to the great prejudice of the Proprietors," recommended further actions to prevent their escape. It also proposed to increase the attractiveness of the incentives to capture or turn them in.[27] The new measures did not discourage some maroons. On March 25, 1729 Eleanor Cusheca, 22, recounted a conversation she had heard around the previous Christmas. A number of enslaved men and women from various places met in the kitchen and quarters of Captain Richard Smith and discussed the recent visit of the African Harry (John Miller), absent "a considerable time," who came back to see his "ship mates." He reportedly said that "there were many Negroes among the Indians" in the Monocacy Mountains.[28]

In Virginia, the threat posed by maroons settling in the Blue Ridge Mountains formed a central part of a geopolitical strategy envisioned by William Byrd II, author, planter, and founder of Richmond. He advocated the exploration of "this important Barrier" (the mountain range) because it might be rich in minerals, and proposed the erection of fortifications in the most vulnerable passes to safeguard against French encroachment and "to prevent the Negroes takeing [sic] Refuge there, as they do in the mountains of Jamaica, to the great annoyance of the Kings Subjects, and these will be the more dangerous, because the French will be always ready to Supply them with Arms, and to make use of them against us on all occasions."[29] To impede this potential alliance of maroons and foreign expansionist powers, he promoted the immigration of Protestants—a proposal he made to the Swiss-born, London-based Quaker Johann Rudolph Ochs—whose settlements, he believed, would hamper any attempt by maroons to establish their own.

Still agitating the specter of Jamaica, where the First Maroon War was going on, Byrd, in a letter dated July 12, 1736, to John Perceval, Earl of

Egmont (first president of the Georgia Board of Trustees), recommended putting an end to the introduction of slaves into Virginia—which he feared could one day be known as New Guinea—and the rest of the colonies, "lest they prove as troublesome and dangerous everywhere, as they have been lately in Jamaica, where besides a vast expence of Mony, they have cost the lives of many of his Majesty's Subjects. We have mountains in Virginia too, to which they may retire as safely, and do as much mischeif as they do in Jamaica."[30]

* * *

To Virginia's south, North Carolina was grappling with its own maroons and those who came down from the North. An early mention of this particular problem appears in the records in 1698, when four "sturdy runaway slaves" who arrived from Virginia in a shallop (a small boat) were accused of having killed three hogs belonging to Roger Snell. The men were armed and resisted when Snell and two others confronted them. In the end the maroons were subdued and taken seventy miles away to be kept in custody.[31]

As had been the case further North, Native Americans' assistance was eagerly sought in controlling the maroons. John Brickell, in his 1737 *Natural History of North Carolina*, noted that Indians were "very expeditious in finding out the *Negroes* that frequently run away from their Masters into the Woods, where they commit many outrages against the *Christians*, as it happened in *Virginia* not long since, where above of *three Hundred* joined together, and did a great deal of Mischief . . . before they were suppressed." He added that Indians generally found the maroons' haunts in much less time than it took white men. Twenty-four maroons were hung, he asserted, after Indians tracked them in the woods where they had found refuge following a failed conspiracy.[32] Brickell was quick to claim that blacks preferred to be captured by Christians because they were terrified of Native Americans, who, according to him, tortured them with delight.[33]

In 1715 "An Act Concerning Servants & Slaves" was passed, at a time when whites in North Carolina numbered 7,500 and blacks 3,700.[34] The statutes concerning runaways were mostly instructions to owners and overseers about the punishments to be administered to escapees and the penalties colonists would incur if they harbored them. In 1741, a more comprehensive code was enacted; amended three times, it remained firmly in place throughout the colonial era. It too referred to maroons by using the expedient phraseology: "And whereas many Times Slaves run away and lie out hid and lurking in the Swamps, Woods and other Obscure Places, killing Cattle and Hogs, and committing other Injuries to the Inhabitants in this Government."[35] And in this colony too, maroons who did not return after a proclamation had been issued against them were outlawed and could legitimately be killed. Since owners were to be compensated on public funds, they had little incentive to preserve the maroons' lives. When Abraham was outlawed in 1774, for example, the person who would bring him back alive was to receive only forty shillings, but he would get five pounds for his head.[36]

In sum, maroons continued to be a vexing problem to North Carolinians for decades. As was the case elsewhere, armed groups who raided plantations and farms aroused fears of insurrections throughout the eighteenth and nineteenth centuries.

THE LOWER SOUTH

South Carolina passed its first "Act to prevent Runaways" on November 7, 1683 and on February 7, 1691 the legislature adopted an "Act for the Better Ordering of Slaves," modeled on Barbadian laws, Barbados being the place of origin of half the colonists.[37] By then the colony counted about 2,500 whites and 1,100 blacks.[38] Article IX of the Act mentioned that a sheriff, having cognizance of "the haunt, residence or hiding place of any runaway slave, [had] to raise a convenient party of men, not exceeding twenty, and with them to pursue, apprehend and take the said runaways, either alive or dead." More generally, if runaways suffered "in life or limb," no one was liable under the law. Other texts followed in 1693 and 1695, and in 1696 another "Act for the Better Ordering of Slaves" was adopted "to Prevent the mischeifs which (as the number of slaves shall Increase) Too much liberty may occasion." Instead of focusing on rewards and fines to whites, it itemized the penalties runaways would incur. Escaping with intent to leave the colony was punishable by death—as was running away for the fifth time—although the death penalty could be substituted by the cutting off of the Achilles' tendon. Males were to receive forty lashes and face branding for the first offense and be castrated if they were over sixteen and repeat offenders; females were to be whipped, branded, and have their ears cut off.[39]

Responding to a specific maroon threat a few years later—at a time when blacks exceeded the white population for the third consecutive year—on June 20, 1711 the Commons House of Assembly passed a resolution asking the governor to take the necessary measures to suppress armed runaways who robbed and plundered houses and plantations, and spread "great fear and terrour" among the white population.[40] One man, whose name was Sebastian, stood out among the people who caused "*barbarities, felonies* and *abuses*" (italics in the original). He was described as a "Spanish Negroe," indicating perhaps that he had come from Florida. He was accused—among other depredations—of burning down a widow's house. In October, the governor offered a bounty of fifty pounds to whoever would take him dead or alive. As was the case in the Upper South too, Native Americans were requested to contribute to the anti-maroon fight. The House asked the governor to "[e]mploy a number of Indians to assist" the men sent to "apprehend, hunt & take the runaway Negroes." Sebastian was surrounded by Native Americans, killed one of them, but was captured and later executed.[41]

In May 1735, South Carolina's militia was ordered to apprehend "several White persons and Blacks" living in the swamp at the head of the Wando River. They were accused of "Outrages and Robberys." The order did not specify the location or the size of the groups.[42] The disturbances continued and "[a] great Consternation" descended in December when it was feared that "the Negroes were going to rise." A large number, believed to be one hundred, gathered in the woods, possibly to plan an uprising, perhaps also to establish a settlement there. What was of particular concern was the fact that they were armed and had ammunition. Some were captured along with their weapons, as well as two barrels of powder, two barrels of shot, and one barrel of flint.[43]

Following the 1739 Stono uprising during which Africans who were trying to reach St. Augustine killed twenty-one whites, a new, comprehensive code was passed in 1740. Among other things, it listed the generous rewards whites and free Indians—but not free and enslaved blacks—could receive if they caught a runaway who had been absent six months on the south side of the Savannah River. They would get fifty pounds for a man; twenty-five for women and boys over twelve; and five pounds for children, provided they were alive. A man's scalp "with the two ears" would bring twenty pounds.[44] The reward doubled for a man or his scalp when brought from the south side of the St. John's River.[45]

At the time, and for many years thereafter, the complicated geopolitics of the region was one of South Carolinians' main preoccupations, with black people at its center. The danger that the enslaved population represented to the survival of the colony was deemed greater than any other threat. The same year as the Stono uprising, Britain started a war with Spain and, as a retaliatory measure, wanted to ban all exports of rice to France and Spain. South Carolinian merchants petitioned the British House of Commons asking for an exemption because:

> at this present precarious Time [this ban] may render the whole Colony an easy Prey to their neighbouring Enemies the *Indians* and *Spaniards*, and also to those yet more dangerous Enemies their own *Negroes*, who are ready to revolt on the first Opportunity, and are Eight Times as many in Number as there are white Men able to bear Arms; and the Danger in this respect is greater since the unhappy Expedition to *St Augustine*.[46]

The petitioners' figures were correct: the colony counted 25,000 whites and 40,000 blacks.[47] And blacks could and did rebel, flee to St. Augustine, find refuge among Indian nations, and form autonomous maroon communities that raided plantations and made new recruits. They could inflict heavy damage and aggravate the colony's precarious position in early America. South Carolina's fears were thus well founded.

In 1751, a new Act concerned "slaves which run away and lie out for a considerable space of time, at length become desperate, and stand upon their defence with knives, weapons or arms." If whites were to arrest any such runaway of at least six month who defended himself with "a knife, sword, cutlass, gun, pistol, or other weapon," they would collect a reward, and if wounded or disabled they would get an additional twenty pounds from the owner. If the catcher was enslaved, he was entitled to only half.[48] The Act is notable in that, contrary to the 1740 iteration, it tried to entice free and enslaved blacks to hunt down the maroons. In addition, it enumerates the various types of weapons maroons were known to possess. But even more important, it clearly—if inadvertently—stated that they used them to defend themselves. There is nothing in the Act about outliers attacking colonists at gunpoint or cutlass in hand as during the Stono uprising. All the maroons did with their arsenal, the Act acknowledged, was to stand up in self-defense. However, this act of self-protection was considered illegitimate as the individuals, by running away, had placed themselves outside the law.

* * *

Like other colonies, South Carolina employed Native Americans in the fight against the maroons. Its strategy was twofold: remote nations were asked to deny sanctuary to absconders and to turn them in when they caught them: while those closest to white areas were used as trackers and hunters of the maroons who had settled autonomously.[49] In December 1736, for example, the Upper and Lower Creeks agreed to bring any runaway who came to them to the garrisons of Savannah or Pallachucola. They would receive four blankets or two guns, or the value in other goods for each live returnee "on the further side of the Oconoy River," one gun elsewhere; and one blanket for a head.[50] A similar treaty was signed by Georgia.[51]

It is important to emphasize that the colonists wanted not only to prevent the loss of property, but more importantly the alliance of Native Americans and African Americans against the white population. As the settlers discovered, the former were not monolithic. They formed alliances with and fought against other Indian nations, colonists of various European stripes, and enslaved and runaway blacks depending on a variety of factors, including the changing politics of the time.

In May 1751, for example, a "half-breed" man from the Cherokee nation enticed six enslaved men to run away to Cherokee land, promising to take them from there to a place where they could "depend on their

Freedom." Three came back, but the others told the Cherokees "the white People was coming up to destroy them all, and that they had got some Creek Indians to assist them so to do." They also made clear that if both oppressed populations cooperated with one another, they could get rid of the colonists. They told the Old Warrior of Keowee (a Cherokee farming town) that "there was in all Plantations many Negroes more than white People, and that for the Sake of Liberty they would join them."[52]

Native Americans either willing or coerced into becoming auxiliaries in the fight against maroons had an evident value to the settlers, but even those who opposed white colonization were deemed useful. Their very presence was seen as a bulwark against potential maroon communities, which were perceived as a more formidable enemy. In May 1760—in a remake of Gooch and Byrd's narratives about Virginia—Governor William Bull of South Carolina wrote to the Board of Trade that the Cherokees should neither be "extirpated" from the Blue Ridge Mountains nor exterminated, because their "inaccessible country" would then become "a plentiful refuge to the runaway negroes of this province who might be more troublesome and more difficult to reduce than the Negroes in the mountains of Jamaica."[53]

Perhaps George Milligen-Johnson—a surgeon who practiced among the Cherokees—offered the best rationalization for an accomodationist policy toward Indian nations,

a natural dislike and antipathy, that subsists between them [Negroes] and our Indian neighbours, is a very lucky circumstance, and for this reason: In our quarrels with the Indians[,] however proper and necessary it may be to give them correction, it can never be [in] our interest to extirpate them, or to force them from their lands; their ground would be soon taken up by runaway Negroes from our settlements, whose numbers would daily increase, and quickly become more formidable enemies than Indians can ever be, as they speak our language, and would never be at a loss for intelligence.[54]

The Catawbas in particular became South Carolina's choice mercenaries. Given their value as maroon hunters, in 1769 when the North Carolina/

South Carolina border was again discussed, Governor Charles Montagu suggested to Wills Hill, then Secretary of State for the Colonies, that the Catawbas "should be comprehended in the proposed boundary as a very usefull Body of Men to keep our Negroes in some awe."[55] South Carolina was thus eager to draw its frontiers in such a way as to incorporate the Catawbas, because the latter would be a deterrent to potential maroons and would destroy those who still dated to settle in the woods and swamps.

* * *

In Louisiana, the first people who came directly from across the ocean—from the Bight of Benin—landed in 1719. By 1723, 863 Africans had disembarked in the French colony and in March, Louis XV promulgated an edict called *Code Noir* specifically for Louisiana, partly modeled on the 1685 *Code Noir* of his father, Louis XIV. Article thirty-two—out of fifty-four—specified that one month from the day their owner reported their disappearance runaways were condemned to having both ears cut off and being branded on the shoulder with a "fleur de lys," the emblem of the French monarchy. If absent for another month, they were to be hamstrung and branded on the other shoulder; after three months, they were to be killed. Free blacks who harbored them had to pay a fine for each day they sheltered the escapees and if they could not, they were to be sold.[56] Despite this and subsequent legislation, Louisiana remained fertile maroon ground whether under French, Spanish, or American rule.

By the end of the eighteenth century some maroons regrouped on small islands in south Louisiana's lakes, and from there launched raids for goods and animals. To put a stop to these activities, the planters of St. Bernard Parish were disposed to pay four pesos for runaways arrested in New Orleans, seven for those caught in the cypress swamps, and up to ten for the maroons who had taken refuge on the islands.[57] Their escalating rewards were a clear indication of the difficulty of capturing the maroons (as opposed to the runaways who settled in the city) as well as the priority given to their eradication.

After Louisiana was purchased from France in 1803, William C. C. Claiborne, Governor of the Mississippi Territory and Governor General and intendant of the Province of Louisiana, on February 21, 1804 published a decree which tackled the maroon problem. He stated that in many cases people stayed in the "woods and swamps, where they are necessarily subjected to continued inquietude, and compelled to seek a livelihood by plundering, to the great injury and terror of the good inhabitants" because they were afraid of the punishment they would receive if they returned. Motivated, as he stressed, by "humanity," Claiborne decreed that if they had not committed any other offence and returned within two months, they would not be punished. Those who did not would be pursued and receive whatever legal penalty their owners chose to inflict.[58]

But in Louisiana as elsewhere, harsh legislation and petty incentives were of little consequence. There, as in the rest of the South, maroons continued to settle at the borderlands and in the hinterland, individually or in communities, well into the nineteenth century.

WARS AND MARRONAGE

While the Revolutionary War generated an increase in runaways it is difficult to assert that it provided a similar impetus to marronage. To be sure, some individuals and groups became maroons during the war and remained in hiding after it was over. But evidence documenting people fleeing to the woods en masse is elusive. Running away, especially to the enemy, is one thing, but being a maroon is another. Tellingly, the Whigs' major preoccupation was to prevent enslaved and free blacks from reaching British ships, and they gave strict orders to that effect.[59]

In Georgia and South Carolina, Tybee Island (in the mouth of the Savannah River) and Sullivan's Island (in Charleston harbor) were still under full British control and runaways gathered there by the hundreds. On Sullivan alone, they were estimated at five hundred by the end of 1775. Although they have sometimes been presented as maroons, they were actually runaways placing themselves under British protection.[60] Slave trader and rice planter Henry Laurens, then President of the Council of Safety, said as much in a letter to the Captain of the *Tamar* sloop of war. He denounced the British ships "harbouring and protecting negroes, who fly from their masters to Sullivan's Island, and on board the vessels." Armed blacks and whites were said to commit daily depredations.[61] As a result, on December 18 a force was sent to destroy or dislodge them.[62] A similar operation was launched against Tybee on March 25, 1776 because, as General Stephen Bull stressed to Laurens, "it is far better for the Public and the owners of the *deserted Negroes* on *Tybee* Island, who are on *Tybee* Island, to be shot if they cannot be taken, [even] if the Public is obliged to pay for them; for if they are carried away and converted into money . . . it will only Enable our enemy to fight us with our own money or property" (italics in the original). And he added, hoping to kill two birds with one stone, "Therefore all who cannot be taken, had better be shot by the Creek Indians, as it perhaps may deter other Negroes from deserting, and will establish a hatred or Aversion between the Indians and the Negroes."[63]

In Georgia and South Carolina, most runaways headed to the coasts to try to get passage to northern and southern cities, Florida, or Indian Territory. A tally of the notices in the *Royal Georgia Gazette* from 1777 to 1783 which suggest a destination, shows that fifty-four individuals were supposed to go to or were seen in a city; sixteen were thought to be harbored on plantations; fourteen followed the army; ten were believed to be on board ships or at the harbor; nine were expected to go to St. Augustine, and eight to South Carolina. Thus only 14 percent (the sixteen harbored on plantations) were believed to have become borderland maroons. In South Carolina, the *Royal Gazette* for 1781 and 1782 yields the following results: twenty-eight individuals were suspected to be or had actually been seen in cities; twenty-two were known to be with the army; seventeen were on board ships; and eight people were being harbored on plantations.[64] There, 10 percent of the runaways were suspected of having gone to the borderlands. Of course these numbers only indicate a trend, because no purported destination was mentioned for many other runaways; still, the little data available does not support the claim of a rush to the woods and swamps. In the end, more than 2,000 black South Carolinians fled to St. Augustine; and in the final months of the war it was estimated that about 9,000 black men, women, and children left with the British from the ports of Charleston (5,327) and Savannah (3,500).[65] If several thousand maroons were "skulking" in the Lowcountry, it would have been noticed. It was not.

In North Carolina a committee was appointed in May 1776 "to enquire [into] ways and means the most probably to prevent the desertion of slaves." It recommended sending all the males capable of bearing arms or helping the enemy from the south side of Cape Fear to the countryside, away from the sea.[66] Slaveholders apparently did not fear that sending them to the interior would incite them to desert by fleeing into the wilderness. Evidently, they were more concerned about cutting the men off from the British. Tony's case exemplifies this fear. He had lived for several years in the woods and swamps of Bladen County and was outlawed in May 1780. But he was not actively pursued until the British troops arrived in Wilmington. It was then that "the Friends of the American Cause determined that no such should be lurking in the Woods for fear of giving intelligence." In September 1783, a posse found Tony and killed him.[67]

Similarly, did enslaved people from Virginia and North Carolina flee to the Great Dismal Swamp and "wage . . . defensive guerilla warfare?"[68] Two sources offered as evidence to support such an assertion are far from being conclusive. Johann David Schoepf, who went through the swamp in 1783–84, noted that there were "runaway slaves, who have lived many years in the swamp." Traveling about the same time, John Ferdinand Smyth Stuart remarked, "Run-away Negroes have resided in these places for twelve, twenty, or thirty years and upwards."[69] There is no indication from either men that the maroons' arrival was due to the war, and Stuart clearly stated that they had lived in the swamp for decades. Elkanah Watson, who toured the north border of the swamp in 1777, noted it was "at this time, infested by concealed royalists, and runaway negroes, who could not be approached with safety. They often attacked travellers."[70] He was referring to Josiah Phillips's band of white laborers and bandits and black runaways.[71] A detailed study of the impact of the war on North Carolina's enslaved population notes the thousands of people who joined the British; a plot or "putative rebellion" in July 1775 in Beaufort, Craven, and Pitt counties that rested on the hope that the British would give blacks their own government; the hanging of the black Loyalist pilot Thomas Jeremiah; but no maroon movement.[72]

If we take as a reference *The Book of Negroes* that lists three thousand blacks who were sent to Nova Scotia, the Caribbean, Quebec, England, Belgium, and Germany by the British, we see that two-thirds came from Virginia, the Carolinas, and Georgia. Among them were 1,336 men; 914 passengers or 30 percent of the total were women; and 750 children (21 percent) left too.[73] Clearly, many families joined the British because they hoped it would be their best opportunity to become free as a unit within what they thought would be a safe framework. That some chose marronage instead is not in question, but it is more difficult to see a direct link between marronage and the escape of families.

* * *

During the War of 1812, the number of runaways increased once more and measures were taken to prevent them from reaching enemy lines. In October 1813 Virginians in Norfolk had "reason to believe that no more negroes will desert to the enemy from Princess-Ann" because in addition to the guards, volunteers were patrolling the deserted zone around the southern part of Lynnhaven Bay, an area where "runaways and outliers" secretly camped while waiting for an opportunity to board a British ship. In Georgia, the governor was quite worried about men making their way to St. Augustine. Since many had succeeded, he stressed the need for constant surveillance.[74] To keep them in the colony the British offered tempting alternatives such as jobs in their regiments and transportation to free lands.[75] Similarly, the Civil War saw an influx of runaways trying to reach the Union lines to enroll in the army or place themselves under its protection.

The broad statement that wars fostered marronage seems logical but it is largely impressionistic and not based on hard facts. Generally, wars did not have a major impact on marronage because more appealing options were or seemed available. During the Revolution and the War of 1812, this included the possibility of becoming legally free in America or

Britain by serving the British. The alternative during the Civil War was a potential general emancipation. In peacetime, maroons were always a minority of the escapees. When they could make a choice, most runaways opted for "freedom" in a slave society (in Southern cities) or in a free state. Maroon life, as most people knew, was dangerous and precarious; if one could escape servitude in another manner—especially when whole families could stay together—it made sense to try to go that route. The maroon way of life was only for a resilient few and a war may not have made it much more alluring.

PERIODS OF MARRONAGE

At the macro level, three main periods can be delineated in the development of Southern marronage and the fight against it. The first stretches roughly from the inception of the colonies until the turn of the eighteenth century. Individuals and groups that stayed close enough to inhabited areas were involved in the appropriation of food and animals. They were a concern to settlers, but the worry quickly turned into anxiety as maroons armed themselves. This led the colonists to link marronage with plots and actual uprisings, whether justified or not. Prevention and repression were then inscribed into slave codes to address the issue. Over the years, reflecting an increasing black population and fear of black people, repressive and punitive measures became more ferocious, with barbaric sentences written into law or simply administered.

The second period started roughly in the early eighteenth century. The arrival of large numbers of Africans, their propensity to run away, the lure of the mountains, European colonial jousting for territory, and events in Jamaica all coalesced to shift the colonists' focus to the eventuality of established maroon communities. In Virginia, Maryland, and South Carolina the mountains became the maroons' shelter but these hospitable sanctuaries evoked specific fears among colonists that went beyond the mere disappearance of their workers. The Maroon Wars in Jamaica greatly alarmed settlers, who were all the more determined to wipe out the fledging communities in their midst. The frightening vision of the Jamaican maroons loomed large in their assessment of the precarious situation they could find themselves in unless they took drastic measures to cut off their own absconders from the Appalachian Mountains. The successes of the Jamaicans proved a bane to the early maroon communities of British North America. Had they not existed or had they been immediately defeated, the development of maroon communities in the American South might have taken a different turn. In addition, French colonial expansion in the west, Spanish expansion in the east, and the presence of Indian nations rendered the situation potentially more difficult for the colonists to handle than was the case in the island. Consequently, a systematic black/Indian divide and conquer policy was put in place while strategic alliances with Native Americans became crucial to prevent the formation of black settlements and to destroy them once they had been established.

The nineteenth century represents the third period. After Native Americans were pushed back and most of their lands invaded and confiscated, they were no longer useful and vanished from the antimaroon strategies. Although large maroon communities did not disappear in the 1800s, documentation shows that they were few; smaller groups were the norm, as they probably had been earlier. Small groups in the hinterland and individuals and small groups at the margins of inhabited areas characterized marronage in the nineteenth century, a phenomenon that existed before but seems to have increased with the development of the domestic slave trade. Stricter control, better communication, the encroachment of white immigrants, deforestation, the drying of swamplands for agriculture and urbanization were among the factors that led to the fading of large communities. Even so, marronage continued to exist until 1865.

[2]

AFRICAN MAROONS

"SOME niggers jus' come from Africa and old Marse has to watch 'em close, 'cause they is de ones what mostly runs away to de woods."[1] Although he was born in 1836, almost thirty years after the United States had abolished its international slave trade, Cinte Lewis knew what he was talking about. He had grown up in Brazoria, Texas, one of the epicenters of the illegal slave trade during which thousands of Africans were smuggled into the Deep South. Lewis's observation about the propensity of newly arrived Africans to head for the woods finds an echo in Lula Coleman's memories of her African grandfather, John Ren, who had been deported to Alabama. He lived "on nobody's place before the surrender," she said, "Couldn't nobody own him. They called him a runaway nigger."[2] Ren rebelled against his enslavement, never spoke English, and refused Western clothes. He lived in a cave and did not allow anybody to stay with him. These two cases are particularly revealing as they occurred after 1830, a period when Africans were a small minority arriving and living in the United States. Yet their response to enslavement was similar to that of many of the Africans who had preceded them.

Philip D. Morgan, analyzing 3,558 runaway ads and 2,041 "captured" notices in colonial South Carolina, has established "the dominance of Africans in the runaway population, particularly among captives."[3] Africans represented between 45 percent of the enslaved population in that colony in the 1760s and 49 percent in 1775, but, based on Morgan's analysis, they made up 68.5 percent of the runaways between 1732 and 1775.

Between the 1750s and 1770s, as the ratio of Africans in North Carolina declined from two-thirds to one-third, they still represented 54.1 percent of the runaways. In Virginia, they accounted for 29.8 percent of the fugitives between 1730 and 1787, at a time when their share in the enslaved population fell from 30 to 10 percent.[4] In colonial Georgia, of the advertised runaways whose origin is known 25 percent were born in the country; 30 percent were Africans who had lived in the Caribbean or North America; and 45 percent were newly arrived Africans. Africans therefore represented 75 percent of these runaways.[5] The prevalence of escapes by Africans held true in other parts of the Western hemisphere; looking for an explanation, the French Ministry of Navy and Colonies concluded that they kept their habits of "laziness and vagrancy" when arriving in the New World.[6]

"NEW NEGROES"

If Africans ran away disproportionately, notices show that the newly arrived among them were the most prone to do so. Slaveholders used various terms to categorize the people born in Africa. There were "new Negroes," outlandish Negroes (in Virginia, Maryland, and North Carolina), and Africans. It is clear from the wanted ads that outlandish was a geographical marker that had no strict relation to time. It meant, primarily, that the individuals were born elsewhere, in most cases Africa, not that they had just arrived, contrary to some assertions.[7] Although many outlandish men and women were newcomers, a significant number of others had the following characteristics: "speaks pretty good English," "speaks English very well," "well acquainted with most of America," "been in the country a number of years," "says he was emancipated," "says he is a freeman. . . . Sued for his freedom." Other outlandish people were familiar enough with their surroundings that they could tell the county they came from and the number of miles they had traveled; some were said to be old or in their late forties or fifties, a sure sign that they had not been introduced only a few months earlier.[8]

Outlandish was not associated with an ethnic or geographical origin. This was perhaps because by the time the outlandish individual was being sought, his/her sojourn in the country had attenuated, in the eyes of the slaveholders, whatever ethnic characteristics were attributed to him/her. The Upper South term "outlandish" is thus a mixed bag that described Africans at various stages of their American experience.

The expression "New Negro," common throughout the Deep South, always referred to the fact that the African in question had been in the country for a shorter period of time: from disembarkation to several months and at most two years. For instance, Simon, an Igbo, called "new," ran away twice after being in the country for two years.[9] Jim was called a new Negro even though he had been in the country for ten months. Rose, a Fulani, had arrived eighteen months earlier when she was advertised as a very "artful . . . New Negro WENCH."[10] The rarity of these examples, though, only confirms that the vast majority of so-called new Negroes had been in the country for less than a year. Actually, a Maryland Act of 1725 defined new Negroes as those Africans who had lived for up to "twelve months here in the Country." It exempted them from branding and mutilation if caught after having been maroons in the backwoods.[11]

A small number of slave owners in Maryland, Georgia, and South Carolina used the terminology "salt-water."[12] After the ship *Providence* landed in Maryland sometime in August 1770 with 132 Gambians on board, John Cooke bought an undetermined number of people on September 3. Soon after, five of these "Salt Water Slaves," as he called them, ran away. They were all in their early twenties, though Jack was only three.[13] In Louisiana, the French called African newcomers *bruts* (*brutes* for females), meaning, in the rough, raw. Further terminology qualified that roughness. If they had just arrived, they were sometimes said to be "absolutely" *bruts*; a while later they could be "almost" *bruts* and when they had lived in the country a few months, they could be referred to as "semi-" *bruts*.[14] Like "new Negroes," *bruts* might have been in the country for more than a year, as were the Congo Magloire and Cesar—two years in Louisiana—advertised in 1807 as "*nègres bruts*."[15]

In most cases, a place of origin or ethnic designation was attached to the term "new Negroes," but they were often vague: Guinea or Guiney Coast or Country was sometimes used for West Africa. Ethnicities and areas of origin did not automatically match and at times names and the ethnicities associated with them contradicted each other. Geographic and ethnic markers in the ads are unreliable on a consistent basis: some were undoubtedly accurate, while others were fanciful. It is difficult, except in obvious cases, to know which is which. The ethnicities relayed here are those given by the owners, whether accurate or not.

Distinct from the so-called new Negroes were established Africans who had lived in the country for several years, including those who had spent their entire childhoods or teenage years there. Their origins were recorded in two ways. When known, guessed, or made up, their ethnicity was often noted; if not they were simply referred to as Africans. In other cases the mention of country marks and/or filed teeth served as a clear marker of foreign origin. Some people whose place of birth was not specified had African names, though this did not necessarily mean they were born in Africa. For example, a Creole origin was listed in the following notices: "Cudjoe . . . this country born"; "Cuffee . . . this country born"; "Quaco . . . this country born"; "Wally and Fatima" (two Muslim names), also "this country born."[16]

The distinction drawn in newspaper notices between newcomers and established Africans is useful because close examination shows that there was not one overarching African maroon experience but several, based mostly on time spent in the country. Needless to say, except in very few cases, Africans who had recently arrived did not run away to join family members, one of the main reasons for marooning among the men and women born in North America. Still, the reconstitution of families or virtual families was sometimes their objective, as they were looking for shipmates or spouses. One case in point was that of Dick who "probably cannot tell his master's name," because he had not been in the country for long. He ran away in February 1781 and was seen at another plantation a few weeks later. Although "new," he had a wife and baby and knew enough of his surroundings and beyond to look for and find his family. He was also savvy enough to organize a group evasion. When he left the Georgia plantation he had been heading to, he did so with his wife, their infant, and another man.[17]

For most maroons, to be free (for African Americans) or to regain one's freedom (for Africans) was a shared reason for escaping; as were brutal treatments. An American-born former maroon recounted how a recently arrived "Guinea man" was terribly abused because of his ignorance of plantation rules and how he reacted to that treatment. As he was being whipped mercilessly the young man did not say, "Do massa," or "Please massa," as he should have according to the humiliating slavery protocol. Incensed at his refusal to plead for mercy, his owner, Col. Billy Mallard of Dean Swamp, South Carolina, swore he would teach the "nigger to beg." The driver and the planter took turns whipping the man, who was first hung by his wrists and later tied to a log, until "they cut a great gash in his side that they had to sew up." The next day, the man ran to the woods. He lived there for five weeks before being caught.[18]

GOING TO THE WOODS

Few avenues of concealment were open to recently arrived Africans. They could hardly settle in a city hoping to melt discreetly into the domestic workforce, their inability to speak English and lack of knowledge of Western urban life would have given them away instantly. Predictably, a very small number of newcomers made their way to Southern towns. An anonymous African was taken captive in the small Georgia town of Ebenezer in May 1768. Another, from Angola, was captured in Charleston; and a teenage Igbo was caught in the same city a month after he had arrived. Caesar, from Angola, who spoke a little English, was caught several times near Savannah.[19] These were exceptions, as the immense majority of African newcomers stayed clear of the urban areas.

To migrate to a free state (mostly in the nineteenth century) was as improbable a proposition as going to town, as it would have implied that newcomers knew enough of the geopolitics and topography of the country not only to be aware that such places existed but also to reach them, a feat that few people born in the country were able to realize. Even so, a man recounted in 1854 the story of an African he said he had secretly helped move from New York to Canada fourteen years earlier. The African spoke almost no English and had evidently been smuggled in. He was "savage looking," famished, and dressed in rags. His back, lacerated by dogs, was ravaged with gangrene. He had escaped six or seven weeks earlier from the Deep South after having heard of the North Star whose direction runaways followed to reach the North, and of "a country where black men might be free."[20]

With Southern cities and the North practically closed to them, Africans had few choices: they could find refuge with Native Americans; settle in the woods and swamps; or attempt to return home by finding their way to the ocean. In colonial Georgia, half the newly arrived Africans for whom a destination is known were going to the backcountry or to the coast; the number fell to 10 to 15 percent for other runaways.[21] In 1896, historian John Spencer Bassett announced what to him and many others seemed like evidence: "Used to the forest life in Africa and accustomed to much severity on the farms of the frontier planters, it was no great hardship to them to live for months or years in camp in the swamps."[22] Bassett could not have been more wrong. Before their deportation, neither urban nor rural Africans had had reason to *live* in the wilderness. In America they went to the woods, the mountains, and the swamps because there was no other place of concealment and freedom for them to go to.

The experience of Ibrahima abd al-Rahman can serve as an illustration. He was one of the sons of Ibrahima Sory Mawdo, the Almamy or Muslim ruler of the theocracy of Futa Jallon (Guinea), and had studied in the reputed Qur'anic schools of Timbuktu before returning at age seventeen to Futa. An army officer, he resided in the capital Timbo, a town of about 9,000. Ibrahima became a prisoner of war in 1788 and ended up in Natchez, Mississippi, where he was bought—along with his compatriot Samba—by Thomas Foster, a small tobacco farmer. When he refused to do manual labor, Ibrahima was whipped and a few weeks after his arrival, he ran away. Searches were abandoned after Foster speculated the young man might have drowned or died of hunger.[23] Ibrahima, the urban aristocrat, the educated man who wrote and read Arabic, and was familiar with the savannah of Timbuktu and Timbo, survived "many weeks" in the forest in the humid and cool Mississippi fall weather. Nothing in his education and life had prepared him for survival in this environment; still, he chose the unfamiliar forest over servitude, and succeeded in remaining undetected for weeks. The Southern woods were as remote from his experience as could be but he endured as best he could.

As with Ibrahima, so too with other Africans—whoever they were and wherever they came from—going to the woods was inevitably more of a challenge than it was for men and women born in the country. The latter knew their surroundings and had sometimes briefly lived in the woods and swamps as truants. They were familiar with the fauna and flora and knew what animals and plants they would find and what they could or should not eat. They knew the weather and its changes, and had family and/or friends around. Newly arrived Africans had no such support system and were still discovering another ecology with cold weather, frost, and snow. As an 1843 newspaper reported after a snowstorm in the Deep South, "the astonishment of the young negroes, fresh from Africa and Cuba was very great, and the capers they cut on the occasion were extraordinary."[24] Although some of the vegetation was familiar, many of the South's most common trees—the pine, the cypress, and the sweet gum—as well as the wildlife and fruits, were new to the Africans. They had never seen a bear or eaten a blackberry.

EARLY ESCAPES

It can be said that Africans, and singularly "new Negroes," ran away as soon as they set foot in the Americas. On a collective level this is accurate; but at the individual level the reality was more nuanced. Some newcomers did get away immediately; others did so a few weeks after arrival and still others several months later. Quick to escape was Arrow (his "country name"). He left two days after being sold aboard the ship that had brought him from the Bight of Benin to South Carolina in 1761. Remarkably, despite his utter lack of preparation and his complete ignorance of his surroundings, he remained securely hidden for years.[25] Another man who ran away without delay was Sambo or more accurately Samba. He had left Gambia on the *Upton* on July 2, 1759. On August 28 the ship landed in Annapolis. The survivors' arrival was described in these terms: "upwards of 200 very likely, healthy Slaves, which are allowed by

Judges to be as choice a Parcel of Negroes as has ever been imported into this Province." Five days later, on September 2, Samba absconded from a plantation near Bladensburg, Maryland.[26] Another early escapee was also a Gambian who arrived in South Carolina on the *Anson* on April 18, 1757 and was advertised in June. He left with shackles on his legs, which points toward a previous escape. That would make two within three weeks.[27]

Juno was barely fifteen when she landed in Charleston on June 16, 1733. She had arrived from Cabinda (Angola) on the *Speaker*, one of the 316 individuals (out of 370) who made it to the end of the voyage. The slave dealer Joseph Wragg had sold her to a planter from Dorchester. She disappeared two weeks later.[28] One of the youngest new deportees to brave the unknown was a Gambian boy between the ages of twelve and fourteen. He got away from South Carolina slave traders John and Edward Neufville by jumping off a wagon on November 10, 1761, five weeks after he had landed.[29]

The overall frequency of those early escapes is impossible to gauge because only the effective getaways were recorded. There is no doubt that some newcomers were either caught in the act or hours or a few days later. Their attempts left no mark other than, at times, a few words in a planter's papers, as happened when seven men left Corotoman in a canoe on July 17, 1727, five days after they had arrived. Robert "King" Carter sent several people in pursuit, and they were arrested a week later.[30] Carter reported the incident in his diary, but other thwarted flights never left a trace, either in a newspaper, a personal journal, or a plantation book. Escapes after a few weeks or months seem to have been more common, or at least they were reported more often, which may distort their actual representation in the sum total of newcomers' getaways. One may argue that someone who had more than two days or two weeks at his/her disposal could carry out a better-planned breakout and stay in hiding for a longer time, prompting an owner to place an ad.

The words "shocked," "bewildered," and "confused" have all been used to characterize the Africans who ran away shortly after arrival.[31] But it is unlikely that this supposed bewilderment was the cause of their escape. On the contrary, confusion allied to their survival instinct should have made them wait until they took stock of their environment. Their early escape, which may appear irrational and impulsive, can instead be seen as the end result of a reasoned decision. While in the factories on the coast and during the Middle Passage, Africans had ample time to reflect on what they would do or try to do once they landed. Even though they did not know specifically what awaited them, they had endured enough hardships ranging from branding, shackling, and whippings, to abject brutality and humiliation to understand that their future would be miserable.

The time in the barracoons, the journey across the ocean, and what awaited them after landing were not three discrete parts of their experience; they formed a continuum. Escaping a day after arrival should therefore not be dismissed as impetuous. Rather, it can be understood as a decision that had matured during weeks or months and was acted upon at the first opportunity, which materialized on American soil rather than during the trek to the coast or in the barracoon. Although weakened by the Middle Passage, often sick or injured or both, the men's ankles and wrists blistered by the shackles they had worn for weeks, the young people who ran away within days of landing seized not the first opportunity that "offered itself" but rather that they sought. They could not have made elaborate plans as to how they were going to endure in the unfamiliar forests and swamps. But the fact that they took their future into their own hands so quickly is an indication of how self-confident and hopeful they were that they could make it. Their actions speak of self-assurance, resourcefulness, and especially for the solitary ones, an extraordinary resolve to effectively bring to fruition their difficult breakout, immersed as they were in an outlandish and hostile environment. It is those very qualities, not their supposed confusion, that enabled them to make their getaway even as the well-known proclivity of "new Negroes" to do so meant they were more closely watched. They were skillful enough to elude detection on the spot, and sufficiently clever to avoid dogs and slave catchers.

One of the difficulties in tracking down the newcomers was that, contrary to people attempting to reconnect with relatives or spouses, their itineraries were unpredictable. The Suffolk mercantile firm Gibson & Granbery acknowledged as much when it put up an ad for a "new Negro fellow of the Mundingo country," said to have arrived only three days before escaping. As the ad noted, "he could therefore have no particular route to prosecute."[32] Still, like native-born men and women, most African newcomers ultimately failed in their endeavor to remain free. Nevertheless, some survived in the woods and swamps on their own or in groups for weeks, months, and sometimes years. But despite the pervasiveness of the phenomenon, little documentation has surfaced about their personal experience. The nineteenth- and twentieth-century sources, such as slave narratives and interviews of freedpeople, which give native-born maroons a voice, are largely absent for eighteenth-century African maroons.

Although they offer few details about personal and communal lives, newspaper advertisements—individually and as a whole—provide some insights into the characteristics of African marronage and the particular experiences of African maroons.

ESCAPES IN GROUPS

As several studies show, one of the Africans' distinctiveness is that they typically ran away in groups. In colonial North Carolina, only a third of the runaways escaped in groups, but 88 percent of the groups whose origins are known were made up of Africans. In colonial Virginia, a little over half the Africans ran away in pairs or more; and in the same period in South Carolina, 50 percent fled in groups of three or more. More generally, based on a sample derived from their *Runaway Slave Database* of 8,400 individuals covering Virginia, North and South Carolina, Tennessee, and Louisiana for the periods 1790 to 1816 and 1838 to 1860—there were few African-born people at this late stage—John Hope Franklin and Loren Schweninger have concluded that two-thirds of the Africans left in groups of two or more and one-third in groups of at least five; while one-third of the American-born ran away in pairs and 14 percent in groups of five or more. In short, almost twice as many Africans as native-born left in groups.

As noted in chapter 1, when American-born men and women ran away in large groups it was mostly during the wars and mostly to "enemy" lines.

In contrast, African groups of five, six, and more were constituted irrespective of wider political events.[33] For example, two men, three women, and one boy, not yet renamed newcomers, escaped from a plantation near Dorchester, South Carolina, in November 1754; while seven Igbo (two women and five men) got away in 1758.[34] In September 1774 a group of five men of the "Guiney Country" escaped from a plantation on Little Ogeechee. Just a year later seven men and women, also from the "Guinea Country," along with one native boy, left a plantation in the same area of Georgia.[35] Among the largest groups of newly arrived Africans who went to the woods was a band of fourteen who ran away from To Ink, the plantation of John Burnley, a wealthy Virginia merchant, at the beginning of August 1773.[36] Leaving Hanover Town behind, they walked, undetected, into neighboring King William County where some were eventually captured, while the others continued on their expedition. Eleven weeks later they were seen near West Point.

Two main reasons explain why Africans, far more than African Americans, escaped in groups. Many of the latter tried to pass as free in Southern cities, an endeavor best achieved singularly; while Africans set their sights on the woods where a group was more likely to be an asset than a liability. More people meant more manpower to cultivate, hunt, fish, gather, fashion tools, and man canoes. In other words, a group had a better chance at survival in the wilds. Moreover, Africans predominantly escaped in groups because they continued to adhere to their own sociocultural framework that valued the group, not the individual.

Therefore, it is truly intriguing that many newcomers went to the woods by themselves. More than anyone else, they were extraordinarily determined to regain their freedom. To the difficulty of living in a foreign environment, they added an acute psychological burden that stemmed from the most fundamental aspect of their cultures. The severing of social links and even temporary seclusion are offensive to African cultures for they do not put a high value on or exalt the individual; rather, the individual's very existence is only intelligible within the group. Prolonged or habitual isolation is strongly frowned upon in Africa, where people seeking even small amounts of solitude are depicted as asocial. For deported

Africans to have been uprooted and separated from family and community was an immense, unfathomable loss; it tore apart the very core of their self-identification as human beings, because to be human was first and foremost to be part of the social fabric. To extract themselves once more from the plantation where they sometimes had shipmates or countrymen and women must have been a tremendously difficult decision whose psychological ramifications are difficult to fully grasp. Escaping as a group was a natural thing for Africans to do; but to do so alone was not. That in itself is a unique indicator of their resolve at getting their freedom back at all costs: not only the physical cost of surviving in the woods but the psychological cost of doing it alone as well.

Charles Ball, the grandson of an African, penned a vivid description of a lone African maroon, Paul from Congo, whom he encountered in the woods.[37] Paul had lived for a few years in South Carolina and spoke enough English to make himself understood. For almost as long as he had been in the country, he had been a maroon. He told Ball that two years earlier he had escaped to the swamps after a severe whipping. For six months he had sustained himself in the wilds while staying in contact with the slave quarters. He sometimes visited a woman, which led to his downfall because she eventually betrayed him. Paul was captured, ruthlessly whipped, and shackled to a heavy block of wood he had to drag to the fields. After three months of this punishment, he found an old file and freed himself. Once again, he ran to the woods. This time he did not last more than a week. Two men who were looking for their cattle found him asleep in the forest. After a third whipping, Paul's skin became "seamed and ridged with scars . . . from the pole of his neck to the lower extremity of the spine. The natural color of the skin had disappeared, and was succeeded by a streaked and speckled appearance of dusky white and pale flesh-color, scarcely any of the original black remaining. The skin . . . was grown fast to the flesh, and felt hard and turbid." To ensure that he would not run away again, Paul was fitted with an iron collar that formed an arch three feet above his head; three bells were fixed to the contraption, which was fastened by a large padlock. Each time he moved, his presence could be detected by sound and sight from far away.

Undeterred by the whippings, resolved to reconquer his freedom, Paul had escaped with the contraption above his head.

When Ball came across him, Paul had lived in the swamps for over three weeks and he already showed signs of distress. His muscular body was naked and his hair was "matted and shaggy." He also looked very hungry. His capacity to hunt was limited by the bells that frightened potential prey and signalled his presence if he dared venture on a plantation to steal or ask for provisions. He had lived on raw frogs, tortoises, and reptiles that he caught with a spear he had fashioned with a long black staff and a piece of iron. Ball promised Paul he would return a week later with a file. But before he came back, Paul had made a rope with hickory bark and hung himself from a sassafras tree. His body, surrounded by buzzards, crows, and ravens, was still hanging two months after his death. Paul's tragic life and lonely death were hardly exceptional in the maroon experience. Disheartening feelings of loneliness—particularly wrenching to Africans—and for some, utter despair, certainly loomed large in the isolated maroons' lives, which led some to kill themselves rather than return to slavery.

Another feature of the Africans' marronage is that they tended to abscond with other Africans, just as most native-born left with other native-born. In eighteenth-century South Carolina, 30 percent of the Creoles escaped with other Creoles, and 11 percent did so with Africans; in Virginia, the percentages were 16 and 5 respectively.[38] In South Carolina between 1804 and 1809, 60 percent of the groups in which Africans were present contained only Africans.[39] Groups were mostly formed by people from the same cultural area, although "mixed" groups were by no means uncommon. However, because of slaveholders' lack of knowledge about African ethnicities—whether real, Western-constructed, vague, false, or artificial—caution is necessary when trying to discern "ethnic" trends or characteristics among runaways based on information given in notices.

Indeed, all that can really be learned with confidence from newspaper notices is that Africans from the same geographic and cultural areas tended to run away together, not that their groups were systematically based on a common ethnicity. Being able to communicate was a manifest advantage, but one should not conclude from this that all group members were required to speak the same language. Multilingualism was and continues to be widespread in Africa, and the presence of even a single multilingual person would have facilitated communication in a multiethnic maroon group from the same cultural and/or geographic area. For example, thirty-five-year-old Betty, advertised in 1785, spoke "tolerable English, " and understood "two or three different African languages."[40] Thus, no theory of creolization and development of an encompassing "African" identity should be built on examples of multiethnic maroon groups—unless they mixed West Africans and West Central Africans, who had no contact with one another in Africa—because multiethnic settings were already a given of life in Africa.

A mixed group consisting of newcomers, established Africans, compatriots, and a man from another origin ran away from a plantation in Fairfax County, Virginia, on Sunday August 9, 1761. Two days later, their owner sent a long advertisement to the *Maryland Gazette*.[41] Such verbosity was not common, but neither was the planter. The prolix writer was twenty-nine-year-old George Washington. The absconders from his Dogue-Run farm at Mount Vernon were Peros, Jack, Neptune, and Cupid. Peros was a "yellowish" bearded man aged thirty-five to forty, who, having been in the country for a long time, had "little of his Country Dialect left." He was, according to Washington's slaveholder parlance, "a sensible judicious Negro."[42] Put another way, he was submissive and loyal. Or so he feigned to be. Jack, about thirty years old, was close to six feet tall and had scars on his cheeks. He too had been in the country for several years and was a "countryman," or compatriot, of the other two escapees, Neptune and Cupid. Neptune (twenty-five to thirty years old) had filed teeth, a shaved head, and small dots from the shoulders down to the waist; Cupid (twenty-three to twenty-five) had no distinctive signs, except that he was prone to pimples. Both talked "very broken and unintelligible *English*." Because the *Molly* was the only ship to have landed in Virginia in the summer of 1759, there is reason to believe that Neptune and Cupid were on board and had arrived from Bonny (in Nigeria) on

July 15.[43] In January 1760, Cupid had fallen ill with pleurisy and by the thirtieth was, according to Washington, "within a few hours of breathing his last."[44] Six months later, though, he was well enough to run away. Jack, Peros, and Cupid were held at Dogue-Run, but Neptune worked at River Farm; still they all ran away together.

In Washington's eyes nothing had motivated their escape: "they went off without the least Suspicion, Provocation, or Difference with any Body, or the least angry Word or Abuse from their Overseers." Because of the absence of a triggering incident, the future president believed the men would not "lurk about in the Neighborhood." They would not lay low for a while and come back when things had cooled down because there was nothing to cool down. Washington envisioned three possible destinations for the runaways. Peros had lived around Williamsburg and in King William County, so he hypothesized that the men may go there. Or they could possibly head toward Middlesex, where Jack had once resided. In either case, by going to a known place the men's likely objective would have been to be "harbored" by Jack's or Peros's relations. In other words, the four Africans would have become borderland maroons.

Washington thought of a third hypothesis as well: he suspected they could have gone somewhere else—he acknowledged he had no idea where—"in Hopes of an Escape." No colony was free of slavery and escape from servitude in the context of the time could mean that the men planned to go to an Indian nation, or to Spanish Florida that still welcomed runaways (Peros and Jack could have been aware of this). Another possibility Washington did not mention was for the men to ensconce themselves in the woods. What really happened is not recorded. How, when, and where Peros, Jack, and Cupid were captured remains unknown. As an additional punishment and a way of avoiding further departures, they were separated. Jack was sent to Home House Farm, Peros to Dogue Run, and Cupid to Creek Farm. Neptune's story appears more complicated. In May 1765, Washington wrote that he paid 3.7 pounds for "Prison Fees in Maryld Neptune."[45] This note suggests that Neptune may have remained a maroon for four years or else he was caught and ran away again. Whatever the case, he did succeed in making his way to Maryland. Upon being returned, he was exiled to Bullskin Plantation in Jefferson County, West Virginia.

Washington's trust in Peros and the fact that he was such "a sensible judicious Negro" suggest that he had not run away before and there is no indication that Jack had done so either. Still, something triggered their decision to take that risk in the absence—at least according to Washington—of any precipitating incident. The influence of Cupid and Neptune may have been the determining factor. Unlike Peros and Jack, they did not have support networks outside the plantation, but what they undoubtedly possessed, as newcomers, was a strong determination to free themselves. Their resolve may well have been what induced Peros and Jack to embark with them on their freedom quest.

THE WATER ROUTE

Newly arrived Africans who sought to escape from bondage appeared to have a penchant for flight by water. In colonial Georgia, between 1763 and 1775 of the twenty men and women who are believed to have been trying to escape by sea and heading for the coast, ten were newcomers, two were skilled Africans, and seven were of unstated origin.[46] In 1780s South Carolina, the reason why many Africans were caught near rivers and creeks was most likely because they were looking for a craft.[47] Small groups of Africans paddled their way out of enslavement at night along bayous like Cook, Castor, and Honoré who, after a month in Louisiana, left an Acadian Coast plantation in a pirogue. Four newcomers, from "the Kifa or Tifa Country," captured near Horry Island in 1797, were found in a red canoe with an indigo sail.[48]

Escapes by water fell into two main categories: either the absconders were on their way to becoming maroons or they were embarking on a trip that they hoped would take them back to their African homes. Illustrative of the first category was a group of three led by Boston, described as artful and cunning. He was a newcomer in 1763, but spoke "Very good English, Spanish and Portuguese," and had traveled "in different Parts of the World." Accompanying the multilingual and well-traveled Boston—probably a former sailor on European ships—went Toney and

Marcellus, two new arrivals who did not speak English. The three men took with them a quantity of clothes, three blankets, and two hats and made their getaway in a neighbor's canoe.[49] The accumulation of clothes and blankets provides more than a hint as to the men's intention: namely, to start a new life in the woods helped by the items they had been provident enough to take along.

Newcomers Mussa, Bob, Bath, Qua, and Bell made an equally well-prepared escape to the wilds: they fled in 1796 in a boat, each having taken with him his shoes, hats, two blankets, two jackets, two pairs of trousers, and flannel robins.[50] In Georgia in the autumn of 1774, six "new" Africans escaped from the plantations of Governor James Wright, stole a canoe to cross the Ogeechee River, and abandoned it in a creek near William Elliott's plantation. A group of Elliott's bondpeople had run away a while before, and they had remained, outlying, in the area. The six Africans were believed to have gone to stay with them.[51]

If their goal was not to establish or join maroon communities via water, another destination that newly arrived Africans sought was the Atlantic Ocean. Polydore and Boatswain, for example, carefully planned their escape with two men who lived on another plantation on Edisto Island, South Carolina. They disappeared on a four-oared boat and it was believed they might be "fool hardy enough to go out to sea."[52]

The story of another group of newcomers reveals what some Africans were planning to do once they reached the ocean. They escaped in a canoe belonging to Georgia Governor John Wright on November 18, 1774. A woman was with them but it is not clear if she was also a newcomer. The four men eventually dropped her off and she revealed that her companions "intended to go to look for their own country" and that the boat being too small, they could not take her along.[53]

What these Africans were embarking on was marronage too: they were going to settle in a place of freedom and self-determination outside white control and power. The fact that this place was their homeland complicated their endeavor; nonetheless it did not deter them from trying. Were their efforts senseless, naïve, or, as one scholar has put it, pathetic?[54] Could they really believe they could reach their home in a canoe?

Just a few weeks or months before their escape, the Africans had lived for four to six weeks on large ships battered by the winds, riding up and down the waves. They knew exactly what the crossing entailed and were well aware of the length of time they had spent on the ocean. They knew that if a powerful ship had sailed, say, for seventy days, a small canoe rowed by one or two men would take an inordinate amount of time to make the same voyage, if it made it to the end. In addition, they had suffered from thirst and hunger and knew that vast amounts of food and water would be needed to travel for months.

Thus, deducing that Africans sought to cross the ocean via small boats misapprehends what they were more likely trying to accomplish. A number of notices point to the fact that they were not looking to cross the ocean in a canoe, only to reach it, so as to embark, as stowaways, on sail ships. Will, a newcomer, was advertised two months after he got away from Jordan Anderson in Virginia in 1768; he had already made three attempts to get back to his country and Anderson warned all masters of vessels against carrying him away.[55] Caesar, who escaped in 1780 from Prince George County, Maryland, "boast[ed] much of his family in his own country . . . it being a common saying with him, that he is no common negro." Caesar was accustomed "to go by water" and his owner believed he might try to board a vessel.[56] Similarly, on August 30, 1817 Sampson, Joe, and Bill, speaking "very broken English, not being long in the country"—they were evidently victims of the illegal slave trade—made their escape from Duplin County in North Carolina. Their owner suspected they were going "to some seaport Town, and try to get on board some vessel." They were caught, but Sampson and Joe tried again and left on October 20 for the same purported destinations.[57] They may have wanted to go North, if they knew of the free states, but the possibility that these newcomers were aiming for Africa cannot be excluded.

During their captivity on the coast Africans had been aware of the great number of vessels that sailed in and out. They knew they regularly linked their side of the ocean to the other side. Once in America, what they could not know was that the ships sailing out before Independence were not going anywhere close to Africa, but rather to Great Britain or

France; and that those that reached the African continent after the war could anchor thousands of miles from their homeland.

CLOTHES, BLANKETS, AND TOOLS

Africans often escaped with only the clothes on their backs, which is not surprising given that recent arrivals were provided few pieces of clothing. When Will was committed to the Isle of Wight jail in the fall of 1773, he wore two cotton jackets but "neither Shirt nor Breeches."[58] Equally ill-clad, Fortune was captured on Hall's Island, South Carolina, with "an old white negro cloth jacket, and a piece of negro cloth round his waist."[59] Flora from Angola ran away with only her blue petticoat on; and Rachael, a fifteen-year-old who had just arrived in South Carolina, escaped in July 1804 with "nothing on but an osnaburgs shift."[60] One man wore only a jacket and two pieces of an old blanket; and another was found with "nothing on but a piece of oznabrugs [*sic*] rapped [*sic*] round his waist."[61]

Some Africans escaped completely naked. When a woman and a man ran away just a day or two after arriving in Purrysburg, South Carolina, she wore "an old brown quilted petticoat" as an interim garment, but the man "had nothing on but a blanket." Also naked was a "tall, slim, black new negro" who had "only a new blanket."[62] The nakedness of the newcomers, distressing as it is, is of special interest because it indicates that some ran away immediately after arrival, before they had received any clothes, a process that could take a few days. When the last Africans brought to the United States disembarked from the *Clotilda* in Mobile, Alabama, in July 1860 they were naked—as was the rule, their clothes had been removed prior to embarkation—and they only received rags and pieces of skins several days later. Real clothes came about two weeks after they landed.[63]

Paradoxically, some African maroons' nakedness can be interpreted as an accomplishment; a sign of early escape. Yet it also speaks of isolation in the woods: they had found nobody who could give them some minimal clothing. Nakedness was unnatural and humiliating to Africans; and the men and women of the *Clotilda* said repeatedly that it was one of the most distressing aspects of the Middle Passage. Fifty years later they still wept at the degradation. Those Africans who ran away naked thus bravely sacrificed dignity for determination to free themselves at any cost.

Amid descriptions of country marks, real or supposed ethnicities, heights, skin colors, and clothes, one item appears disproportionately often in newspaper notices targeting African newcomers: the dual, Dutch, or duffel blanket.[64] In Georgia, for example, David, a Gambian who spoke no English, ran from a brickyard with the clothes on his back and his blanket.[65] So did two young men, about twenty, who were brought to Charleston on the *Alert* on June 11, 1806 and ran away on August 31. Three months later they were still free, and their owner advertised for them, stressing that they had taken their red and yellow striped blankets.[66] Also gone with their blankets were one Calabar (from Nigeria) and seven Coromante men (from Ghana), who escaped from True-Blue, a South Carolina indigo plantation.[67] Jack was captured with his "old Dutch blanket" in November 1774 and had not been "reclaimed" four months later.[68]

While only a minority of Africans took off with their blankets, this action is noteworthy when compared with the habits of native-born runaways. Less than 1 percent of African Americans in Virginia left with their blankets; and although Africans represented about 4 percent of the people advertised between 1736 and 1803, they were 22 percent of those who took their blankets.[69] In South Carolina, 92 percent of the people who brought their blankets with them were Africans; but those who had been in the country for a long time were not particularly inclined to do so. Interestingly, when three West Africans—Martin, Pompey, and Joe—ran away together in May 1773, only Pompey and Joe, who were new, took their blankets.[70]

Why are these blankets significant? Coming from more clement climes, Africans knew that a blanket was indispensable to their welfare in the woods. But besides comfort, the item tells of long-term plans; by taking it with them the Africans involuntarily signaled their intention to stay away. The blanket was a sign that truancy was not at play, and slaveholders understood the message: one South Carolinian stressed that he was sure Cudjo had gone back to Georgia because he had taken two blankets with him.[71] The blanket signified that the person intended to stay in the woods permanently.

African maroons also displayed a greater tendency than the native-born to take along tools. Axes, hoes, and a canoe belonging to a neighbor were items that three men from Angola took when they escaped from a Wando Neck (South Carolina) plantation in February 1734.[72] Likewise, in the fall of 1761 three Gambians recently arrived in Charleston carried their blankets and their axes, and two Igbo newcomers grabbed their blankets and their axes and escaped in the cold month of February from a Stono plantation.[73]

Some native-born runaways also took their tools but there was a striking difference between them and the Africans. The former were almost invariably skilled men: coopers, carpenters, shoemakers, or sawyers; they needed the tools of their trade because their objective was to establish themselves in a city where they could pass as free artisans.[74] The Africans' tools were those of field hands: axes and hoes. Useless in town, they were essential in the woods.

AFRICAN COMMUNITIES

Although two-thirds of the Africans who escaped did so in groups, sources reveal next to nothing about the existence of African communities. No African maroon settlement, at least any that was described in the sources as such, was discovered in the Southern colonies or states. And "described" is the operative word, as evidently most black men and women in the 1600s and early 1700s were Africans and there was no need for the records to stress that point. "Negro" maroons were thus mostly Africans (some had stayed a while in the Caribbean) until a later generation born in the country was old enough to run away to the woods. As such, even though the early records do not explicitly reveal the existence of African maroon communities, they do so implicitly.

Some sketchy details about a colony that might have been made up entirely of Africans were revealed in a letter to the Lords of Trade in London written by Lieutenant Governor William Gooch of Virginia. Sometime in the spring of 1729, a group of about fifteen people escaped from a new plantation at the head of the James River. They planned to establish themselves as a community and took weapons, ammunition, food, tools, as well as their clothes and bedding. Gooch's letter describing the episode contains no indication as to the origins of these maroons, but some historians have asserted without any corroborative documentation that they were Africans.[75] An account by local amateur historian T. E. Campbell is often cited as substantiation.[76]

In 1728, according to Campbell, many recently arrived Africans ran away from plantations on the Upper James River and some established themselves near present-day Lexington, where they "built a town of boughs and grass houses in the manner of the homes in their native land, and set up a tribal government under a chief, who had been a prince among his own people before slave traders brought him across the Atlantic." The community grew crops and prospered and it is only the following year that soldiers from all over Virginia destroyed the camp, killed the chief, and returned the settlers to slavery. Unfortunately, as is the case throughout his book, Campbell does not cite any sources—not even Gooch's letter. In addition, his version contradicts the Lieutenant Governor's letter on one important point. Gooch stated that the group's escape occurred "Sometime after my Last." He had sent a letter to the Lords of Trade on March 26.[77] He further established the short existence of the camp—three months—when he mentioned that the settlers had "already begun to clear the ground." If they had been established for a year, the land would already have been cleared.

Nonetheless, it is quite probable that these maroons were Africans. Although it cannot be asserted as an established fact, significant clues point to an African origin and more precisely to a particular subgroup. As mentioned earlier, to take tools and blankets and all the necessities of life to the woods was characteristic of African newcomers who did not intend to go back to the plantations to get supplies, as was running away in a group, especially such a large one. In the eighteenth century, the largest group of Virginia escapees was made up of fourteen newcomers.[78] Whereas Africans who had been in the country for several years and the native-born were the most likely to have access to firearms and ammunition, it happened that "new Negroes" absconded with guns. In any event, the group could have been "mixed." Thousands of Africans had landed in Virginia since the early 1600s and the established African and native-born populations were substantial. However, the probability that the community was mostly or exclusively made up of newcomers cannot be discounted, as 1,567 Africans had arrived between 1728 and the first quarter of 1729.[79]

According to Gooch, as the community was putting down its roots in "a very obscure place among the Mountains," a group of men, including the maroons' owner, went searching for them. There was a short exchange of fire—"a shot or two"—and one maroon was wounded. Gooch stressed that they were all captured and taken back to the plantation. He did not provide any description of the settlement, let alone of its organization.

Another reason for the lack of visibility in the sources of African maroon communities may be that rather than forming large settlements, they lived in small groups, although the former certainly existed as well. Notices of newcomers brought to jail give credence to this hypothesis. They often concern three to five Africans "taken up" together. For instance, four men—each with a blanket—who seemed "to have been lately imported," were committed to jail in Onslow County (North Carolina) in October 1769. Four "New Negro Fellows, of the Angola country," supposed to "belong to one master," were captured, with their blankets, a few miles from Charleston in August 1785. When Dautra, a newcomer from Congo, was arrested he stated after multiple examinations that he had been in the company of four other men.[80] On March 27, 1814 four Africans "having the marks of their country or village" and coming from two different towns, were captured at Etienne Trépagnier's Louisiana plantation.[81]

As may be anticipated, the capture of a few individuals attracted much less attention than the discovery of a settlement of two dozen people. With one major exception: regardless of size, groups made the news when they were accused of having committed "diverse depredations." One may argue that the African groups' arrests did not elicit attention because they were not known to have been involved in raids. This proposition dovetails nicely with what will be shown later: that newcomers set out, from the start, to count primarily on themselves with no intention of going back to the plantations to take food and other items.

Several ads suggest that some African newcomers were harbored at the borderland of plantations. For example, two Gambians, Prince and Chopco, who talked "but little English" and had escaped seven months earlier, were supposed "to be harbour'd at some plantation." Another Gambian, Samba, ran away in 1785 and was captured at the plantation of John Deas—a wealthy planter and partner of the international slave trading firm David and John Deas. Samba managed to escape and was believed to still be "lurking thereabouts." On the same plantation, another "new Negro," Dembo [Demba], arrived less than a year later. Yarrow, a "Surroga" newcomer not yet renamed ran away in September 1789 and was seen on a plantation on the Savannah River in October. According to his owner, he had "lost" the clothes he was wearing when he left. More probably they were so worn out that he had to change them. He had found helping hands since he was now dressed in an old pair of breeches and had a brass watch around his neck.[82] The same was true of Charles, a Gambian who ran to the woods three weeks after landing from the *Yaminarew* in August 1770. He left Amherst County, Virginia, wearing a cotton jacket, a pair of long cotton breeches, and a linen cap, but when arrested ten months later in Fairfax County he was wearing "crocus trowers" and a felt hat.[83]

Prince, Chopco, Demba, and Samba were going to places where they had not lived before. Isaac Porcher—a planter from South Carolina who owned seventy-five people—believed he knew why: Clawss, a newcomer from Angola, escaped from his plantation in 1737 and, "As there is abundance in this Province of that Nation," Porcher explained, "he may chance to be harbour'd among some of them."[84] His hypothesis seems just right; it was only logical that a concentration of people of the same origin would result in extended complicity.

Another case further bolsters this premise. On February 19, 1775, five newcomers—four men and a woman—escaped from the house of

Edward Batchelor and Co. in New Bern, North Carolina.[85] The men were Kauchee, Boohum, Sambo Pool, and Ji. The woman was named Peg Manny. They all left with their blankets, and none spoke a word of English. Where they came from is unknown, but it was most likely Senegambia. "Sambo Pool" was evidently Samba a Pullo (singular of Fulbe, the name the Fulani give their ethnic group). Boohum could be Bocoum and Ji is most likely a rendering of Njie, a common last name among the Wolof of Senegambia. In the same newspaper issue as the one in which he advertised the runaways, Batchelor also reminded readers of the sale of men, women, and children who had arrived on the schooner *Hope*, the ship the five Africans had traveled on.

When Samba and the others escaped in February, they had been in the country for only two months. A man named William Gatling caught them about ten miles away. On April 26, two months after their first escape, Boohum and Kauchee ran away again. Batchelor thought he knew where they might be: Gatling had since "purchased a Wench who was imported with them" and they might be "lurking about that Neighbourhood."[86] It is possible they had been attracted to Gatling's plantation the first time because they knew their compatriots lived there and could provide assistance and comfort, and they went back a second time to connect with their shipmate. That newly arrived Africans were able to find shipmates/compatriots is supported by another case: the intriguing story of a man who spoke no English and has remained anonymous. He was captured numerous times on the same plantation at Santee in South Carolina; and although he was repeatedly sent to jail in Charleston, he always returned.[87] The fact that he kept going back to a particular place despite the risks suggests that he found assistance and companionship there.

In the alien and closely monitored environment Africans lived in, to find shipmates and coutrypeople demanded a method. As has been well documented, the plantation communication system was particularly effective and news flowed even from dozens of miles away. With the help of more settled countrymen and women and without leaving the quarters, newcomers could get information as to the whereabouts of their compatriots living in the area. Once they had located them, the next phase was to establish direct contact, which could be done by joining the nightly expeditions enslaved men regularly made to visit loved ones on other plantations. While there, plans could be made for a harboring scheme in the vicinity or to prepare a coordinated escape. Collective flights from different plantations were indeed organized by newcomers. Sanco, Doo, and Lufa (or Luther), who talked "but little English," fled together in early January 1839 from different plantations in Brazoria County, Texas. Although they lived on different estates, the three men nevertheless succeeded in synchronizing their breakout. They were maroons for close to three months before being caught and delivered to the sheriff. Once locked up, they escaped again.[88]

The harboring of newcomers on distant plantations and their absconding in concert from different places is significant. In light of what some people were able to accomplish, it becomes clear that newly arrived Africans who became maroons were not devoid of resources. If some made it on their own two days after arrival without any assistance, others elaborated strategies, created opportunities, made use of the existing social structures of the quarters, or created their own to get out of the plantations and into the woods.

RECIDIVISTS AND LONG-TERM MAROONS

Some African newcomers showed a tremendous amount of resolve to recover their freedom; these recidivists ran away not once but several times, were jailed, whipped, shackled, and closely monitored, but still tried to return to the woods. George of the Gold Coast (Ghana), enslaved in Albemarle County (Virginia) first went to the woods in January 1767. For two years he "rambled" as far south as King William and Hanover counties, more than a hundred miles away. After being caught and sent back to Green Mountain, he escaped again in the spring of 1770. He was still unaccounted for in February 1771.[89] When newcomer Dick ran away on June 3, 1777 it was his fourth attempt. Following his three previous escapes, he was jailed in New Bern (North Carolina) and three of his toes were cut off.[90]

Recidivists were, by definition, caught at least once but some were savvy enough to carry on their lives in the woods for long stretches at a time in between captures. This was the case with Homady, from Angola (he may also have been Hamady, a Muslim from Guinea/Senegambia), and Dick. They ran away together in August 1770 from a plantation on the Santee River in South Carolina and were still gone the following January. Homady was caught, but escaped in July 1772 and was advertised eight months later.[91] On and off, he had been able to remain in the woods for at least thirteen months.

The story, stretching over at least two years, of two men from the "Kissee country" (Sierra Leone) is typical of the kind of determination some maroons exhibited. Massa was about twenty-five, and Barra eighteen when Andrew McCredie, a Savannah slave merchant, sold them to planter Jacob Russell shortly after their arrival. On July 6, 1788 they deserted Russell's plantation. Barra was caught but, although under guard, he succeeded in escaping from a boat on November 21. At some point Massa was also captured; and eventually so was Barra for the second time. In July 1789, a year after his first escape, Massa absconded again. Barra did too but was captured for the third time. Undeterred and singularly focused, in July 1790 he hopped his way out of the plantation with an iron on each leg.[92] Within two years, Barra tried to gain his freedom back four times; whippings, close watch, and shackles did nothing to discourage him.

Because newcomers were by definition the least experienced maroons in terms of knowledge of topography and slave patrol habits, it might be deduced that their marronage was short-lived. Yet despite the specific obstacles they faced, some were able to survive in the woods and swamps for months and even years. In April 1738, South Carolinian Thomas Wright posted an ad for the four Africans he was looking for: Trampase had left in 1736 and was still unaccounted for two years later, Paul escaped in August 1737, and Will and Summer followed in January 1738.[93] Yoat and an anonymous companion were gone for almost a year. When captured in June 1754 in Surry County, Virginia, both men were interrogated. By their own reckoning, and using an African way of counting time, they said they had been in the woods for "ten moons" or ten months.[94] Two men supposed to be Mandinka had also been out "ten moons" when committed to Onslow prison in North Carolina.[95]

The fascinating story of two men who lived on the same plantation and escaped within a two-month interval of one another shed important light on these long-term escapes. Lymus got away from lawyer James Parsons's plantation in Colleton County, South Carolina, in September 1761 with another man, not named, who was captured before long on a small marshy islet near Long Island. Although Parsons interrogated him, the man did not say anything. Lymus was finally captured but escaped once more in September 1762. In January 1763, Parsons advertised for him again. This time, Lymus was described not only as "a very black tall likely young man," but he had another characteristic: he was frostbitten and one of his big toes had lost some flesh. The rigors of life in the woods in winter had taken their toll. Lymus was arrested again. He had run away twice and was caught twice in sixteen months, and Parsons was determined to put a stop to his marooning. He put him in irons and cut off part of his right ear, as a new ad revealed: in addition to having frostbite, the young African had now "lost" a piece of his ear. But as seen in other cases, punishments, devices, and the hardships of life in the woods did little to discourage the most strong-minded. In November 1763, Lymus broke away with shackles on his legs.[96] After three years, three escapes, and more time spent in the woods than on a plantation, his body scarred by his rejection of enslavement, Lymus was still not ready to relinquish his hope of freedom.

Another case of long-term marronage unfurled just before and after the abolition of the slave trade. In December 1809, Nicolas Villain of Fausse-Rivière, Louisiana, offered two hundred dollars for the capture of Pyrame (Birame) from Senegambia. Birame was a newcomer bought at auction on June 26, 1806. He escaped a month later, on July 25, and was captured on August 15. Jailed in Baton-Rouge, he managed to run away as he was being transported back to Villain. From August 1806 to the end of 1809, Birame lived in the woods, but in December, he was caught and locked up in Iberville. Put in irons and confined to a jail cell, he filed off his shackles and made his getaway. By January 1811, a year after his latest escape, he was still at large.[97] Between June 1806 when he arrived and at least until the beginning of 1811, Birame had lived as a maroon for about four years and four months, and as a slave for eight weeks.

Arrow arguably provides the most spectacular example of successful marronage by a newly arrived African. He was, according to his owner, a "Papaw." This was the term used for Africans who had embarked at Grand Popo in present-day Benin. Arrow had probably been transported on the *Marlborough*, the only recorded ship that came from the Bight of Benin in 1759. She landed in Charleston on July 29, with 293 men, women, and children on board; 105 individuals (26 percent) had died during the Middle Passage.[98] Arrow escaped two days after arrival, on July 31. Sixteen months later, in December 1761, James Parsons advertised for his capture, manifestly following a sighting.[99] A year passed without any actionable news and in January 1763 Parsons again put up a notice to no effect. Arrow had been a maroon for more than two years already. Exactly a year later, Parsons placed still another ad.[100] He speculated that Arrow was "perhaps the same advertised to be in Savannah goal." Whether he was or not, Arrow had already accomplished a tour de force: he had been a maroon for at least three years, just two days after setting foot on American soil.

CAPTURES AND SURRENDERS

African newcomers were captured in the woods, the swamps, and on plantations, and a great number of them were thrown in jail and advertised. It was necessary to publish these jail and workhouse notices when the men who captured the runaways and maroons had no idea who their owners were, most often because they were not from the neighborhood or even the county, colony, or state. The ads consequently help map the maroons' itineraries because the first valuable information they yield is that many newcomers did not live in the areas in which they were apprehended. They came from somewhere else, often far away. Sampson, Molly, and their two-month-old were captured twenty miles from Augusta, Georgia, in January 1769 after having walked from a place "near the salt-water," at least a hundred and seventy miles away.[101] More impressive still, a man from the Gold Coast jailed in Wilmington, North Carolina, had come all the way from Indian Land, South Carolina, almost two hundred miles away.[102] From far inland, he was getting close to the coast. Omar ibn Said of Senegal walked two hundred miles too, from South to North Carolina. James and Dick, sent to the Richmond County jail in Virginia, "told so many different stories in what part of the state or continent their owner lives, and speak such broken language, it is impossible to say where they belong," complained the sheriff. He finally showed them rice and they made him understand that "their owner makes it in great abundance," which led him to believe they had come from "the southern states."[103] Another Dick and his companion Will ran away from two adjacent plantations on the Congaree River in South Carolina and made their way to Virginia, close to four hundred miles away. They were caught "almost naked" in December and thrown into the Sussex County jail.[104]

These captures in unknown and distant territory beg the question: why would Africans travel hundreds of miles when cover could be found closer to where they were enslaved? Apart from those whose destination was the Atlantic coast, it can be argued that it was their lack of knowledge of the geography and society of this new land that pushed some to venture so far away. They may have been exploring the landscape in search of the ecological systems to which they could best relate: savannahs for the Sahelians, or tropical forests for the Central Africans. In a familiar environment they could better procure food, heal themselves, and cultivate the land. It is equally possible that they hoped their journey would take them to places where they would find people different from the slaveholders with whom they had been in contact thus far. In Africa, diverse populations and social organizations could be found within reasonable distance from one another. Some societies practiced slavery, others did not; some were based on a rigid caste system while others were egalitarian. Thus, newly arrived Africans may have thought or hoped that diversity—namely, free society—also existed in the South. Another question raised by arrests on faraway plantations is, what course of action were the Africans planning on these distant estates? Shelter from the weather was one reason for maroons to venture to plantation grounds, but some people probably stumbled upon unmarked, wild territory without realizing they were encroaching upon someone's property and that people were on the lookout for runaways and maroons. Such incursions on planters' land were always dangerous and sometimes fatal, as two newcomers who entered Elias Ball's estate at St. John, South Carolina, on August 14, 1772 realized too late. They may have been looking for friends—or for food, since they were in a cornfield. They fled when discovered. Although one got away, the watchman shot the other in the back, and he died three days later.[105] He was unknown in the area and Ball put up a notice in the newspaper asking his owner to come forward.

Africans who were arrested obviously had hoped to remain under cover, free to pursue their lives as maroons either close to the place where they had been caught or further away. But others—like Primus, for example— gave themselves up. Primus was not "taken up" or captured but had "come" to the plantation of Nathaniel Polhill in St. Matthew's Parish, South Carolina, in the early fall of 1780.[106] His reason for doing so was not documented. Nor was any explanation recorded when two Igbo, Billy and Sue, walked to the plantation of James Butler by the Great Ogeechee River in Georgia on March 3, 1781. They said they had come from Stono, South Carolina, and had been on the run "a long time."[107] Although they were not explicit about it, the reason they gave themselves up may be surmised from the "long time" they survived on their own. They may have come to the end of their strength.

As might be expected, sickness or exhaustion ended some Africans' lives in the wilds. They were captured when they became too vulnerable. Too sick to remain in the woods after four months, Tom, a recent arrival, gave himself up at a Parker's Ferry plantation in South Carolina. Illness was also the cause of a young Senegalese couple's demise. They had arrived in Louisiana on July 16, 1720 on the *Ruby*, the first slave ship from Senegambia to land in the French colony. When the Senegambians landed, naturalist and historian Antoine Simon Le Page du Pratz traveled from Natchez to receive his share of the captives. "My stay at New Orleans appeared long," he wrote, "before I heard of the arrival of the Negroes. Some days after the news of their arrival, M. Hubert brought me two good ones, which had fallen to me by lot. One was a young Negro about twenty, with his wife of the same age; which cost me both together 1320 livres, or £55 sterling." About six months later, during their first winter in the colony, the young people ran to the woods. Du Pratz viewed their courageous attempt at freeing themselves as little more than laziness. Of the man he wrote, "his youth and want of experience made him believe he might live without the toils of slavery." The couple was eventually found "by the Tonicas [Native Americans], constant friends of the French." They were about sixty miles from Natchez. The husband "died of a defluxion on the breast, which he catched by running away into the woods."[108]

Other maroons, however, did not surrender. One frail man who did not speak English was caught in a swamp after he had swum across the Santee River in the spring of 1765. He was very feeble, wore old clothes, was suffering from starvation, and his feet and hands were so crippled that he could not walk.[109] Life in the woods had taken its toll; still, he was desperately trying to leave and in the absence of a canoe took the risk of swimming across the river.

Two men from "Guiney," Pompey and Sambo, were captured in January 1771 one mile from the plantation of William Heatly of St. Matthew's Parish, South Carolina. Although they were entirely naked, they had not run away shortly after arrival. Through an interpreter they revealed that they had already been bought twice.[110] Life in the woods was hard on them but they survived there for about twenty months. Their feet and legs were extremely swollen due to their "lying in the Cold," according to Heatly. Even so, naked in the dead of winter, exhausted, and feeble, Pompey and Sambo had not renounced their precarious freedom.

* * *

Of all maroons, African newcomers were the least cognizant of what it took to survive in the American wilds; yet, by default, it was the only place where they could find refuge, the only place where they could exile themselves from the inhuman foreign world into which they were thrust.

The equally foreign world of the woods and swamps was the only one where they could try to create a new life, different from the one they had just ran away from, but just as different from the African one they knew. Despite their unfamiliarity with the wilderness into which they were going, by taking their hoes, axes, and blankets, they seem to have prepared for their stay as best they could. Their organization and foresight also suggest that they envisioned their new existence differently than native-born maroons did. The latter remained connected with the black and white sections of the plantations and the larger world in multiple ways; they maintained family ties and friendships, and while in exile, continued to appropriate or trade for food and useful items. But most African newcomers had little use for the plantations once they left. They could hardly count on extended networks over a neighborhood or a county and often had little or no knowledge of the topography of plantations, making it challenging to distinguish between a building that housed cured meat and one for the storage of tools or grain. What their preparations hints at is that they had no intention of secretly returning to the plantations. Even if, in the long run, they realized they might have to establish contact with people in the quarters to survive, most, it appears, ran away with the intention of relying primarily on themselves.

The lives of African maroons whose fragmentary stories can be reconstructed—particularly those of people who had arrived recently—illustrate to what extremes they were willing to go to recover their freedom. Records show that they displayed a high degree of resourcefulness and organizational skills ranging from finding shipmates and countrymen and women and coordinating escapes from different plantations, to trekking in secret for weeks and managing to flee with shackles on their feet. All suffered, some succeeded, and most failed, but like no other group of maroons, they literally stepped into the unknown with bravery and confidence in their ability to create a new life for themselves.

[3]

BORDERLAND MAROONS

J OHN SALLY "runned away an'
didn' never come back. Didn' go no
place either. Stayed right 'roun' de plantation."[1] Like Sally, most maroons
did not look for freedom in remote locations; instead they settled in the
borderlands of farms and plantations. If not caught by men and dogs, and
depending on their health, survival skills, and their families' and friends'
level of involvement, they could live there for years. These men and
women have become the most invisible maroons although their (white
and black) contemporaries were well aware of their existence. As is true
for most maroons their lives have remained partially unknown but several
individuals who later got out of the South, or had loved ones who went to
the woods, described that experience in autobiographies and memoirs. In
addition, detailed and intimate information about their existence can be
found in the recollections of the formerly enslaved men and women gathered by the Works Progress Administration. Some were former maroons
themselves, others were their kin, acquaintances, and protectors.

Pieced together, these stories offer a striking portrait of a unique population and delineate how and why one became a borderland maroon; who
the men, women, and children who settled by the plantations were; and
what skills they needed to master in order to survive in the woods.

FAMILY CONNECTIONS

South, North, Indian territories, the periphery or the hearts of cities,
remote swamps, or the edges of their own habitations—it was not always

immediately apparent to slaveholders where their escaped workers were headed or if they planned on being away for a few days, a few weeks, or hoped to remain at large forever. In other words, it was difficult to tell whether the absconders were truants, maroons, or runaways. Unless one was confronted with a habitual fugitive whose routine was known, or someone whose tentative destination could be guessed, it was often assumed that the escapee would go to the woods and stay there for a short time. Absconders were thus often treated as truants before some were reclassified as runaways headed for a Southern city or a free state. However, when the absence continued, the individual would be labeled an outlier (or still referred to as a runaway) if known to be "lurking about" or "skulking" in the neighborhood.

It goes without saying that the people who chose to settle close to the farms and plantations had crucial reasons for doing so. Frederick Law Olmsted's conversation with an overseer indicates one of their major motivations. The overseer said of the runaways he knew, "[T]hey almost always kept in the neighborhood, because they did not like to go where they could not sometimes get back and see their families."[2] When people left—for Spanish Florida, Texas, Mexico, or the North, depending on geography and time—they did so with little hope of seeing their loved ones again. The latter, in turn, could spend a lifetime wondering if their relative had made it to safety or died trying. To sever the relations that sustained an otherwise dreadful life was a difficult, heart-wrenching decision both for those who remained and for those who left. Runaways accepted this as the unavoidable price of their desire to be free; but for others, the priorities were reversed. They escaped to avoid being separated from their relatives or to reconstitute their families.

Newspaper ads are a good tool to map this geography of love, migration, and defiance, but they must be treated with care. When a slaveholder wrote that he "suspected" or "believed" that someone was going back to a relative or spouse, he made it clear that he was not fully certain this was the case. That some people had other plans in mind is a given; still, slaveholders made sure they kept track of family connections as best they could because they knew that reunification was a strong motivating factor in desertions. In colonial South Carolina, apparently four times as many escapees were said to have been looking for relations rather than trying to pass for free; 66 percent of the male runaways and 80 percent of the females were thought to have run off to relatives or spouses.[3] In colonial Chesapeake, between 29 (Virginia) and 54 (Southern Maryland) percent of the runaways were expected to be heading to their relatives or acquaintances.[4] In North Carolina (1775 to 1840), 57 percent of 1,380 advertised individuals for whom a destination was provided were believed to be attempting reunification, while only 7 percent were thought to be going to a free state.[5] Reflecting on these numbers, historian Philip Morgan has concluded, "A considerable number of advertised runaways were said to be visiting acquaintances, friends, or relatives."[6] In reality, they were not "said" to be "visiting" because that terminology was not used. Among the thousands of notices gathered from New York, New Jersey, Pennsylvania, Georgia, Virginia, Maryland, and South Carolina newspapers, the word "visit" appears only five times.[7]

Morgan equates what he considers visits with *petit marronage*: people went to see a loved one in the neighborhood and came back after a few days. These activities, illegal as they were, were expected and did not translate into manhunts and notices. However, when slaveholders posted ads stressing that runaways were thought to be going to relatives, especially in distant places, not only did they not use the term visit, but the mere fact of advertising for their capture shows that they did not expect them to come back quickly and voluntarily. To be sure, occasionally someone would go and see a spouse faraway, as did a man from Virginia who visited his wife in Alabama and returned; a transgression for which he received two hundred blows with a paddle.[8] But was a family visit Lucy's objective when she left Saint Thomas Parish in South Carolina with her four children, the older aged eight, to join her sisters in Georgia?[9] Or the goal of a man, his pregnant wife, and their two sons, aged five and two and a half, when they departed from Georgia supposedly headed for "Carolina neighboring plantations," where the man had "a great number of relations and acquaintances"?[10] The parents took enormous risks—including being sold separately if caught—with two small children in tow and one on the way. They went away equipped with clothes, provisions, and blankets for what could only be a long stay. The stakes were just too high for them to envision a simple visit to relatives, followed by a return home. There were, indeed, visits meant to be just that: brief encounters, and there were reunifications—or attempts at reunification—that took place at the borderlands, because once successfully reunited with their families, runaways had few options. The only places that were close to their loved ones and also relatively safe were the forests and swamps that bordered the plantations.

Men, mostly, and some women, attempted to permanently reunite with relatives following the dislocation of families that was all too common in slavery. When a slaveholder migrated, he sometimes sold some individuals to help finance the move and took along the rest; but even when everyone was part of the journey the separation of some families was inevitable, because husbands and wives often resided in different places. They were said to have "broad" husbands or wives, as in abroad. It was especially frequent when they belonged to small farms and plantations where prospective mates were in short supply. These "broad marriages" were often judged problematic, at least by the males' owners.[11] "When a man and his wife belong to different persons," warned an 1833 essay on the management of slaves, "they are liable to be separated from each other, as well as their children, either by the caprice of either of the parties, or where there is a sale of property. This keeps up an unsettled state of things, and gives rise to repeated new connections." What was at issue was not the agony of dislocation but its potential harm to the slave system. Men, out of the "control of their master for a time" as they visited their wives, got a dangerous "feeling of independence." But even worse, "wherever their wives live, they consider their homes."[12] And this was exactly what precipitated a large number of men's escapes: they wanted to stay with their wife and children.

Couples or families who decided to stay together permanently when one person was slated for sale or migration essentially used two strategies to achieve their goal. In the first case, the spouse who was to move away escaped and hid in the woods, like a North Carolina woman did when she learned that her owner was migrating west with his workforce. Because she had a broad marriage and was determined to prevent a separation, she took her infant girl with her and settled in the swamps close to her husband.[13] Some families chose to stay where they were, with all their relatives. When Samuel Andrews moved to Camden, South Carolina, sometime in 1777, eleven men, women, and children failed to follow. Andrews believed they had stayed behind in the neighborhood of his old plantation.[14]

The second strategy was the opposite of the first: the spouse who was to stay followed the departing one to new and unknown territory. Such was the decision made by Randol, who ended up being wanted in four states. Randol was believed to have "marks of shot about his hips, thighs, neck and face, as he has been shot at several times." He was fired at as he was escaping from a plantation in Franklin County, North Carolina, in January 1817. The wounded young man likely stayed in the woods near his wife, who lived on another plantation. In February 1818, a year after Randol had absconded, his spouse was taken to the Deep South. What Randol did was expected: his owner was certain he would follow his wife. To thwart this project, the planter put up ads in North Carolina, South Carolina, Tennessee, and Georgia newspapers.[15]

To follow his family was also the choice made by Will, a man who had "the incisions of the whip on his back," an indication that he had run away before and/or stood up to authority. He was believed to be heading for a plantation by the Coosahatchie River in South Carolina. Just a week before, his wife and five children had been sold to a planter living there.[16] Other examples help reveal the profound attachment that bonded spouses and led them to become maroons. Strongly suspected of migrating South, was Tom from Virginia. "I have reason to believe, from what he told my overseer a little before he went off, that he intends for South Carolina, as his wife was sold to a gentleman there a few months ago," wrote his owner.[17] Will ran away for the same reason. Embarking on a six hundred mile trip, he absconded from Maryland "in pursuit of his wife, who was purchased in Somerset by a Mr. Lewis, from Georgia."[18] Another poignant case which relveals strong spousal devotion is the trek on which

Sip embarked. He was fifty years old and, proof of an "intractable character," had bullet scars on his back and shoulders. Sip left Bertie County, North Carolina, intent on reuniting with his wife en route to Alabama.[19]

The decision to go on these hazardous journeys was all the more courageous given that people were moving deeper into the South, which made the prospect of escaping to a free state more remote than ever before. What they expected, at the end of their journey, was a reunion, which they knew would be complicated and could only be half-realized.

While some people left the Upper South for the Deep South in pursuit of a spouse or relative, others, also in search of loved ones, made the voyage in the opposite direction. With the development of the domestic slave trade, men, women, and children sold down the river had gone on forced journeys to Georgia, Alabama, Mississippi, Louisiana, Florida, and Texas. As some tried to reconnect with their families, they began walking back to Virginia, Tennessee, Maryland, and the Carolinas. Their reverse journeys of several hundred miles via discreet paths, and through forests, swamps, and deserted fields were long and perilous. Two men who escaped from northern Alabama walked for three months to reach New Bern, North Carolina.[20] Ned of Nash County, North Carolina, was sold to Georgia in 1816; he returned and was a maroon in Nash and neighboring counties for nine years before being captured in 1825.[21] Sylvester from Maryland, sold down to Alabama, was caught in North Carolina after being in hiding for five years, and George came back from Kentucky to Virginia, "skulked" for three years, and finally took away his wife and young daughter.[22]

Determined to reunite with her loved ones, Tamar of North Carolina walked for three weeks. Her tragic life story was far from atypical. She had seen five of her children put up for sale before she too, along with her sixth child, was finally sold to slave traders. On her way to the Deep South she managed to escape, without her infant, after trekking more than a hundred miles in the speculators' coffle or slave caravan. Traveling at night and hiding in the woods during the day, she made her way back to her family and settled in the woods nearby.[23] William Kinnegy's saga paralleled Tamar's. A native of Jones County, North Carolina, he was sent to Richmond, Virginia, to be sold, leaving behind his wife and four children who lived on another plantation. From the slave pen in Richmond, Kinnegy was auctioned off to an Alabama planter who put him, with another hundred people, on a train to Wilmington, whence they were to board a ship to the Gulf. Kinnegy jumped off the train and settled in the woods near his wife.[24]

When people tried to reach loved ones, the first difficulty in locating them stemmed from a simple question: which relative were they looking for? Unlike any other community, the family networks of enslaved people were extremely far-flung. Families were broken up and scattered in all directions—even before the onslaught of the domestic slave trade, as some of the following examples show—because of a slaveholder's debt, relocation, bankruptcy, marriage, gift to a relative, divorce, or death. Enslaved men and women's large sets of widespread connections reflect the scope of the community's dislocation. But they also offered the maroons a choice of destinations. For instance, where was twenty-four-year-old Hagar, a mulatto with "a sulky impudent look," heading? She had left her South Carolina plantation with her blanket and bedding, and it was thought that she was being harbored either on a James Island plantation, or in White Point, where she had a husband, or then again at another place where her mother lived.[25] As for Aaron in North Carolina, he could have been with the "notorious Jonathan Rector," a white man who was "lurking in the woods [of Iredell County] for a year . . . [with] runaway negroes"; or perhaps he was in Lincoln County near his wife; or close to a plantation near Salisbury, Rowan County, where he had a brother; or in Mecklenburg County, where another brother stayed.[26] Ben had an even more extended network of disrupted relations. He lived in Wilmington, North Carolina, but he had had three previous owners in different counties, and a fourth residing in Virginia. It was thought that he had gone to any of these places or that he was being harbored near Cape Fear or on the Sound, where he probably had relatives as well.[27]

As they reunited with their families, the runaways became de facto maroons, living secretly in the woods by the plantations and farms, close to the world of slavery, but free from white control.

Following his getaway, John Little first stayed near his mother: he lived "in the bush," as he put it, for two years.[28] Suck, a young woman who escaped from Edenton, North Carolina, in 1778, was believed to be staying near her husband "in the woods between the creek and the plantation of her late master's."[29] After she came back to her homeplace, Tamar lived for several years in the woods close to her mother and brother, giving birth to three children. Kinnegy settled "in a close jungle, so thick that you could not penetrate it, except with the axe." He stayed there for five years.[30] Andrew Johnson of Virginia ran away in October 1809 and was advertised the very next day, a hint that his absence was not expected to be a simple visit. His wife lived on a farm five miles from Alexandria, and his owner conjectured he might be "harbored by her at night, and skulk[ing] about the neighboring woods through the day."[31]

Unlike "visit," the word "harbored" (or "harboured" and sometimes "entertained") can be found in countless newspaper ads. To understand the borderland maroons' specific experience, it is essential to appreciate what harboring meant. Enslaved people were not able to conceal anyone clandestinely—except for brief moments—in their cabins as these could (and legally had to) be searched any time by overseers, militia, and patrollers. Freedman William H. Singleton noted, "Nights they [the patrollers] would go around to the houses where the slaves lived and go in the houses to see if there was anybody there who had no right to be there. If they found any slaves in a house where they had no right to be, or where they did not have a permit to be, they would ask the reasons why and likely arrest them and whip them."[32] Naturally, slave quarters were the first places to be checked when a runaway was advertised; this was why "Ben dare[d] not stay very long at a time in his wife's cabin, as a strict watch was constantly kept, that the runaway might be apprehended."[33] William Kinnegy concurred, "I never dared to stay at my wife's cabin more than a few minutes at a time, although it was always night when I visited her."[34]

Still, Isaac Jones of South Alabama took the risk. He "dodged about for sixteen months, sleepin' in de woods when it were warm, an' when it were cold hidin' in a cabin."[35] When Riley of Kentucky returned to his homeplace, he first hid in his mother's cabin, but was sent to the barn as a precaution because of the owner's anticipated search. His next destination was a hole under his mother's house, where he stayed for a year and a half.[36] Like him, William Singleton succeeded in spending three years in a potato cellar below his mother's cabin until he was tricked out of the house. After he was captured, he escaped again but this time he was more cautious: he only went to the cabin at night and left before sunrise to spend his days in the woods.[37]

The danger inherent in remaining too long on plantation grounds is illustrated by what happened to Tom, a maroon known to have committed robberies in the vicinity of Fishing Creek, North Carolina. His owner's son, William Mace, finally decided to put an end to his activities. He scoured the swamps and the woods for five days, but discouraged by his failure to find any trace of Tom, went back home. Stopping on the way to visit a farmer, he approached the quarters and became suspicious when a light was immediately put out. When he entered the cabin, he found Tom, shot him—he stated that he had only wanted to frighten him—and killed him.[38]

To avoid detection, borderland maroons sometimes hid in outbuildings and some were even smuggled into the Main House rather than the quarters, because it was safer. For instance, Maria and Betsy escaped from Charles Manigault's Gowrie plantation in South Carolina, and stayed near a neighbor's place. They "often hid in the kitchen as it is known that search would only be made for them in the negro houses."[39] Landon Carter was incensed when he learned that Johnny, his gardener, "had harboured Bart & Simon all the while they were out, sometimes in his inner room and sometimes in my Kitchen Vault." Of course, they "were placed in the Vault in particular the day my Militia were hunting for them."[40]

A remarkable case of harboring that unfolded in South Carolina in the summer of 1853 illustrates the subterfuges, solidarity, secrecy, and widespread complicity that often went into harboring borderland maroons. At an unknown date, Alfred of Alabama ran away and made his way to Anderson County, South Carolina. On the plantation of Hugh Gantt, he benefited from the active or tacit solidarity of several people. He lived at Bob's and then at Dina and Mahalah's. Throughout his stay, Alfred, a tall man, passed as a woman, wearing a white and blue dress. Everyone in the quarters and at least three people from other plantations saw him and knew who he was. Alfred did not stay in the cabins for long because of safety issues; he was soon transferred to one of Gantt's cellars. When slave hunters came by, Bob contacted Harriett on another plantation, asking her to conceal Alfred, whose odyssey took him from the woods to the quarters to a planter's cellar and on to another plantation.[41]

To harbor was to give food and assistance as well as occasional refuge; or as the law defined it in South Carolina, it meant knowingly entertaining and giving victuals to runaways.[42] It was of course illegal and resulted in trials and punishments. Harry of South Carolina was tried for harboring Sylvia who left on January 1, 1838 with a number of possessions, such as baskets, clothes, and her bedding. Harry concealed them in the planter's kitchen and brought her food when she stayed in someone else's barn, and hid some of her clothes, wrapped in a blanket, under the floor of his cabin.[43] In Anderson County, South Carolina, Mary went on trial on March 9, 1843. She was accused of harboring Simon, who had lived in the woods from November 1842 to February 1843. She knew he was a maroon but she did "harbour said Simon a Slave, by carrying to him victuals, and spirits and by sleeping with him the said Simon in a camp in the woods not far from the house of the said O. R. Broyles."[44]

Free blacks were also harborers. In many cases, the people they helped were their enslaved relatives.[45] But others were friends, acquaintances, and strangers. There was enough complicity between free blacks and runaways and maroons that it had to be controlled by law.[46] As explained in chapter 1, as early as 1740 South Carolina decreed that free blacks "harbouring" could be fined ten pounds for the first day, and twenty shillings for every succeeding day. If unable to pay, they were to be sold at public auction. Because there was sometimes insufficient evidence to punish the free individuals who harbored, entertained, and concealed, the Act specified that any free Indian or slave could testify without oath against "any free negroes, Indians (free Indians in amity with this government, only excepted,) mulattoe or mustizoe."[47] A new law passed in 1821 condemned free harborers to corporal punishment only; nevertheless, in August 1827 Hannah Elliott, her daughter, and her son were sold into slavery in Charleston for harboring a fugitive. In the nineteenth century, throughout the South free and enslaved blacks guilty of harboring were liable to corporal punishment, short of mutilation and death.[48]

"Serial harboring" was one of the problems slaveholders confronted when trying to catch borderland maroons, who could be as itinerant as their networks and sense of safety allowed them to be. This was true mostly of people not encumbered with children, like Amy of Jones County, North Carolina. First harbored by Sam, she was then "entertained" on a second plantation. She crossed the Neuse River and found refuge and help on two other estates before being captured on a third. Less than three months later, she disappeared again. She moved between five places.[49] Also quite mobile was Harry, about twenty-four, of Dinwiddie County, Virginia. He ran away in 1765 and was caught near Williamsburg in May 1767. In a matter of hours, he escaped once more. A year later, in March 1768 Henry Brodnax advertised for him and believed he was "lying lurking" in the neighborhood of Indianfield, York County, where he had previously lived. Harry was finally caught six months later and brought to prison in James City. He escaped and was brought back to the same jail on April 13, 1769.[50] On and off, Harry succeeded in remaining free for five years, harbored in three counties in a radius of about one hundred miles.

While maroons hoped to remain unseen via harboring, numerous notices reveal that many were spotted in the vicinity of various plantations. Abram, a middle-aged sawyer, absent for two years, was known to be "harbored sometimes about *Four Hole Swamp*, sometimes about Mr. Baccots at Goose Creek, and sometimes on the Town Neck, he having been frequently seen about them Places, and not long since on the latter."[51] Bella was seen on the Augusta road "in company with some Negroes of Major Douglas's, on their way to their master's plantation . . . those negroes will probably endeavour to conceal her on the plantation."[52] A group of seven men, four women, and their five children living in the woods near their former South Carolina plantation was noticed in broad daylight in the quarters. When not around, they were "near Mr. Rowland's Mowberry Plantation or Mr. Dawson's with whom negroes they are also connected." Their owners even laid a plan for slave catchers to follow, as they offered $200 for their capture. They indicated the four points—two plantations, a boat landing "where they constantly cross and re-cross Wappoo Cut," and a store—that "if watched will insure success. . . . And if one is taken, he may be induced by reward, or constrained by punishment," they ominously announced, "to show where the rest are."[53]

Harboring and sightings expose the extent and the depth of the complicity many maroons enjoyed. There is no question that once someone was spotted the entire community was questioned, often fruitlessly, as the repetition of ads attests. Moreover, the hiding places must have been well-chosen as, despite obvious clues as to their whereabouts, some maroons were able to stay hidden in the borderlands for years.

* * *

The maroons who settled close to the plantations where loved ones were enslaved lived in a paradoxical situation. While their objective was to reunite with their families, they remained separated from them. But by keeping members on the plantation, the family optimized the chance for the maroon(s) to remain at large—hence to keep the family together—because the enslaved relatives could provide food, clothes, and precious intelligence. That it was the best solution dislocated families were able to find to stay together speaks volumes not only about the system they lived under, but even more importantly about their willingness to make extraordinary sacrifices to circumvent it.

No one went to the woods mentally unprepared. Most runaways and maroons were caught and subjected to barbaric punishments administered in public as a deterrent, so absconders were well aware of what awaited them were they to become maroons. They exposed themselves to a hard life if successful and to ghastly reprisals if they failed, all in the hope of keeping their families together. These maroons delivered three blows to the slave system. They denied slaveholders the legal ownership of their bodies, they deprived them of the product of their labor, and they refused them the authority to manage and control what they considered their personal sphere: their family. Even though, by law, they did not have authority over their own bodies and movements, let alone those of their spouses, children, and relatives, they took that power knowing full well what this particular type of opposition to the institution of slavery could cost them.

VIOLENCE AND MARRONAGE

If the preservation of families was a significant objective that led men and women to become borderland maroons, severe whippings and other cruel treatments were a frequent catalyst to escape. "De slaves used to be badly treated, so dey would run off de woods and hide for a long time," recalled Sally Snowden of Louisiana.[54] However, it was rare for a slaveholder to attribute an escape directly to a whipping or the promise of one. Charles Yates's notice in the *Virginia Gazette and Weekly Advertiser* of September 20, 1783 was one such anomaly. Anthony, he explained in a rambling ad, had run away three months earlier: "He hath formerly had two or three severe whippings (which his back will show) for his obstinacy and bad behaviour to his overseers, and his consciousness of deserving further correction, probably made him abscond." Also exposing a direct link between brutality and running away was a notice in the *Virginia Gazette* of August 6, 1772 for a twenty-two-year-old "Mulatto Wench named PHEBE": "A Propensity for Pleasure in the Night brought a little Punishment from the Overseer, which I suppose made her run off." Moses, who ran away on May 1, 1823 had been flogged a week before and his owner expected that the mark of the whip would remain for some days, and Reuben had many scars on his back "from flogging . . . which he justly merited."[55] The overwhelming majority of wanted notices, though, did not mention violence, other than to imply that the scarred backs, broken limbs, and severed ears and toes were relics of the past. If one is to believe slaveholders, no one ever escaped because of their brutality. While most people who left for violence-related reasons did return after they had healed or recuperated, others intended their departure to be permanent.

The men and women who fled because they had decided not to submit to an impending beating, or had just received one did so on the spur of the moment. Nonetheless, lack of planning in the breakout did not inevitably mean failure. Harry Grimes of North Carolina went to the woods after being threatened with a hundred lashes and even death because he had gone without a pass to visit his wife five miles away. Although he left unprepared, Grimes was a successful maroon for twenty-seven months.[56] When S. Coutrell of St. James Parish, Louisiana, struck Octave Johnson with a big stick and ordered him to be whipped, Johnson dashed for the swamp located a mile behind the plantation sugarhouse. He outran his pursuers and lived in hiding for eighteen months until he enrolled in one of the Corps d'Afrique regiments during the Civil War.[57]

The story of the Heard family illustrates the failures and successes of people who took refuge in the woods to escape violence.[58] Sylvia Heard's owner, Peter Heard, a rich planter near Lagrange in Troup County, Georgia, was reputed to be mean and cruel. He whipped and beat his workers without mercy and Sylvia, a midwife, endured lashings on a regular basis. According to her family, the main reason for Heard's brutality was that she used to pray every morning. Heard forbade any expression of faith by his bondspeople because he believed that they prayed for freedom. Despite the beatings, Sylvia kept on praying. But one day "the master heard her and became so angry he came to her cabin seized and pulled her clothes from her body and tied her to a young sapling. He whipped her so brutally that her body was raw all over." All day long, Sylvia, who was reaching the end of a pregnancy, remained tied to the tree. At night her husband Anthony released her. Too weak to walk, Sylvia crawled to the woods. After she found a place to hide, Anthony greased her back to ease her pain and hasten healing. Then he went back to their cabin. The very next day, Peter Heard started to hunt Sylvia down. When he finally caught up with her, she had given birth to twins. Because she was captured, there is no way of knowing what her long-term strategy could have been. She may have planned to settle in the woods for good and raise her children there, as other women did. If this was her intention, Peter Heard and his dogs put an end to it. But the story of the runaway Heards continued with Sylvia and Anthony's son William.

One night, patrollers caught him off the plantation without a pass. After he was seized, the patrollers, as was their duty, beat William, who then ran off to the woods. His plan was not to nurse himself back to health only to go back to another whipping or worse. He decided to make his escape permanent and came to the conclusion that his family had to join him. To that end, he built a home in the woods and when it was finished, he returned at night to his cabin. It was a perilous move that could have ended his attempt at living free, but he succeeded in taking his wife and two children. The family made it safely to their new home. No patrollers, no hunters, dogs, or passersby ever found them and several years later, in 1865, they emerged from the woods. By then William's family counted two more children, born free in the forest that bordered Heard's plantation.[59] William had gone to the woods on the spur of the moment, in the middle of the night, empty-handed, wounded, and full of frustration and rage. But he quickly planned an alternative life for his family, complete with a secret home, means of procuring food, and of evading slave catchers and bloodhounds.

It was not the fear of violence that motivated people like Grimes and Heard. Bishop William H. Heard, a former runaway himself, understood that going to the woods under those circumstances was not a sign of defeat: "The blood would run from their heads to their heels," he wrote, "yet many of them were never conquered. They would go to the woods and stay there for months, yes, some of them years."[60] The maroons' determination to take control of their lives reflects the confidence they had in themselves and in their ability to create new lives even when physically diminished by the torture they had endured. Overtly disallowing anyone the right to assault them, they "would not yield to punishment of any kind," wrote former runaway from Virginia, Henry Clay Bruce (brother of the first black U.S. senator, Blanche K. Bruce), "but would fight until overcome by numbers, and in most cases be severely whipped;

[they] would then go to the woods or swamps, and [were] hard to capture, being usually armed."[61]

Violence cut both ways, and the woods were also the refuge of men and women who had attacked whites or were about to do so. Elizabeth Ross Hite of Louisiana joked in the 1930s, "We used to hear about de slaves beatin' up dere master and runnin' away. I wished I had de dollars for de slaves dat beat up dere masters, I would be rich."[62] Actually, records show that slaves were prosecuted for killing whites in about every state and every year.[63] William Ballard of South Carolina remembered how a man had whipped the overseer and "had to run away in the woods and live so he wouldn't get caught."[64] Men and women who assaulted or killed whites had few options other than to remove themselves from society and disappear into the woods, as William Robinson did after he knocked down his owner with an ax handle because he had cursed and kicked his mother. He made it to the swamps, where he knew he could join a group of maroons.[65]

FAMILIES AT THE BORDERLANDS

In addition to people who lived in the borderlands near their loved ones, families also settled there. Naturalist John James Audubon came across such a family in a Louisiana swamp in the 1820s. Eighteen months earlier, the man—whose name Audubon did not give—his wife, and their three children were sold at auction, and all ended up with different owners. With great optimism and resolve, the father devised an audacious plan to free his kinfolk. He settled in the swamps and made methodical and daring excursions at night to the plantations where his wife and children now resided. One after the other he "stole" them. The family lived close to their first homeplace.[66] In the fall of 1831, Henry fled from Little Rock, Arkansas. He remained in hiding in the area, and in January 1832 was joined by his wife and their three children, who lived on a plantation north of the city. They took a bed with them, indicating that they did not expect to be on the move but rather planned to settle down in a place where they would not find furniture.[67] Ned, his wife Bella, and their three children escaped in February 1827 and settled near a plantation in Christ Church Parish, South Carolina. More than a year later they were still being looked for.[68] Families started in the woods too: Pattin and his wife had fifteen children in the fifteen years they stayed in hiding. They left their refuge only after the end of the Civil War.[69]

The borderlands also sheltered groups consisting of several families. Perhaps the best example of such a community—as mentioned earlier—began its journey on February 21, 1825 after escaping from Kershaw and Lewis, one of the most prominent business houses in Charleston. Three months later, they were known to be living together in the woods near The Oaks plantation from where they had been bought a year earlier.[70] Among the seven men and four women, there may have been up to four couples.

Children taken to the woods and the swamps near the plantations as well as those who were born there were spared the brutality and oppression of slavery, but they still led a dangerous, restrictive, and stressful life. Although nominally free, they were virtual prisoners, their movements restricted to a small perimeter mostly accessible at night, condemned to a life of whispers. The children of a woman from North Carolina experienced severe constraints: "by the strictest discipline, she prevented them ever crying aloud, she compelled them to stifle their little cries and complaints, though urged to it, by pinching hunger, or the severest cold. She prohibited them from speaking louder than a whisper."[71]

Yet the parents, to whom family was so precious that they went to the greatest lengths to keep it together, were willing to maintain these young children and adolescents in a state of social deprivation; a decision that illustrates how much they found the alternative—servitude or life in a Southern or Northern city under white hegemony—incomparably worse. What they could have envisioned as a long-term future for their children can only be conjectured; but they doubtless had to contemplate their forced reentry or entry into the world of slavery. Parents knew that this highly traumatic experience could be compounded by the possibility of the family being broken up by sale.

Family life had its obvious advantages but was also taxing: a family demanded more food and other necessities as well as bigger accommodations. This could have two negative consequences: in some cases it pushed the maroons to take more risks to provide for their loved ones, leading them to lose the very freedom they diligently sought for them. For others the challenge became too hard to face, and they had to give up, turning themselves in.

THE WOMEN'S EXPERIENCE

Gender—to which were linked violence and family—was an important variable that predicted who would most likely get away. "The women are always beat worse than the men. The more they whip the men, the more likely they are to run into the swamp, but the women don't run away so much," a former borderland maroon explained.[72] He was certainly right, as the overwhelming majority, up to 81 percent of runaways, were young men.[73] In the workplace, whether they were young, old, single, or married females did not enjoy the limited ability to move around, as some males did. Their tasks rarely took them outside the plantation: they did not go on errands, drive the coach that took the slaveholders here and there or the cart that transported goods, or row the canoes or man the boats. In the personal sphere, they were not the ones going out at night to see a spouse or fiancé. Although they were familiar with parts of the borderlands—where some had gardens and/or gathered medicinal plants—and the neighboring plantations, their knowledge of the outside world was more limited than that of men, as were their networks. Their presence on the roads was more conspicuous, and more readily questioned than men's.[74]

Children also prevented women from escaping as often as men. James Curry, a runaway who reached Canada, recalled how his mother had escaped at fifteen, and again sometime later. She was captured both times and before long had children. "This ended my mother's running away," he concluded. "Having young children soon, it tied her to slavery."[75] The alternative for women was to leave their children behind, as did Anney of Virginia, who escaped with a quantity of clothes but left her still suck-ling infant behind.[76] For personal or social reasons, this was a choice few women made.

Though the number of female runaways was low, a new picture emerges when harboring is taken into account. In colonial South Caro-lina, where 17 to 21 percent of those who ran away were women, 80 percent of them were suspected of having gone to stay with relatives or spouses.[77] In Georgia (1783–1795), about 44 percent of the females whose destination was mentioned were believed to be harbored or to have gone to family and friends.[78] Also in Georgia, between 1822 and 1829 close to 60 percent of all female runaways were thought to be harbored.[79] They were harbored either in town or at the plantations' margins. Some were undeniably visiting, or were out for other reasons, and expected to return after a few days or weeks. But others had gone to stay.

There was little doubt as to where a Georgia woman and her two chil-dren could be when they were sold in absentia "for ready money"; they were "supposed to be in the woods."[80] Another Georgia woman, Sally, escaped in May 1764 with her "two mulatto children" a few days after they were all bought. Their former owner had died, and they had been auctioned off to Alexander Wylly, a Justice of the Peace in Christ Church Parish. Wylly believed the family had "run away into the woods," and he was so anxious to get them back that he placed twenty-two ads for their return. At least ten months after they had escaped, Sally and her children were still at large.[81] Haly and Amy Tyler, who escaped from Moseley Hall at Bear Creek, North Carolina, in July 1838 were "supposed to be lurking about George's Garnes's in Craven County near Newbern."[82] They likely had relatives or friends there. Their "lurking" seemed to have been quite successful as their owner was still running his notice two years later.

For some women determined to escape slavery, even pregnancy was not a deterrent. Moll, eighteen and "very big with child," ran away with her Angola-born husband.[83] Because it was more difficult for Africans to pass for free in a city, it is reasonable to infer that the couple chose the woods instead, perhaps staying close to Moll's relatives since she was born in Virginia. In Georgia, Betty, "big with child," was believed to be "harboured at some plantation."[84] Expecting a child may actually have been the reason why some women escaped in the first place, hoping to reunite with a husband or relative who would provide them and their child with support and love.

In some crucial respects, isolated women were at a clear disadvantage. To sustain themselves and their children in the woods, they needed to build shelters, fish, hunt, and trap. Few were familiar with, let alone proficient in these activities. They had to learn how to do these things as they went along, and some never did. The young North Carolina woman, cited earlier, was not good at hunting and fishing, and when her husband did not bring them food, she fed her children frogs, terrapins, snakes, and mice. When, as in her case, a woman was staying near her husband's farm or plantation, he played the traditional role of provider that slavery denied him. He became the supplier of food and other necessities and her link with the outside world; but therein lay an inherent danger. Maroons, whatever their gender, but especially those who did not hunt, could not rely exclusively on a spouse. When her husband "deserted" her—the circumstances remain unknown, he may have been sold, fallen sick, or died—she was no longer able to feed her family and after seven years she surrendered.[85]

However, few women on the borderlands seem to have been on their own. The available evidence indicates that most of them lived as couples, in families, or in mixed groups where they benefited from a support network of husband and relatives. Tamar, cited earlier in this chapter, relied on her mother, brother (the memoirist Moses Grandy), and husband, and delivered three babies as a maroon. She lost one, but even in her difficult circumstances, her children's survival rate was better than that on any average plantation. Nonetheless, pregnancy and delivery were times of particular vulnerability; tellingly, Tamar was captured before she had had time to recover from the birth of her youngest child.[86]

Caring for infants in the wilds was a challenge, as attested by the experience of Hannah, a habitual runaway from Virginia, who escaped repeatedly with her two children. She lost one, and when she was captured, the other was, according to her owner, "lingering from the effects of . . . exposure." In 1855, pregnant again, Hannah remained in hiding most of the year and lost her third child "from neglect and exposure."[87] In the woods, exposure to the elements and lack of adequate food and clothing compounded the health issues that originated on the plantations.

AD HOC GROUPS

Many borderland maroons lived in nonkin groups. The interrogation records of a group of six arrested in the fields in Attakapas County, Louisiana, in July 1771 shed light on the composition of these ad hoc groups. One of its members, Mariana, was looking for food when she was caught in the dairy of the prominent Mr. de Saint Denis. She said she had come from New Orleans and had been away for eight months in the company of another woman, a man, and a young child. She stayed briefly on Louis Harang's plantation before meeting Louis, a maroon of two years, who took her and the other woman to the woods. Joining them were Charlot, who had run away from New Orleans and was absent for fourteen or fifteen months; Gil, also from New Orleans and a fugitive for two years; and Miguel, who had left the city three months earlier and spent most of his time in the woods. Jean-Baptiste Raoul had been away from New Orleans for seven months, and had lived in various places together with other maroons.[88] The six members of the group, formerly held by different planters over 130 miles away, had gathered at different times and pooled their resources together in order to survive.

Another Louisiana group of twelve arrested by the slave patrol in October 1805 in St. Charles Parish was international, an apt reflection of the diversity of the enslaved community of the time that counted men and women born in Africa, Louisiana, and the Caribbean.[89] Celeste, aged forty, was born in Congo and lived in New Orleans before she ran off. Her husband James was Creole. Augustin Kernion, a mulatto, was part of the group, as was John, a nineteen-year-old from Jamaica, who had escaped from New Orleans. Other members were Marie, Charles, and Lucie enslaved by a man named Joachim; Senegaux and Etienne from different plantations; and two individuals whose gender was not specified. They all lived in the cypress swamp near the La Barre plantation, but when they saw Joachim searching for his three escapees they thought it more prudent to split up. Eight people hid near a Ms. Pain's place, while four remained at La Barre. Celeste revealed that she and three others lived for two weeks with other maroons whose leader was a François from New Orleans and that she knew of still another group "hiding in the swamps along the shore of Lake Pontchartrain." The group was disparate, made up of small subunits (Marie, Charles, and Lucie; Celeste and James; and the two anonymous members) having come together as circumstances dictated. It was also mobile, moving from borderland to borderland, and fluid, associating with and separating from other groups. Its regrouping was opportunistic, based on need and efficiency, as was its dismantling in response to circumstance.

The comings and goings of three men arrested in the spring of 1808 in St. Charles Parish offers further details on the wandering life of some of these groups and the temporary nature of their relations. Honoré, one of the members of the trio, ran away from François Piseros, captain of the Hussards and chief of the slave patrol, and hid in the swamp behind his farm. There he came across Gabriel and Lindor, who had two guns. The three decided to move back of the Delhomme farm. They built a shack and got food at the slave quarters. They also hunted near two other farms. They then proceeded to the Cabaret farm where Louis and Celestin, who like Honoré had escaped from Piseros's estate, joined them. Honoré, Lindor, and Gabriel then settled behind Pierre Renine's farm for two weeks, and later established a camp between the Fortier and Saint Martin farms. They later stayed for two months with a band of maroons living in the cypress swamps by the Destréhan plantation. After this Lindor spent a week in Ceba's cabin on the Fortier plantation. A free black man—and slaveholder—Charles Paquet housed him and Gabriel for five or six nights while Honoré remained close to the Fortier farm, where he was ultimately discovered.[90] Honoré thus moved around between eight farms and three maroon groups in a matter of months. Closeness to friends, safety, the possibility of procuring better or more food, the risk of being hunted down after too much plunder, and immediate danger dictated his and other maroons' wanderings.

To live successfully at the margins of plantations and towns, maroons had to develop a number of new skills and devise protective measures that would increase their chances of remaining undetected. Staying close to inhabited areas, they were vulnerable at all times. For example, contrary to runaways to the North or to the Southern cities who, when successful, rarely had to confront dogs again, maroons were constantly at their mercy. Not only were dogs unleashed after them when they escaped, but they could also be sent to search for the people who lived in the woods at any time. For that reason, the maroons' antidog methods were varied, had various purposes, and were used at different stages. Over time, people concocted, experimented with, discarded, talked about, shared, celebrated, or cursed a number of strategies designed to neutralize or annihilate the bloodhounds.

The simplest and most common tactic was to use a kind of dog repellent, most often made of pepper, black or Cayenne. Texan freedman Walter Rimm explained that all people had to do was to "take black pepper and put it in your socks and run without your shoes. It make de hounds sneeze." Another method was to make a deep impression in the ground with one's heel and sprinkle the hole with pepper. Some people added ingredients such as saltpeter or turpentine. They put the mixture in their shoes and rubbed their soles with pine tops as an extra precaution, hoping to repel the dogs and mask their own odor. Trying to cover up one's scent was a prevalent tactic. Borderland maroons would run amid the people working in the fields, attempting to make their scent disappear in the midst of everybody else's. Sometimes they exchanged their shoes with a friend, expecting that the ruse would throw the dogs off track.[91]

According to Albert Patterson of Louisiana, the people who lived in the "great big woods in de back where de niggers would hide when they run away," could not be caught because "they put Bay Leaves on de bottom o' their feet an' shoes, then they go an' walk in fresh manure an' a dog can't track them." Charles Thompson from Atala County, Mississippi, escaped after taking his precautions: "I had provided myself a preparation called 'smut' among the negroes, which, when spread thinly on the soles of the shoes or feet, destroyed that peculiar scent by which blood-hounds are enabled to follow the trail of a man or beast." This smut could be composed of snuff mixed with hog lard or rabbit grease. Likewise, Octave Johnson and the ten women and nineteen men who lived with him "[c]arefully rubbed the soles of their feet with the feet of rabbits, with which they had previously supplied themselves for this purpose, and dragging these after them to deceive the scent of the hounds."[92]

Water was considered an almost infallible ally in the battle against canines. Maroons crisscrossed creeks, springs, rivers, and bayous, because dogs could not pick up a scent in the water. That ploy could be supplemented by tree climbing, as a man who was hunted by dogs several times testified: "The only way to do when I heard them coming, was to go across water, and put them off the scent, and then climb a high tree in the thickest part of the swamp where the overseer can't come."[93] Knowing how to swim was often a prerequisite to escape, if not to distract the dogs, at least until one reached a safer place. Essex, a maroon for three years, "wanted no better sport than to slip into the river and kiss good-by to hound and hunter. When necessary, he could remain in the river as long as an otter."[94]

Another of the maroons' survival skills was the ability to devise strategies that enabled them to make a quick getaway at any given moment. Jim Bow-Legs, who dwelled in a cave, always observed the surroundings meticulously when he wanted to take a nap: "he took care, first, to decide upon the posture he must take, so that if come upon unexpectedly by the hounds and slave hunters, he might know, in an instant, which way to steer to defeat them."[95] When living in a family or group unit, people created codes to announce their approach. The maroon Audubon met in the Louisiana woods "emitted a loud shriek, not unlike that of an owl," when he came close to home, to inform his wife and children of his arrival. "A tremulous answer of the same nature gently echoed through the treetops," his wife's signal that everything was clear.[96]

* * *

To be a borderland maroon could appear to be a half failure, a consolation prize for someone too scared to join a community in the hinterland or to cross the Mason-Dixon Line. But it took as much courage to stay South as to go North. Henry Gorham, who lived in hiding for eleven months, was ready to "die in the woods, live in a cave, or sacrifice himself in some way . . . rather than remain a slave."[97] The borderlands were home to people who, like him, exiled themselves for reasons linked fundamentally to integrity and free will: the exact opposite of what slavery was about.

Maroon life on the borderlands was full of diversity. The woods and swamps hid a range of people whose experiences varied widely: from isolated individuals, families, clusters of strangers, itinerant and settled groups, to people who had moved just a few yards away from their cabins, and others who had walked hundreds of miles to unfamiliar locations. The borderlands were places of creativity, innovation, exchange, and transformation; they were also places of anxiety and struggle. Borderland maroons knew they were in for a tough time. They could be discovered and suffer extreme punishment, be shot, injured, or killed by wild animals, poisoned by unknown plants, or be debilitated by diseases they could not treat. They endured because they found support in the borderlands, autonomy, a free life outside white control and a particular kind of security that only they could cherish. Reflecting on his life in the woods, Tom Wilson could say, "I felt safer among the alligators than among the white men."[98]

[4]

DAILY LIFE AT THE BORDERLANDS

As they settled down at the margins of the slave world, borderland maroons embarked on a life that had little in common with the old one. Working under duress from "sun up to sun down" was over. Although they were now free to manage their own time and organize their own lives as they wished, their closeness to inhabited areas brought tremendous risks and imposed many restrictions on that independent existence. Coming and going in broad daylight, and making the noises that the most ordinary tasks generate, were prohibited. If self-determination was their guiding principle, self-sufficiency, in contrast, was never on their minds, as their environment prevented them from growing the crops and breeding the animals that could ensure their survival. Borderland maroons enjoyed few of the freedoms that a hinterland refuge provided, and yet their location also had its rewards, closeness to loved ones being the most important.

Finding adequate shelter, victuals, tools, utensils, information, weapons, ammunition, and clothes became the maroons' major preoccupations, as was outsmarting the patrols, slaveholders, overseers, and drivers constantly making their rounds on farms, plantations, and the surrounding areas. To succeed in their endeavor they had to find the best ways of profiting from the nearby world from which they had exiled themselves but could still easily access, and of solidifying the social networks that would help them make the most of their unique situation.

FROM TREES TO CAVES

The new life of the borderland maroons started with the obvious: their living quarters had to blend into the landscape to the point of becoming invisible. Some "homes" were so rudimentary that they could scarcely pass for shelters and were truly indiscernible from the outside: for example, Harry Grimes lived in a tree trunk.[1] A hollow gum "sufficiently large to contain 6 persons with much comfort" was the home of Jack Stump and Bristol near Edenton, North Carolina.[2] The top of trees also provided refuge to some maroons, who built platforms of branches and covered them with leaves and grass for comfort.[3] Louis from Alabama established his quarters in a big oak tree behind the pasture on his owner's plantation, about a hundred yards from a path. He carried poles and grass up the tree and made himself a bed that doubled as an observation point: "[B]ut you can't see it from de groun'. When I get up dar I can see all 'roun," he recalled.[4] One Louisiana man was known to have lived for three years in the crown of a large cypress tree.[5] Joe Sims from Virginia had nothing more than a bed he had fashioned out of moss and branches, and two men devised an unusual stratagem: they put cotton seeds in the fields to rot and lay on the natural fertilizer to keep warm.[6]

The maroons' habitat could change over time, from a simple refuge at first to a more elaborate structure, as tools and additional materials later became available. William Kinnegy lived in a densely covered area and he upgraded his shelter as soon as he could:

> I slept under the boughs and on a bed of pine blooms for a month or two (mid-winter and plenty of rain) until spring, when I began to build me a hut. I cut down small trees, and from an old fence got some boards, and soon built a place large enough to sleep in. I had to get a saw, so as not to make a noise; the sound of an axe would be heard a much greater distance.[7]

Maroons also lived in caverns. They were a natural refuge that offered more space and better protection than trees, as Josh of Richmond County, Georgia, found out. He first tried to live inside a hollow trunk, but when a bear got the same idea, he had to find other accommodations: large caverns bordered his owner's plantation and Josh appropriated one.[8] George Womble of Valley, Georgia, knew a couple who stayed in a cavern near their plantation and raised their children there. Their cover was so good and they were so successful at eluding capture that they only reappeared after the Civil War.[9]

The borderland maroons' most emblematic lodging, though, was neither a tree, nor a cabin, nor a cavern, but a cave. The description given by Martha Jackson of Alabama, explains the difference. She knew a man who "wa'n't gone nowhur but right up de big road a piece, livin' in a cave whut he dug outer de side uv a clay bank."[10] These caves, also called dens, were dugouts, underground houses: the ultimate man-made invisible shelters. Once they entered them, the maroons literally disappeared from the face of the earth. William H. Heard, a freedman who became a bishop in the African Methodist Episcopal Church, knew people who "would dig caves in the ground and live in them" for years.[11] Another freedman remembered that a man who ran away because of cruel treatment, lived in a cave for fifteen years before "Lee's surrender."[12] Well camouflaged, these dens sometimes harbored maroons right on the plantations. On Oliver Bell's place near Livingston, Alabama, one cave was dug near the slaves' burial ground. Interviewed in the late 1930s, Bell recalled other such dugouts on the De Greffenreid plantation. His cow had just fallen into one.[13]

Information about caves, their construction, what kind of shelter they provided, and how one lived underground can be found in two major sources. One consists of the recollections of maroons themselves, their friends, and their relatives. Interviews of people who were not maroons, but were aware of the process of cave building and other survival techniques, reveals a transmission of knowledge within the community. Cave dwellers passed on their skills, either while they were still hiding in the woods and secretly came back to the quarters, or after they returned or were caught. This knowledge constituted an important social capital for the community. Before he was fifteen, for instance, William Webb of Mississippi already possessed the requisite know-how. While still living on the plantation he dug a cave in his spare time, just in case. Then he "made another den, so that if they found the first cave [he] would have another one to go to for safety."[14]

The other source of evidence on cave digging and dwelling, more surprisingly, can be found in the remembrances of North Carolina Confederate deserters who borrowed the maroons' know-how. They were most likely former patrollers, militiamen, and slave hunters who had previously pursued, discovered, and captured borderland maroons.[15]

The construction of a cave required serious planning. First, the builders had to survey the area to find the location that offered the best cover. This meant that the selected spot could be accessed from various directions, each providing sufficient security. The digging, with few tools, had to be done quickly. A quilt was laid on the ground and the dirt was piled upon it, so that no particle of fresh soil would be found next to the needles and leaves that naturally covered the ground. Sometimes family and friends on the plantation gave a hand, as did Ishrael Massie of Virginia who helped his half-brother Bob, his wife, and their two children build a comfortable cave.[16]

Oliver Bell explained the process: "You digs an' starts low an' pushes de dirt out an' digs up an' make a big room up so de water won't git you."[17] The dugout he described was located on a riverbank, as proximity to a body of water was essential. Water was of course necessary for drinking, bathing, and cooking, but this was not the first reason why maroons built their bunkers in the vicinity of a river or a creek. Rather, they needed water because they had to dispose of all the dirt they had dug out, since nothing could reveal their presence better than a mound of freshly moved soil. The most efficient and inconspicuous trick for getting rid of the dirt was to dump it into the water.[18] The people who transported it had to constantly change their itinerary to avoid tracing a conspicuously trampled path from creek to cave.

The minimal dimensions of a cave were six feet by eight feet, and six feet deep; but some could be much larger and deeper. Across the rectangular hole, below the surface, solid poles were laid out and boards were placed above them to form a ceiling. All that timber had to be cut down or stolen, both major endeavors. Planks and dirt amassed on top of the cave kept the rain from seeping in.[19] Some sloped back gently to prevent leaks. Pine needles and leaves were carefully rearranged on the surface as camouflage. The finishing touch of the cave, arguably one of its most critical features, was its opening. In order for the hideout to be inconspicuous, its trap had to be well hidden. The simplest way to conceal it was to cause a tree to fall close to the den. The boughs hid the trap from view and the tree trunk, serving as a walkway, enabled the maroons not to leave any footprint by the cave.[20] When that trick was not feasible, other cover-ups had to be found. Only one description of a trap has come to light: it closed the cave of Goober Jack. Because Jack was a habitual runaway who lived in the woods for weeks at a time, Colonel John T. Sloan (later Lieutenant Governor of South Carolina) sold him to someone in Mississippi. Jack made his way back to South Carolina. He dug a cave in the canebrake by a stream. Its trap was "an old plank window shutter ingeniously constructed into a suitable cap for a ventilator shaft." Jack bored holes in it with an auger and "twined a few pieces of laurel and cane twigs, the whole having been covered over with leaves in such a way as completely to hide the existence of the shaft."[21]

Such a well-camouflaged trap was of the essence. In Georgia, a woman who lived with her three children in a cave had a trap "door so covered with leaves that no one could see it, and so well constructed that one might walk over it without guessing what was beneath."[22] Leaves, straw, dirt, or moss: the disguise changed according to the location and the seasons. Bob in Virginia covered his trap with "sticks, pine beard, and trash on top to kiver de hole." His brother remembered decades later with obvious jubilation how good their work was: "Ha, ha, ha. Ya could stan' right over dis hole an' wouldn't kno hit."[23]

While most caves were dug in inconspicuous places, some were daringly situated in plain view and one has to marvel at how fast and how discreetly they were built. In 1838, one such den was discovered near Washington Spring in Georgia. It was located in sight of several houses and near a road and fields. Its opening was concealed under a pile of straw made to look like a hog bed. Below the trapdoor was a six-foot square room home to two occupants: a man who had been in hiding for a year, and a woman who had been a maroon for even longer. They had enough space to store ample provisions of food.[24] The Georgia woman and her three children, already cited, lived in a cave in an inhabited area, but it was so well conceived and concealed that even though people passed over it many times, nobody ever suspected a family was living right under their feet.[25] Near water and in an open area was the location Jack Gist chose for his underground home. He dug his cave near a road, by a bridge that crossed a creek close to the property of William H. Gist, state senator and then governor of South Carolina. The bridge, the creek, and the road were far from secluded; people passed by Jack's den constantly. Nevertheless, no one noticed it or him.[26]

Maroons usually came and went from their caves at night, when nobody was supposed to be around, but sometimes they had to go out during the day and one wonders how those who lived in plain sight were able to accomplish this feat. Exiting was especially problematic, since from underground one could not know what was going on around the hiding place. Fine-tuning one's senses to the environment was certainly essential: perhaps the sounds of nature guided the maroons. Louis, from "Guinea," who lived in the woods in Alabama, learned the forest's language there: "Can't nobody come along without de birds telling me. Dey pays no min' to a horse or a dog but when dey spies a man dey speaks."[27] Still, one question remains: why did some maroons build caves in frequented areas? Since their freedom and sometimes their very lives depended on their invisibility, it is clear that they did not take the decision lightly. Perhaps they gambled that nobody would be looking for them in an open space, so close to settled areas. Some may have lived in a place where land had been cleared and no good cover remained close enough to the plantations where their families were enslaved.

The caves below the discreet traps were much more than holes in the ground: they were homes, not mere human lairs. In Virginia, Martha Showvely's uncle dug a cave after running away following a beating; he covered it with leaves and, according to his niece, it was "a nice place."[28]

A cave the police discovered near Norfolk was

quite a commodious apartment, regularly excavated in the bank, and prepared for an abode of some permanence, being ceiled within, and stored with fresh and salted pork, several bushels of potatoes, and corn, some green peppers and other articles of sustenance. The apartment was also furnished with some cooking utensils and crockery ware, and two sleeping bunks.[29]

Like this cave, some maroons' living quarters were real homes, complete with furniture, either hand-made or appropriated from the Big House. One woman said of her father-in-law's dugout in Virginia that it was as large as her own room. He had a bed and blocks for chairs, and to be more comfortable, he had taken whatever he needed from the planter's mansion.[30] Also in Virginia, Bob, his wife, and their two children lived in a ten-foot square dugout. Their beds were made of rails; the mattresses were fashioned out of the woman's old dresses and other garments they had appropriated. They had built a fireplace with stones and bricks and sawed-off tree trunks served as their chairs. As for cooking utensils, they had gotten them from a place where they were in abundance: slipping at night to the plantation, the parents had helped themselves to old pots and pans discarded from the Big House.[31]

Another cave, hidden near a plantation in Georgia, was even more sophisticated. It was the achievement of a young man who, to protect his wife from an upcoming beating, took her to the woods and built a cozy underground home for her.[32] He brought a stove and ran the pipe through the ground into a swamp, fashioned a ceiling with pine logs, and built beds and tables out of pine poles. Because tables and chairs were rare in slave cabins, their presence in caves is a good indicator of how successful some maroons were at making a comfortable living for themselves.

Good ventilation was a prerequisite for cave living: one had to dispose of the smoke of stoves and fireplaces. But first, the cave dwellers had to have something with which to build a fire. They generally had tinderboxes, flint, and steel, or flint, steel, and spunk; and if nothing was available, they struck a rock with a piece of steel. Others regularly got matches from family and friends.[33] Fire to get warm, to reduce the moisture that covered walls and floor, and to cook was indispensable, but it could become a major problem. When fire burned in a dugout fireplace or a stove, it had to be evacuated; and, if the cooking was done outdoors, it had to be contained. In both cases, smoke was a signal that someone was living where no human being was supposed to.

Not surprisingly, smoke was some maroons' downfall. One way of avoiding detection was to dig a cave in the densest part of the woods or in areas where fires were frequent.[34] Another common tactic was to locate it near a dead tree already blackened by fire. Sometimes a tree stump was purposely charred and planted above the chimney so that the smoke rose through or around it. To minimize potential sightings, maroons used hickory or oak bark, which did not emit as much smoke as wood.[35] But still, timing was essential. Cooking had to be done late at night when one hoped that nobody was around. In Alabama, a woman who lived with her three children in a dugout for four or five years did hers before dawn. "If early in the morning you went out to the swampland and looked very carefully along the ground," recalled three witnesses, "you might see a little line of smoke: that meant the woman was doing her cooking."[36] Handy maroons made and installed pipes that ran underground and ejected the smoke at a safe distance. A man and a woman who lived near Washington Spring in Georgia concocted such an evacuation system, and despite the fact that their underground home was near a road and houses, their smoke was never detected. A man in Petersburg, Virginia, had "some piping—trough-like—made of wood" that ran for several feet under the ground; they carried the smoke away from his cave.[37] Isaac Williams and Henry Banks combined strategies: the long pipe, the dense wood, and the fire-prone location.

> In order that we would not be smoked out, we dug a hole from the top of the bank clear through to our cave, a distance of some fifteen feet, and then fixed the top of our earthen stovepipe so it wouldn't be noticed, by covering it up with light branches and leaves. The trees grew so thick, and fires in the woods were so common, that we did not apprehend much danger of discovery from that source

anyway . . . whatever smoke issued from the small aperture at the top of the bank was lost out of sight before it passed through its leafy way.[38]

Cave dwellers had to perform a great many of their tasks indoors: they stocked and prepared food, ate, washed and dried their clothes, underground. Pattin and his wife's bunker, no doubt big and sturdy, housed the couple and their fifteen children. As Arthur Greene, who recounted their story explained, it was large enough to let them do all their daily chores. "Dis den was er—I guess 'bout size of a big room, 'cause dat big family washed, ironed, cooked, slept and done ev'ythin' down dar, dat you do in yo' house."[39] The wife and children never came out. Spending the greater part of their day underground, the cave occupants were more susceptible than other maroons to the ills associated with a lack of sunlight. Children who were born and lived for years in dugouts were at risk of developing rickets and depression. No complaint about the caves could be found, though, only positive recollections of how comfortable and spacious they were. Tellingly, since they were used to more comfort than slaves and did not have the same stakes as the maroons, the Confederate deserters, who only spent a few hours at a time in their caves, were more critical: "Even under the best of circumstances," their chronicler explained, "in the fairest, warmest weather, and in the driest soil, a cave was a dismal abode. There was a darkness, a chilliness, a strange and grave-like silence down there. . . . When rainy weather came . . . the walls oozed water."[40]

Caves were dug all over the South, as the above examples from Alabama, Georgia, Mississippi, North Carolina, South Carolina, and Virginia attest; and they may be typically American. References to this type of dwellings do not appear in the historical literature on maroons in other parts of the Americas. It may be an academic oversight; or perhaps the presence of denser cover close to the plantations that offered better camouflage precluded the use of dugouts elsewhere. In any event, the pervasiveness of the phenomenon in the American South makes it truly emblematic of marronage in the United States. Mention of caves continued to be made until the end of the Civil War. The dugout even made its entrance in literature in William Wells Brown's 1853 novel, *Clotel, or the*

President's Daughter. One of the protagonists, Picquilo, from the "barbarous tribes in Africa," resided for two years in the Great Dismal Swamp and married another maroon. They "built a cave on a rising mound in the swamp."[41]

Caves were an expression of fierce independence, and a manifestation of technical skills and resourcefulness. They demonstrated an uncommon resolve on the maroons' part to be and remain free. By the same token they were a stark illustration of the gruesome nature of slavery, as men, women, and children were willing to live underground for years in precarious, challenging, and potentially dangerous freedom rather than go back to bondage. It was as strong an indictment of slavery as they came, but one that did not register in the larger society. Although Southern newspapers reported cave discoveries and their Northern counterparts relayed the information, the shocking reality of people finding refuge under the ground did not elicit comments, interrogations, or perplexity, not even in the abolitionist press. Cave dwellers were as invisible to American social and political consciousness as they wanted to remain to slave hunters.

GETTING THE NECESSITIES

For the people of the woods life really started at night, particularly, as one former maroon stressed, when the moon was not too bright.[42] It was then or in the early morning hours that they looked for victuals. They could gather provisions on their territory, help themselves in the plantations' outbuildings, and receive supplies in the quarters. Each locale had its risks and rewards, and the maroons generally combined all three sources. In the borderlands and deeper into the woods, they gathered nuts, roots, parched corn, persimmons, pawpaws, grapes, and berries. Edinbur Randall lived several months in the Florida woods "on berries, the stem or pith of Palmetto leaves, and other vegetable substances."[43] It is possible that a few maroons planted vegetables. But given their locations near populated areas, it would have been perilous to cultivate: a garden would have clearly signaled their presence, unless it was located among those that plantation people sometimes grew into the marginal lands. Maroons trapped, snared, or shot deer, rabbits, squirrels, turkeys, geese, ducks, opossums, raccoons, wild cats, and wood rats.[44] They fished in rivers, creeks, and swamps, and slaughtered the cattle and hogs that belonged to white farmers and planters but lived half wild, in the woods and marshes. Nobody kept a precise count, and maroons, bondspeople, and poor whites alike preyed on them.[45] Most accounts establish that the provisions maroons managed to get on their own were in general insufficient, both in quantity and diversity. In some areas, as the clearing of land increased, what was left of the woods bordering plantations had little game and other foodstuffs and the lizards that rested on fences were game for the most famished or the least skilled.[46] Moreover, a number of items that people grew accustomed to could simply not be found in the wilds. Regularly, then, they reached into the outer limits of the maroon landscape to fill their needs. What they wanted, as Solomon Northup—the free New Yorker kidnapped and sold into slavery in Louisiana— put it, often "escaped from smoke-houses."[47]

Dora Franks of Mississippi, recounted that her Uncle Alf "would come [at night] out on de place [the plantation] an' steal enough t' eat an' cook it in his little dugout."[48] Echoing her, a woman from North Carolina said of her own uncle, who was raised by his family in a cave, that he lived on berries and "stold stuff."[49] Essex, who spent three years in the swamps and forests of Georgia and South Carolina, "did his foraging for food after nightfall. The henroosts along the Savannah he knew much better than some of their owners knew them, and thought it not a crime to levy toll whenever his appetite called for fresh, fat fowl," recounted the son of his former owner.[50]

"Stold stuff" was an important supply of food for the maroons and the people on the farms and plantations. "Fak' is dey didn't call it stealin', dey called it takin'," explained Sarah Fitzpatrick of Alabama.[51] This was also the assessment of a maroon: "I did not think it was wrong to steal enough to eat. I thought I worked hard to raise it, and I had a right to it."[52] John Little, who lived for two years in the woods near his mother's cabin in North Carolina, acknowledged, "I ate their pigs and chickens," and added, "I did not spare them."[53] The reappropriation was as much a practical measure to better one's welfare as it was an act of covert resistance, but the maroons went one step further than the people who still labored in bondage. They took what they needed from the planters and farmers even though they had stopped working for them. Their prior years of free labor were more than ample compensation, in their view, for whatever they pilfered.

In the fields, pastures, and gardens, maroons plucked corn, dug up potatoes, and milked cows. They butchered livestock on site or took them alive. It is difficult to imagine anything more conspicuous than a wanted man walking away from a plantation with a hog or cow in tow, but examples are abundant.[54] In Louisiana, for instance, Jean Deslandes declared to the court in June 1748 that two weeks earlier he had found one of his cows coming from the woods with a rope around its neck; he was sure the people of the swamps had taken it. As another cow went missing he sent two men to patrol the area behind his plantation, where they saw a group of maroons armed with guns and hatchets, smoking meat.[55] Joel Yancey, Thomas Jefferson's overseer at Monticello, was incensed at the maroons' raids. He informed his employer, "Billy is still out and have joind. a gang of Runaways and they are doing great mischief to the neighboring stock, considerable exertions have been made to take them, but without success." He added, "[H]e and his comraids takes a shoat or lamb every day from us."[56] Similarly, planter Thomas B. Chaplin of Tombee on St. Helena, South Carolina, complained in his journal: "[O]n Friday night, 6th inst. [July 1855], 2 sheep were stolen out of my pen. Followed the tracks the next morning to a swamp . . . but saw nothing of meat or rogues. I am sure they are two of Isaac Fripp's Negroes, runaways & the same fellows, by the tracks, that broke into my corn house a while back."[57]

Recollections about domestic animal thefts by the maroons and their acquaintances are consistent with the planters' recriminations and denunciations. Arthur Greene stated that Pattin, who had seventeen people to feed, "got food by goin' bout nights an steal a hog, cow, er anythin' an' carry down dar [his family's cave]."[58] Jack Gist was discovered with a hog, chickens, and geese, he had appropriated much earlier.[59] A live animal offered much more than whatever meat an individual or a small group could carry on their back or their head. The piglet, once fattened, would supply a great number of meals. The strategy of taking live animals, dangerous as it was, enabled the maroons to abstain from raiding for longer periods of time, thus increasing their chances of remaining undetected.

A major problem for the nightly visitors was the presence of guard dogs on the farms and plantations, and they had to find ways to neutralize them. The fact that maroons were able to regularly walk the grounds without the dogs sounding the alarm made Solomon Northup wonder. "It is a fact," he stated, "which I have never been able to explain, that there are those whose tracks the hounds will absolutely refuse to follow."[60] Emily Burke of New Hampshire, who lived in Georgia in the 1840s, had a down-to-earth explanation. "You may ask where the watch dogs are all this time, when these depredations are going on in the fields and yards," she wrote. "[T]hose who are on thieving excursions, are careful to go where they are acquainted with the dogs."[61] Harry Grimes from North Carolina concurred: "I had been in the habit of making much of them [the dogs], feeding them, [so] they would not follow me."[62] Even more intimate with the plantation hounds was Jake of Greenville, South Carolina. He lived in the cane thickets, going back to the quarters at night to get food; and when it was cold, he slept with the dogs to keep warm.[63]

With the dogs silent, the maroons could start their cautious approach to the most desired outbuildings where meat and other hard-to-get products were stored. All the activities in the fields, and hog and cow pens, regardless of how risky, paled in comparison to those that took place in the more exposed and tightly controlled territory. The landscape surrounding the Big House was, by design, not conducive to secrecy. It was mostly bare, except for flowerbeds and decorative trees that stood at regular intervals. Treading on that ground was to expose oneself with little chance for cover; so every incursion had to be very carefully planned and executed. Despite the danger, even kitchens were visited, sometimes with the complicity of the cooks. Burke was aware that maroons went into the same kitchen night after night, to cook their stolen vegetables and meat. You may ask . . . why the cook did not lock the kitchen door? . . . the very cook who is so loud in her vociferations about the operations that have been going on all night in her kitchen, in all probability is accessory to the whole affair.[64]

Some people were quite inventive when trying to get food from their old places. One man, arguably a unique case, devised an audacious plan to get his hands on provisions. He killed snakes and dried and strung them around his neck, his wrists, and his waist. In this garb, looking wild and fearsome, he walked openly on to the plantation. The planter's wife ordered his companions to catch him but they refused, telling her they were scared. It was as good an excuse as any to support him without getting whipped for not following orders. The man grabbed meat and meal and went back to the swamps. It was said that he was never caught.[65]

Although one might think that a few people foraging for food could not inflict much harm, it goes without saying that the borderland maroons' thefts came in addition to those perpetrated by runaways, hinterland maroons, and enslaved people themselves. The exasperated Patrick Mackay of Hermitage plantation on Sapelo Island ran a notice for three months that exposes vividly the kind of activities that could go on at night on some estates:

> WHEREAS the Subscriber's plantation, lately Chief Justice Grover's, now named Hermitage, is grievously and insufferably annoyed and disturbed by negroes, who come there by land and water in the night-time, and not only rob, steal, and carry off hogs, poultry, sheep, corn, and his potatoes, but create very great disorders amongst his slaves, by debauching his slave wenches, who have husbands, the property of the subscriber; and some are so audacious to debauch his very house wenches: These therefore are to give notice to all proprietors of slaves, that, after the 16th September 1763, the subscriber is determined to treat all negroes that shall be found within his fences, after sun-set, and before sun-rise, as thieves, robbers, and invaders of his property, by shooting them, and for that intent he has hired a white man properly armed for that purpose.[66]

The quantity of goods carried off by just two men, Tom and Patterson of South Carolina, gives an idea of the damage that determined and well-organized individuals could inflict in a single night. They made off with one piece of pork, a piece of bacon, sixty pounds of flour and molasses, three pairs of pants, two coats, one shirt, one bag, one pocketbook, and one handkerchief. They managed to carry their loot to the edge of another plantation.[67] In Louisiana, three men got away with three shirts, two pairs of pants, one jacket, some money, a petticoat and a woman's chemise, a sheet, a woolen blanket, three sacks, a bucket, a sifter, half a barrel of rice, a third of a barrel of salt, two pounds of meat, some fresh cheese, and five barrels of corn.[68]

The mention of clothes being part of these men's booty is noteworthy. Maroons, whether they lived on the borderlands or in the hinterland, were constantly in search of clothes. Those who had left with only what they had on were hard pressed to replace their rags, as Edinbur Randall explained: "At length my clothes were nearly all scratched off by the brush and briars; my torn shirt and coarse blanket were the only pieces of clothing I had left."[69] After he escaped several times and was either caught or returned, Charles Thompson of Mississippi went to the woods in a piteous state: "I tore my already much-worn clothes almost in shreds," he recalled, "and lacerated my flesh severely, especially on my arms and legs."[70] At best, the maroons who settled close to their homeplaces could get access to the clothes they had left behind before going to the woods. As planter Edward Thomas acknowledged, "At night they would leave their hiding places and sneak to their respective cabins to get a change of clothing from mother or wife."[71]

How quickly clothes could disintegrate and to what lengths a maroon could go to get his hands on a new set can be inferred by an ad posted in the summer of 1777 in the *North Carolina Gazette*. Two men, Dublin and Burr, were hired out to Richard Blackledge on February 12 and immediately escaped. Because they were "supposed to be lurking about committing many Acts of Felony," they were outlawed. Anyone could legally shoot them on sight. Dublin, about thirty, was a newly arrived African who had "never since surrendered, or been taken." Burr, sixteen and country-born, returned to Blackledge shortly after he left, but he was already "quite naked." After being clothed, he escaped again.[72]

The maroons' shortage of clothes was so well-known that each time somebody ran away from the McWhorter plantation in Greene County, Georgia, Aunt Suke would go to the spring, ostensibly to do her laundry, but in reality to leave old clothes there for the fugitives.[73] Clothes were hard to procure and the fact that maroons sometimes used sand in lieu of soap—also a rare item—to clean them did not help in their conservation.[74]

COMPLICITY

A distance from the Main House, the smokehouses, and stockrooms, the slave quarters offered the maroons their third source of food and supplies. As Julia Brown from Georgia acknowledged, "How did they get along? Well, chile, they got along all right—what with other people slippin' things in to 'em."[75] Even though slave narratives and freed people's interviews are replete with memories of inadequate victuals, they also mention that food was shared with those in even greater need. A former maroon, Robert Williams, recalled that at night, before he went to sleep, he would go around the "slave quarters an' git food. I got me all I wanted to eat an' plenty of rest."[76] From their weekly rations, the food they grew in their gardens, and what they had reappropriated, relatives and friends helped feed some of the people of the woods. When runaways were only passing through on their way to somewhere else, giving them something to eat once or twice was one thing; but with maroons like Williams, the sharing was constant and could last for years.

A woman from Georgia recounted how she and her husband routinely helped a borderland maroon. Every night at 11:00 p.m. he would come to their cabin and they handed him whatever they had saved from their meals.[77] Kitty of South Alabama fed a young man, Isaac Jones, for sixteen months. She explained their arrangements in 1910 at a time when Jones owned a nice house and one hundred acres of land. "He weren't much mo' dan a boy and when I come in my cabin and see his woolly head down dere I wouln't seem ter notice, but I'd leave somethin' lying about ter eat. When I come back it' ud we gone. Sundays I'd go a piece down de road to de woods an' leave some corn."[78]

Some maroons did not even have to venture to planter territory, because relatives and friends would meet them at an agreed-upon spot at the edge of the plantation to give them the food they hoarded.[79] A Georgia man who had built a cozy cave for his wife and children devised a plan that served them well for seven years. His friends gave him bits of their own food; he gathered whatever he got and left it at a certain place where his wife retrieved it and took it to her cave.[80] These support systems minimized the maroons' risks while they actually increased them for their families and friends. Some people willing to help the maroons but wary of the risks chose a more careful approach. Aware that a woman and her children lived nearby in a cave, people knew that "it was not wise to go near the place, but one might drop a piece of food at the wood's edge confident that it would reach a little hungry stomach."[81]

The sharing of food could even go beyond the immediate vicinity, as illustrated by an episode on Gowrie, Louis Manigault's plantation in South Carolina. Jack Savage, a carpenter, escaped in February 1862 and settled with several men in a swamp near another plantation. His friend, Charles Lucas, in charge of the stock at Gowrie, let "eight of the choicest Hogs" disappear, for which he was whipped. Manigault believed Charles had butchered the pigs and sent the meat to Savage's camp. Tellingly, soon after the punishment, Charles joined Savage.[82]

It was not uncommon for youngsters to be part of the chain of solidarity; some were directly involved because they had relatives at the borderlands, but others had no family connection to the maroons. Children who had not yet started to work in the fields were under less scrutiny than teenagers and adults; their greater mobility was an asset, as some could sneak into the woods to bring people food.[83] Many had to surmount their fear because white adults made maroons and runaways the ultimate bogeymen. Henry Clay Bruce heard white mothers quiet their babies with "so many horrible stories told of their brutality" that he too was afraid.[84] To compel Julia Brown to work fast, she was told "that if Ah got behind a run-a-way nigger would git me and split open my head and git the milk out'n it."[85] According to James G. Blaine, who was in favor of enlisting enslaved men into the Union army, they would be useful, because "the perfect terror" of the South was a "runaway negro in the canebrakes." To this, one who dissented with him on this subject, belittling the maroons' ferocious reputation, replied that they "would do for a bugaboo, to frighten negro children and white children into propriety."[86]

Children's helpfulness is well illustrated by the testimony of a woman who, as an eight-year-old, discovered her uncle hiding under corn shucks in the barn. He had been living in the woods in the vicinity for a year. He told her, "Don't holler, Honey; just go back to the house and tell your mammy to send me something to eat." The girl managed to get food by herself and did not say anything to anybody, "I knowed if Ole Partee (his master) caught him, he would whup him to death."[87] She also stole bread from the Big House to give to other maroons. The children's responsibility was heavy: carelessness or misguided trust could have terrible consequences; a naïve tattle could spell disaster for a great number of people on and off the plantation.

Some white people also supported the maroons. An intriguing case comes from North Carolina. When Burrus went to the woods, he got help from an unexpected source. He was hiding near the henhouse, in plain day, when his owner's wife, Sally Moss, saw him lying in the pokeberry bush, looking famished. She whispered to him to stay put: she was going to bring him something to eat. Burrus complied. He had good reasons to trust her: earlier she had thrown herself in front of the gun her husband was pointing at Burrus's brother. Sally Moss put some meat and bread for Burrus under the chickens' cornmeal dough.[88]

Moss's actions were uncharacteristic because it was usually poor whites—a small fraction of them—who were most likely to lend a hand. According to Julia Brown, whose grandmother lived in the woods, "Some white people who didn't believe in slavery," helped the absconders.[89] Some were taking their revenge at slaveholders who despised them; others employed the maroons and were simply trying to get cheap help. A few were genuinely concerned about the fate of individuals they had befriended.[90] Allen Parker stayed briefly in the forests of North Carolina, taking refuge in the house of "a poor white woman who had been a friend to [his] mother."[91] Poor whites also provided meals and companionship to Peter Bruner from Kentucky. He got food in the quarters but after a while he "[s]tayed with the poor white people in the mountains."[92] He played hide and seek with his owner, sometimes being just a few yards from him, and then enjoying his dinner at the white families' tables. William Kinnegy established a relationship with poor whites. He could not let himself "be seen by a white man for months, and then only by one or two of the very poorest, who traded with me in small things."[93]

COMMUNICATION AND INTELLIGENCE

Slaveholders and overseers knew that theft and other prohibited activities occurred on a nightly basis. As a former runaway asserted, "The white folks down south don't seem to sleep much, nights. They are watching for runaways, and to see if any other slave comes among theirs, or theirs go off among others. They listen and peep to see if any thing has been stolen, and to find if any thing is going on."[94] His observations were echoed by a white woman, who recounted: "Many a planter, with his rifle over his shoulder, or his revolver in his hand has nightly passed hour after hour patrolling his plantation in order to catch marauders, or to watch for runaways."[95]

Despite their vigilance, overseers and slaveholders often failed to catch the men and women who, for months and sometimes years, came back secretly. One reason some maroons could return to the plantations night after night without being caught was that they had developed efficient but simple communication systems. Ben's actions, as described by his nephew Charles Thompson, exemplify this:

> [He] stayed under cover in the woods, in such lurking places as the nature of the country provided, in the day time, and at night would cautiously approach his wife's cabin, when, at an appointed signal, she would let him in and give him such food and care as his condition required. The slaves of the South were united in the one particular of

helping each other in such cases as this, and would adopt ingenious telegrams and signals to communicate with each other. . . . Ben's wife, in this instance, used the simple device of hanging a certain garment in a particular spot, easily to be seen from Ben's covert, and which denoted that the coast was clear and no danger need be apprehended. The garment and the place of hanging it had to be changed every day, yet the signals thus made were true to the purpose, and saved uncle Ben from capture.[96]

When it was too dark to see, Ben and his wife had another means of communication, "a bright light shot through the cracks in the cabin for an instant, and was repeated at intervals of two or three minutes, three or four times." This signal "was made by placing the usual grease light under a vessel and raising the vessel for a moment at intervals." Ben had his own "signature" when coming to the door: he rapped on it three times, and after a short pause rapped another three times. In addition to these tactics, when going from one place to the next during the day, maroons probably drew on the community's repertoire of vocal signals when they approached a plantation: field calls, whoops, and hollers that carried special meanings.[97]

Apart from love, friendship, food, clothes, and other items, proximity to the plantation grounds also provided borderland maroons with instant information. News and rumors, from the mundane to the critical, could be gathered night after night and could mean the difference between life and death to people constantly on the alert, hunted down by motivated men and well-trained dogs.

The intelligence he got from a woman he knew helped Francis Fedric map his stay in the woods. From her, he learned that a $500 reward had been offered for his capture, that a watch had been placed along the Ohio River, and that neighborhood people had been warned not to help him with food. She also told Fedric that if caught he would receive a thousand lashes.[98] The young man planned his movements accordingly. Similarly, Charles Thompson's wife was a source of useful intelligence. "My wife knew of my hiding-place," he recalled, "and when night came she sought me [out] and reported what had been done for my capture." She warned him that professional slave hunters with dogs had been summoned and were scattered all over the region, looking for him. "This information put me on my guard," he continued, "and gave me time to consider what direction I had better take in my flight. . . . After bidding my wife farewell I . . . started in the direction of the hills, beyond which was a large swamp, the refuge of many a poor runaway."[99]

When maroons had extensive family and friendship networks, the information grapevine could involve several plantations. The story of a South Carolina man who stayed in the woods near his sister, visiting her every night, is a case in point. She informed him that Davy Cohen had offered $50 for his capture. Cohen's plantation was located about twelve miles from Charleston while the woods where the maroon was hiding were thirty-five miles from the city. Communication between the plantations was occurring nevertheless and news was flowing from one place to the other, and in between. Two Georgia delegates to the Continental Congress—as famously recounted by John Adams—could not agree more as they remarked in 1775, "The negroes have a wonderful art of communicating intelligence among themselves: it will run several hundreds of miles in a week or fortnight."[100] Coachmen were a source of information; so were the draymen, boatmen, domestics, and the people sent on various errands. Historian W. J. Megginson, writing about South Carolina, argues that in the course of a week, a man engaged in these activities could have brief encounters with a hundred people from thirty plantations, representing a community of about eight hundred people.[101] Charles Manigault described this chain of intelligence gathering and sharing that stretched from the youngest house children to the people in the swamps in a letter to his son Louis:

> 10 of them gentlemen & overseers turned out with loaded guns & 9 hunting Dogs to scour the country from Silk Hope down to the mouth of Eastern branch of Cooper River, & back from it, as many Negroes were known to be out thereabouts. . . . But they did not meet one, & attributed it Solely to their intention having been Communicated by

house Negroes, who became acquainted with their intention & it is justly said that no overseer, or Planter should speak on such subjects even before a small house boy, or girl, as they communicate all they hear to others, who convey it to the spies of the runaways, who are still at home. If any preparation for hunting them be made the day before they will be informed that night.[102]

Their ancestor Gabriel Manigault had observed long before: "[I]t is *extremely* [emphasis in the original] difficult to prevent runaways from being informed of a search after them being in preparation."[103]

Their precautions notwithstanding, the maroons' forays to plantation grounds could end violently. Many were caught, wounded, or killed, like Quath, who had lived in the woods for six or seven years. He doubtless was a good hunter-gatherer, and certainly possessed a strong social network that provided him with needed supplies. He was cautious for many years, but one night in March 1734, he was cornered in the kitchen of the Big House on a South Carolina plantation. He managed to run up the stairs and jumped out of a window. The planter fired at him; though wounded, Quath was able to run for a while, before being caught and sent to jail.[104]

ARMED AND DANGEROUS

Like the people who lived deeper in the woods and swamps, borderland maroons were often armed. Their way of life as hunters and butchers of planters' sheep, cattle, and hogs demanded it. They also had to defend themselves from attackers, whether wild beasts, men, or dogs. Their arsenal comprised a variety of tools necessary to life in the woods that could be used as weapons, such as clubs, axes, butcher knives, corn knives, hatchets, hoes, shovels, and scythes. Strong, sharp knives were found, stolen, or made to order through the maroons' networks of accomplices. South Carolinian Jacob Stroyer revealed that "[s]ome [maroons] had large knives made by their fellow negroes who were blacksmiths."[105] Scythes were easy to procure and fitted with a short, straight handle, they became valuable arms against bloodhounds.[106]

More unusual weapons could be found in maroons' hands. In Louisiana, a group had a bayonet that had belonged to a German soldier.[107] Donum, Todge, Jack, and Ben of Jones County, North Carolina, had guns, knives and, borrowing from Native American material culture, they also had tomahawks.[108] Emmanuel, a maroon for several months, also had unusual weapons. He regularly walked the grounds of Peru, his old homeplace in Georgia, armed with a sword and a piece of lead.[109]

Firearms were forbidden by law to enslaved men, and generally only one man per plantation was allowed a gun—accompanied by written permission—so that he could provide game for the slaveholder. The men charged with protecting backwoods estates from Native Americans, wild animals, and birds were also allowed to bear arms. While the number of men with authorized guns on any given farm or plantation was low, firearms were surprisingly common in the hands of escapees, whether runaways or maroons.[110] Touring the South in the 1850s, Horace Cowles Atwater, a Northern Methodist Minister, pointed out that the men who lived in the wilds "in different ways, not unfrequently [*sic*], manage to obtain fire arms and ammunition, which places them in quite independent circumstances."[111] His observation is supported by the mention of guns in black men's hands in newspapers and court documents. For example, John, a maroon for at least six months in 1818 was seen "lurking about Vine Swamp" and in his former owner's neighborhood, with "a gun and other weapons for defense."[112] When Tom escaped with three of his children, aged twenty to twelve, he took a shotgun and two pistols.[113] A group of seven ran away from a Louisiana plantation with a shotgun "very long . . . in the barrel, at least five feet long." Jack went off with his "Master's Gun and a Grenadier's Sword," while Scipio had "a Militia musket and powder horn."[114]

These advertised cases notwithstanding, wanted ads that mention guns are not frequent; historian Betty Wood, reviewing notices for 453 runaways (1730–1775) in Georgia, found only four who were said to have taken firearms.[115] Similarly, Philip Morgan found that about 1 percent of advertised runaways in Virginia and South Carolina (1736–1790) had weapons.[116] Out of 3,900 Virginia ads (1736–1803), only thirteen mentioned a gun.[117] But when we probe court documents, personal testimonies, and newspapers articles relating to the capture of maroons (and runaways), a different picture emerges; one that shows how frequently they were able to acquire firearms *after* they had left.[118] Interestingly, these sources do not question the weapons' provenance because Southerners generally knew how the absconders got them. But to inquisitive Northern readers, Stroyer provided an answer:

> Of course the runaways were mostly armed, and when attacked in the forests they would fight. My readers ask, how had they obtained arms and what were they, since slaves were not allowed to have deadly weapons? . . . [Some] stole guns from white men, who were accustomed to lay them carelessly around when they were out hunting game.[119]

As Stoyer pointed out, maroons had plenty of opportunities to seize guns lying around. In Louisiana, Honoré stole one from the pirogue (canoe) of a white peddler, and Charles took his from a boat tied up in a bayou.[120] These firearms happened to be "found," but more forceful approaches were also used, such as burglarizing homes. This was the method chosen by Luke, a man from North Carolina who was sold down to Georgia and two months later made his way back to his homeplace near Wilmington. Living secretly nearby, he waited until everyone was away. Then he went to the planter's bedroom and took a gun and some ammunition. He later acquired a rifle, another gun, and a sword.[121] Guns were also seized directly out of people's hands as illustrated by an incident that occurred in Bringier, Louisiana. In April 1854, a white man discovered a maroon fishing for crawfish. Pointing his gun at him, he walked him out of the woods, but the man turned quickly, grabbed the weapon and ammunition, and melted back into the forest.[122]

But most firearms and ammunition found their way into maroons' hands through exchange and purchase. They traveled through an underground network of trade and barter, run by the friendship or self-interest of enslaved and free black men, and whites. The latter were a vital part of the system, being the main providers of the forbidden items. Some, like Le Ber, a French Louisianan sailor and habitual thief in the King's galley, had stolen them in the first place. He was accused in 1749 of having pilfered a gun, a horn of powder, and a bag of lead bullets. He acknowledged he gave the powder to a maroon.[123] William Kinnegy devised a discreet arrangement with a poor white man who, like Le Ber, was an occasional barterer. For their first transaction, Kinnegy killed and dressed a pig and left it in an agreed-upon spot. The man took the meat and left a gun. For their second transaction, a cowhide was exchanged for shot and powder.[124]

UNDERGROUND ECONOMY

Maroons traded goods in the underground market because they needed articles they had grown accustomed to and could not find in the woods or had trouble getting on plantations. Besides guns and ammunition, salt, flour, cornmeal, and bread were the items most difficult to acquire.[125] The maroons who had an abundance of meat, either from hunting or stealing, exchanged their surplus for these commodities if they could not appropriate them. Well-known to most blacks near Florence, South Carolina, a man who lived for several years in the swamps and woods killed hogs and cattle and traded the meat from plantation to plantation in exchange for clothes and bread.[126]

Instead of bartering in the woods or on plantation grounds furtively at night, some maroons traded openly in the cities. Seven men, four women, and five children, who escaped from Charleston and lived in the woods near The Oaks plantation—their former homeplace—were probably some of the most adept at doing business in an overt manner. "They are not only supported by the people of the adjoining plantations," complained their owners, who received reports of numerous sightings, "but pick black moss, make baskets, and take them to the City in boats through Wap[p]oo Cut." The audaciousness of these entrepreneurs is all the more remarkable as they had escaped from a prominent Charleston business and returned to a city where they could be easily recognized. They "cross[ed] and re-cross[ed] Wappoo Cut" during the day and brought their products to a store located near the lumber mills of Thomas Bennett, Jr., the former governor of South Carolina.[127] A group made up of three brothers, the wife of one of them, and their three children did business in the city too. They lived in the woods near their former plantation, received assistance from the people of several estates, and used boats—"borrowed" from a slaveholder—with which they went to town to trade.[128]

One of the occupations of the maroons who lived close to New Orleans was to gather wood during the day. Cutting and selling firewood for the steamships that plied the rivers was one way enslaved men earned small amounts of money and the maroons took advantage of the common sight of black males involved in that business to conduct their own transactions.[129] They entered the city after sunset with their loads and sold them on Rampart Street between St. Louis and Canal Streets. Some then retreated to the nearby swamps and came back again between 10:00 p.m. and midnight. On their second incursion, they broke into stores and houses if they needed items they could not buy and they sometimes attacked passersby. They also violently repulsed those who tried to capture them.[130] One group, arrested in 1848, consisted of eight individuals who had been maroons for years and made a living cutting wood for a white man. When their camp was discovered, three men were in town procuring provisions in broad daylight. Their five companions were arrested and jailed.[131]

A noteworthy case of exchange comes from the Eastern Shore of Virginia. In 1724, Caesar, who had lived for several months in the vicinity of several plantations, was outlawed. Notwithstanding the risk, a free black couple gave him food, and enslaved men and women fed and sheltered him. In contrast, his own wife refused to make him a shirt with fabric he had stolen. Rebuffed by his spouse, who even informed her owner, Caesar found help from two poor white women. With one he bartered cornmeal for the berries he had gathered in the woods. As for the other, he brought her and her three children the fresh pork and corn he had appropriated, and the game he had hunted. He also offered the family some of his fabric. The woman reciprocated with food and a place to sleep. For this she received twenty-five lashes and spent a month in jail.[132]

Some borderland maroons participated in the underground economy by working on the side for wages. They hired themselves out during the day while continuing to hide at night. One South Carolina man, who lived near a plantation for a year and a half, and another who stayed there for two months, found work on a canal.[133] In Louisiana, Lindor and Gabriel cut posts for the free black man, Charles Paquet.[134] Maroons were a cheap source of labor and their illegal status made them vulnerable and thus unlikely to complain; but by engaging in illicit dealings the employers also exposed themselves to opprobrium and reprisals if discovered. The deal between both parties rested on the most improbable trust.

If employers had good reason to hire maroons, the latter had good reason to want to be hired. They made money, even if it was not much. This enabled them to acquire the items they could not produce or appropriate. The arrangement, mutually beneficial, is an apt illustration of the maroons' pragmatism, entrepreneurship, and self-confidence as they diversified their activities and widened their networks—in a potentially perilous manner—in order to preserve their independence.

COOPERATION IN THE QUARTERS

With all the interaction, communication, and various transactions going on between the plantations, their borderlands, and towns and cities, for each maroon hiding in a cave or atop a tall tree, many people were in on the secret. On farms and plantations, cabins were close to one another and on many estates two families shared a double house—two single cabins joined under a common roof by a wall or a chimney. It was therefore hard to hide any activity, clandestine or not. When a maroon came back at night, at least a dozen persons within a few feet could be aware of his/her presence. Within a radius of fifteen yards, there could be sixty people. Nevertheless, it was a danger that few borderland maroons seemed to have feared: without confidence in their companions, they could not have chosen to remain in the neighborhood and walk regularly to the quarters. William Singleton, who lived in the woods and came back to his mother's root cellar at night, acknowledged, "Of course I could not have done this if the colored people had not been friendly with me."[135]

It was common knowledge, including among the white population, that bondspeople were for the most part supportive. Samuel Huntington

Perkins, a Northern tutor working in North Carolina, noted this solidarity: "Their fidelity to each other is almost proverbial," he confided in his diary. "When one has run away they all take interest in his escape; and though there are usually 30 or 40 who know where he stays and who supply him with provisions, yet no instance has ever occurred of the most extravagant rewards inducing one to betray him."[136]

The people who assisted the maroons did so knowing they could suffer severe repercussions. With some exaggeration, Kitty of Alabama, who secretly fed Isaac Jones for sixteen months, stated, "[I]f I'd got co'ght den, oh my! My! Dey wouldn't have stopt at a hundred lashes, it 'ud ha' been a thousand." Fearing the potential outcome of her actions did not stop her, though. Jones, looking back at the community that took care of its people in need, concluded, "Colored folks was more together in dose days dan dey are now. Dey'd take risks in dose days."[137] Ishrael Massie, whose half-brother Bob lived in a cave, put it simply: "[A]ll us slaves knew whar he wuz but, in dem days ya kno', nigger didn't tell on each other."[138]

Slaveholders and overseers knew perfectly well that the maroons living around their plantations (and even those who settled in the hinterland) kept in contact with their families and friends, and concocted various strategies to catch them. The colorful story of a man named John, a borderland maroon of four years, attests of such efforts. He was wanted for a long time and a trap was set to catch him. As he was known to like good food, a quilting party was organized with an abundance of chitterlings and hominy. John, who was invited by his unsuspecting friends, joined the crowd. The patrollers were on the lookout for him and once they knew he was in, they galloped toward the door. When he saw them coming, John grabbed a shovel full of hot ashes and threw them in their faces. He ran off yelling, "Bird in de air!"[139] A more simple and widespread trick was to deposit food in plain view. William Singleton recalled how "[t]hey would put food on the fences where a slave they suspected of being in hiding could see it in the hope that he would get hungry and venture out."[140]

Rather than—or in addition to—attempting to trap the maroons, some farmers and planters resorted to psychological warfare by putting pressure on families. Charles Thompson, his sister, and his uncle Ben's wife were kept in close confinement so that they could not communicate with Ben or help him. As Thompson stressed, "[A]ll of us had to suffer."[141] When three men ran to the Alabama woods where they lived in a cave, the overseer gave their wives only half their weekly allowance, so that they would have no surplus "to feed the rascals." As they complained, he exhorted the women to hunt their husbands down. If they brought them back, he assured them, their allowance would return to normal.[142]

Sometimes the whole workforce was threatened because slaveholders were aware that the community knew, in varying degrees—from the general to the specific—the whereabouts of the maroons and truants. After Burrus escaped, Jordan Moss told his three hundred workers that he would shoot them if they housed or fed him; and he searched inside and under their cabins every day.[143] James H. Hammond of Silver Bluff stopped giving out meat until the maroons returned. He also severely whipped the people who sheltered their companions.[144]

In spite of strict surveillance, the families and friends of the maroons who spent years in hiding were adept at keeping up the charade, even when the continued relationship was noticeable. A good example is that of Lettie, who maintained her ignorance of her husband Jesse's whereabouts in the face of obvious clues. Colonel Calloway of Georgia believed she was still seeing her husband, who had been away for several years, because she gave birth to two children, Jesse and Macon, who looked just like their father. They were born in 1859 and 1861 during the seven years he was hiding in the vicinity of Calloway's plantation. But Lettie always claimed that the last time she had seen Jesse was the day he ran away. Actually he came back to stay with her two or three times a week. In 1865, the year he left his cave when he learned of the end of slavery, he and his wife had a girl, Hettie, conceived like her brothers while her father was a maroon.[145]

William Kinnegy's wife was just as adamant in her denials. While her husband stayed in the woods for five years, she had two children who looked strikingly like her other four. Her owner constantly badgered her to reveal Kinnegy's whereabouts, but to no avail.[146] Slaveholders and overseers walked a fine line between bullying people into talking, but not pushing them to run away. When violent, disproportionate threats were made to relatives, they could be counterproductive and induce them to escape to avoid the threatened whippings.

Sometimes the protection given to the maroons turned into the ultimate sacrifice as relatives declined to talk, even when they knew the consequences could be dreadful. Such a tragedy happened in Mississippi, near Magnolia. A man lived in a cave and the overseer knew he came back regularly to see his wife and get food, yet he could not catch him. One day, though, he saw him on the road talking to his relative, Terry. The man swiftly ran away. When Terry refused to give the overseer any information, he beat her to death.[147] Isaac Throgmorton recounted a similar occurrence. He had not witnessed it but heard his owner and overseer talk about it. A man from the neighborhood settled back in the area and it was believed that a woman knew where he was hiding. According to what Throgmorton heard, when she refused to talk "the men hold her over a log heap until she was burned to death."[148]

Regardless of the dangers, solidarity with the maroons appears to have been strong. This was not systematically the case for unknown runaways.[149] Unlike the latter, the maroons were asking for assistance not from strangers but from people they knew: family, friends, and neighbors. Some helpers may have been returning a favor: they had been in the woods before and received support from the very people who were now in need. Others may have thought that one day it could be their turn too. Besides, betraying the maroons would have meant betraying their relatives who were neighbors and friends; and the social ostracism this disloyalty would have engendered may have been enough to silence some.

But there is still another side to the story: for all the camaraderie between the people of the plantations and those of the woods, stressed by blacks and whites alike, there was duplicity as well. A monetary reward, a better work assignment, a promotion, indulgence for a family member, or a personal grudge were all reasons to denounce a maroon. Informers could also be looking for something more trivial like "a little tobacco, or a few pounds of meat," as freedman William J. Anderson stated; or as mentioned by a former maroon, a new coat, or two or three dollars.[150]

John Little, who lived in the woods near his mother's cabin for two years, was betrayed by an acquaintance, a free black man who knew his whereabouts but kept silent until $50 were promised for Little, dead or alive. "Some poor white fellows" offered him $10 (pocketing the rest), and he led them to Little's hideout.[151] Love gone sour could also turn into disloyalty: Essex, a maroon for three years, was betrayed by "his Georgia girl." They had a falling out one night and the next day she told on him. "I could fool de dogs," Essex said, "but when dat yeller gal tell dem white folks, dey trap me."[152] Jack was deceived by one of his old companions, Anderson. They met by chance at night, when Jack was crossing a creek, and they talked for a while. Jack returned to his cave, confident his secret was safe; but the next morning Anderson appeared at Jack's trap door with Governor Gist in tow. They took everything he had: the hog, the two geese, the chickens, and the meat. Gist marched Jack to the plantation, whipped him, and put him back to work.[153]

Maroons, perpetually on the defensive, could be aggressive when they suspected duplicity. "They'd try to snatch you and hold you, so you couldn't tell," remembered Green Cumby of Texas.[154] His negative view was shared by Julia Brown, who recalled that the people who "runned off and stayed in the swamps . . . was mean. They called them runaways. If they saw you, they would tell you to bring them something to eat. And if you didn't do it, if they ever got you they sure would fix you."[155] When the chain of solidarity was broken, the maroons were known to be pitiless. If they were able to find the informers in the woods, they beat them up or killed them or came back to the plantations for the traitors and punished them.[156]

Like informers, the black men assigned to hunt the maroons could face retribution, as did Isaac on January 11, 1843. He was hired to catch George, who was living in a cave with his friend Jim. The men were well-armed and threatened Isaac several times. A measure of their resolve to exact vengeance can be gauged by the plan they hatched to get rid of him. They did not ambush him in a discreet spot but walked to the plantation, got into the Main House, and put a bullet through his head as he was sleeping on the kitchen floor. A hunt was ordered and Jim was discovered hiding in his cave. After a short trial, he was hung and his body, ending up in physicians' hands, as was the custom, was said to have been cut into pieces and thrown into Smith Fork Creek.[157]

THE MAROONS' EXPERIENCES

There was no one typical borderland maroon experience. Some people were well adapted, their material life better than their enslaved companions'. Others barely survived. Francis Fedric did not stay long in the woods and the details of his life there attest, *a contrario*, to the ingenuity of those who did well. Fedric settled in a natural cavern and had extreme difficulty feeding himself. He plucked berries, but some made him vomit and he was afraid others might kill him. His first endeavor to get food led him to a young woman he knew. She was shocked at seeing how emaciated and distraught he was. She brought him two ounces of bread. Two days later he ventured at night into a white couple's log cabin where he stole a hambone with an ounce of meat on it. It lasted for four days. Walking four miles, a famished Fedric came across a goose; he blissfully caught it, only to realize it was actually a sleeping dog. He finally was able to steal a loaf of bread from an outdoor oven. After nine weeks, unable to devise better ways to feed himself, Fedric went back to the plantation.[158]

By contrast, the maroons who throve best enjoyed vast stocks of food and their accommodations compared quite favorably with the basic interiors of the average slave cabin. The home of three men—found by accident by a group of hunters in December 1856 near a plantation in the vicinity of Springfield, Louisiana—was well furnished with a full bed and had kitchenware and abundant food. The maroons had obtained a good amount of pork, flour, cornmeal, sugar, and salt. They even had a large bottle of whiskey, guns, powder and shot, and to entertain themselves, a deck of cards.[159] Likewise, when the police near Fort Jackson, Georgia, raided a camp in 1855 they found abundant provisions: beef, pork, whole hogs, cooking utensils, a musket, and several musical instruments.[160]

It is impossible to gauge the average standard of living among borderland maroons. However, one thing is certain: although life in servitude was cruel and degrading, only a small minority of men and women exchanged it for survival in the woods, even close by.

To be a borderland maroon was not for everyone. By venturing to the farms and plantations night after night, by stealing, trading, bartering, and retreating just a stone's throw away, the maroons were taking considerable risks. Not only did they face dreadful punishments if caught, but their freedom and even their lives were at stake. Each step they took on plantation land was a gamble that could turn deadly. Courage and skills were a prerequisite, as was network loyalty. Planters, overseers, drivers, patrollers, and disloyal companions lurked around, searched, set traps, monitored, and eavesdropped. But remarkably, communities—often scattered over several locations—were able to organize themselves in such a manner that they could hide, protect, and sustain some maroons for years.

5

HINTERLAND MAROONS

THE farther reaches of the maroon landscape harbored secluded communities, large and small. The experience of their members was similar in some respects to that of the people who settled at the margins of plantations, but their design was different. Whereas borderland maroons relied heavily on the black and white plantation world for survival, hinterland maroons planned on generating some of their own resources in order to be more independent. By choosing an environment that hid and protected them much more efficiently than the borderlands, they enjoyed a degree of autonomy, self-sufficiency, and freedom of movement that only isolation could provide.

Some evidence about their specificity can be found in first-hand accounts by captured maroons. However, the bulk of the information comes from the men involved directly or indirectly in their elimination: petitioners to the courts denouncing—and often exaggerating—their "depredations"; officials directing their suppression; officers raiding their settlements; and journalists reporting their capture and the destruction of their sanctuaries. Despite their limitations, these sources still offer considerable detail about the hinterland communities' habitat, how they were formed, established themselves, developed, and survived with the help of various economic and protective strategies.

THE HINTERLAND HABITAT

The establishment of a group in a secluded area was not a small matter. First, a thorough work of reconnaissance had to be completed. Seasoned

individuals had to scout the woods and swamps on foot and canoe, looking for the best site. This could take weeks, because the most important attribute of the prospective refuge was that it be hard to find. Its
topography had to offer a strategic advantage against possible attacks:
vantage points for sentries, proximity to an escape route, and discreet
means of access to a rear base. It also had to be close to a source of clean
water—but not by a river where people traveled constantly—or one had
to find indices revealing the probability of underground water that could
be reached through a well. The soil had to be suitable for cultivation and
not be susceptible to flooding. The surrounding area needed to provide
edible fauna; the type of flora that could be used for food and medicine;
and creeks or streams with rich supplies of fish and shellfish. The scouting
party would also be looking for a good vegetation cover but one where
a clearing would not stand out from afar. The potential refuge had to be
distant enough from any place where someone could venture so that the
noise of axes felling trees could not be heard and fires could not be seen.[1]
And although it was imperative that it be hard to reach, it also had to
provide convenient access to the plantations and towns where some items
would continue to be traded or appropriated.

Once the scouts had selected a site that provided concealment, inap-
proachability, invisibility, and sustainability, the community could settle
down. As was true elsewhere, in some cases it was only then or even after the
crops had matured that some men fetched their families still on the farms
and plantations, as evidenced in some of the stories detailed in this chapter.[2]

Although it seems that because of these constraints maroon settlements could only be found in faraway areas, this logical conclusion has
been shown to be inaccurate. Given the immensity of the continent,
as opposed, for example, to the Caribbean islands, North American
maroons could have spread out hundreds of miles away. While this cannot be be ruled out, they commonly stayed within reachable distance of
inhabited areas. For example, a large community prospered eight miles
from New Orleans; another was hidden less than five miles from South
Carolina plantations; and in the same state the trail leading to a settlement started two miles from plantations.[3] It was outsiders' difficulty in

navigating a particular terrain that led to its selection as a place of refuge, not necessarily its distance from plantations and towns whose accessibility and proximity were actually a plus since they facilitated raids and trade. Although geographically insulated, hinterland maroon communities did not choose to function in social and economic isolation.

COMMUNITY FORMATION

Hinterland communities were often made up of people who had come together at different times, from different places, with different stories. Some joined alone; others were couples, families, or friends. The development of a community from one determined individual to several, spanning twelve years and straddling international borders illustrates how a group could be drawn from various places and in various ways, and how it could expand and contract. On July 18, 1785, sixteen-year-old Titus, a waiting man—personal menservants were the elite among the domestics—ran away with Tice of the same age from the Savannah River plantation of George Morel. On September 8, Morel informed the readers of the *Gazette of the State of Georgia* that he was still looking for Titus (Tice must have been captured) and for Ishmael, fourteen. They were frequently seen together at Yamacraw. Titus was eventually arrested but he escaped again and four years later, in April 1789, he was advertised along with the African blacksmith Hector who first escaped in 1786.

Thus far, Titus and his friends had just been a small group of maroons but soon the young man was accused by Peter Morel (George's brother) of having "enticed away" Patty, nineteen, who left with her nine-month-old Abram, and fifteen-year-old Daniel.[4] "If they are not gone to Florida," suspected Morel, "it is supposed they are in the neighbourhood of Kilkenny, on Great Ogechee Neck." As it turned out, they were still in Georgia and the community was growing. When Titus finally arrived in Florida, Tice and another dozen people—including Jeffrey, John, Beck and her two children, and Rose with one—accompanied him. But the community made it across the border too late: it was after September 1790 by which time, following an agreement between Spain and the United States, East Florida no longer offered sanctuary to runaways. The group returned to Georgia and at some point its members were back at the Morels'. On January 12, 1795, six years after their return from Florida, Tice, Jeffrey, John, Rose, and Beck and her child escaped from Ossabaw Island with a two-oared canoe, their pots, blankets, and clothes. Morel offered ten dollars for each, but he was ready to give fifty dollars to whoever brought Titus back:

> A known villain, who has been concerned in most of the robberies that have been committed on the inhabitants of this city and the neighborhood for these three years past. It is supposed that the foregoing Negroes have been inveigled away by this fellow; his haunts are on the hammocks on the sea coast bordering on this and Bryan county, that part of Carolina adjoining Chatham county, and on the swamps of Savannah river as high up as Purysburg.[5]

The search for the maroons must have been intense, for soon Titus and his companions were, once again, on their way to Florida where, despite the collapse of the American-Spanish collaboration, runaways were not simply considered free. By February, fifteen people, including Titus, were caught.[6] The community's leader remained in custody in St. Augustine until at least August 1796 before returning to Georgia where he was suspected of having "enticed" another two men to join his community. According to Commissioner James Seagrove,

> The notorious Titus with some negroes from Florida made their way along the coast until they got into Savannah River and among the nice plantations where he was well acquainted. There Titus soon formed a party with some other outlying negroes who became very troublesome to the people by plunder and as a receptacle for runaways. A party of armed men were sent after them with orders to kill all who would hesitate to surrender. The armed party came up with the Negros in their camp who fled at its approach. The Negros were fired on but it being a very thick swamp, most of them escaped.[7]

While the settlement was found and attacked, the maroons' prompt escape avoided a disaster.

Although this community was distinctive in its crossing and recrossing of international borders, its activities, response when attacked, and the different locations of its settlements make it representative of other hinterland communities. And so does its formation. Titus first ran for freedom at sixteen; within seven years he had become the leader of a maroon community: some members joined him, others he actively recruited. Between 1791 and 1795, the group covered a large area, establishing camps from the Georgian coast to Purysburg, South Carolina, thirty miles away. They roamed the entire maroon landscape, from hinterland to plantations to city, and chose for their last known settlement a thick swamp in the Savannah River.

This thick swamp was the sort of hard-to-find place that maroons took great care to appropriate. To join a hinterland group, escapees would thus have had to face days or weeks of paddling through muddy swamps, overcoming quicksand, searching in all directions for people whose raison d'être was to remain invisible. But this search, as the story of Titus's community shows, was not a solitary affair: there were social, if not necessarily geographical, shortcuts to the backwoods. The simplest, easiest way to join a hinterland community was to be recruited by the maroons who came to the plantations at night to stock up on food, visit family, and gather intelligence. Another path to a hinterland settlement was to have been a borderland maroon first. As they went foraging, borderland and hinterland maroons interacted, and the former sometimes followed the latter to their secluded areas.

Finding one's way to a community was also done singularly but with information passed on by former maroons who shared their experiences, stories, and knowledge, and talked about hiding places. Armed with this information, William Robinson, a native of Wilmington, North Carolina, joined a community when he was only eleven. He knew the general location of the camp because he had heard former maroons talk about it, and even passed in the vicinity several times. But to find it he needed a detailed itinerary, and so he went to see an elderly woman who he knew could put him on the right path. His complicated expedition through canebrakes and swamps evidence of how well concealed the camp was:

> Quite late that night I got opposite the hiding place. It was a low swampy place back of a thick cane brake. It was so dark and the cane so thick when I got to the place where I had been directed to turn in I was afraid to venture. . . . Sometimes I could walk upright, sometimes I was compelled to crawl through the cane. About three o'clock the next morning I came out of the cane brake on the banks of a large pond of almost stagnant water. I could see the rocky mound or cave that I had heard so much talk of. . . . There was no boat around and I was afraid to go into the water, but the same impulse that drove me into the cane brake caused me to go into the water. With a long reed for a staff I waded into the water.[8]

Once close to his goal, Robinson was stopped by a sentry. He had reached one of the most crucial moments in his journey. Before he could go any further—in a scene that doubtless played or should have played throughout the South—he had to show his credentials as a bona fide runaway, he had to establish his trustworthiness:

> I heard the voice of a man, in the real coarse negro dialect, "who is dat?" My hair was not extremely long, yet it seemed so to me, as I imagined I felt my hat going up, and I answered "dis is me." (Of course he knew who "me" was.) He then began to question me as to my name and my parents' name. It was necessary for him to be very cautious whom he admitted, because white men often disguised themselves and played the role of a runaway, and in this way many runaways had been captured. I finally succeeded in convincing him that I was not a spy but an actual runaway.[9]

The sentinel's precautions were necessary because black men and women could never be trusted blindly. Most conspiracies, revolts, and paths to maroon settlements, throughout the hemisphere, were revealed by people who acted as spies from the start or were coerced into betrayal.

What is more surprising, as Robinson noted, was that white men—in blackface, no doubt—ventured into the swamps and the woods trying to pass for would-be maroons.

A COMMUNITY IN TRANSITION

On November 15, 1765 the Georgia House of Assembly took affidavits from people who complained that "a number of fugitive slaves . . . have assembled themselves together in the River Swamp on the North Side of the River Savannah [South Carolina] from whence they have of late frequently come into the plantations on the South side [Georgia] . . . and Committed several robberies and depredations." The legislature resolved to allocate one hundred pounds sterling at the most to their eradication. Slave hunters were to receive five pounds for each male aged sixteen or up caught armed or in the company of an armed man, provided he was brought to jail before the end of the month. If someone resisted arrest or tried to escape he could be killed on sight and two pounds would be paid for his head. Women and children above five were valued at two pounds. Within ten days of being informed of the House's recommendations, Georgia Governor James Wright sent rangers and the militia after the maroons. Having searched every probable place of refuge they found nothing: neither people nor canoes.[10]

Soon, details about the community emerged from the deposition of "John a Negro fellow." Interrogated by Alexander Wylly, the speaker of the Georgia Royal Assembly, he reported that he had learned a great deal about the maroons from a certain Theron. Theron was a slave of George Cuthbert, a Scot who owned Drakies, a rice plantation of more than a thousand acres worked by twenty-nine people. According to John, sometime in October 1765, Theron was walking on the road coming back to Drakies after having spent the day working on the widow Douglass's (Cuthbert's sister's) plantation when he came across Ben—whom he knew to be a maroon—and two or three of his companions. Ben told him he planned on freeing his wife and children still enslaved by Douglass. That done, perhaps fearing that Theron would talk, Ben kidnapped him. At least this was Theron's version. The episode does not make much sense, and given the absence of other recorded abductions by maroons in the country, it is highly possible that Theron followed the group willingly and concocted the story afterwards to exonerate himself.

Whatever the case might have been, the new maroon settled in a camp "opposite to a large Savanna in which were many Negroe men, some Women & Children." He was forced, he alleged, to go on raids shortly after his arrival. If Theron had really been abducted, Ben was showing an evident lack of judgment by allowing a man held against his will to go back to planters' territory.[11] Theron's first sortie occurred on Champion Williamson's plantation. He and his companions killed an ox and carried it to their settlement. Theron took part in several other raids, the last one on November 11. That night the group made its way to Vale Royal, the plantation of Lachlan McGillivray, a Scot immigrant and famous Indian trader. They killed an ox and dismembered it. Theron was ordered to carry a quarter to their canoe. After he did, as no one was around, he made his escape. He had not done so before, he later claimed, because Ben had shot a man who wanted to go back to Mrs. Douglass. Whether the story was true or not, it was entirely plausible. For safety, Ben would indeed have had to kill any potential deserter or move immediately to another sanctuary if he let him/her go. Theron returned to Douglass's plantation, and confided in John.

Following John's testimony, the authorities proposed that Colonel Thomas Middleton, chief of the militia of Granville County, send men and if possible "some of the Indians in the Settlement" to Governor Wright in order to lay a plan "to Hunt out & disperse those Nest of Villains & to cooperate with the partys he should send out for the purpose." Upon receiving the information, Wright charged Captain Braddock with ambushing the maroons at the mouth of a creek they frequently passed and to "apprehend Some of them."[12] But the governor's order came too late. Unbeknownst to him and to his great chagrin, on the night before Braddock was to launch his offensive Roderick McIntosh sprang into action.

McIntosh's version, spelled out in a letter to attorney Isaac Young, was different on two crucial points from John's testimony.[13] John mentioned that Ben wanted to free his wife and children. But, according to

McIntosh, Ben "had declared his intention of going with a party of his [to] said Mistress Plantation burning her House & killing every white Person on the place & also every Negro who should refuse to join him."[14] McIntosh's dramatic version lacks plausibility: Ben was certainly aware that any lethal descent on a plantation would condemn his community to annihilation. In addition, the massacre of blacks would cut him off from the vital assistance provided by plantation people. By the time McIntosh wrote his missive he knew that Governor Wright was furious at his initiative. His sensational account reads like an attempt at justification: by acting swiftly he had saved the lives of several whites and prevented the desertion of untold numbers of individuals who would have joined the maroons and brought more destruction to the white community.

Acting on his own, McIntosh hired four white men and the free William Martin and, guided by Theron, they started their trek toward Ben's settlement. En route, they came across two of Archibald Bullock's bondsmen—Bullock was a future delegate to the Continental Congress and first president, then governor of Georgia—and took them along. McIntosh and his men arrived around nine at night at the head of a creek between Nelville Plantation and the plantation of James S. Bullock, Archibald's son. They knew from Theron that the maroons would pass there, and an hour later they indeed saw men in three canoes, paddling softly. Even after Theron's defection, the maroons had not changed their routine. Still, they were alert enough to spot the intruders. When McIntosh, his plan to surprise them having failed, ordered the men to surrender, they returned a volley of shots. The search party riposted and the maroons jumped into the water. Leaving their canoes behind, they vanished into the foggy night.

The next morning the sight of blood in the largest canoe—which, according to Theron, was Ben's—comforted the raiding party. Certain that the group was weakened, McIntosh decided to attack its camp. As he proceeded a quarter of a mile up the creek, three men appeared; McIntosh thought they had mistaken his group for the maroons and had come to take their share of the "plunder." The three men ran away. The party kept on going, treading through the swamps, waist-deep in water and mud, for at least another four miles; their travails illustrate how well the maroons had selected the location of their refuge. Finally McIntosh and his men stumbled across a strange sight. They saw "two Negroes on a Scaffold one Beating a Drum & the other hoisting Colours." Both men jumped off the structure firing their guns, ran away, and were not seen again.

Some scholars have concluded that the drum and the flag were a sign of military organization, "probably copied from the militia system in which slaves often served."[15] However, there is an alternative explanation. During the 1739 Stono uprising in South Carolina, the Africans from Kongo had also "marched on with Colours displayed, and two Drums beating."[16] The use of drums to alert and galvanize the participants was duly noted and as a consequence, the following year, the South Carolina legislature—Georgia quickly followed suit—passed an act forbidding drums.[17] As for flags, they were customarily used for military purposes in West and West Central Africa.[18] The fact that the men were on a scaffold points to a surveillance system and suggests that they were sentries who, seeing the approaching party, sent a forewarning by sound and sight. Indeed, it is common in Africa for a specific message to be relayed via a specific rhythm. For instance, the drummer could have "told" his companions at the camp to regroup at another base, or to take the canoes and flee to a different part of the swamp. The flag, signaling danger, would have warned those outside drumming range. These features point to the presence of at least some Africans in the community. Although there is no indication whatsoever that Ben and Theron were anything but native-born, nothing is known about the others. Given the dearth of documentation about African communities in the colonies studied here, Ben's settlement is the closest one can come to uncovering features of discernibly African cultures that may have survived among maroons.

The sentries' message was well received and the maroons acted swiftly, for when McIntosh and his group reached the settlement they found it deserted. The effortless way in which they entered the premises suggests that although the maroons had a warning system, they did not erect fortifications. The settlement's location was well chosen—and if not for Theron's betrayal it may never have been discovered—and the difficult terrain, added to the warning system, undoubtedly seemed sufficient to the community. The retreat was hasty: kettles were still on the fire boiling rice. The maroons took their guns and ammunition but left behind the blankets, pots, pails, shoes, axes, numerous tools, and about fifteen bushels (675 pounds) of rough rice.

The settlement was a square on which four buildings had been erected. McIntosh called it a "town." Four houses would hardly qualify as a town anywhere, but when referring to maroons it was not unusual—throughout the Americas—to use the word indiscriminately to describe anything from a few shacks to large villages. The overstatement was not gratuitous; besides the genuine fear maroons inspired, inflating their numbers and their strength and therefore their potential threat often led more men to be dispatched and enhanced the stature of the commanders who defeated the innumerable enemies armed to the teeth. In this particular case, McIntosh may have chosen his words in the hope of talking up the invaluable service he had rendered the community. Consistent with this reading, he also called the four buildings "houses," not sheds, shacks, huts, or cabins. He did not specify what they were made of, but if one takes him at his word, they may have been sturdy and made to be permanent. They could have been built of wood (the maroons had axes), palm leaves, and perhaps mud. The combination of the abundant wet soil of the swamp mixed with sand, animal dung, and rice hulls would have made perfect adobe.

The houses were spacious by slavery's standards. Whereas the typical plantation cabin in the Georgia/South Carolina area was twelve feet square, each house was about seventeen feet by fourteen. John was vague about the number of occupants—"many" men, and "some" women and children—but McIntosh indicated that he knew from Theron that the camp counted forty residents. If that is correct, the density was normal to low for North American slave quarters. According to Theron, the maroons had thirty guns, which could indicate the presence of perhaps thirty men out of a community of forty, and about ten women and children. With forty residents, the community was large and had the potential to grow quickly. One clue as to how it could have done so may be found in the very reason why it was "discovered." Ben wanted to free his wife and children, and other men would certainly have wanted to do the same. If only fifteen men out of thirty had succeeded in bringing their families, the colony could have easily doubled.

His reconnaissance over, McIntosh set out to destroy the "town." Everything in it, including the rice, was set on fire. It was a hard blow to the maroons, but none was killed or captured, and they even killed one of their pursuers. Two months after the raid, Archibald Bullock asked for compensation for his "Negro Fellow named Colly killed" in the "Skirmish with the Runaway Negroes."[19] Colly was one of the two men McIntosh had recruited on his way to the maroon camp.

There was no further news about the maroons. They likely regrouped in one or several locations better concealed than the one they had lost. Their strategy of disappearance, based on their warning system, had paid off. While they lost most of their possessions, they may have hidden some in other parts of the swamps, a precaution taken by maroons elsewhere.

The story of Ben's settlement offers rare insight into a large hinterland colony: its recruitment, activities, strategies, and travails as it navigated threats to its existence. But it lacked one important feature of hinterland communities: a certain degree of self-sufficiency. Colonists started to complain about the maroons' "depredations" in November, stressing that they were recent. Thus there is reason to believe that the community's fifteen bushels of rice indeed came from raiding neighboring plantations since this cereal is harvested in late September/early October. The scale of the thefts tells of a well-run organization; of men paddling through the swamps, landing at plantations, walking the grounds to locked outbuildings, and helping themselves to hundreds of pounds of rice, carrying back their loot to the canoes, and gliding back home. But raids for food could only satisfy part of the community's needs. To better sustain themselves, especially if more people were expected, as Ben's own project indicates, the residents needed to be more autonomous—they had to turn their settlement into a farming enterprise. However, this could only have happened the following year after the men cleared land in January, and men and women planted rice in the spring. In November, when the colony was attacked, it still faced almost a year of living dangerously because to get food the men had to keep on raiding plantations. Inevitably, as was true for this community, repeated nightly forays exacerbated militias' vigilance and thus increased the risk of detection and destruction of the settlements.

The conversion to an agricultural colony was fraught with danger; but if the maroons could succeed in raising crops, sheep, poultry and cattle, they could attain a much higher degree of autonomy.

FARMING SETTLEMENTS

On the night of June 26, 1788 Thomas Maclaine's cellar in Wilmington, North Carolina, was robbed.[20] Intruders forced a door open with an iron tool and carried off a number of items. Two days later, a search of Barnet's Creek uncovered a maroon village. It contained some huts, but no number was given. Fires were still burning, proof of a hurried exit and a successful, if tardy, alarm system. The place seemed to have been inhabited for a long time and was believed to have been the repository of many goods stolen in the city. The settlers had accumulated several hoes, axes, and cooking utensils; and even had "instruments for breaking locks," a sign that betrayed how they effected their surreptitious visits to the city's cellars and storehouses.

What they brought back from their latest excursion is of interest: one hogshead of tobacco, another of molasses, and two barrels of beef. The sheer weight and volume of these items spirited away from a cellar, transported through the streets, and brought aboard their canoes illustrate how well-organized and efficient the maroons were and hint at a substantial community. A hogshead of tobacco weighs between 900 and 1,000 pounds, a hogshead of molasses is the equivalent of 140 gallons; and two barrels of beef weigh 400 pounds. The products they took were typically those that maroons were accustomed to but could not manufacture or raise on their own or in adequate quantity. On the plantations, molasses served as a sweetener, accompanied cornbread, and sometimes substituted for meat as a stimulant. Besides being smoked, tobacco was used as protection against mosquitoes, a necessary item in the swamps.[21]

Although they helped themselves in town to what they could not produce, the maroons also relied on their own resources. They had cleared
about an acre and planted corn. The yield at harvesttime in October
could have been between thirty and forty bushels. Based on the average
plantation rations of two pounds of corn a week per person, the field
could have fed no more than two individuals yearly. But increasing the
size of their field was impossible because the needed acreage would have
been noticeable. Therefore, the men still had to embark on precarious
journeys to plantations and farms or even more audaciously to town,
covering several miles by boat and carrying back thousands of pounds
of food. The more loot they got in one raid, the fewer expeditions they
would have to launch and the less vulnerable they would be.

Another farming settlement (made up of people "of bad and daring character") for which some details have emerged was located in Big
Swamp, between Bladen and Robeson counties in North Carolina. Big
Swamp, about four miles wide and several miles long, was a maroon and
runaway refuge for many years. The site in question, discovered in 1856,
was situated on an island in the "almost impenetrable" swamp. The settlers were a diverse group. According to the twenty-two petitioners who
brought their grievances against the maroons to the governor, "Many
[belonged] to persons unknown."[22] In other words, they were not locals.
They may have followed displaced relatives or been attracted by the seem-
ing impregnability of the refuge. The rest of the colonists were enslaved
in the area and people knew who they were. One of them, Henry, was
typical of many maroons who peopled the Southern wilderness: he was
from the neighborhood but had been sold to a man in Arkansas and had
come back to live in the swamps, close to his loved ones.

The maroons had cleared land to make a garden and brought cows,
"&c. out in the swamp."[23] It is unfortunate that we cannot know what
the "&c." were, though the presence of cows is noteworthy. Apart from
milk and, at some point, meat, they produced manure that could serve
as fertilizer to increase the output of the future garden. The Big Swamp
group—whose size is not known—started to build a farming operation
but continued to visit the surrounding plantations and farms, and was

so "destructive to all kinds of stock and Dangerous to all persons living by or near said swamp," that on August 1 more than a dozen men set out to hunt them down. The maroons fired at the intruders and mortally wounded one man. To add insult to injury, they ran off cursing and swearing, and told the posse "to come on, they were ready for them again." Taunting, a tactic used by maroons elsewhere, served as a double-edged psychological weapon.[24] It was intended to discourage adversaries by inducing them to think that the men, utterly confident in their own strength and that of their weapons, were sure of their ability to defeat the hunting party. Once their general location was uncovered, maroons had only two options: they could leave or they could try to discourage any further incursion. It was easier to migrate when camps were rudimentary, but established communities had investments to protect, so the settlers of Big Swamp chose to scare off the intruders and stay put.

A week after the confrontation, the maroons put deed to words: they twice shot at a white man who approached their camp, but missed him. Such was the outrage that a group of citizens petitioned Governor Thomas Bragg for help. They said they had raised money, but it was not enough to induce "negro hunters to come with their dogs"; therefore they were counting on Bragg to offer a "suitable reward." Their appeal exposed once more the fact that sometimes slave hunters were reluctant to venture into the swamps to dislodge maroons because the latter had succeeded in building a reputation as fierce enemies ready to kill. The governor turned the petitioners down. He explained that he could only offer a reward for people who had committed a capital offense and fled the state. He advised the solicitors to ask the sheriffs of Bladen and Robeson to call out a force to scour the swamp. It is not clear what happened next, but the maroons' daring strategy, based on defensive aggressiveness worked, at least for a while.

The Big Swamp's settlers' incomplete story exposes the quandary many maroon communities had to face. To be autonomous or at least more so, they needed to grow crops and raise cattle and hogs; to get the seeds and the animals, they had to steal; before they could live on their own crops and meat, they had to steal some more; their raids attracted counterraids;

to deter incursions, they sometimes had to become overtly aggressive, whereas their objective was to remain undetected.

The Barnet Creek and Big Swamp farming communities shared one characteristic: the men who described them made no mention of the existence of individual plots, which is in sharp contrast to a great number of plantation quarters, especially in the Lowcountry. The fact that individual plots were uncommon among maroons might be seen as the continuity of an African tradition, but it is not. Africans do work collectively when clearing land, for example, but fields are family "owned." It could also be viewed as a slavery-related practice: enslaved people worked cooperatively in the fields. But the existence of slaves' personal plots directly contradicts this hypothesis. Maroon communalism may have been the result of a deliberate decision to create cohesive, strongly knit communities by shunning individualism and enforcing egalitarianism. In the American South, an additional reason was the particular limitations maroons faced due to their closeness to inhabited areas. Dozens of individual lots would have required the clearing of larger tracts of land that would have been conspicuous.

Examining what the maroons cultivated in their communal fields and their breeding activities sheds additional light on their lifestyle.

THE MAROONS' CROPS AND DOMESTIC ANIMALS

A woman who had been a maroon for sixteen years and ended up betraying her companions provided a glimpse into the farming activities of a secluded community about eight miles from New Orleans.[25] She left the settlement in the fall of 1827 and revealed that it was home to fifty to sixty people. They had put together a fully diversified operation: they cultivated corn, sweet potatoes, and other vegetables, and raised hogs and poultry.

Two South Carolina farming communities operating at different times reveal helpful details about the breeding activities and varied crops of Southern maroons. The first community sheltered itself in an "impenetrable swamp" in Gadsden's Bay. Its residents had built a hog pen and had "a fat sow." They also raised and/or stole cattle. Large quantities of beef drying on scaffolds and four hides were the signs of a recent and significant butchering.[26] Because salt was notoriously difficult for maroons to obtain, and smoking—depending on where the settlement was located—could attract attention, drying was the most convenient way to preserve meat and fish for months. The hides could be used to make shoes, hunting and foraging bags, and containers to haul water. The fifteen white men "and several trusty negroes" who invaded the village in June 1826 after having looked for it "assiduously for several hours," also found pots, clothes, "and every necessary preparation for a long residence." One sign of actual or intended permanence was without a doubt the camp's wells. Digging a well required tools, know-how, and extensive work. It was only done by those who had a long-term perspective. The slave hunters saw several men, fired at them, but were unable to capture any.

On "a knoll in the swamp," the second community—discovered in 1861 in Marion County—grew corn, squash, and peas.[27] The search party soon came across a second settlement. It had meal, cooking utensils, blankets, and tools, and nearby was another patch of corn and vegetables. The farmers could thus count on the yield of two fields. To spread their settlements and fields over at least two locations was a protective strategy maroons used when circumstances were favorable.

There does not seem to be much continuity, in the Southern maroon settlements described here, of African crops (such as yams, millet, rice, and plantains), as was most often the case in the rest of the hemisphere.[28] Although millet and sorghum were grown on North American plantations to feed enslaved people and animals, they do not appear in the known maroon crops. Similarly, African Americans cultivated sesame—brought from West Africa, it was also called benne (or benni) seed—in their own gardens for soups, puddings, and oil; but no reference to its presence in maroon settlements is made in the documentation. Rice, on the other hand, was cultivated in South Carolina and Louisiana maroon colonies, just as it was on the farms and plantations of these two states, where it was a major cash crop. Unlike rice, the crop (planted and/or stolen) that can be found wherever a camp description exists is corn. This was also the most common fare on farms and plantations throughout the South.

Maroons seemed to favor the food they were used to: corn universally, and rice in rice-growing regions.

The preponderance of "non-African" foodstuff can be explained by the late date of the available examples, a time when the vast majority of maroons were born in the country. The fact that communities were short-lived must also be taken into account. One can imagine that Africans cultivated crops they were familiar with in their early settlements; and if these had survived it is likely that the following generations would have kept on raising the same crops. However, the short lifespan of North American communities precluded that kind of transmission.

Squash, peas, various vegetables, and sweet potatoes were also cultivated in maroon fields. Squash was valuable not only as food but also because the dried gourds were widely used as recipients and spoons.[29] On farms and plantations, peas were planted between the cotton rows and African Americans often grew them in their gardens. Mashed, rolled in cornmeal, and fried, the peas became pea cakes. One advantage to cultivating peas was that they matured in early spring when corn, rice, and sweet potatoes were months away from being ripe. Sweet potatoes were hardy, easy to conserve, and nourishing. Roasted in cabbage leaves on an open fire, they provided sustenance during winter. So by growing corn, peas, rice, and sweet potatoes, in theory maroons could feed themselves throughout the year. The main problem they faced was, as noted above, the small size of their fields. This prevented them from cultivating on a scale that would have made them more self-sufficient.

If not African crops, the maroons did use African cooking methods, just as on the plantations. William Robinson has left an invaluable account of the way food was prepared in his maroon camp:

> The cook came out, made a hot fire of hickory bark, thoroughly wet the chickens and wrapped them in cabbage leaves and put them in the bed of ashes; then he proceeded to make his bread by mixing the corn meal in an old wooden tray and forming it into dodgers, rolling them in cabbage leaves and baking in the ashes. These are known as ash cakes, the most nutritious bread ever eaten. Of course the chickens

retained all their nutriment because the intestines had not been taken
out of them. But now he returned to them and catching them by both
feet he stripped the skin and feathers off, then took the intestines out
and put red pepper and salt in them and then returned them to the
oven to brown. Parched some corn meal for coffee.[30]

The cook made a fire with hickory bark, which, as already noted, was,
with oak bark, the maroons' preferred combustible because it emitted little
smoke. His cuisine shows the kind of ingredients maroons looked for on
plantations and farms. Meat, poultry, and flour were the most obvious, but
they were not the only items that formed the basis of pilfered maroon fare.
Salt and red pepper were highly sought after. The latter not only seasoned,
flavored, enhanced, and masked the taste of inferior meat, but it was also
used for medical purposes, in conjure (occult activities), as a widespread
antidog repellent and, put into shoes, it was said to prevent the chill.[31]

The presence of cabbage is also notable. Not just another vegetable, it
was the main component of a cooking method prevalent in African and
African Diasporan cuisine. Cooking in leaves—generally banana—is a
common way of preparing food in many African cultures, and Africans
brought the technique over to the Americas. In the United States the cabbage leaf substituted for the banana leaf. On Southern plantations, cabbage
leaves wrapped chickens, corn pones, and other foods put to bake or roast.[32]
They were handy in the kitchen but, like pepper, they had other functions
as well. African Americans made cabbage poultices to treat bruises, and
when wrapped around the body the leaves were reputed to reduce fever.[33]

Robinson's companion used another African culinary procedure: open-
hearth cooking or cooking in ashes. One of his productions, the ash
cakes, figures prominently in slave narratives and interviews. "Ash cakes
was a mighty go then," recalled John F. Van Hook of Georgia.[34] They
were typical black fare: "the famous negro 'ash-cake,'" as one white soldier called them; while a Southern white woman remembered the "'ash
cake' of the cabin" and "the 'Dixie cake' of the big house."[35] Cornmeal
could be turned into bread, naturally, but also into coffee, an inferior
brew reserved for the workforce.[36] Open-hearth cooking was particularly

adapted to the special situation of itinerant maroon groups as it did not require utensils. However, the presence of pots and kettles in settled camps shows that other cooking methods were used as well.

Hinterland communities, in contrast to those on the borderlands, grew a variety of crops and raised animals to sustain themselves and achieve some level of self-sufficiency. But their economic activities extended well beyond the heart of the maroon landscape.

MAROON COMMUNITIES AND TRADE

To husbandry and raids, communities often added a third activity they deemed indispensable to their survival: trade. A colony involved in trade, well-established, and dispersed over three locations, flourished in the vicinity of Georgetown, South Carolina.[37] The chain of events that led to its destruction started on December 17, 1824 when about twenty armed maroons attacked three men who were in pursuit of runaways. The slave hunters' small number indicates that they were probably looking for no more than one or two people and did not expect to be confronted by a large group of armed men. What likely happened is that they came dangerously close to a settlement and were fired upon and otherwise hunted out of the area by the maroons who, by the same token, revealed their general location.

Outnumbered and outgunned, the slave hunters withdrew. But the next day the sheriff and companies of the Georgetown militia went after the maroons, who were said to have been committing numerous depredations in the neighborhood. In three boats, loaded with provisions and weapons, the men reached the settlement. It consisted of three parts: two were large and located at some distance from each other, while of the third nothing is known. The site had been judiciously chosen on small elevations surrounded by extensive areas of marsh. From high above on tall trees one had a complete view of the bay, the creeks, and the neighboring islands. Although the lodgings were not described, clearly they were not rudimentary huts or crude cabins as they were depicted as "snug little habitations" that could have accommodated twenty people.

The maroons had gathered fine cabbages recently uprooted from one of the slave hunters' gardens. Relics of ducks, turkeys, vegetables, and beef "proved that they had been abundantly provided with delicacies as well as necessaries." Each part of the settlement had a well, and both had a rice processing operation. When the militia reached the village, it was empty, and after a long chase only one man was captured. His name was Newton. He was the brother of the leader, Will, a forceful chief who did not keep a low profile. Will had sent a message to John Thompson—he was among the three men who had been looking for the runaways—and a Mr. Fraser, warning them that if he ever came across them he would kill them.

Newton revealed that he and his companions, far from staying in the safety of the settlement during the day, often went to town. They paddled to Georgetown and moored their canoes at the foot of the fort. In the city, they "often amused themselves with promenades through the streets, unmolested by police or patrols." They carried on an extensive trade, sometimes by themselves, sometimes through agents. Soon, two black men were held on suspicion of having communicated with the maroons and the authorities had no doubt that many others were involved. It is doubtful that Will and his companions could have peddled their own corn, rice, or potatoes; their raids onto farms and plantations to procure foodstuff only underlined their continued reliance on the outside world. But the "fishing apparatus" found in the abandoned settlement suggests what they could have been selling.

In South Carolina, black men virtually dominated the fishing business and some fishermen were known to be maroons, like the men from Sullivan's Island who regularly brought in oysters and fish to market.[38] Will and his cohorts might well have been selling their catch in town. Other examples of maroons involved in the fishing business have surfaced. A network of enslaved and maroon fishermen provoked the ire of fifty-six residents of Craven County who felt compelled to petition the North Carolina Assembly in 1831. They lived by the Neuse River, north of New Bern, and denounced the bondsmen from the city who, official passes in hand, came to their neighborhood to "sell, buy, traffick [*sic*], and fish." They were said to induce the petitioners' laborers to run away. Now turned maroons, in addition to committing depredations on the farms they worked at dragging skimming nets, and selling or bartering their catch with the New Bern men.[39] In Louisiana, the maroons of Terre Gaillarde sold their fish at night in New Orleans. With the money they made they bought necessities and ammunition.[40]

Maroons gathered, raised, and manufactured timber, honey, fish, shell-fish, game, baskets, black moss, and articles made of willow or wood in order to trade with the outside world. This commerce, while illegal since the maroons themselves were considered outlaws, was legitimate in the sense that they were trading in their own goods, not in stolen items; but they also sold and exchanged stolen goods. An anonymous traveler reported such activities taking place during nocturnal encounters organized a few miles from Charleston in 1772. Around midnight, a kind of "maroon time," when they felt safe enough to get out, he had seen a dozen men join the festivities. Eight, on horseback, were probably horse thieves. The maroons brought mutton, lamb, and veal— not the kind of meat they could have butchered from animals hunted in the forests. They received liquor and other articles and left an hour before dawn.[41] In Louisiana, Octave Johnson's group roped cattle and dragged them to their camp; they butchered the cows and gave the meat to field hands in exchange for cornmeal.[42] In South Carolina, maroons who lived in the swamps and marshes by the Combahee and Ashepoo traded stolen goods from river to river. The items came from the plunder of plantations and attacks on the inland coastal traffic. According to Governor David Williams, the "ill-disposed and audacious" gravitated to the maroons, who were numerous and armed. They transformed the numerous creeks, marshes, water sources, and cuts between rivers—supposed to be kept wide and deep, but narrow and shallow because of neglect—particularly one between the Ashepoo and Pon-Pon into a maroon landscape that the governor had baptized a "Negro thoroughfare." These activities enabled them to sustain themselves for several years.[43]

* * *

Whether they traded the fruits of their labor or stolen goods that were actually the fruits of slave labor, the hinterland maroons were part and parcel of the informal economy, just like the borderland maroons. Like them, they entered into commercial relations with white men of various persuasions—storekeepers, patrollers, small farmers, and the underclass. Each transaction could end up in loss of freedom or death for the traders themselves; but even more importantly, in the destruction of their community. Because of their particular situation they had to test and establish exceptionally loyal networks of free and enslaved blacks as well as whites. The maroons who were able to maintain these setups for months and years were not only commercially savvy; they also possessed the skills necessary to assess the reliability and retain the fidelity of people who could have an obvious interest in betraying them.

White men who entered into commercial transactions with the maroons overlooked racial divisions and the law in order to make a profit. Although far from disowning whiteness and its privileges, they knowingly involved themselves in a series of actions that could have lethal results for their own community. This was because what the maroons wanted most were guns and ammunitions and to some degree, tools. Firearms shot cows and deer but they also wounded and killed militias, slaveholders, slave hunters, and others.

COMMUNITIES' DEFENSIVE STRATEGIES

All the hinterland settlements studied in this chapter share a number of characteristics. Safety measures were clearly lacking in these cases. When a colony with women and children invested time and resources establishing a farming operation, security had to be an absolute priority. Basic safety dictated that a settlement be erected at a distance from the fields. If it was destroyed, the community might still continue to function if its food supply had remained undamaged. Cabins could be rebuilt, and tools and pots could be appropriated, but fields took months of constant work to turn out crops. An added protection was to spread the fields over several locations. At Gadsden's Bay, the maroons wisely worked two fields but their security system was deficient. The settlers had no sentry and heard or saw the invaders only at the last moment. As they hastily fled, they abandoned twelve guns. This number of firearms suggests that the camp may have harbored over twenty people—including women and children. The loss of the weapons was a massive blow to their survival capacity, but there was worse: they left behind two children, each about a year old.

Similarly, the Marion settlement, although well planned, lacked elementary safety features. While the path leading to the camp was winding, a "party of gentlemen," who were looking for maroons thought to be hiding only two miles from town, found the trail. Trails and tracks were telltale signs of human activity and communities of dozens of individuals had to take extra precautions not to leave behind heavily trampled paths. One solution was to enter and exit the settlement from different directions to minimize the impact on the ground. It was an imperfect tactic, one that could not fool expert trackers. Given these constraints, it is striking that some communities did not take elementary precautions, or simply lowered their guard out of a false sense of security.

But increased protection was very much on the minds of a group that established itself in Mobile County, in the fork of the Alabama and Tombigbee rivers.[44] However, as often happened, its location was revealed by one of its inhabitants. On June 12, 1827 a Mr. Dupree saw two canoes hidden under willow trees by his plantation. Suspecting that they belonged to runaways, he called on a neighbor and his men and they all proceeded to the spot. As they approached, they saw the canoes, this time manned by five males, come down the river. One transported Hal, the group's leader, another man, and a teenager; although they quickly paddled away, the second canoe was overtaken. On board were Adam, who had escaped from a plantation near Claiborne, and Bush, originally from Mississippi. They were arrested. The next day, Bush, trying to make his escape, managed to grab a gun. As he was firing at the men who held him prisoner, he was killed. Adam was brought to the house of John Johnson, Sr., who promised him no jail time and a favorable intercession with his owner if he cooperated. Adam took the offer and that night, accompanied by a party of nine, he stood guard by a lake frequented by his companions. As the maroons approached on two canoes, there was an exchange of fire but no capture. The next morning Adam led the expedition to the settlement about twelve miles away.

When the men reached it they found Old Hal, a "very noted bad fellow" described as tall and powerfully built. He had been a maroon for several years. With him were Hector, Pompey, Bob, and Charles. The men did not see or hear the group's approach; when they seized their guns it was too late. Johnson recounted, "The negro man Pompey who is now living, tried to get his gun fresh primed to shoot, after he was shot through the thigh. Old Hal shot at Daniel Rain, not more than 3 or 10 paces. Harwell's Bob's gun flashed; Pompey's snapped; Hector fired in Brother Joseph's face with a French musket, but fortunately missed." Pompey was injured, Hal was wounded and died twelve hours later, and Hector was killed. Charles ran off with a wounded Bob, his wife, and children. In valiant maroon style, some men fought to the end to let the women, children, and wounded get away.

Johnson admiringly described their last stand: "[O]ld Hal and his men fought like Spartans, not one gave an inch of ground, but stood and was shot dead or wounded, and fell on the spot." In that sense, their heroic effort was a success: of the fourteen people present at the time of the attack, nine escaped. Yet the men's courage and valor cannot hide their carelessness. With two companions already captured and liable to betray them, and an encounter on the lake, prudence should have made them disappear. Short of leaving the area altogether, Hal should have posted sentries; if he did, they were quite ineffective.

The settlement had no cultivated land—at least none was found—and it was assumed the group lived on plunder. Thirty barrels of corn identified as belonging to two neighboring planters, and cowhides branded with a third man's mark, were sufficient proof that at least some of the maroons' necessities had "escaped" from plantations. To move about and to conduct their raids the maroons had six canoes at their disposal. They had carefully selected a difficult to access location, but they wanted to make it more secure. According to a newspaper, "They say they were about to commence a stockade fort, when a great number of negroes in the secret were to join them."

The large quantity of corn found in the camp can be interpreted as a sign that they were indeed expecting more people. The small number of settlers and the big ambitions they were said to harbor seem to indicate that this particular camp was in transition: its first occupants were involved in securing recruits who, they hoped, would make the fort a reality and, as a result, would enable the development of a larger and more secure colony. If this had been the case, the authorities believed that a canon might have been necessary to wipe out the defenses.

The possibility cannot be excluded that some communities in the South erected fortifications and other defensive mechanisms, as Hal and his companions were perhaps on the verge of doing. But no documentation has surfaced to confirm this, rumors and misinterpretation notwithstanding. For example, on July 23, 1841 the *St. Louis Argus* reported that a community of "600 negroes from Florida, and runaways from the Choctaws and Cherokees and from the whites" had gathered "west of Arkansas" (in Oklahoma) and built "a very tolerable fort with logs, surrounded with a ditch," from where they were said to raid the Choctaw settlements. After they allegedly repulsed the Choctaws and a company of U.S. dragoons, the infantry defeated them, and two cannons destroyed the breastworks. However, there is no official record of this purported event and *Niles' Register* concluded a week later that the story "is likely to turn out to be a false alarm." In addition, *The Annual Report of the Commissioner of Indian Affairs* did not mention the incident, which would have been recorded had it happened.[45]

One early eighteenth-century reference to an African defensive system does exist, but it concerns Hancock's Fort held by the Tuscaroras in North Carolina. It was the brainchild of Harry, an African from South Carolina who had fled to North Carolina when sold to a slave owner in Virginia.[46]

Despite the existence of striking but isolated examples of war camps in the rest of the Americas, there, just as in the United States, most maroons relied on the difficult terrain of dense forests and treacherous swamps rather than on the man-made works that would have reinforced these natural defenses. While this approach may seem to indicate a lack of foresight, it did not. Trenches, ditches, spikes, and breastworks, however useful, were not an absolute deterrent to militia or army assaults, and they did not necessarily prevent the settlements' annihilation because the attackers had superior firepower and the maroons opted for their preferred guerilla strategy of disappearing.

* * *

One major issue maroons confronted was the sustainability, in the long run, of large communities. The people who decided to migrate to the hinterland wanted the kind of self-sufficiency that only growing crops and raising animals could provide. But while individuals and families could live for months and years scattered about various borderlands without making their presence unduly felt, when they regrouped their raids increased in frequency in fewer locations, as did the quantity of items pilfered. The establishment of a larger community in the hinterland thus usually signaled itself by the increased disappearance of hogs, cattle, and grain. As the community grew its first crops, the raids would subside but not cease altogether.

Larger communities could only hope for a degree of autonomy because a common feature of their settlements was their small sizes. Complete self-sufficiency was difficult to attain for another reason. The demand for articles the maroons could not produce—particularly guns, powder, lead, and textiles—meant that raiding and trading were unavoidable. Some communities in the Great Dismal Swamp—and perhaps elsewhere—were self-supportive, but most others developed a diversified economy based on gathering, small-scale farming, hunting, fishing, raiding, and trading. These last activities connected them to the larger world and helped them sustain themselves but they also exposed them to dangers they pragmatically accepted because they significantly improved their material lives.

6

THE MAROONS OF

BAS DU FLEUVE, LOUISIANA

From the Borderlands to the Hinterland

THE most famous maroon community of Louisiana was formed, lived, and was destroyed in the early 1780s in St. Bernard Parish in the region called Bas du Fleuve, or Lower River, southeast of New Orleans. Its saga is well documented because the authorities charged to eliminate it left a voluminous correspondence and other documentation.[1] What make this story especially valuable, however, are the interrogation records of a number of maroons. Their first-hand accounts offer unique insights into the dynamics of their community. When pieced together, their testimonies draw an intimate portrait of a fluid group of men, women, Creoles, Africans, and at least one free woman. Their community of close to forty people regrouped, separated, migrated, lost, and gained members, and was undermined by spies and traitors.

Theirs is a long and instructive story of ingenuity, determination, duplicity, carelessness, solidarity, and courage that unfurled at the edges of several plantations and at Terre Gaillarde in the hinterland, as they covered the entire maroon landscape determined to preserve their community and freedom.

BONNE'S BORDERLANDS

On Saturday May 26, 1781 Juan Bautista Bienvenu, captain of the New Orleans militia, noticed that one of his cows was gone.[2] He sent some of his slaves, armed with sticks and three guns, to search for it. When they got to the woods located behind the king's arsenal, they discovered two maroons: Juan Bautista, who had run away from Mr. St. Amant seven months prior to the encounter and Pedro, who had come all the way from the plantation of Mr. Tounoir of Pointe Coupée—about 130 miles northwest of New Orleans—two and a half months earlier.

Brought to Bienvenu for interrogation, both men denied stealing the cow but said they knew the culprits, other maroons, and offered to take a search party to their camp. While Juan Bautista was shackled, Pedro led the expedition.[3] At 9:00 a.m. on Sunday, the troop came upon a number of shacks hidden in the canes behind Mr. Raguet's plantation. They arrested three women: Maria Juana, Margarita, and Nancy. Although they were vastly outnumbered by more than twenty armed men, three maroons managed to escape: Zephir, who had run away a year earlier from Tounoir of Pointe Coupée; Tham, who had escaped from St. Amant; and Samba, from Duparc. As the men were fleeing, the slowest was wounded in the back by birdshot after ignoring orders to stop.

The six maroons were part of a larger group that had also included their betrayers Juan Bautista and Pedro. After making their getaway from St. Amant's plantation around November 1780 with a barrel of rice, half a barrel of corn, two guns, and two knives, Juan Bautista, Tham, and Margarita had stayed in the woods behind Duparc's plantation for two weeks before migrating to another borderland. Their new refuge was the land situated behind Albert Bonne's plantation. There they joined Zephir and Lorenzo who had guns and "enough" provisions of powder, lead, and birdshot. The little group lived on the provisions brought from St. Amant's storehouse, and ate fish and turtles. They stayed in close contact with ten people from Bienvenu's estate, revealing the networks that linked borderlands and plantations.

Over time, Bonne's marginal acreage became genuine maroon land. The community of twenty-one (in two camps) consisted of individuals and small groups from fifteen plantations who came together at various times. At least three men—15 percent—were Africans of various origins. One was from Congo, and Samba and Mustapha were from Senegambia. The five women represented almost a quarter of the community. The people whose ages were recorded were between thirty-six and forty-two. One teenager was fifteen and there were no children.

The reason so many people had regrouped behind Bonne's was because they had struck a deal with the planter: he owned a sawmill and needed cheap manpower, while they needed money, supplies, land, and trading partners. Every morning Samba, Zephir, Tham, Pedro, Jacques, and others went into the woods to cut trees, square the timber, and drag the logs to the canal from where they floated down to Bonne's mill. Every week Bonne paid them one and a half *reales* for each piece. The "boldest and most daring" would go to the plantation at night to collect the money, usually Tham, as "he was the bravest." The maroons shared the money equitably according to the work each one had performed.

The arrangement with the planter did not end there. The maroons had obtained from Bonne the use of a lot where they planted corn, squash, and other vegetables. And they engaged in yet another venture: they made baskets, sifters, and other items out of willow and entrusted them to Bonne's bondspeople, who sold them in the city and brought back corn flour and other necessities.

To be as self-reliant as they possibly could, the maroons thus forged a profitable relationship based on hard work, assertiveness, and resourcefulness with the black and white inhabitants of the plantation. However, some men continued to raid neighboring plantations, expressing an emblematic maroon sense of having a rightful claim to whatever the slaveholders accumulated. According to Zephir, Joseph, Santiago, and Samba stole an ox or cow from Guido Dufossat, and an ox from Mr. Marand. Sometime later, they committed a major burglary stealing half a barrel of sugar, a barrel of salt, a barrel of lard, about one hundred bottles of wine, two soup dishes, twenty sifters, and a large churn to make butter. They also took two oxen and six pregnant cows. This robbery makes plain the kind of heavy damage maroons could mete out in a single expedition.

The group had been living on Bonne's land for about three months when in April the planter, through one of his bondspeople, warned them that Macarty—who was "missing" the maroons Thomas and Santiago—and St. Martin were coming after them. One night, led by a maroon who had just been captured, the two planters followed a trail that took them to the hut of an old man who lived on Bonne's land. Close to it they saw a path "covered with interwoven cane palms," as one witness described it, whereas another only mentioned dry leaves. The casual remarks are significant. It means that the maroons had devised a simple but ingenuous alarm system. They were alerted by the noise made when people walked on crackling leaves. Given the scarcity of information about them, this detail adds significantly to our corpus of knowledge about Southern maroons' protective strategies.

Dry leaves notwithstanding, St. Martin and Macarty were able to walk a short distance undetected before they heard the maroons talking. Knowing they were at a disadvantage, they left and went to ask Bonne for help. Bonne and his overseer took a gun each; they gave St. Martin a bayonet and together they returned to the camp. Hatching a quick plan, they assigned each man a post, but the noise they made walking on the dry palms—the stratagem worked this time—alerted the maroons, who vanished into the night. The next day St. Martin, Mr. Cazelar—whose Maria Juana and Joseph were among the maroons—and three others followed the same path further up and found the hut. It was burned down. The only traces of its occupants were a few dishes, skins, and some meat. The maroons had returned, taken everything of value, and torched the place.

St. Martin and his troop went back to Bonne's plantation and confronted the planter's brother, Juan Arlu, telling him that Bonne's slaves must have informed the maroons they were coming. Arlu vehemently denied having had any relations with the maroons. Alexandro Dupont, a tutor employed by St. Martin, replied that he was not accusing him, but only noting that the slaves must have known of the maroons' presence because their squash field was located on Bonne's land. Arlu claimed he had planted the squash himself. To this Dupont retorted, "[I]f you planted them, you must have done it with your eyes closed if you did not see the maroons' hut so close by."

After leaving Bonne's hospitable borderland, the maroons had to find other quarters. Zephir, Tham, Samba, Nancy, Maria Juana, Margarita, Pedro, and Juan Bautista moved behind Raguet's plantation at Cane

Bayou. But in late April Pedro and Juan Bautista left the group for the swamps behind the king's arsenal. According to Pedro, they were "disgusted by the injury the neighborhood residents suffered because of the negroes' robberies." By making such a claim they obviously hoped to ingratiate themselves with Bienvenu who was interrogating them after the theft of his cow. In reality, their disgust is likely to have stemmed not from sympathy for the planters, but rather from fear that too many thefts would result in an expedition to root out the culprits. And this is exactly what happened. In May, Zephir and Samba stole Bienvenu's cow and Pedro and Bautista were arrested for it.

When Bienvenu and his men arrived at the maroons' camp, all they found of the cow was its hide and some meat in Nancy and Maria Juana's hut. But they discovered the maroons' arsenal: an axe, hatchet, file, knife, and bayonet. The latter came from the German Waldeck regiment that had fought alongside the British during the Anglo-Spanish War of 1779–1781. About two hundred Germans had surrendered at Baton Rouge and were taken to New Orleans.[4] Through an underground network of traffickers one of their bayonets had reached the maroon camp, further proof of the vitality of the maroon networks.

Following the theft of the cow, six maroons were captured, but many of their companions were still living in the swamps. As for the prisoners themselves, some would make their way back there too.

LIFE AT TERRE GAILLARDE

Two years later, a community located in the same part of Bas du Fleuve, in an area called Terre Gaillarde, caused major concerns in the colony. Its leader acquired quasi-mythical status, although little is known about him, not even his name. He was alternatively called St. Malo, Juan Malò, and San Malò. St. Malo (from Saint Malo, a patron saint of Britanny) was a slave port, the place of departure for numerous French immigrants to Louisiana and one of the colony's trade partners. There was at least one white man named St. Malo in Louisiana in the 1720s.[5] According to the *Síndico Procurador General* (public advocate) of the New Orleans Cabildo (city council), Leonardo Mazange, the maroon leader was known as Juan

Malò when enslaved.[6] Juan Malò—*malo* meaning bad—is a common first name/surname combination in Spanish. However, the Spaniards were in the habit of translating French names. Thus he might have been Jean Malo (or Jean St. Malo) rather than Juan Malò, Malo (without the accent) being a French family name. His language was French, not Spanish, which indicates that his original owner must have been a French speaker who would have given him a French, not a Spanish, name. His previous (and perhaps only) owner, Pierre Frederick d'Arensbourg—a son of Karl Friedrich d'Arensbourg, the founder of the German Coast settlement on the east side of the Mississippi above New Orleans—called him St. Malo.[7] No physical description has surfaced; his age remains unknown, as does his life as a slave, his reasons for running away, and even when he did so.

St. Malo's community was composed of families, couples, and single men and women who coalesced over time. Several had been maroons for a few months, others for a few years. Some were part of the community that lived at the margins of Bonne's plantation. Captured and whipped, they escaped again. Like them, several people had started their marronage in the borderlands. The particular stories of two families, based on their own accounts, are our point of entry into the community.

Goton had run away because she was regularly punished.[8] She left with her husband Huberto, their adult children, and the youngster Bautista. Their daughter Catiche followed because she did not want to be separated from her mother and stepfather; and their son Cupidon's wife, Theresa, joined to be with her husband. They had escaped from Attorney General and officer of the militia don Henrique Desprez, and for two months the family of six lived right behind his plantation. Like other borderland maroons, they diversified their food supply to sustain themselves. They took the precaution of appropriating some rice before escaping, and obtained additional rations as well as corn from friends. They lived on ducks and birds and the meat Huberto received from four maroons he met in the woods.

Desprez's plantation was fertile ground for maroons. Apart from the six people who freed themselves from his rule, "many others" were living off his land. Some, like Goton and her family, were borderland maroons, but Jacob and Scipio who frequented the area, lived several miles away in Terre Gaillarde. They came to the plantations to steal, gather information, visit friends, and as with Huberto, to exchange and/or give what they had produced or hunted. There was active, tangible solidarity between the people of the borderland, the hinterland, and those who lived on the plantations. Desprez was not able to put a stop to it and apprehend any of the maroons.

After two months, Goton and Huberto's family decided to leave Desprez's borderland. Perhaps prodded by Jacob and Scipio, they wanted to move to Terre Gaillarde. *Terre* means land in French and the word *gaillard(e)* (both as adjective and noun) means someone full of life and drive, strong, robust; it was a good name for a maroon refuge. According to Acting Governor Esteban Miró, St. Malo himself had baptized the place.[9] In contrast to what transpired elsewhere in the country, the name of the maroon territory became widely known by white Louisianans and made its way into official correspondence. The fact that Louisiana was Spanish at the time was quite significant. Spaniards—in contrast to the British colonists of North America—acknowledged the reality of marronage and either named settlements or called them by their maroon names.

Terre Gaillarde was not a village per se but a territory on which a settlement had been erected. Mazange of the Cabildo of New Orleans lamented that the site was located far enough from settled areas to provide safety and was hard to reach due to its unknown and inaccessible paths. According to Governor Miró, to get there one had to wade through reeds in chest-high water.[10] The zone that abutted it was scarcely populated; by 1785 only 586 people (mostly Spaniards from the Canary Islands and two free blacks) lived in what was then named San Bernardo Parish, also known as Terre aux Boeufs, a land that could not be cultivated beyond the banks of the creek due to the presence of marshes.[11] Terre Gaillarde was thus ideally located amid wild land and, as an added safety feature, it could only be entered through small waterways from Lake Borgne.

En route to their new home, Goton, Huberto, and their children met Dota, Maria, Margarita, La Violette—a man, despite his female name—and another man whose name Goton did not know. They too were on their way to Terre Gaillarde. Margarita was the same woman who, two years earlier, had been living at the borderland of Bonne's plantation.

Terre Gaillarde's maturity and seclusion as a maroon haven were underlined by the fact that its settlement consisted of many cabins, some new, some old, and it had enough of them to accommodate the eleven newcomers in communal cabins. Goton noted that eleven people already lived there when she arrived; but when her daughter Catiche was interrogated she gave thirteen names. The mother and daughter's lists do not entirely match. After each name is taken into account, the total comes to sixteen people from nine different plantations. Among them were five women. Colas, one of the maroons who lived behind Bonne's and Raguet's, was part of the community too. The lists are interesting for what they do not mention: children. Just like the groups who gathered behind Bonne's plantation, it appears that Terre Gaillarde was made up of mature people, some of whom were old enough to have adult children.

With the eleven newcomers, the settlement was now home to twenty-seven people, but they were not all sedentary. The place was a rallying point of sorts. Some maroons lived there but others came and went. St. Malo had built a cabin and came frequently, but he lived part of the time at Chef Menteur and on the borderlands of Chabert and Bienvenu plantations. Jasmin lived behind Charbert's but his wife stayed at Terre Gaillarde and he visited her. The principal person in the settlement was not St. Malo but Juan Pedro, and his second was his son Joli Coeur.

Juan Pedro, his wife Maria, their daughter Pelagie, and Joli Coeur had decided to run away three years earlier because Maria was repeatedly punished by Mr. de Mazilliere. It was the same reason—violence against a woman—that pushed Huberto and his family to escape from Desprez. De Mazilliere also threatened to inflict the same treatment on Juan Pedro. After their escape, the family wandered through the woods. For the first year Juan Pedro (and perhaps the rest of his family) took refuge by a lake, in a place secluded enough for him to cultivate his own crops. He raised and consumed four barrels of corn. Not surprisingly, he also helped himself to whatever he could find on the neighboring plantations. The following year, the family moved to Terre Gaillarde.

At Terre Gaillarde Juan Pedro (and doubtless others) raised provisions but they were far from sufficient. Actually, when Catiche and her mother Goton were interrogated, they did not even mention the crops. Both said that the maroons lived on roots and herbs. They pounded the root of China-smilax into flour. It was a meager diet and Maria acknowledged that they took provisions from the neighboring plantations. They also hunted and fished and Juan Pedro took the catch to town at night to sell in order to acquire the items they needed.

On his second and final year at the settlement, Juan Pedro embarked on another income-generating activity. He worked on Mrs. Mandeville's plantation for the enslaved Colas. What he did is not clear, but in the light of the tasks maroons performed on other estates, he could have worked in Colas's garden and/or helped him with his chores in the woods, such as felling trees and making staves. Juan Pedro and the people of Terre Gaillarde, just like those at Bonne's, combined all the activities in which maroons could engage to enhance their standard of living. They gathered, hunted, fished, cultivated, traded, and worked for money or necessary items on the side.

Also like most maroons, they acquired firearms and organized an ammunition supply network. Before his escape, Juan Pedro secured a horn full of powder and he later bought ammunition in town with the proceeds from his fishing activities. He worked for Colas in exchange for half a pound of powder, half a pound of ammunition, and five or six balls. St. Malo made money as an artisan building large tubs, mortars (or troughs), and other items made from the abundance of cypress wood that surrounded him. Those he exchanged with the enslaved Alexandro for ammunition. Through his legitimate business St. Malo got a regular stock of balls and powder. Jasmin, who had run away only three months before he was captured, took ammunition from his owner and bought some in the city, "on the Plaza."

The maroons of Terre Gaillarde were mobile, moving around well beyond New Orleans. One day Juan Pedro, St. Malo, Joli Coeur, Bautista,

Prince, Henri, Maria, and Carlota (Joli Coeur's wife), each with a gun, went on an expedition to a plantation fronting Mrs. Assemard's on Bay Saint Louis in Mississippi.[12] Once there, according to Juan Pedro, a white man confronted them: he wanted to know where they were going. They responded that they were heading for Mobile to meet Don Bernardo de Galvez. Their joke was quite impudent, not to mention potentially perilous, emanating as it did from a group of maroons. They were telling the man in no equivocal terms to mind his own business: Don Bernardo de Galvez was the governor of Louisiana and Cuba. An elderly American Juan Pedro believed to be the plantation owner, asked if he would exchange guns with him. Juan Pedro was tempted because his own was in poor condition and lacked a hammer, but his companions discouraged him.

The maroons left, yet the next morning, Juan Pedro, accompanied by the unarmed Bautista, Prince, and Henri paddled back to the plantation to conduct the transaction. Their naïveté might seem astounding, but not all encounters between maroons and white men resulted in bloodshed. As already emphasized, some were based on economic interest that benefited both parties. Juan Pedro and his companions obviously thought the meeting with the American was of that nature. As soon as they got onshore, though, eight gun-toting men jumped them. Juan Pedro was shot in the neck and Henri, Bautista, and Prince were tied up. The white men then paddled to where the other maroons were encamped. They surrendered without resistance and were all tied up, except St. Malo. The Americans' objective was to deliver the eight maroons, a good catch, to the authorities in New Orleans. In the evening, on their way to the city, they stopped their two pirogues at Pointe des Rigolets to look for wood to cook dinner. St. Malo seized the occasion to commandeer a carbine and untie his companions. He grabbed a hatchet and struck the man who was guarding the prisoners and the unloaded guns. Joli Coeur took the hatchet from him and St. Malo put his right foot on the American's stomach while Joli Coeur struck him repeatedly on the head and killed him. Removing his clothes—always an important bounty—he threw him overboard. From what Juan Pedro divulged, only one person was killed.

St. Malo and his partners appropriated the pirogues and whatever was in them. They went to Chef Menteur where they stayed three months, until Juan Pedro's wound had healed. He and St. Malo then went their separate ways but kept in touch, the chief and his lieutenant Michel often visiting Terre Gaillarde. On one of these occasions he confided that he and Michel had killed four Englishmen who had left a plantation near Conway's Bayou loaded with provisions. They took the goods and St. Malo gave Michel the only gun found in the boat.

THE FIRST ATTACK ON TERRE GAILLARDE

With white people murdered, maroon activity becoming more taxing on farms and plantations, and the Anglo-Spanish War behind them, the authorities decided to more forcefully tackle the maroon problem. They enlisted Chacales/Chacala to help locate St. Malo and his people. Chacales was Colas's father. Since Juan Pedro had once worked for Colas, both men knew the maroons' whereabouts. On March 1, 1783, guided by Chacales who was promised two hundred pesos, a force gathered under the command of Don Guido Dufossat.[13] It consisted of five white and several free and enslaved black men, spread out in seven pirogues. Patrick McNamara, three of his bondsmen, Juan Luis—one of Regidor Francisco Maria de Reggio's slaves—and three free people of color occupied one. The pirogues made their way through the bayous toward Lake Borgne and less than three miles from shore, they sighted a group of people moving their baggage around. The raiding party's intention was to surround them, but when the maroons realized they had been discovered, they tried to flee. The raiders fired at them, killing one, probably La Violette, as mentioned by Goton.[14] Twelve people were captured and ten escaped. Among the prisoners was Juan Luis, a maroon for five months. Hoping to spare himself further trouble, he helped the expedition capture his comrades.[15]

Chacales then led the party to Terre Gaillarde. At that particular moment, there were only eight people there: Goton, Catiche, Scipio, and Theresa; Juan Pedro, Maria, Pelagie, and Joli Coeur were fishing in the bayou nearby. Feeling quite secure in their hard-to-reach settlement, the maroons had no sentry and no protective mechanism. When the raiding party pounced, one man offered some resistance but the others surrendered. They were tied up and dispatched to the pirogues.

Where were the rest of the maroons? According to Juan Pedro, the night before, St. Malo and his wife Cecilia Canoy (sometimes spelled Canuet or Conway), Samba—who used to work for Bonne—and six others went to the German Coast to look for Samba's brother. While on this trip, through the well-oiled maroon-plantation grapevine, St. Malo heard that an expedition was in preparation: "the mulattoes"—the militia of free people of color—were getting ready to hunt and kill the people at Terre Gaillarde. He told his friends he had to warn their companions that the "mulattoes" were on their way. Esteban, Carlos, and Jasmin accompanied him. Carlos, a twenty-two-year-old African from "Guinea," who had been a maroon for three months, wanted to retrieve his clothes from the settlement. Jasmin, twenty-eight, also a maroon for three months, was going to get his wife.

At least that was what Jasmin and Carlos explained when they were interrogated. But fifteen-year-old Alexandro contradicted them. He said he was fishing when he saw the raiding party take the first group of prisoners and went to Terre Gaillarde but found the settlement deserted. When he reached Bayou Bienvenu on his way back, he met St. Malo, Carlos, Jasmin, and Esteban who told him they wanted to try to free the prisoners. Alexandro's version was more plausible than that offered by Carlos and Jasmin. It is indeed hard to believe that St. Malo and his three partners were unaware of the first arrests and the subsequent expedition to Terre Gaillarde. The whole episode unfolded over several hours and the numerous maroons in the hinterland and the borderlands who were in contact with one another could not have ignored what had been going on.

St. Malo and his men went away on their rescue mission well armed. Esteban had a gun, hatchet, and a kitchen knife tied around his neck. St. Malo had a gun, machete, and big knife; Jasmin carried a gun, knife, and hatchet; and Carlos had a knife and a gun that did not work. St. Malo lent him a functioning one. He had also received six balls from Esteban and Maria. They all had powder, balls, and birdshot. To justify their arsenal, which was truly fit for an attack, when he was interrogated Jasmin insisted that maroons never went anywhere without their weapons, because the only way they could get food was by hunting for it. And, of course, they could not leave their weapons in the bush, for they would be stolen.

As they rowed their pirogue, St. Malo at the helm, the four men came in view of Patrick McNamara's boat, which was a distance from the others. Jasmin and Carlos both told their interrogators they wanted to go back to shore to avoid any confrontation, but St. Malo warned them he was going to shoot. He did, killing de Reggio's slave, Juan Luis. Almost simultaneously, Esteban fired his gun. The maroon Scipio, who was sitting next to Juan Luis, was wounded in the right hand. McNamara riposted and shot Jasmin, who fell into the water, overturning the boat. The maroons went under. Carlos maintained he first tried to reach land but upon McNamara's order to stop, he turned around and told him he was going to surrender. The four men swam toward McNamara, who testified that they all grabbed the side of the boat to try to capsize it, screaming "use force." The black men on board beat the maroons with their guns and oars. Carlos, afraid of being shot and of the strong waves that agitated the lake, swam toward shore. He did not see what happened next but heard the men in the pirogue scream "kill him, kill him." His three companions grasped the boat again and Esteban was hit so hard on the head with the butt of a gun that he drowned. At that point, Jasmin and St. Malo swam away, the raiding party hot in pursuit. McNamara managed to grab Carlos on the banks of the bayou and Luis captured Jasmin on land. St. Malo disappeared into the night.

The deadly encounter on Lake Borgne highlights not only St. Malo's sense of responsibility to his people as a leader but also his impulsiveness, as well as divergent strategic visions among the maroons. It is clear that nobody else was willing to undertake the risky rescue. None of the other maroons agreed to accompany St. Malo, Esteban, Carlos, and Jasmin on their mission. With more men and more guns, the operation might have ended differently, but evidently most men disagreed or were not about to risk their lives to find out.

The whole episode was a disaster. Two maroons were killed, twelve were rounded up in the woods and another eight at Terre Gaillarde, and Jasmin and Carlos were captured by Lake Borgne. Other arrests were made as well, as a year later Governor Miró affirmed that forty-three maroons were captured.[16] Following the depositions of all parties—whites, free men of color, and maroons—on May 15, prosecutor Pedro Bertonniere asked that Carlos and Jasmin receive "the greatest and more severe punishment" allowed under law. This would "serve as a warning to the rest of the slaves who are running away every day."[17] Perhaps fearing a loss of property, or out of genuine concern, Francisca Pigeaule, widow of Domingo St. Amant, mounted a vigorous defense of her slaves.[18] The only criminal, she argued, was St. Malo, as he had done the shooting. As to the accusation that the men tried to capsize McNamara's boat by grabbing it, she answered it was a natural gesture for someone about to drown to grasp a branch to save himself. The fact that the men swam to the boat was proof of their innocence, she claimed; otherwise they would have fled with St. Malo. She therefore asked that the two maroons be declared innocent of the crime imputed to them. But on August 29, Miró decreed that Carlos and Jasmin were to be charged. On December 23, 1783 they were condemned to receive three hundred lashes and to be exiled about three hundred leagues (nine hundred miles) away.[19] The rest of the maroons were sent back to their owners.

Despite this successful expedition, the Spanish authorities were only half satisfied. St. Malo was still free, as were many more maroons, and the raids on plantations had not abated. Miró came up with a new strategy. In the fall, he sent a slave posing as a maroon to spy on the Terre Gaillarde community. However, whatever elusive pieces of information the man brought back were useless and Miró fired him.[20] Winter that year was unusually frigid and no campaign could be organized, but in the spring Miró sent Bastien—a former maroon— to infiltrate the group. If he could lead a raiding party to the community, he would be handsomely rewarded: he would get his freedom from his owner Charles Honoré Olivier.[21]

* * *

Meanwhile, after the devastating raid at Terre Gaillarde, St. Malo's community had to find another safe haven. The maroons took a bold decision: they opted for the borderlands. The easy accessibility of food and intelligence was likely a factor. They settled at the edges of Mr. Prevost's plantation at *Détour des Anglais*—English Turn, also known as English Bend, a bend in the Mississippi—about twelve miles southeast of New Orleans. Over time other people joined.[22] In an approach that ensured solidarity and minimized the risks of betrayal, St. Malo's group entered into a mutually beneficial arrangement with the men and women who labored for Prevost. The maroons helped them with their tasks, doing all their work in the woods, making stakes, and cutting timber. They even cultivated the slaves' small gardens. In return, their partners stole domestic animals and brought them to the edges of the woods where the maroons killed and butchered them. In another confirmation of the kind of spaces of autonomy enslaved men and women succeeded in creating, they all ate together every day in the forest. Significantly, the people at Prevost's also provided St. Malo with all the powder and ammunition he needed. But the tight relationship went beyond work and trade, it was also very personal: both groups intermarried. And it was a dispute over a woman that provoked "a war" between them.

As friends became enemies, the maroons had to leave Prevost's borderland. Conscious of the harsh existence they were bound to face, St. Malo told his companions who had not committed any "crime" other than marronage that they could return to their owners. In April, he left accompanied by a group believed to number thirty to thirty-five individuals, including the spy Bastien. Michel—who, with St. Malo, had killed four Englishmen—stayed behind but was supposed to join them later. In another unexpected move, the group migrated back to Terre Gaillarde. Chacales and the raiding party he had led just a year before knew how to get there, but this may have been precisely why a return made sense. No one would imagine that the maroons were so foolhardy as to return to a safe haven whose safety was thoroughly compromised. Some people did not follow but settled on Bienvenu's borderland. It was about six plantations away from Prevost, towards Terre aux Boeufs, closer to Terre Gaillarde, and people in the quarters were known to be helpful.

THE SECOND ATTACK ON TERRE GAILLARDE

While St. Malo and his companions were settling back into the hinterland, the authorities were busy planning their destruction. On April 28 and 29, meetings with concerned planters organized respectively by Miró and the Cabildo concluded that a new campaign had to be launched. Expecting casualties, the planters agreed to compensate the owners of the people killed in action or executed—two hundred pesos per person—and the Cabildo to advance the funds. On April 30, in an attempt to thwart marronage the Cabildo proclaimed a series of regulations concerning the control of slaves.[23] The first of its eleven articles stated that any slave found any time, on foot or on horseback, with or without a weapon, and without a pass would immediately receive twenty-five lashes. If a runaway he was to be sent to jail, "where he would receive the punishment his crime deserved." Given what was already clear and had been made even clearer by the interrogations of Juan Pedro, Jasmin, and Carlos the year before, the decree reiterated that it was forbidden to sell powder and ammunition to slaves under penalty of fines and "other punishments." Moreover, the name of the owner was to be written on the guns delivered legally to enslaved hunters so that if they were found in maroon hands, the ownership could be proved and the proprietor punished. Slaveholders were ordered to search slave dwellings frequently and to arrest any runaways or strangers and send them to jail along with the people who harbored them. Since it was impossible "to distinguish by sight a free negro or mulatto from a slave or a runaway," free men and women had to carry their certificates at all times.

The next day, Miró issued an identical order to post commandants, with a telling preamble.[24] Free blacks and mulattoes would be held particularly responsible for any damage to the public if they had information about the maroons and did not report it to the authorities. The paranoia that commonly accompanied any suspicion of extensive black solidarity cannot be taken as evidence of collusion, but some free people of color certainly had firsthand intelligence about the maroons. Among them were those who were part of the underground economy and those who had enslaved relatives and friends at Prevost, Bienvenu, and perhaps even among the maroons themselves.

After the promulgation of his order, Miró departed for Pensacola and Mobile to attend meetings with Native American leaders. During his absence, two men were to assume his functions: military affairs were entrusted to Lieutenant Colonel Francisco Bouligny, while civil affairs were assigned to Francisco María de Reggio, whose slave Juan Luis had been killed by St. Malo on Lake Borgne. On May 18, Bouligny called a meeting of militia officers and told them that rather than regular soldiers, men used to the bayous and lakes were the best suited to hunt for the maroons.[25] Henrique Desprez, officer of the militia, volunteered to draw a list. Given he had been so inept at finding the numerous maroons who, like Goton and her family, lived at the margins of his own plantation, reliance on his expertise was ironic.

Two days later, the authorities got a break. Guido Dufossat's bondspeople captured Pierre, a Creole who had been a maroon for six months. He had spent time on Prevost's borderland and had had a falling-out with the people in the quarters. To take revenge, he explained that several maroons lived behind the plantation, including St. Malo's group for a while. He also told Bouligny that twenty to twenty-five men and nine women were with the leader at Terre Gaillarde but no one knew exactly where or how to find them, except Michel, who had stayed behind for reasons unknown to him. He knew, however, that Michel was going to join them.

Pierre also revealed the presence in the woods of four maroons who had escaped from Mrs. Doriocourt, whom Prevost's bondspeople continued to help. He agreed to lead Guillemard with six grenadiers and a dozen free men of color to their camp. The party departed at sunset and waded for hours through treacherous terrain, waist-deep in mud. When they finally got to the refuge at two in the morning, they found it deserted. Bouligny suspected that the people at Prevost's had alerted the occupants. The expedition was a failure, a waste of time and money.

A dejected Bouligny reported that the maroons were scattered around in the swamps and without a trusted guide it was impossible to attack the camps. Never did more than three or four people live in each hideout. In addition, the sound of a raiding party warned the maroons who could find refuge ten steps from their huts by jumping into the water that reached up to their necks. A single shot alerted them all. Acknowledging the comings and goings between hinterland and borderlands, he concluded that the situation in the country was disastrous, especially because the maroons found refuge on all the plantations.

But Bouligny was to get another break the very next day. Another maroon, the third in almost as many days, was brought in. He was, according to Bouligny, "*medio bozal*" or "half bozal," which means he was an African who had lived in the country for several years. Having recently fled from Mrs. Leconte, he was living behind Bienvenu's plantation. Several people who Pierre had said were with St. Malo at Terre Gaillarde, were, according to him, still on Bienvenu's borderland. Pierre, who now came under suspicion for having lied or shaded the truth, offered to bring Michel's head to redeem himself, but Bouligny refused to let him go. He feared that in another bout of duplicity Pierre would inform the maroons of the latest plans to catch them. He also believed that the best strategy to get rid of the St. Malo group was to offer a bounty of two hundred pesos and his freedom to any slave who could bring the leader's head; and freedom without reward to those who would do the same for his lieutenants Michel, Philippe, and Etienne who had distinguished themselves with their "audacity and impudence." Miró, however, rejected the idea.

Bouligny knew that St. Malo's community counted about two dozen people and he thought they could be isolated and cut off from food supplies. But for the time being the maroons had the upper hand. On May 17, they launched an expedition of their own. They organized a raiding spree on the storehouse of a German Coast planter and appropriated twenty barrels of corn, eight barrels of rice, and one barrel of flour. About six miles away, they stole a large pirogue. Although the theft was spectacular in reality it did not amount to much. With the flour the maroons could make about five breads per person. The eight barrels of rice could feed thirty people for roughly three weeks and the corn for about six. They would soon have to organize several other raids, or a major one.

On May 28, at the weekly Cabildo meeting, the Public Advocate Leonardo Mazange launched into a diatribe against the enslaved population in general and the maroons in particular. According to him, the former, being treated with too much leniency, were no longer showing the submissiveness expected of them and had fancies of independence. As a result they committed crimes ranging from armed robberies to murders. Never before had they had the audacity and the cruelty to stain their hands with "white blood." The problem was so acute that some plantations were left unfarmed because their labor force had deserted. Widows and orphans were clamoring for protection. All the criminal activities going on enabled the maroons to form large communities in various places, especially at Terre Gaillarde. Mazange warned about the potential for a Jamaica-like situation. The maroons had become so bold that they attacked travelers, he continued. They had cruelly murdered five Americans of Bay St. Louis as they returned home. Moreover, they were sustained by people who remained "in their masters' power" for no other reason, seemingly, than to assist the maroons and join them later.

Wanting to show the complete control St. Malo exerted over his troops and how bloodthirsty and pitiless he was even with his own people, Mazange claimed that he had killed his wife because she wanted to return to her owner and that he had executed a man who refused to slaughter a calf. His second in command—Joli Coeur—was known as the "Knight of the Ax" for having split a white man's head open with an axe. The Public Advocate went on to recount the attack against McNamara's pirogue a year earlier, making it appear as if it had just happened. Invoking widows, orphans, massacre, Jamaica, and a bloodthirsty black man on the loose, Mazange was as inflammatory as he could possibly be in order to jolt the authorities into action. He concluded by exhorting the present assembly to ask Bouligny to hunt the maroons down. The council members agreed.[26]

The same day, from Pensacola Miró sent a letter to Bouligny proposing a plan of action. He argued that a force of fifty men would be sufficient to go to Terre Gaillarde. While one group of twenty men mounted guard on Lake Borgne at the entrance to the bayou that led to the settlement, another twenty would guard another bayou to prevent the maroons from escaping. He still left it to Bouligny to increase or decrease the number of men depending on the latest news he was able to gather.[27]

Around May 28, the maroons attacked Mrs. Mandeville's storehouse. Francisco, a slave, interposed himself and was killed. The maroons also stole rice, flour, and corn at Ms. St. Amant and other estates.[28] Following these raids, on June 2 Bouligny and his forces, which numbered about one hundred, jumped into action.[29] Fifteen hunters were posted on the waterways of Chef Menteur and Isles of Pines. Fourteen free militias of color went into Chef Menteur; thirty militias moved toward Terre Gaillarde. Eight militiamen were sent twelve miles below the last plantation in the area and twenty soldiers set ambushes on three consecutive nights on Prevost, Bienvenu, and Mandeville plantations. Two groups of four soldiers were to be discreetly posted near storehouses. Bouligny urged the planters to safeguard their stockrooms and boats because he believed the maroons were in need of provisions. He also encouraged them to send trustworthy slaves and free mulattoes to comb the areas known to harbor maroons. It was an elaborate strategy, one that covered all the maroons' known bases.

According to this plan, Pierre de Marigny and thirty of his men were to move toward Terre Gaillarde and meet up with Guillemart. But on June 3, when he was still at home instead of in the field, Marigny heard a knock on his door at 3:00 a.m.[30] The visitor was Bastien, surfacing after his two-month stint as an infiltrator. St. Malo had sent him, Michel, and two others in two pirogues to steal provisions and spy on the mounting expedition; evidence that the group, far from being completely isolated, knew something was going on. Michel and the two maroons were arrested, and Michel was wounded in the action.

Marigny now had a direct conduit to St. Malo, and rather than obeying orders, he decided to catch the leader and his community by himself. Following Bastien, he and his men entered the bayou that led to Terre Gaillarde. Instead of discreetly encircling the village, they started firing, thus alerting its occupants. This ill-conceived maneuver enabled the maroons to flee. They left behind the injured Isidore. All the raiding party could do was torch the huts. It was another spectacular failure.

The same day Bouligny sent Miró a list of the people thought to be with St. Malo.[31] The fact that he listed Bastien shows that he still did not know that the spy was guiding Marigny toward the maroons' settlement. Michel, wounded and captured by then, was also on the list. Bouligny enumerated thirty-two people and mentioned that he did not know the names of another four or five. The maroons came from twenty-four plantations and—except for six individuals from Leconte's—they were held individually. This congregating of people from so many estates speaks of cross-plantation networks and of regrouping born out of numerous encounters at the borderlands. There were fifteen women; such a high proportion (47 percent) was quite unusual in any maroon settlement.[32] Once again, there was no mention of children. Bouligny listed only two couples, Cecilia and St. Malo and Janneton and Esteban, giving credence to the contention that some maroons' spouses were indeed among the people at Prevost's.

For Cecilia, Bouligny used the Spanish word *a* (of or belonging to) like he did for the others, implying she was enslaved. But later on she was referred to as a *negra libre*, a free black woman.[33] There is reason to believe this was the case. By the time her free status was mentioned in an official document, she had been in jail for several months. During this time her legal standing must have been verified. The choice this free woman made to lead a life full of uncertainty, danger, and lack of comfort was notable. Some free blacks helped, traded with, and harbored runaways and maroons, but few lived among them.

Meanwhile, in the swamps and bayous Marigny and Guillemard continued their search.[34] Bouligny believed that while ten or twelve maroons had settled at Barataria, Chapitoulas, and La Conception, almost all the most "criminal" ones were at Terre Gaillarde. He thought they would be incapable of getting out of the area and was determined to support and reinforce Guillemard's expedition with a force of sixteen militias under Nicolas Olivier's command.[35] The party returned to Terre Gaillarde, and finally Captain Juan Bautista Hugon, a free *pardo* (of mixed black, white, and American Indian origin), a veteran of the antimaroon fight and an officer of the colored militia, discovered the maroons' tracks and informed Guillemard, who arrived with his men. After cruising the waterways for two hours they heard the maroons and saw them scattered along a bayou. As they reached shooting distance, they opened fire. The maroons, the militias on their heels, fled across a meadow full of holes and dense rushes with water up to their waist. Guillemard could not follow because of an old leg injury, but he climbed atop a live oak and directed his men, shouting and agitating his handkerchief and his hat toward the fleeing maroons. Olivier ran after a man for more than three miles and in the end shot at him from a great distance. He saw him fall, wounded in the arm. When he came close, he realized it was St. Malo.

The successful operation evidenced once again one of the maroons' fatal weaknesses: their lack of vigilance. They had escaped a raid four days earlier but instead of quickly scattering into small groups and trying to leave the area altogether, they remained clustered in the same general place. They did not post sentinels and did not see or hear the approaching militia. Once attacked, the men did not return fire to try to slow down the assault. St. Malo's own actions may explain why. When wounded, according to Olivier, he asked him to finish him off as he knew "his crimes deserved death." Obviously, he was not afraid to die and was aware he would be hung. He could have killed himself before Olivier finally got to him, sparing himself the humiliation of defeat, the agony of torture, the gruesomeness of hanging, and the triumph of his enemies. He could also have fired at Olivier. He did not, possibly because he could not. There was no mention of him fleeing with a gun. Nor did the other men shoot back. Everyone ran away. As already stressed, disappearing was the maroons' preferred strategy. Their flight was thus to be expected, but the absence of a protective last stand was unusual. It is possible that they had no ammunition.

In the end five men escaped, and seventeen people were rounded up and can be identified.[36] Almost half were women: Janneton and Nelly (both present during the first attack on Terre Gaillarde in 1783), Venus,

Genevieve, Francisca, Julia, Naneta, and Cecilia. Five had lived in the woods for between one and two years; and three for three to eight months. St. Malo and Juan Guenard were maroons for an unknown number of years; Bautista for five, and Esteban for two. Cesar, Juan Luis, Francisco, Luis, and Jason were new recruits, from one to six months out. Of the men who escaped, Telemaque had run away six months earlier, Philippe was a five-year maroon veteran, and Colas was involved in the events of 1781. Of Etienne and Printens nothing is known. The reality is glaring: only about half the men were experienced maroons. As such Terre Gaillarde did not correspond to the image that was painted for months, that of a nest of dangerous murderers, formidable maroons ready to start a general insurrection and transform Louisiana into Jamaica. But when Miró gave an account of the expedition to Bernardo de Gálvez, he did not spare the hyperbole. He assured the governor and captain general of Cuba that the maroons were about to attack the plantations "*a fuerza abierta*," that is, openly. He feared they could build a *palenque*—a fortified camp—like the maroons did in Jamaica, because the place they had settled in could be defended by five hundred men against any number of attackers. He was conveniently omitting that the maroons numbered less than thirty. He added that through the bayous they could reach Terre aux Boeufs, a zone favorable to human sustenance where corn abounded. As noted earlier he stated that St. Malo himself had named the maroons' land "La Terre Gaillarde." According to what Bastien had told him, St. Malo had struck his ax in the first tree, declaring (in French), "Malheur au blanc qui passera ces bornes," or "woe betide the white man who crosses these bounds." His companions had yelled their approval.[37] Miró's is the only source explaining how the site acquired its name. However, if the maroon leader did bestow it, it was not on that day in April, as the area was referred as Terre Gaillarde in written records three years earlier, in 1781.

* * *

After the fruitful raid, the prisoners were taken to New Orleans in chains. White crowds along the Mississippi cheered their capture, praying to heaven, and blessing the expeditionary forces.[38] The maroons reached the city on June 12; by the 14th forty men and twenty women were in detention, in addition to the forty-three from 1783.[39] Twelve people were arrested for being the maroons' accomplices. Bouligny believed a dozen maroons had disappeared into the heart of Barataria and Terre Gaillarde. St. Malo was so gravely wounded that he thought he might not survive. He had gangrene. According to Bouligny, "Full of remorse, he hides nothing of his crimes nor of those of his companions."

The judicial proceedings against the maroons were started straightaway by Francisco Maria de Reggio, who took testimonies for less than a week. Because they involved the murder of whites, the first order was to get information on the incidents at Bay St. Louis and Conway's Bayou. Bouligny, in a letter to Miró on June 19, summarized what St. Malo was said to have confessed concerning Bay St. Louis.[40] Eloquent and acting as a kind of prosecutor, in Bouligny's words, St. Malo pushed his friends to admit their guilt. He acknowledged that he gave the first blow to the man who guarded the guns; then Joli Coeur, leaping from a pirogue with a half axe in hand, attacked the American. But it was only when St. Malo put his right foot on the man's stomach that Joli Coeur was able to smash his skull into a thousand pieces. All the while, Prince stood passively, encouraging his companions but not taking part in the action. From then on he was known as a coward. Bautista did nothing, because the Americans— who distrusted him more than they did the others—had tied him very carefully. Henri repeatedly beat a woman and a boy with the butt of a "half rotten" gun. Bouligny added that St. Malo also stated that Michel had helped him murder the four Englishmen near Conway's.

Reggio had interrogated Juan Pedro just a year before and was therefore already knowledgeable about both affairs. Juan Pedro had told him that his own son, Joli Coeur, had killed an American and Michel and St. Malo the four Englishmen, but did not give details about what the secondary characters did or did not do. Armed with revelations about Prince's coaxing and actually nothing against Bautista, Reggio acted swiftly. Bautista was apprehended. He was still enslaved by the Capuchins and had hired himself on a plantation despite the edict of April 30 that forbade slaves to do so. This arrest infuriated the clergy, who later refused to cooperate with the authorities.[41]

On June 18, six days after the maroons arrived in New Orleans, Reggio delivered his verdict. St. Malo, Joli Coeur, Henri, and Michel were condemned to death. Cecilia was condemned to death too for no other reason than that she was St. Malo's wife. She could not be accused of being a maroon since she was free; she had not killed anyone and was not even present during the murders. But Cecilia, judged guilty by association, was not disposed to let herself be hanged. She let it be known she was pregnant and two physicians acknowledged that she seemed to be. Her sentence was suspended.[42] Bautista and Prince were condemned to receive two hundred lashes. The next day, St. Malo, Joli Coeur, Henri, and Michel were executed on the *Plaza de Armas* (Jackson Square) and Bautista and Prince were flogged at the gallows. Some people said they heard St. Malo exculpate both men just before he was killed. Bouligny himself heard Bautista tell St. Malo he should have done it before it was too late.[43] In truth, if Bouligny's summary of the interrogation reflects reality, St. Malo never implicated Bautista. But did St. Malo talk at all or did he refuse, as one scholar insists?[44] There are likely embellishments, self-serving interpretations, and half-truths in Bouligny's narrative of St. Malo's declarations to Reggio; but on the other hand there are no solid grounds on which to dismiss his entire account as pure fantasy.

On August 7, judgment was rendered against close to fifty maroons and their accomplices. Four were condemned to hang.[45] Five men who had assisted the maroons and traded with them were sentenced to be led to the gallows with a halter around their necks, bound to a pillar, and branded on the cheek with an "m" for *marron* before being returned to Prevost and Bienvenu. Printens, who escaped the Terre Gaillarde raid and was caught or surrendered, received the same "lenient" punishment because he had not robbed or assisted in committing any crime. Reggio believed they all deserved death, but since the principals had already been hung there were no more examples to be made; in addition their death might "ruin an innocent and poor master."

Samba, a maroon of five years but who did not associate with the "insurgent and famous thieves," was to receive three hundred lashes and be exiled from Louisiana forever. This was also the punishment reserved to Bautista—also five years a maroon—an associate of St. Malo, and a "great thief," and Luis, a "great thief" too. Six women were condemned to wear a halter around their necks, to be flogged two hundred times at the foot of the gallows, and to be branded with an "m" on the right cheek.[46] More severe—no reason was given for the difference in treatment and no association with St. Malo was mentioned—was the sentence passed against eleven women, all maroons for less than a year.[47] They had to suffer three hundred lashes and be loaded with twelve-pound shackles for three months. Nineteen males, maroons for one to six months, were condemned to two hundred lashes and to having their feet shackled for three months with a twelve-pound chain.[48]

On October 25, Cecilia, who should have delivered a child by then was reexamined.[49] She said she was pregnant again. The physicians, stating it was too early to make a determination, asked to see her two months later. Playing on a pregnancy that seemed as fabricated as the first—unless she had miscarried—Cecilia escaped death a second time and nothing is known of what ultimately happened to her.

* * *

Within a year, more than a hundred maroons and some of their helpers were arrested. Three were killed during the 1783 attack, eight were hung in 1784, close to fifty were severely whipped, four were lashed and exiled, and expenses incurred during the 1784 expedition include compensation for seven maroons killed during the raid.[50] It was the strongest, most spectacular retribution Southern maroons had to sustain. Yet as far as can be ascertained—except for the murders at Bay St. Louis, and Conway's Bayou for which only four men were directly responsible—they never fired a shot at whites. As was true of many maroon communities throughout the hemisphere, their activities, hypothetical objectives, strength, power, and influence were grossly inflated. But their mere existence, the freedom they flaunted, and their autonomy—perhaps even more than the depredations they caused to sustain their way of life—could not be tolerated because they influenced others and were, in and of themselves, an attack against slavery.

The story of the maroons of Bas du Fleuve exposes, perhaps better than any other, the symbiotic relations that existed between the men and women who peopled the maroon landscape, from the hinterland to the borderlands to the plantations. All improved their standard of living thanks to the contributions of the others. Borderland maroons lightened the workload of their enslaved friends and loved ones, who compensated them by acting as their intermediaries in trade. Both groups shared and enjoyed planters' stolen property. Alternatively, borderlands and hinterlands served as refuge when external pressure demanded it. When staying in the hinterlands, maroons got information, ammunition, food, and support from friends and spouses not only on the plantations but on the borderlands as well. They formed a triangular community of sorts and multiple lines united them. Needless to say, even the people in the quarters who did not take part in these activities were involved, if only through their silence. They could not ignore the fact that maroons were cutting timber and tending their neighbors' gardens. It was this kind of cohesion that enabled the maroons to survive. But the lines that united—family, friendship, love, work, and trade—could also divide. Ultimately it was disloyalty that led to the demise of the Bas du Fleuve communities.

In 1781 Juan Bautista and Pedro betrayed their friends who lived on Raguet's borderland; the enslaved Chacales and the maroons Antonio Delery and Juan Luis Chabert led the militia to Terre Gaillarde in 1783. In 1784 Pierre and two maroons disclosed to Bouligny what they knew about St. Malo and his group. The people at Prevost who were so intimate with the maroons chased them away and they or others on the plantation arrested the few who stayed. And of course Bastien's duplicity brought about the destruction of the community.[51] Money, freedom, a pardon were powerful lures; and the promise or reality of torture an equally potent incentive. Maroons' continued subsistence was greatly dependent on the solidarity of the many, but their very existence hinged on the betrayal of the few.

This story is also invaluable in that it defies stereotypes. Terre Gaillarde challenges the widespread notion of large hinterland settlements as established enclaves of families and single individuals who lived there for as long as they were not discovered. This particular type of community did exist but a more flexible kind did too. The comings and goings of the maroons of Bas du Fleuve between borderlands and hinterlands were the result of personal and familial choices, as well as collective threats; and the same must have been true for other communities. As this case reveals, maroon life was fluid, adaptive, and pragmatic; it had to adjust constantly. Terre Gaillarde was a refuge for a diversity of people: families with adult children, couples, one half of couples, single men and women who spent time when necessary, moved to various borderlands, came back, left again, individually and collectively. The group's migrations to the borderlands attest that a large community could flourish—even if only for a time—at the margins of plantations.

* * *

More than a century after St. Malo was hung, in 1886 a woman named Madeleine sang a song in Creole in his honor which was published in *The Century Magazine*.[52]

> The Dirge of St. Malo
>
> Alas! young men, come, make lament
>   For poor St. Malo in distress!
>   They chased, they hunted him with dogs,
>   They fired at him with a gun,
>
> They hauled him from the cypress swamp.
>   His arms they tied behind his back,
>   They tied his hands in front of him;
> They tied him to a horse's tail,
>   They dragged him up into the town.
>   Before those grand Cabildo men
>   They charged that he had made a plot

To cut the throats of all the whites.
They asked him who his comrades were;
Poor St. Malo said not a word!
The judge his sentence read to him,
And then they raised the gallows-tree.
They drew the horse—the cart moved off—
And left St. Malo hanging there.
The sun was up an hour high
When on the Levee he was hung;
They left his body swinging there,
For carrion crows to feed upon.

In the original Creole version, it is a beautiful ode to St. Malo. But despite its seemingly documentary tone, it strays, significantly, from reality. The raiding party did not bring dogs to Terre Gaillarde; St. Malo was not dragged behind a horse; he was not accused of having conspired "to kill all the whites"; there is no proof he did not talk; he was not hanged on the Levée.[53]

That a folk song is not an infallible historical source and aggrandizes its hero is a given, but what is significant is the fact that St. Malo was eulogized, that a song to his memory was composed at least a decade after his death, and that he was still remembered a hundred years later. What he represented as a maroon—freedom, defiance, courage, and resistance—struck a chord. As did the ignominious manner in which he and others were treated. No other maroon has been so honored.

The hierarchical plantation world is clearly rendered in this anonymous painting showing the Big House at the top and the slave quarters below. Wooded borderlands—maroons' places of refuge—surround the property. American School. The Plantation. ca. 1825. Oil on wood, 19 1/8x29 ½ in. Gift of Edgar William and Bernice Chrysler Garbisch, 1963 (63.201.3).

The Metropolitan Museum of Art, New York. © Image copyright The Metropolitan Museum of Art. Image source: Art Resource, New York.

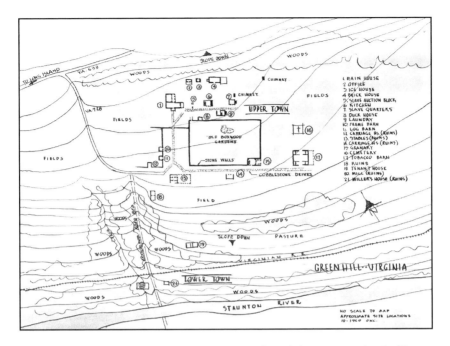

Green Hill, Campbell County, Virginia. In "Upper Town" stood the mansion and outbuildings and in "Lower Town," the slave quarters. As in many estates, woods bordered the plantation on almost all sides. Library of Congress, Prints & Photographs Division, HABS VA,16-LONI.V,1-1.

View of Upper Town. Library of Congress, Prints & Photographs Division, HABS VA,16-LONI.V,1-12.

Cabin in Lower Town. Library of Congress, Prints & Photographs Division, HABS VA,16-LONI.V,1K-1.

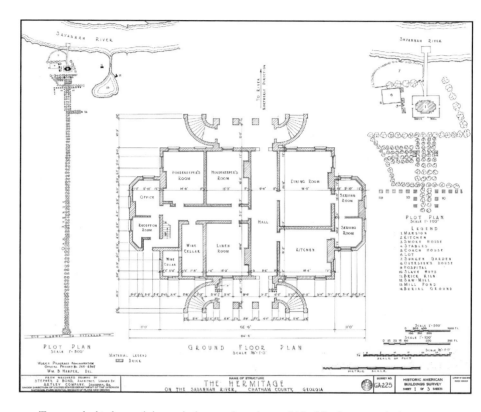

To get to the kitchen and the smoke house, where they could find food, maroons had to come dangerously close to the Big House, as evidenced in this map of the Hermitage Plantation in Chatham County, Georgia. On some plantations, rows of trees hiding them from view offered some privacy to the slave quarters, an arrangement that enabled maroons to visit their loved ones undetected. Library of Congress, Prints & Photographs Division, HABS GA,26-SAV.V,1.

Slave cabins on the Hermitage Plantation. Courtesy of the New York Public Library, Schomburg Center for Research in Black Culture/Jean Blackwell Hutson Research and Reference Division.

Because of the proximity of the cabins, neighbors were generally aware of the maroon activity taking place nightly in the quarters. Their active and tacit solidarity was central to the maroons' survival. "Slave Quarters, South Carolina," by photographer Clifton Johnson. *The Pageant of America Collection—Toilers of Land and Sea.* Courtesy of the New York Public Library, Stephen A. Schwarzman Building /Photography Collection, Miriam and Ira D. Wallach Division of Art, Prints and Photographs.

The plantation borderlands were spaces of freedom that provided enslaved people autonomy, mobility, enterprise, and a sense of physical security. To maroons, they offered a refuge close to family and friends. But, as the presence in this painting of the owners (right) and the overseer (left) shows, the borderlands were also a contested terrain that slavers strove to control and frequently invaded. *A Plantation Burial.* The Historic New Orleans Collection. 1960.46.

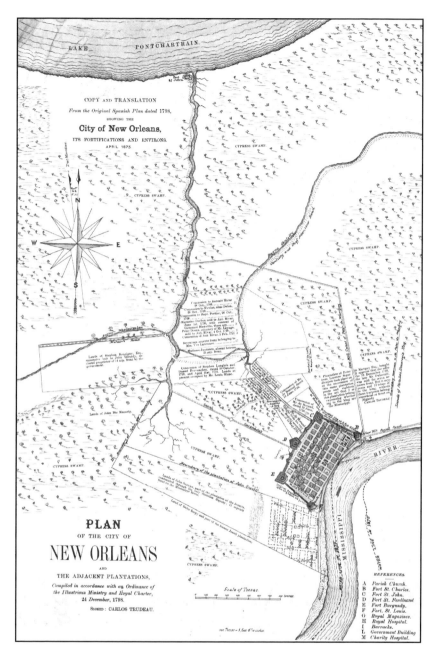

This reproduction of a 1798 Spanish map of the plantations around New Orleans shows the numerous cypress swamps—inhabited by maroons—that covered the territory and surrounded the properties. Plan of the City of New Orleans and adjacent plantations /compiled in accordance with the Ordinance of the Illustrious Ministry and Royal Charter, December 24, 1798. Carlos Trudeau. Copy April 1875 by Alexander Debrunner. Library of Congress, Geography and Map Division.

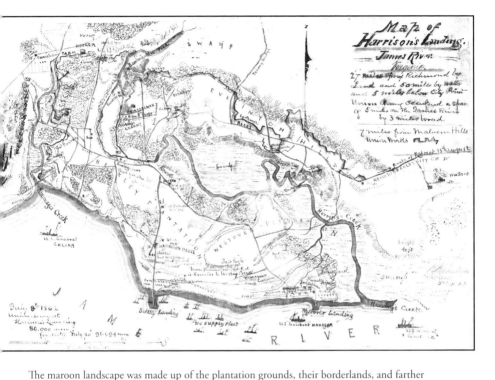

The maroon landscape was made up of the plantation grounds, their borderlands, and farther away from the seat of white power, the hinterland. Visible on this hand-drawn map are the plantations, their wooded borderlands, and the various waterways, rivers, creeks, and ponds that led to the hinterland of woods, swamps, hills, and more swamps that offered refuge to maroon settlements. Scrapbook Page, Map of Harrison's Landing, James River, Virginia, by Robert Knox Sneden. The Virginia Historical Society (1994.80.179.B). Photograph from the Library of Congress, Geography and Map Division.

The development of the domestic slave trade in the nineteenth century gave an impetus to marronage with people sold to the Deep South going back to live in secret at the borderlands of their former plantations. Frank Holl, Gang of Slaves Journeying to Be Sold in a Southern Market. Courtesy of the New York Public Library, Schomburg Center for Research in Black Culture /Manuscripts, Archives and Rare Books Division.

Trees were one of the borderland maroons' shelters. "Living in a Hollow Tree," in William Still, *The Underground Railroad*, 1872. Courtesy of the New York Public Library, Schomburg Center for Research in Black Culture / Manuscripts, Archives and Rare Books Division.

Some borderland maroons lived in natural caverns and caves. The caves they dug six feet below ground were an expression of their fierce independence. These maroons demonstrated an uncommon resolve to remain free as they were willing to spend years underground. "Living in a Cave," in William Still, *The Underground Railroad*, 1872. Courtesy of the New York Public Library, Schomburg Center for Research in Black Culture / Manuscripts, Archives and Rare Books Division.

Whippings and contraptions made to impede movement did not deter the most determined from running and staying away. "Instrument of Torture Used by Slaveholders," *Harper's Weekly: A Journal of Civilization*, February 15, 1862. Courtesy of the New York Public Library, Mid-Manhattan Library/Picture Collection.

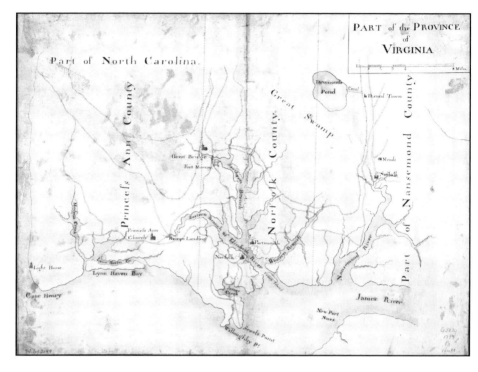

This circa 1791 map shows the Great Dismal Swamp—between Virginia and North Carolina—called Great Swamp. The map also shows the future location of part of the canal that enslaved men (and some maroons) would start to dig in 1793. After the canal was completed, the main industrial activities were linked to timber. Numerous maroons worked in the swamp as "shingle-getters." Library of Congress, Geography and Map Division.

The Great Dismal Swamp was reputed to harbor the largest concentration of maroons in the country. David Cronin, *Fugitive Slaves in the Dismal Swamp*, 1888, oil on canvas. The New-York Historical Society.

Porte Crayon (David Hunter Strother) sketched Osman, an African maroon he claimed to have come across in the Great Dismal Swamp. "Osman the Maroon in the Swamp," by Porte Crayon. David Hunter Strother, *Harper's New Monthly Magazine*, September 1856. Courtesy of the New York Public Library, Schomburg Center for Research in Black Culture /Photographs and Prints Division.

Some maroons lived in the Great Dismal Swamp's hinterland for decades, but by the 1850s those who settled close to work camps were systematically hunted down. Thomas Moran, *Slave Hunt, Dismal Swamp, Virginia*, 1862. Gift of Laura A. Clubb, 1947.8.44. © 2013 Philbrook Museum of Art, Inc., Tulsa, Oklahoma.

After the uprising he had organized and led in 1831 was crushed, Nat Turner lived for two months as a borderland maroon on various plantations. His final hiding place was a cave he dug with a sword. Its opening was hidden by a fallen tree, a common trick among maroons. "The Discovery of Nat Turner," in E. Benjamin Andrews, *History of the United States, From the Earliest Discovery of America to the End of 1902.* Courtesy of the New York Public Library, Schomburg Center for Research in Black Culture / Jean Blackwell Hutson Research and Reference Division.

Unlike runaways to the North or the Southern cities who, when successful, rarely had to confront dogs again, maroons were constantly at their mercy. "Rymning" [Running], from Cecilia Baath-Holmberg, *Kampen för och emot negerslafveriet.* Courtesy of the New York Public Library, Schomburg Center for Research in Black Culture/Jean Blackwell Hutson Research and Reference Division.

Countless dogs died at the hands of maroons armed with axes, scythes, and knives. Richard Ansdell, *The Hunted Slaves*, 1861, oil on canvas, 184 x 308cm, WAG 3070. Courtesy of National Museums Liverpool.

[7]

THE MAROONS OF BELLEISLE
AND BEAR CREEK

ONE of the most intriguing and long-lasting maroon communities established itself in the 1780s in the southern part of Georgia and South Carolina on both sides of the lower Savannah River. A number of scholars have briefly mentioned its existence but its story has not been told. Yet it is one of the best documented in the country, thanks to official correspondence, runaway and jail notices, newspaper articles, and the testimonies of three maroons.[1] Born during the Revolutionary War and expanding in its aftermath, this community was unique in its size, longevity, and the personal experiences and tribulations of some of its members. The study of the various schemes it devised to survive and protect itself when attacked provides an exceptional perspective on maroons' strategies as they exploited the hinterlands, the borderlands, and the plantations. Moreover, the types of settlements its members founded, one of which was a fortified camp comparable to the *palenques* and *mocambos* of Latin America, make it a distinctive case among known American maroon communities.

This colony of several dozen men, women, and children stood up to some of the most prominent citizens of the Lowcountry. Esquires, notables, officials, Whigs, and Tories, they were the gentry, the top rank of the planter and merchant class. They had been given or had inherited thousands of acres of Indian land along the rivers, and put their bondspeople to work carving out large indigo and rice plantations. Some of these men were slave traders, like John Graham who made his first money supplying Africans to the markets of Georgia, South Carolina, and Florida. By 1774 he owned 277 individuals, and more than 26,000 acres.[2] A Loyalist, he was a member of the Georgia provincial council, became Lieutenant Governor and Superintendent of Indian Affairs in 1782, and lieutenant colonel of the militia. Commodore Oliver Bowen, a native of Rhode Island who settled in Georgia and distinguished himself in the navy during the Revolution, was awarded 1,500 acres as a bounty in 1784.[3] A year later, he was dabbling in the transatlantic slave trade.[4] Godin Guerard, a Huguenot justice of the peace in Beaufort District, South Carolina, was the son of a well-known merchant and international slave trader and the brother of a future governor.

The most notable of the notables was Alexander Wright, the son of Sir James Wright, himself the last colonial governor of Georgia, reputed to be the second largest slaveholder—with more than five hundred individuals—in the colony. Alexander Wright owned several plantations.[5] Among the men who hunted the maroons down were James Jackson, a future U.S. senator and governor, and James Gunn, who had just been elected one of five delegates to represent Georgia in Congress.[6]

THE MAROONS

Contrary to the expansive biographies of their foes, the lives of the majority of the maroons remain unknown. Still, runaway notices, newspaper articles, and claims by slaveholders whose bondspeople had been killed help fill in the personal stories of thirty-six maroons, about a third to half of the community. In addition, the trial records of Lewis, the maroons' second in command, include three invaluable first-person short narratives that offer priceless information about some maroons, their activities, the dynamics inside their settlements, and what happened during and after their discovery.

Two women, Fatima and Hannah, were the property of Lieutenant Governor John Graham. As part of the succession of eminent planter, once acting governor, and slave dealer James Habersham, who died in 1775, Fatima was sold at auction in 1781 along with another sixteen men, women, and children.[7] Graham, Habersham's friend and colleague in the transatlantic slave trade, had bought her. Fatima, Hannah, and several others had been through many tribulations before joining the maroon colony. In July 1782, when Savannah was evacuated, Graham had chartered five ships to transport about four hundred slaves (his and those of his friends) to East Florida where he had previously acquired 2,500 acres on the Matanza River. He took 102 men, 67 women, and 56 children there "in full confidence of enjoying the fruits of the labor of his Negroes."[8] In this new environment, they carried out the intensive, backbreaking labor required to carve out three plantations from the swampy wilderness. They dug ditches and drains, cleared the land, fenced it, planted rice, corn, and indigo, and built houses for the overseers, barns, and small lodgings for themselves. But all their hard work was in vain because after East Florida was ceded back to Spain, Graham decided to leave and sell them all to Jamaica. However, because the price he was offered was not to his liking, on December 21, 1784 he sent the group from St. Augustine to Beaufort.[9] After two and a half years, the twice-displaced men, women, and children were back in the Lowcountry. Some were sold to Godin Guerard. On May 1, sixteen people from the Graham group escaped from Guerard.[10] They included seven women and at least three children aged eighteen months to eight years. One of the men was the African Mahomedy/Mahomet, a noted multirecidivist who first ran away in 1771.[11] Guerard believed they would "attempt to conceal themselves on or near Savannah river." Sometime in 1785, the planter also "purchased a considerable number of Negroes then at Saint Augustine."[12] At least five people from this group—Frank, Sechem, Dembo (perhaps a Senegambian actually named Demba), Cook, and his wife Peggy—ran away.[13] Two groups of Florida returnees thus escaped from Guerard and joined the maroon community.[14]

The core of the maroon group was reputed to have fought at the Siege of Savannah, which took place from September to October 1779. Its leader, a slave of Alexander Wright, was named Sharper. His *nom de guerre* was Captain Cudjoe. There was, of course, quite a famous Captain Cudjoe who preceded him as a maroon chief: Captain Cudjoe of the Leeward maroons in Jamaica. Could it be that Sharper had heard about him from Jamaicans introduced into the Lowcountry? It is also possible that Cudjoe—the most common African name in the United States even among country-born men—was his "basket name," given to him by his parents. Sharper could have added "Captain" because of his involvement in the Revolutionary War, when he along with 200 other African Americans fought on behalf of the Loyalists.

Captain Cudjoe's second in command was the aforementioned Lewis who ran away from the plantation of Commodore Oliver Bowen because the overseer "used him ill." He acknowledged he was absent "near two years," which means he was a newcomer, joining Captain Cudjoe in Martin's Swamp sometime in 1785. Like Cudjoe, he was also called "Captain"— Captain Lewis.[15]

THE FIRST SETTLEMENT

The existence of a large maroon settlement in Belleisle Island in the swamps of the Savannah River came to officials' attention after some plantations suffered repeated robberies. In early October 1786, the Grand Jury of Chatham County denounced the fact that "large gangs of runaway Negroes are allowed to remain quietly within a short distance of this town" and blamed the militia officers for their inaction.[16] The maroons had been living on the island for years, so why did they suddenly become a problem? The response lies in the demographics. When he joined Captain Cudjoe's community in 1785, Lewis said, it was composed of only ten men "and a number of women." It is impossible to know if they had branched out from another larger community of Savannah fighters or if they had always been a small unit to begin with. In any event, they only became a major problem in 1786. It is likely that the community expanded and retracted as individuals and families joined and left, first after the 1779 siege of Savannah and then following the evacuation of the city in 1782. The addition of the Florida returnees greatly increased its size. It is thus after and not during the war that the Belleisle Island settlement was the largest, thanks in part to the "Floridians." When various groups and individuals consolidated in 1785–1786 into one large community, more food and supplies than could be produced were needed and the raids increased.

The Grand Jury's admonition had immediate effect. On Wednesday 11, a few men from the Chatham artillery militia, which had been formed just six days earlier, were sent in pursuit of the maroons who were assumed to be more than a hundred strong. The militia located and attacked the settlement—whose name is not known—on Belleisle Island (now Abercorn Island) on the Savannah River, about seventeen miles north of Savannah.[17] The engagement resulted in the death of three or four maroons and the wounding of four militiamen. Running low on ammunition, the latter thought it prudent to retreat; but at sunset a fresh force of fifteen from the Savannah light infantry accompanied by three or four other men made a second attempt.

By that time the maroons had devised a plan. Placing sentries at strategic points in advance of the base camp, they waited. The infantrymen fell into the trap; as they launched an assault on one of the sentinel posts they were taken off guard when a large party of maroons descended upon them. Overwhelmed, the soldiers beat a hasty retreat to their two boats. The maroons tried to cut them off but were repelled when a lieutenant fired a small canon from a craft. It was loaded with grapeshot, the type of ammunition that had a devastating effect when used at close range. The cannon was discharged three times and killed and wounded several maroons, whose blood was later found all around. But despite the cannonade, for the second time in a day the militia had to withdraw. The maroons knew this was only a reprieve and a larger operation was in the making. And indeed on Friday morning, a third party was dispatched to destroy the settlement and seize or kill its inhabitants.

It is a reflection of the seriousness with which the officials took the situation that the man now in charge was planter James Jackson, a famous brigadier general, hero of the Revolution, justice of the peace of Chatham County, and a future U.S. senator and Georgia governor. Captain Cudjoe and his people did not wait for him. Like most maroons, they did not want to fight unless they had to, and after having lost a number of men two days earlier they thought it more prudent and efficient to disappear. When Jackson arrived, he found their settlement empty. Methodically, he set out to destroy it. From Friday morning until Saturday afternoon, he and his men burned, looted, and wiped out everything the maroons had built, planted, raised, harvested, and raided.[18]

They burned down "a number of their houses and huts." The distinction is noteworthy because it traces the contours of a settlement intended to be permanent. Its occupants built dwellings that may have been comparable to plantation cabins—the "houses"—as well as what probably were the sheds—the "huts"—necessary to a farming operation. Unfortunately, Jackson did not mention how many buildings he saw and torched, but his use of the phrase "a number" points to a significant settlement. Another sign that the community was sizable can be inferred from the fact that it owned at least fourteen or fifteen boats, enough to transport a community of up to a hundred people. The militia found the canoes at the landing and took them away. The maroons had either fled on foot deeper into the island carrying their most precious belongings, or they had other boats at their disposal and left the area altogether.

Apart from the houses, the huts, and the canoes, the settlement—whose size is not known—had its own field, of about four acres, planted with "green rice."[19] There was also a stock of rough rice already harvested, which after threshing and pounding would have yielded twenty-five barrels (about 3,400 pounds) of clean rice. This rice was either stolen—a feat in and of itself—or the maroons had another plot, more mature, that the militia did not find. These two pieces of information relayed by Jackson's party about rice in the field and rice in the camp give precious insight into the maroons' activities. The rice cycle in the Deep South started in January, when men cleared the land. The preparation of the field took place in March and the actual planting was finished in April or early May.[20] To plant their rice paddy the maroons needed up to twelve bushels of seed or rice that they must have originally taken from plantations. By mid-September to early October, when it started to turn yellow, the rice—about thirty-two barrels of it—would have been harvested. Based on the average ration on South Carolina plantations of eight quarts a week per person, the field would have fed no more than six individuals per year.[21] Even with the addition of the rough rice and the eighteen barrels of corn—likely raided from plantations—found in the settlement, less than twenty people could have lived on these provisions. Raiding was not an option, it was a necessity.

Following Jackson's actions a newspaper rejoiced, "The loss of their provisions, it is expected, will occasion them to disperse about the country, and, it is hoped, will be the means of most of them being soon taken up."[22]

THE MAROONS' CAMPAIGNS AND THE CAMPAIGN AGAINST THE MAROONS

After the destruction of the Belleisle Island camp in Georgia, Jackson informed the governor of South Carolina, Thomas Pinckney, that the "daring banditti of slaves, who some weeks since, attacked two of my detachments, & were at last with difficulty dislodged from their camp," were his problem too.[23] Jackson, who was conveniently rewriting history—the maroons had not attacked his men, it was the other way around—had learned that the "banditti" were at or near Hartstone's Swamp in South Carolina. One hundred, he wrote, had been seen in the area. From there they made frequent incursions into Georgia. The swamp, located at Great Swamp in the Swiss colony of Purrysburg—about twenty miles north of Savannah—was the property of Joachim Hartstone, a former Representative, who was also the captain of the Purrysburgh militia company.[24]

Evidently, the destruction of their Georgia settlement had not crushed the maroons. Despite the loss of their canoes they were still mobile, which suggests they had concealed some. But after the wreckage of their field and the theft of their corn they needed food and were resolved to get it on both sides of the Savannah River, aggravating citizens in two states. On November 29, a group of twenty maroons burglarized the house of a Mr. Wolmar, taking "every valuable he possessed." According to Jackson, they even planned to kill him because one of their leaders, once enslaved by Wolmar, was slain—presumably on October 11 during the second attack—and his severed head was posted on the road. Jackson believed the maroons wanted to go after Wolmar in order to avenge their companion, but the planter was absent that day.[25] They also paid a visit to Godin Guerard's plantation and carried off "whole stacks of rice at a time to compensate, as they term it, for the incredible magazine of provisions we destroyed at their camp." According to Jackson, the booty the maroons got and the freedom they flaunted were attracting recruits. The actual or potential desertion of bondspeople inspired by the maroons' example seriously alarmed farmers and planters.

In Georgia, Governor Telfair issued a proclamation on December 21, 1786, stating that "a certain banditti of run-away negroes, who have been outliers before and since the evacuation of the town of Savannah, lately embodied themselves, and with arms opposed the militia ordered out to suppress them, and also committed depredations on the property of sundry inhabitants."[26] He offered ten pounds for each man brought to trial on sufficient grounds and the same amount for each one killed. The proclamation, in effect a call to indiscriminate executions, was published in newspapers in Georgia and South Carolina the first week of January 1787, as the new Georgia governor, George Matthews, was about to take over.

This was insufficient for James Jackson. In a letter similar to the one he had dispatched to Thomas Pinckney, the South Carolina governor, concerning "the formidable numbers of runaway slaves," he now wrote to Matthews. He stressed that their provisions having been destroyed, "They are compelled to maraud, for their daily subsistence." He added:

> If something cannot be shortly done, I dread the consequences—they are as daring as any & from their independent state, from the ease they enjoy in S. Carolina, forbode what I dread to express, a capital insurrection. Their leaders are the very fellows that fought, & maintained their ground against the brave lancers at the siege of Savannah, & they still call themselves the King of England's soldiers.[27]

The maroon threat was certainly a problem, but by theorizing an upcoming general insurrection, Jackson was grossly exaggerating the danger in order to get as much assistance as possible in his efforts to eradicate the community. Prior to his alarmist letters, little action had been taken. Fewer than twenty men had been sent out to get rid of an estimated hundred people, among whom were armed men who had proved they could fight. Jackson's failure to defeat what Governor Telfair had called a group of "banditti run-away negroes" may have been particularly stinging. To get what he needed to crush them once and for all he had to convince the governors that the danger was already extreme and could turn even worse. For the first time, the Patriot hero mentioned that the maroons had been active enemies of the Revolution and continued to be so, as they still called themselves the King of England's soldiers. He also obliquely paid them homage—no doubt to underline the menace they posed—by stating that they "maintained their ground" during the war against the brave Patriots. There is no evidence to refute his claim, but there is no reference other than Jackson's to the maroons calling themselves the King of England's soldiers. The trial records make no mention of it, though such a statement could have served the prosecution by emphasizing the ancient and entrenched "disloyalty" of the maroons. The reference did not appear in other correspondence or newspaper articles either.

As Jackson waited for "plans of cooperation" between South Carolina and Georgia, the maroons were busy looking for food. On March 14, 1787, they raided the plantation of John Bourquin, Jr. A future South Carolina House Representative for St. Peter's Parish, owner of a thousand acres and forty-five individuals, Bourquin was considered the leader of the Purrysburg Township, and at least one of his slaves had joined the maroon community. The incursion was violent: the maroons killed the black driver and slightly wounded Bourquin. It was the first time that a killing had been attributed to the community. The maroons' actions that day illustrate how resolute and perhaps how desperate they were to get provisions. Bourquin moved quickly: he sent a letter to the captain of the militia, Joachim Hartstone. Like Jackson, he speculated that very soon procuring provisions would not be the maroons' only objective, "as they have in my hearing," he wrote, "threatened the lives of many of the citizens."[28]

If the statement attributed to them is true, the maroons were playing with fire. They may have wanted to appear so menacing that the militia would not go after them, a strategy that sometimes worked with ordinary slave hunters, but the tactic could also have exactly the opposite result. The danger they potentially posed could prompt the deployment of a large force to annihilate them. It is also possible that the threat was

Bourquin's invention, the hyperbole of a man who wanted to attract immediate attention. He complained that the militia was willing to do its duty but given the scope of the task, which would require several days of service, the men wanted to be provided for adequately. In the end, he stressed that the maroons were a menace in and of themselves, but as could be expected, he also raised the possibility that they would inspire others. If nothing was done immediately, white families could be "surprised by them & probably by our own indoor domestics." It was a frightening prospect that he knew would trigger vigorous action.

Hartstone was all the more sensitive to Bourquin's request because the community lived in the vicinity of his swamp. Acting swiftly the following day, he recommended that measures be taken to annihilate the maroons, either in the form the Georgians had adopted, "so much per head—dead or alive," or by any other method.[29]

On March 19, South Carolina Governor Pinckney sent a message to the House of Representatives giving them intelligence—Bourquin's and Hartstone's letters—on the "Depredations committed by a party of Armed Negroes" in the south, which evidenced the necessity of establishing "an Effectual Militia and patrol Laws or of adopting other measures as you may think the Occasion requires."[30] The governor's message and its accompanying letters made their way through the House and on March 20, the representatives recommended that the governor "be requested immediately to adopt the most decisive and effectual measures to extirpate the Runaway Negroes committing Depredations in the Southern parts of this State." They also asked that he "be authorized to issue a proclamation offering a reward of Ten Pounds sterling for each said Negroes killed or taken in this State."[31] The next day, the Privy Council agreed unanimously that volunteers be selected and placed under the leadership of Colonel Thomas Hutson, the owner of Cedar Grove Plantation in Prince William's Parish, a former member of the General Assembly, and a major in the militia during the Revolution.[32] The legislators agreed that sixty to one hundred men should be retained for one month and perhaps as many as three with a pay of one shilling a day, rations, and a ten dollar bounty for each "Negro" caught dead or alive.[33]

Finally, nine days after Bourquin had sent Hartstone his cry for help, Governor Pinckney instructed Hutson to engage a company of no more than one hundred minutemen for at least one month to "extirpate the runaway Negroes," cautioning him against unnecessary expenses.[34] He also informed Hutson that he hoped to recruit twenty Catawbas, although he evidently had little confidence in them, and warned that they "should be suffered as little as possible to act alone, as the reward offered by the Proclamation . . . may be a temptation to abuse. I doubt not you will be particularly careful to prevent any wanton destruction of property, or unnecessary effusion of human blood." With a proclamation that called for a bounty for dead blacks, the fear was that some people—conveniently, only the Catawbas were mentioned—would kill or maim any black man, that is, planters' property, a serious loss for slaveholders. The man who was to deliver the Catawbas was Colonel Robert Patton. Pinckney asked him to recruit up to twenty to serve for at least one month. Their salary would not be one shilling a day like their white counterparts, only two blankets; but they would receive the same bounty as whites for each maroon they caught or killed.[35]

On March 23, 1787 the governor of South Carolina issued a proclamation offering ten pounds per person, dead or alive. He then turned to his Georgia colleague, informing him officially of the upcoming assault and asking for his cooperation: "As the Citizens of both States are interested in the reduction of these [people,] I have no doubt your honor will see the expediency of a joint exertion."[36]

THE SECOND SETTLEMENT

A few months after the maroons had regrouped at Hartstone's Swamp they headed for Bear Creek, back in Georgia, close to their first settlement. The total area of the place they settled in was 700 yards by 120, or seventeen acres. There is no way of knowing if it was smaller or bigger than the first one, but it was a much more efficient sanctuary. Because the maroons knew they could be attacked they set out to make sure they could protect and defend themselves. Once the men had felled the trees and the canes, they built a breastwork around the camp. About four feet high, it had a small opening that admitted only one person at a time.[37]

The breastwork was actually the maroons' defense of last resort. Two miles below camp, the men had piled large trees across the creek to prevent boats from passing through. Only their small canoes could go by at high water. One hundred and fifty yards from their settlement, they had placed a sentry. They had learned from their devastating experience at Belleisle and built a veritable war camp, the only one documented among maroons in the United States. It was capable, they hoped, of sustaining an assault thanks to its four-part defensive system. Slowed down by the trees in the creek, unable to come near in large boats, their approach signaled by the sentries, their enemies would find the maroons hidden behind the breastworks, ready to shoot. It is possible that this settlement was already operational, a sort of backup in case the Belleisle camp was found, a frequent strategy used by maroons. But if the camp was previously in existence, they evidently built its fortifications only when they returned. It would not have made sense to live in a defenseless Belleisle settlement while a fortified one was available. If this village was entirely new, they cleared the land, erected a defense system, and built several houses in record time; another sign that the community was large and efficient.

But as it was re-creating itself and mounting its defenses the group was weakened by a power struggle between Captain Cudjoe and Captain Lewis. The latter, who had been a maroon for only two years, resented Cudjoe's authority. One incident Lewis recounted illustrates how much he contested Cudjoe's power. Cudjoe had given a gun to Jimmy and ordered him, as a sentry, to shoot at whites. He had also told Lewis to stand guard, but Lewis refused to obey, perhaps because he thought it was below his position as second in command. Cudjoe then told him to move off, which Lewis also refused to do.[38]

Despite the internal strife, the community remained together until "the White people first came up": when Jackson attacked the camp at Belleisle in October 1786. At that moment, Cudjoe and Lewis separated. With the settlement and the provisions destroyed, the breaking up of the community was strategically necessary. It was easier to hide and feed several scattered small groups than one large one. Captain Cudjoe went his way with twenty soldiers and presumably also women, children, and noncombatant men. The split was only temporary. By January 1787 both Cudjoe and Lewis, as well as dozens of men and women, were living in the new camp at Bear Creek. According to Juliet, Lewis and Cudjoe continued to quarrel frequently. "Lewis wanted his own people as Sharper took all his men," she explained. When the community separated, Lewis was finally a chief; but when the maroons joined forces again to establish their new camp, "his" men had passed back under Cudjoe's authority.[39]

The Bear Creek fortified settlement consisted of twenty-one houses. No description of these dwellings exists, but given the known density in plantation quarters and in other North American maroon camps, they could have housed at least one hundred people, which is what officials and others estimated the size of the colony to be. The maroons set out to plant the cleared land—no indication was given as to the size of the field—in an effort to become more autonomous. They planted rice and potatoes. Given the life cycle of both crops, they faced at least eight months without access to their own food. In the meantime, as the women stayed in the camp, the men organized raids on plantations on both sides of the river to make up for their destroyed provisions at Belleisle.

The men went back to known territory, the places they had escaped from. Ulmer and Lowrman in Georgia and Bourquin and Guerard in South Carolina all received nightly visits from them. When the maroons went to John Lowrman's plantation they got powder, and Lewis stole one of the planter's coats and some white linen. To obtain these particular items the men had to have entered his house. They also took powder from a woman in South Carolina. Lewis plundered corn from James Greenhow, a planter and merchant near Abercorn, and Peter stole a sheep from him. The latter may have taken unnecessary risks because Cudjoe and Lewis rebuked him for that theft. Joe and Lewis had their own networks and strategies to get hold of meat and they were the regular providers of beef. These and other raids that took place in March and April show how much the maroons needed to find food as they were unable at the time to feed their large community with their own resources.

Then came a most bizarre episode. Captain Cudjoe, Captain Lewis, and ten others who went on an expedition to round up provisions came across two white men manning a boat full of potatoes and corn. Cudjoe called on the men, who at the sight of twelve armed maroons could do little else but to obey. The Captain talked to them, and decided to let them go. It was an unexpected decision as the maroons could easily have taken the provisions and killed the men for safety reasons. Later Lewis once again came across one of the white men, John Casper Hershman, who begged the maroon to take him to the settlement. Lewis refused but, not discouraged, Hershman built himself a fire and remained in the field all night, waiting for Lewis to pass by on his way back home. At dawn, Lewis arrived and, manifestly won over by Hershman's arguments, took him to the settlement.

There is no record of what Hershman had in mind, but his and Lewis's actions suggest that he had a proposition he believed the maroons could not refuse. Bypassed for large tracts of land, Hershman had to ask repeatedly for a few hundred acres. He was a slaveholder, but of the small farmer category.[40] To complement his workforce, he may have been interested in getting maroon labor, the cheapest manpower available as it did not require any investment. Hershman would have had good reasons to insist on getting to their village if he wanted to offer the maroons a business deal and Lewis would have had equally good reasons to take him there.

When Lewis and Hershman approached the settlement, things did not go as planned. Captain Cudjoe told his second he "had no business to bring White people to camp." Then, according to Lewis, Sechem killed Hershman. Juliet added that Cudjoe ordered Sechem to shoot, and Peggy said that Sechem took Hershman's clothes and threw his body into a pond. The episode reveals some of the tensions at the top echelons of maroon leadership. Captain Cudjoe harshly rebuked his second in front of the other men and by having Hershman killed without even listening to him, he affirmed his authority while exposing Lewis's lack of judgment.

Shortly thereafter, the maroons prepared for a momentous excursion. Their forays into plantations were by and large organized to procure food, ammunition, and intelligence. But on April 21, they had an added objective. Lewis, Dembo, Frank, and others took four canoes and went off to fetch people at Godin Guerard's plantation. Several men and women from Guerard's were already living in the settlement and the maroons were going to get their relatives or other individuals who had expressed a desire to join the community. The need for four canoes suggests that perhaps eight to ten people were expected to make their escape that night; a significant addition to the already large colony. The maroons were doing exactly what slaveholders always dreaded and denounced: actively attracting and even transporting new recruits.

But on their way to the plantation, they were ambushed. Dembo and Frank were killed. After the deadly encounter, the maroons knew that their general location had been identified. Yet they did not evacuate, probably thinking that their defense system—the logs in the creek, the sentry, and the breastwork—would be enough to protect them from an attack.

THE ATTACK

By early April 1787, dozens of South Carolinian minutemen, 20 Catawbas, 150 weight of musket powder, 700 weight of lead, 300 flints, and 110 gallons of rum were assembled in preparation of the assault.[41] Colonel Hutson took position in Purrysburg with his men, awaiting the cooperation of the state of Georgia in the form of additional troops. On April 21, he decided to send Captain Winkler and twenty-five men in three boats to Collins (or Collis) Creek to set an ambush.[42] That is when the exchange of fire between the militias and the maroons on their way to Guerard's to fetch more people occurred. This raised the hopes of the militia: they erroneously believed that Lewis had been killed because his boat was seized. But it would take another two weeks for the militia to locate the settlement, proof that the maroons had chosen the site wisely.

During the night of May 5, after four days of intense searching, Lieutenant Colonel Howell learned that Cudjoe's village was located at Bear Creek.[43] He informed Colonel Gunn at 1:00 a.m. The search continued and at 10:30 a.m. Gunn discovered some signs of life in a swamp and organized the assault. In the end, all the defensive work the maroons had built proved inefficient. First, the militiamen killed the sentry. Then, they were able to reach the settlement and enter it despite the fortification. As eight men rushed in, fourteen infantrymen charged with bayonets. Captain Tattnall moved from the right and Major McPherson with South Carolina militiamen and fifteen Catawbas formed the second line of attack.

What followed was classic maroon strategy. Captain Cudjoe ordered the women to flee.[44] His men fired a few shots to slow the assailants' progress—they wounded a lieutenant—and they too ran away. The white men and the Catawbas pursued them two miles in every direction the treacherous terrain allowed. Six maroons were killed and a number of blankets covered with blood were recovered. Some of the maroons' possessions—seven boats and provisions—were taken and the Catawbas "got as many good blankets & clothing of different kind, as they were able to take with them."[45]

At 5:00 p.m. Gunn gave the order to torch the twenty-one houses and the breastwork. The following day, as they continued to explore the area, the Carolinians and the Catawbas killed two maroons while Captain John Martin Dasher, leading a small company of the Effingham militia, came across eighteen men, women, and children. This group's plan, Dasher believed, was to get to the "Indian nation," the Seminoles of Florida.[46] The militia killed a man and a boy and took several women and children prisoner, as well as a man they erroneously thought was Lewis.

As for Captain Cudjoe, he was believed to have been in the party of eighteen on their way to the "Indian Nation." When interrogated during his trial, Lewis said he believed the maroon leader was still alive, giving added stimulus to the manhunt, perhaps his way of taking revenge on his chief. Interestingly, shortly after the encounter with Dasher, a man named Sharper and his wife Nancy asked for sanctuary in St. Augustine. According to historian Jane Landers, they were the maroon leader and his spouse and were subsequently freed.[47] On May 14, 1787, Juliet was captured and two days later, it was Peggy's turn. They acknowledged that "they were amongst the runaway negroes in Abercorn swamp."[48]

News of the destruction of the colony and the killing and capture of some of its occupants brought relief to white citizens. Gunn had finally destroyed "the confidence and strength of the runaways." The settlement was denounced as having been a "general asylum" where many more people would have gone to "on the approach of hot weather."[49]

LEWIS'S TRIAL

Lewis, who was in the party of eighteen that escaped, hoped to make it back to his former place, Commodore Bowen's mills. In other words, he wanted to be near friends who could provide food, assistance, and intelligence. Once a maroon leader, he planned on becoming a borderland maroon, even if only for a time. To sustain himself on the way, he killed a calf. That was his demise. He was discovered and taken prisoner by two slaves of Israel Bird, a captain of the Effingham militia.[50] The arrest took place sometime during the week of May 14 and on Saturday 19, Lewis was brought to Savannah.[51] On Monday, he was tried.

In *The State vs Lewis a Negroe*, the maroon was accused of "the Murder of John Casper Herman [*sic*, his real name was Hershman], Robbing Philip Ulmer, John Lowerman of Georgia and Coll Bouquin of South Carolina." The trial was held in front of four justices of the peace and seven jurors. Lewis had no lawyer. Three people testified: Lewis and fellow maroons, Juliet and Peggy. Lewis tried his best to exonerate himself of the murder charge. He acknowledged that the coat he wore belonged to Lowrman and that he took corn from Greenhow; but he denied having killed Hershman. He sought to distance himself from Cudjoe and the most serious accusations by stressing that he had separated from the leader at least twice. Lewis also attempted to get leniency by stating he had been helpful to three planters. He said he told Thomas Pollhill to "take Care" of the maroons or they would come and hurt him, and he saved John Bourquin's and John Walthour's lives. As for the murder of Hershman, he asserted that Sechem was the culprit; and after the killing, he stated, he separated from Captain Cudjoe.

Juliet, whose husband Pope was killed, testified that Lewis was present when Sechem murdered Hershman and threw him into the pond. She was not there, she conceded, and all she knew was hearsay. She added that Lewis had killed a cow and was part of the group that had robbed Lowrman. She also testified he was in the camp, and armed, when the militia arrived. Peggy, like Juliet, had lost her husband, Cook. Her statement, also like Juliet's, was not favorable to Lewis. She implicated him in the plunder at Philip Ulmer; the bloody incident at Bourquin's; the expedition to Guerard's; and the shootout with Winkler. She also confirmed that he was present when Hershman was killed. Finally, she too stated that Lewis was armed when the militia raided the settlement.

The three testimonies clearly established that Lewis did not kill Hershman, and in truth if he had wanted to he would have had ample opportunity to do so when he saw him sitting alone by the fire. But whether he was the perpetrator or not, Lewis was present when Hershman was murdered; he raided plantations, and he was a maroon leader. The jury returned a guilty verdict. Lewis was condemned to be hung on the South Common in Savannah, "[a]fter which his head to be Cut of and Stuck upon a pole to be sett up on the Island of Marsh opposite the Glebe land in Savannah River." The jury and the justices acting together as slave appraisers assessed his worth at thirty pounds sterling. On Saturday June 9, Captain Lewis was hung.

THE AFTERMATH

Six maroons were killed during the attack as they withstood fire to let their companions escape. The Catawbas slayed four and brought their scalps, for which they were to receive forty pounds. Jacob Winkler and Nath Zettler each killed one man.[52] At some point Sechem's head was cut off and brought to Spring Hill.[53] After the assault, Dasher killed one man and one boy. The men who were after the maroons had no financial interest in taking them alive. They were not slaveholders intent on safekeeping a neighbor's property. As Gunn pointed out, they were "chiefly men of small property." The wealthy men, he explained, who were the most interested in the destruction of the settlement, had paid a fine rather than be part of the militia draft.[54] Like the poor whites, the Catawbas had no financial motivation to be careful. They too were paid ten pounds per maroon, dead or alive. Thus by keeping the fighting to a minimum and by disappearing into the swamps, the maroons avoided a massacre. The total number of recorded dead seems to have been less than a dozen out of a population of perhaps a hundred.[55]

What happened to the Bear Creek survivors is only partially known. On May 17, the press reported "some of them are coming in daily to their owners."[56] The punishment they received must have been particularly cruel; not only had they been maroons for years, but they had also "committed depredations," and defended their freedom rifle in hand. The men exchanged fire with the militias on several occasions, including in October 1786 and the following April and May. As the self-proclaimed or so-called King of England' soldiers, they had a reputation, whether justified or not (since most had not taken part in the war), of being violently anti-American.

Apart from Captain Cudjoe and his wife, some maroons may have found refuge in Florida, while a few may have regrouped in small bands or family units. Still others may have settled as borderland maroons in familiar territory and a number of people could have left the area altogether. It is perhaps not a coincidence—though there is no direct evidence—that about two months after the destruction of the Bear Creek settlement, maroon activity picked up on the Stono River, about eighty miles east. On August 1, William Drayton sent a letter to Governor Pinckney, informing him of the presence of "runaway Negroes," many of them armed, in the neighborhood of Stono, a notorious maroon area. Pinckney contacted Arnoldus Vanderhorst, planter and Berkley County militia colonel (and future governor), letting him know that the maroons were "very troublesome, and dangerous to the planters."[57] He added that because they were too numerous to be "quelled by the usual parties of patrol," he wanted Vanderhorst to take matters into his hands.[58]

The maroons of Belleisle and Bear Creek did inspire some sympathy. A piece written in New York lauded the brave and hardy sons of Africa, [who] will occasion those States [Georgia and South Carolina] the loss of much blood and treasure, before they are subjugated—as notwithstanding their sufferings in their present exposed situation—their want of military apparatus to defend themselves—and their late defeat, the appearance of submission is not discoverable among them—Though vanquished they are not disheartened—and they seem wisely to prefer a precarious existence, in freedom, on the barren hearth, to the chains of their oppressors, whose avarice is augmented by their earnings, and whose tyranny, cruelty and barbarism encreases [*sic*] with their wealth—in short the spirit of liberty they inherit appears unconquerable—Heaven grant it may be invincible.[59]

But the general sentiment among slaveholders and their allies, of course, was that a calamity had been narrowly avoided. The examples of Jamaica and Suriname were brought up. There, it was emphasized, the once "contemptible fugitives" united, increased in numbers, harassed their owners, forced them to sign treaties, and formed independent colonies. The Carolina maroons, it was acknowledged, were despised and neglected, their robberies left unpunished; all these mistakes may have led them to think of themselves as being on par with their counterparts in Suriname and Jamaica.[60]

* * *

The story of the maroons of Belleisle and Bear Creek offers a privileged view into the formation of large communities made up of small groups, families, and individuals intersecting over time to create what they anticipated would be a stable, safe, and autonomous colony. It also provides fascinating insights into the inner workings of a community destabilized by a power struggle at the top while being under siege, and into the approaches maroons used to protect and defend themselves.

Over the course of their community's existence, the maroons devised two strategies to maintain their independence. The Belleisle settlement was not protected and they chose to withdraw when attacked, this being the most widespread maroon tactic. The second approach, at Bear Creek, was to build a defensive camp. In light of what unfolded next, it is clear that this innovation gave the residents a false sense of security. Contrary to what occurred at Belleisle—where they evacuated in time—at Bear Creek they were caught by surprise. But there again, they chose to put up just enough resistance so that most could evacuate. Breastworks or not, ultimately the strategy was to withdraw. Even those maroons who built impressive defense systems with trenches and stakes in other parts of the Americas retreated once discovered.[61]

This is not to say that fighting was always a losing proposition, as the maroon wars in Jamaica, Panama, and Suriname, for example, attest, but in North America as in the rest of the hemisphere, most maroon communities avoided a frontal fight. They knew that if they successfully repulsed a first attack, another, better organized one would likely follow. Moreover, they were generally outgunned; and even when they did have enough firearms, ammunition was often in such short supply that they had to resort to improvised bullets like pieces of iron, buttons, coins, or small stones. In the end, the treacherous terrain, the well-hidden location, and the exit strategy were more effective in most cases in ensuring the residents' survival than the erection of defenses that mostly had the effect of slowing down the attackers and killing or wounding only a few. Moreover, in several instances slave hunters were able to obtain the cooperation of or coerce individuals into providing information on the maroons' defenses so that they could safely reach the war camps.

Retreat, far from being a sign of defeat or weakness, was a deliberate strategy. Killing some maroons, taking most of them prisoner, and making an example of their defeat to discourage potential followers was precisely what the authorities hoped to accomplish, but the strategy of disappearance frustrated these efforts. At both Belleisle and Bear Creek, the community lost the settlements it had built with great care, as well as several members either to death or imprisonment. But others were not captured and remained in the woods. In the end, even though the defenses failed them the maroons were able to ensure a high a rate of survival, which was obviously their objective.

Modern historians have presented the maroons of Belleisle/Bear Creek as revolutionaries with "a collective consciousness for large scale revolt" who "launched a series of guerilla attacks . . . boldly attacked two detachments of Georgia state troops"; carried on "the armed struggle for freedom"; and "continued to harass local planters."[62] But the maroons did not attack. When attacked, they counterattacked. There was no wanton destruction of property, they did not set crops or buildings on fire, slaughter cattle, and kill white people. The only person they did kill was a black man, a driver. Their raids on plantations were restricted to taking food, and there is no indication that they envisioned a large-scale revolt. What is clear from their actions is that their main preoccupation was not to fight whites. They linked their raids to their need for food, not to a more general struggle against slavery. They clearly expressed how much safer it would have been to let them live in peace: the plunder would not have happened if they had not been hunted down and their settlements destroyed. Their objective was the development and self-sufficiency of their community and they applied themselves diligently to achieve it. They were willing to fight to protect it—and only to a point—but that fight was a consequence of the defense of their objective, not the objective itself. This in no way diminishes their valor, their vision, and the significance of their endeavor. Like all maroons Captain Cudjoe's people defined their freedom on their own terms. It was more than a refusal of slavery, it was the right to self-determination. And that in itself was revolutionary.

8

THE GREAT DISMAL SWAMP

"**O**NE could imagine that there may be many negroes living still in the swamp, who have not yet heard that the war is over and that they are free."[1] Such was the reputation for isolation of the Great Dismal Swamp maroons that two years after Emancipation, one could hypothesize that some of them still did not know they were legally free. For the longest time, the swamp and its elusive inhabitants loomed large in the popular imagination. Mysterious, wild, savage, primitive, dreary, gloomy, dismal, oppressive: negative terminology almost always followed any mention of the people and the place, a 2,000 square mile area—until the early nineteenth century—that stretched from southern Virginia to northeast North Carolina.

The existence of hidden families, groups, and individuals in the swamp had been known about since the early 1700s but it was not until the mid-nineteenth century, as they were being aggressively hunted down, that the maroons of the Great Dismal Swamp burst onto the national scene. In 1842, Henry W. Longfellow published his celebrated six-stanza poem, "The Slave in the Dismal Swamp":

> In dark fens of the Dismal Swamp
> The hunted Negro lay;
> He saw the fire of the midnight camp,
> And heard at times a horse's tramp
> And a bloodhound's distant bay.[2]

Madison Washington, the hero of Frederick Douglass's *The Heroic Slave*, published in 1853, hid there in a cave for five years, to stay close to his wife. Williams Well Brown's novel *Clotel* put Nat Turner and hundreds of his followers in the swamp. In Harriett Beecher Stowe's hugely successful novel *Dred: A Tale of the Great Dismal Swamp*, published in 1856, Dred—the son of Denmark Vesey and a Mandinka mother—the leader of a group of maroons, advocates revolution; and Martin R. Delany's "Blake; or, the Huts of America" has the runaway Blake/Henry Holland meet old colleagues of Nat Turner and Gabriel, who assure him that "the Swamp contained them [warriors] in sufficient number to take the whole United States."[3]

Novelists immortalized imaginary maroons ready to fight the slave system, but the reality was quite different, more complex and more intriguing than fiction. While some maroons' way of life was not unlike that of their counterparts in the rest of the South, the swamp was also home to two distinctive groups, who lived in two distinctive areas and whose experiences were simultaneously vastly different from each other and specific to the place.

Past the outskirts of the swamp lay the two sociogeographic zones that formed the larger part of the maroons' landscape. The borderlands in this case could be well within the swamp but they were borderlands in the sense that they formed the margins of places of industrial activity: the canal, logging areas, small stores, and workers' camps. It was the domain of mostly male maroons, while the hard-to-reach hinterland, surrounded by miles of marshes, sheltered isolated families. How both groups organized their lives, what contact, if any, they had with the outside black and white world, and what kind of safety the swamp provided these exiles are questions to which a variety of sources, including firsthand accounts and archeology, provide some responses.

"UNCOUNTED NUMBERS"

Numerous accounts claim that the swamp held the largest number of maroons in the United States, but estimates vary. The *Zion's Herald* mentioned in 1848 the presence of "hundreds of fugitives" in "this damp and dreary region."[4] During a lecture on December 8, 1850 Frederick Douglass told of "uncounted numbers of fugitives," no doubt the most accurate comment on the issue.[5] Abolitionist Edmund Jackson stated ironically in 1852: "From the character of the population it is reasonable to infer that the United States Marshal has never charged himself with the duty of taking the census of the swamp."[6] Nevertheless, Jackson, who wrote about "a large colony of Negroes," believed their numbers to be "considerable." A Norfolk merchant had told him that the estimated value of the maroons living in the swamp was $1.5 million lost to the people who once owned them. Jackson calculated that there would thus be close to 40,000 maroons in the swamp, which he thought was much too high. His calculations were incorrect: according to his arithmetic, a slave would have been worth $37.50, whereas the average price was $926 between 1846 and 1850 and $1,240 from 1851 to 1855.[7] Of course, prices fluctuated with age, gender, and skills, but with an average of $1,000, and according to the trader's estimation of "lost wealth," there would have been about 1,500 maroons in the swamp. With a lower average of $600 to include the aged, children, sick, and unskilled maroons, the number could have been around 2,500.

These numbers are close to an earlier estimate. In 1831, when Nat Turner's revolt focused attention on the maroon insurrectionists supposed to live there, the militias of Norfolk, Nansemond, and Princess Anne counties were ordered to scour the swamp, in which "it was asserted that from 2000 to 3000 blacks were concealed."[8] The *Norfolk Herald*, for its part, mentioned "a formidable number."[9]

In 1939 Herbert Aptheker thought it "likely that about two thousand Negroes, fugitives, or the descendants of fugitives" lived in the swamp, but in his *American Negro Slave Revolts*, published four years later, he stated that reports of two to three thousand maroons were "no doubt greatly exaggerated."[10] He did not give sources for these numbers in either case. Scholars have generally cited his earlier estimate, without mentioning his second thoughts.[11] Because of the unreliability of the documentation, it may be that all that can be established with certainty is that hundreds of maroons lived in the Great Dismal Swamp at any given time.

But beyond the numbers, what is of interest is what the maroon experience was like. Or rather, what the experiences were like for the people who inhabited the swamp from its borderlands to its most secluded areas.

In 1792, the Dismal Swamp Canal Company, eager to start work on a canal connecting the Chesapeake Bay in Virginia to the Albemarle Sound in North Carolina, launched its first labor recruiting effort. It was "desirous of purchasing a number of good Slaves, for whom a liberal price will be paid in cash," or shares of the corporation. These men needed to be "able bodied negroes," not over thirty, and perhaps more important, not "addicted to running away."[12] This was the wisest of precautions, given the reputation the swamp already had by then. After the canal had been completed, the main industrial activities in the area were linked to timber. Cypress and juniper shingles from the region were in great demand, as were planks used to build ships and fence rails. In the 1830s the Land Company and individual landowners employed an estimated five hundred men.[13]

Typically, starting in early February, companies of men, under the supervision of a slave driver or an overseer, were sent to the swamp with several months' worth of pork, flour, and cornmeal. They built huts on high ground and lived there until the end of June.[14] The wilderness offered them a modicum of freedom not found on the plantations: they fished, hunted, and worked at their own pace, the requirement being that each person produce a given number of shingles. Moses Grandy, hired out for a year as a carboy driving lumber, was quite satisfied with the deal: "I had plenty to eat and plenty of clothes. I was so overjoyed at the change, that I then thought I would not have left the place to go to heaven."[15]

To the company's satisfaction, Grandy was not "addicted" to running away, but most black men and women entered the swamp because of their "addiction" to freedom.[16] Predictably, as they penetrated deeper into its recesses to cut down trees and to make shingles and staves, some men seized the opportunity to free themselves, as did Ned, a young man who adopted a "pleasing and submissive countenance," and smiled a lot in order to fool his way into marronage. In April 1812, the twenty-four-year-old and several others started to look for timber; rapidly Ned took the lead and left the others far behind. He disappeared and was still at large five months later.[17]

In addition to the shingle-getters who became maroons, were maroons who worked in the timber camps to sustain themselves. Stephen, a musician who commonly had "a fiddle hung to his back," escaped in July 1806 and five years later was still transporting shingles down the canal.[18] One man who eventually made his way to Canada recounted why and how he first chose to live and labor in the swamp. Separated from his wife and subsequently threatened with sale to the Deep South, he escaped. Before disappearing, he went to bid farewell to his brother, his wife, his mother, and a friend—all living in separate locations. The friend told him "he knowed folks in de Dismal Swamp, and p'raps he might 'ceed for me, an' get me 'casion to work dar."[19] The recommendation worked and the friend's connection hired the runaway for two dollars a month. The arrangement, common between maroons and lumbermen, was mutually advantageous.[20] For every thousand shingles they produced, slaves were credited a fixed amount of money; the value of their food and clothing was then deducted, as was the fee their owner received. The surplus was their pay.[21] Once they had hired maroons to help them, they could double or triple their output. They drew on their rations and money to compensate them.

When Frederick Law Olmsted visited the swamp in 1854, a man named Joseph told him the maroons received "enough to eat, and some clothes, and perhaps two dollars a month in money."[22] Everyone along the chain found the deal beneficial, including the overseers. They did not get in the way, explained a white man, "especially as the runaways were the hardest workers of his gang; and, as he was supposed to be unaware of their existence, he never paid them anything."[23]

Maroons also hired themselves out directly to white men, who added them to their regular crews. Some knew their status, others probably had a hint, and still others could have been fooled by fake free papers. Passing for free is what Aaron from North Carolina had in mind when he escaped in February 1799. If not "lurking" near Nixonton where his wife lived, Aaron, who had previously worked in Lebanon Swamp, was thought to be in possession of fake papers in order to try to pass himself as a free man and work as a shingle weaver on the Virginia side of the swamp. His owner asked contractors to apprehend him should he apply for a job.[24]

Some men worked entirely for themselves. These entrepreneurs brought their shingles to the "Swamp merchants" or "Nigger traders." They were paid in money, meal, flour, meat, clothing, whiskey, "salted provisions," Indian corn, coarse cloth, and tools. A maroon who lived in the swamp for nineteen years recalled that he received "plenty of whiskey and tobacco" in exchange for his work.[25] Of greater concern for the authorities and the neighboring planters and farmers was the fact that the maroons turned shingle-getters also got powder and bullets.[26] They used them primarily for hunting, but the authorities also feared—with good reason—that they could turn them against those who stood in their way.

Maroon-white complicity was denounced as early as the 1720s. As William Byrd, an elite Virginia elite planter, deplored:

> It is certain many slaves shelter themselves in this obscure part of the world, nor will any of their righteous neighbours discover them. On the contrary, they find their account in settling such fugitives on some out-of-the-way corner of their land, to raise stocks for a mean and inconsiderable share, well knowing their condition makes it necessary for them to submit to any terms.[27]

A flagrant case of such connivance was that of a slaveholder named Sullivan who struck a deal with a group of maroons. He provided them with meal, bacon, tobacco, coffee, and other items, while they procured him fish, wild turkeys, and venison. The liaison between the parties was an elderly African, a carriage driver. When Sullivan needed to build a dam but was reluctant to take his own farm laborers off their tasks in the corn and cotton fields, he contracted with the maroons, who constructed the dam at night by the light of fires, protected by scouts posted all around to sound the alarm should any patrollers make an incursion. The maroons received rations, whiskey, and money, and Sullivan established a lucrative business thanks to his waterpower.[28]

Dispossessed slave owners were particularly incensed that whites conspired to defraud them of their property. James White offered one hundred dollars in June 1816 for the capture of George Hicks—a likely recidivist since he had already been shot six times in the arm, thigh, and wrist—who had escaped in August 1815 and, according "to satisfactory evidence," was employed by "a *White Person* [emphasis in the original] in procuring Shingles and other Lumber" in the swamp. In addition to the reward for Hicks's apprehension, White was ready to give another one hundred dollars to anyone who could furnish proof that George had been hired.[29]

This collusion with the maroons came to the legal forefront on January 18, 1847, during the 1846–1847 session of the North Carolina General Assembly, when the legislators ratified "An Act to provide for the apprehension of runaway slaves in the great Dismal Swamp and for other purposes." It was claimed that the legislation became necessary because "many slaves" escaped to the swamp and, with the help of free blacks and whites, eluded capture. Through their contact with free people, they became defiant. This in turn corrupted the enslaved population, whose submission declined, thus diminishing their monetary value. As the Act stipulated, "Consorting with such white men and free persons of color, they [the maroons] remain setting at defiance the powers of their masters, corrupting and reducing their slaves, and by their evil example and evil practices, lessening their due subordination and greatly impairing the value of slaves in the district of country bordering on the said great dismall [*sic*] swamp."[30] In an effort to better control enslaved and free blacks the legislature put in place a system of registration for the men and women legally working in the swamp. The description of each laborer was entered into a book. Akin to the minute descriptions of runaway notices, all physical particularities including age, complexion, and so on were duly noted.[31] Free men and women had to go through the same routine and keep a copy of what amounted to an identity card with them at all times; they risked a fine, imprisonment, and a whipping if found without.[32]

* * *

One advantage of working on the canal or as a shingle-getter was that the maroons could keep abreast of developments at home. Fresh information circulated when new gangs of workers made their way into the swamp; and life was not all work. The maroon who left for Canada fondly remembered his time in the swamp. He and his companions moved around freely in their bark canoes: they worked in the Company Swamp and hunted wild hogs and cows in Gum Swamp. They lived in shacks not far from the corduroy roads cut and used by loggers. When bears came too close to their camps, they chased them away with shots. They were not afraid of the wild beasts nor, he boasted, of anyone else: "Hope I shall live long enough to see de *slaveholders* feared to interrupt us!"[33] His group of tight-knit men had its own preacher, Ole Man Fisher, who led energetic singing sessions.

But inevitably, there was another face to the maroon experience. Joseph said that it was easy for the drivers to tell a fugitive from a regularly employed slave in the swamps. He described it to Olmsted as follows,

"How do they know them?"
"Oh, dey looks *strange*."
"How do you mean?"
"*Skeared* like, you know, sir, and kind o' strange, cause dey has n't much to eat, and ain't decent [not decently clothed], like we is."[34]

Hungry and poorly dressed, the maroons Joseph knew were at the mercy of the slave hunters who roamed the more accessible areas of the swamp. Yet they chose to continue working, taking risks for meager pay, still determined to live their lives as free men.

MAROONS IN THE HINTERLAND

Other maroons inhabited the Great Dismal. They were the secretive men and women who inspired writers and inflamed the popular imagination precisely because not much was known about them, even though they had been written about for decades. In 1790, the *Daily Advertiser* informed its readers that the swamp was a sanctuary for "run-away negroes, many of whom live here to be old, without the least danger of being discovered, in short, this is the general asylum for everything that flies from mankind and society."

Johann David Schoepf, who visited the area in 1783–1784, reported the existence of "runaway slaves, who have lived many years in the swamp." The existence of multigenerational households was hinted at in the 1780s when John Ferdinand Smyth Stuart noted that maroons lived in the interior parts "for twelve, twenty, or thirty years and upwards," during which time, presumably, they had children and grandchildren. As the anonymous former maroon confirmed when he reached Canada: "Some runaways went dere wid dar wives, an' dar childers are raised dar." They were the people Joseph had told Olmsted about: "Children were born, bred, lived, and died here. . . . There were people in the swamps still, he thought, that were the children of the runaways, and who had been runaway themselves all their lives."[35]

The enigmatic existence of these individuals and families was revealed when they were found, gave themselves up, or emerged after Emancipation. Samuel Huntington Perkins—a Yale graduate tutoring the daughters of slaveholders in Hyde County, North Carolina—recounted in his diary in 1817: "[N]ot long since a woman was discovered in the center of the Great Dismal Swamp. There she & her six children had lived for years."[36] Another household that made the news in 1846 had given itself up. As a raging fire in the swamp drove away a number of maroons, an elderly woman went in search of her former owner, taking with her her eleven children, "serving as an indemnity or remuneration for her long absence," commented a journalist sarcastically.[37] Another of these long-term maroons was Davy, a former carriage driver. He had killed a white man with a hatchet over a disputed fish and buried the body in a pond under the mud. Following his father's advice, the young man disappeared into the swamp and remained under cover until 1865.[38] He went into hiding before 1817 and lived in the swamp for at least forty-nine years.

If Davy ran away from white men he knew too well, other maroons were said never to have seen any. In 1848, an anonymous writer remarked in the newspaper *The Non-Slaveholder*: "So extensive is this place, and so inaccessible to the population, that many of its inhabitants have never seen a white man."[39] His statement was confirmed by the maroon shingle-getter who recounted his life while in Canada: "Dar is families growed up in dat ar Dismal Swamp dat never seed a white man," he confided, "an' would be skeered most to def to see one."[40] Another witness, a Northerner who was stationed with his company at the northern edge of the swamp during the Civil War, saw a "family of nine negroes [who] came into our lines, the seven children of which had never looked upon the face of a white man before."[41]

But what of other black people? Did the children of the Great Dismal Swamp see black people other than their relatives and other members of their community? If so, it would prove that contacts took place between the hinterland dwellers and the black men, enslaved and free, who worked in the swamp. The testimony of a maroon shingle-getter offers one clue. He stated that he had never seen a woman: he never encountered the women and children who lived in the remote areas.[42] And what about the men? Did some of the maroons from the hinterland hire themselves to the shingle-getters? Olmsted believed that by the time of his visit there in 1854, there could not be many "natives" left, because they could not have sustained themselves without raiding the plantations or working for the lumbermen. Another visitor agreed; the people who raised families, he conjectured, lived by "woodcraft, external depredations, and more frequently, it is probable, by working for the task shingle-getters at reduced wages."[43] If so, it would have been through them that the shingle-getters could have learned about the hinterland people, without having gone where they lived. Because to avoid betrayal, these maroons had to maintain the tightest secrecy about their settlements. Even those who dwelled at the edges of the swamp made sure that other blacks remained ignorant of their location. As Sis Shackelford emphasized, they "never would let you foller 'em." They lived in "holes in de groun' so hidden dey stay dere years an' white folks, dogs or nothin' else could fine 'em."[44] The precautions taken by these maroons at the swamp's margins were certainly not superior to the hinterland maroons' safety measures.

When he visited the swamp in 1856, the illustrator David Hunter Strother—also known as Porte Crayon—immortalized one man who may have straddled both worlds. He seems to be the only maroon whose portrait exists and appeared in the pages of a national magazine.[45] Strother longed "to see one of those sable outlaws." After leaving a causeway, he crawled his way through the undergrowth until exhausted. He heard footsteps and soon saw "a gigantic negro, with a tattered blanket wrapped about his shoulders, and a gun in his hand. His head was bare, and he had little other clothing than a pair of ragged breeches and boots." The middle-aged man had iron hands and "purely African features" that bespoke strength and energy. He looked both fearful and ferocious. Strother had chanced upon what had to be a rarity in the late 1850s Upper South: an African maroon. After sketching him, Strother said he left his drawing where the two black boatmen who had accompanied him could see it. He heard them talk about "Osman," but when interrogated they denied knowing anything about the man in the picture.

Strother's story is perplexing. The illustrator came, on his own, across a man who had been hiding for years, perhaps decades, a man so in tune with his environment that he had so far escaped detection but who had failed to notice a newcomer's presence a few feet away. Yet if Strother had wanted to invent a story about an African, chances are he would have given him an easily recognizable African name such as Cudjoe. But the name he said he heard was Osman, a Muslim name, which would tend to give some credence to his story. But did he really see him? Did he only hear about him and sketch a man described to him? In any event, the main point of the story is that in the sketch Osman holds a gun. Hence he needed ammunition, and if he was one of the secluded maroons, he was clearly in contact with the outside world. This raises some questions as to some hinterland maroons' isolation and degree of self-sufficiency.

Daniel Sayers of American University has led promising archeological digs in one area of the swamp and asserts that work on the canal and logging significantly changed the swamp's culture, with isolated maroons going to work in the camps and getting commodities. There is no doubt that the industrialization of the swamp brought change. Once secluded maroons had to move further away because of encroachment. Although some may have decided to work on the canal, the scale of this involvement is difficult to assess. They may have opted for part-time industrial work, returning to their homesteads with much needed items such as axes, guns, knives, nails, cloth, all available through enslaved and free blacks as well as white traders. Yet Sayers's digs have unearthed very few manufactured items: one iron nail, parts of a white clay pipe, and small pieces of lead shot, glass, and flint.[46] They may have been traded but they may also have been brought along during someone's escape.

However, the significant point is that, whatever their origin, such objects were recycled almost into disappearance. If they could have been found on a regular basis at the camps, there would have been little need to reutilize them indefinitely. Their scarcity, the immense care with which they were repaired, and their very longevity show that they were highly prized items not easy to replace. This points to isolation rather than contact. Actually, the seclusion of the hinterland dwellers was such that pieces of Native American ceramics dated 1200–800 B.C. were found sustaining a more recent round post, indicating that they were used, probably by maroons, who even recycled the flakes of stone left over by sharpening prehistoric tools.

Sayers's archeological excavations have focused on one site. More locations need to be explored to get a better picture of maroon life in the inner swamp. But what can be cautiously concluded on the basis of current fieldwork is that families or small communities of isolated maroons found ingenious ways of surviving without having to interact with the outside world, while others may have had limited communication—through the men—with outsiders.

MATERIAL CULTURE

Before archeology can help answer some questions, one has to probe other sources, some of which are dubious. Secrecy and seclusion go to the heart of the way the maroons organized their existence in the most remote parts of the Great Dismal, which explains why fables born of ignorance and prejudice surrounded them. However, it is possible to partially reconstruct how they lived from the evidence provided by contemporary writings, oral history, and from the descriptions of the people who remained in the swamp after 1865.[47] Although a magazine claimed in 1896—without elaboration—that "the remains of a large colony" established in the recesses of the swamp had been discovered, there is reason to doubt that sizable settlements of, say, a hundred people or more existed. Elementary safety militated against large regrouping and the very topography of the swamp would have precluded the development of large villages in most cases. Archeological excavations conducted by Sayers unearthed the remnants of at least five cabins on a site dated sometime between 1600 and 1759.[48] They could have harbored two or three dozen individuals at the most.

In the humid and waterlogged swamps, the maroons settled on knolls and small islets that rose two or three feet above water. They were located far inland, surrounded by miles of marshes, a choice of setting that clearly exposed the maroons' efforts at complete isolation. This was all the more necessary because, as a WPA writer remarked, "Sounds that warned the fugitive and also betrayed him could be heard for immense distances."[49]

How the hinterland maroons lived can only be partially reconstructed, helped by accounts of the particular way of life of post-Emancipation swamp dwellers. These flesh out the numerous gaps that still characterize the maroons' story. Shortly after 1865, descriptions of "families of Negroes completely isolated from the outer world, and evidently the descendants of runaway slaves," were published in newspapers and periodicals. They provide indications as to the former maroons' habitat, diet, and appearance. Structures well adapted to the particular terrain of the swamp were noted as follows in an 1867 article: "[T]he deepest recesses of the swamp were always inhabited by negroes, who built their cabins elevated upon stilts above the water."[50] Some could still be seen in the early 1900s.[51] They may have been similar to the shingle workers' cabins, described in the 1880s:

> The shanties of the negro laborers are always built over ground, the nature of the soil preventing any other manner of building. One of these dwellings was a curiosity in its way. It was constructed by bracing scantlings against four cypress-trees that happened to grow at regular quadrangular distances, and then lifting the house upon those supports several yards above the water. This roost was approached by a skiff, and entrance effected by climbing a ladder that hung from the door, so that its residents literally and truly abided in the treetops.[52]

Even on knolls, an elevated house was not superfluous: it was a protection against muddy ground drenched by heavy rains, a defense from floods and rodents, and it helped circulate the air. In addition to the shingle-getters' cabin, the home that a family of nine built in the Georgia swamps can serve as an example:

> First they drove posts into the ground upon which they could lay a foundation above the water, then with branches of trees skillfully and ingenuously woven together, they constructed the floor, roof, and walls of this their most rural habitation. To complete the structure they over-laid the whole with long marsh grass and the tough palmetto leaves, till it was quite comfortable even during the winter season.[53]

Given the dearth of artifacts and the absence of axes and other tools in the excavated five-house settlement, one wonders how the preliminary work of cutting timber to make the posts was conducted.

While some hinterland people certainly had axes, those who did not had to find alternative ways to build homes. One tantalizing clue as to how they could have done it is provided by two different sources. Poet, editor, and journalist Henry Clapp, Jr., wrote in the 1840s that they erected shacks made of mud, sticks, and bark.[54] He did not say how he knew this; but consistent with this source, elders from the area, inter-viewed in the twentieth century, were told when they were growing up that the maroons lived in bark cabins.[55] American Indians and European lumbermen routinely built these types of dwellings. Bark had other uses: the men who worked in shingle camps and had all kinds of tools at their disposal to build wood canoes made theirs out of bark. The maroon shingle-getter who settled in Canada remembered: "De boys used to make canoes out ob bark, and hab a nice time fishin' in de Lake."[56] With a bark canoe, isolated maroons without axes could do just the same. Bark houses and canoes, and wooden pegs would not leave many traces for archeologists to uncover.

How and what the maroons hunted and what they ate also reveal details of their experience. In the summer, game migrated to cooler and wetter areas in the deeper parts of the swamps, which was a boon to the inland dwellers.[57] They could feed on squirrels, deer, otters, beavers, ducks, partridges, and quails. According to what elders said, they hunted with bows and arrows, and like maroons elsewhere, built log traps and deadfalls to catch wildlife.[58] One such trap was used by the shingle-getters:

> a great log, some eight feet long, is laid on the ground, and fenced in by shingles or palings being driven down on either side, thus when one of the logs is raised there is, apparently a hollow running beneath it. A trigger is set and baited, and the coon has his life crushed out if he meddles with the dead chicken or fish on the end of the blade.[59]

A maroon recounted how the high lands teemed with wild hogs, cows, wolves, and bears.[60] The presence of wild cattle, called cattle-beasts, was mentioned in the eighteenth century. Even by the very end of the nineteenth century there were still "plenty of cattle in the swamp—small, dark and very wild. . . . the progeny of animals that have strayed from domesticated herds."[61] Moreover, a study conducted in 1897 and 1898 by the Department of Agriculture found that some black sharecroppers who lived by the swamp also ate muskrats, opossums, frogs, turtles, and snakes, a diet probably similar to that of the maroons.[62]

Winter was a more difficult time; it brought frost, cold winds, and sometimes snow. The rain could be heavy and stagnant waters turned into ice sheets. Although some animals and birds migrated South, the maroons were not without resources. In the early 1780s, Stuart noted that in the more elevated areas not subject to floods, they cleared small fields where they grew corn and raised hogs and fowl. Another eighteenth-century traveler remarked: "[T]hese negro fugitives lived in security and plenty, building themselves cabins, planting corn, raising hogs and fowls." In the nineteenth century Edmund Jackson added that they also grew sweet potatoes. Confirming the viability of cultivated lots in the swamp, the post-Emancipation "swampers" lived in small farms on higher ground, growing a variety of produce. They gathered fruits and honey; and bark, roots, and herbs to heal themselves. In their cabins, "stock of native remedies h[u]ng in festoons from the smoke-blackened rafters," recounted a visitor in 1881.[63]

Although they were disconnected from the plantations where other maroons helped themselves to and received food from relatives and friends, the hinterland maroons were not at a disadvantage. Their remote locations enabled them to conduct agricultural and breeding activities on a scale that closer proximity to inhabited areas would have precluded, which in turn made them independent from the plantation world. From a strictly economic point of view, they had the least impact of all the maroons on the slaveholding world: they did not raid homes, farms, plantations, or stores. And if some did, it was minimal. One account published in 1866 stated that the maroons lived on game and roots; but "when corn is fit for use, they would travel miles to obtain it, and return again to their hiding places before daybreak."[64] Out of the swamp wilderness, the hinterland people had created pockets of sustainable life.

An intriguing aspect of maroons' material culture concerns their clothing. Witnesses regularly noted the sorry appearance of the people who came out of the woods after months or years. Reinforcing the point about marronage and clothes, tales abounded about naked men and women living in the Great Dismal Swamp and white commentators often wondered how they resisted mosquito bites. It was a well-accepted notion that blacks were immune to mosquitoes: "[T]he negro's skin is impervious to the bite of the ordinary mosquito," claimed a writer in 1855, "but those that live in the Dismal Swamp have a proboscis that will pierce the hide of a ox."[65] A dozen years after Emancipation, a journalist stated: "Some people say that in the center of the swamp there are living a naked, semi-civilized colony of negroes who escaped from plantations in slave times, and who have become innured [*sic*] to the attacks of the insects."[66] Similarly, at the beginning of the twentieth century a man who knew the area quite well mused: "How the runaways existed under these circumstances is a mystery, for domestic cattle turned into the swamp to browse during the Winter months are invariably driven out by the insects in the Spring, maddened by the torture."[67] In the presence of fierce mosquitoes, it is more likely than not that maroons covered themselves.

The men and women who lived in the swamp for decades and were not able to get fabric had to draw on what they found in their environment: likely a combination of skins, fur, and bark treated to look and feel like leather. The shingle-getters, who had access to plantation clothes, used an abundance of raccoon skins, out of which they fashioned coats, hats, and waistcoats, and hinterland maroons were known to have done the same. "There are known cases where runaways lived thirty years or more in the swamp," wrote Frederick Street, "depending chiefly both for food and clothing, on the 'coons.'"[68]

Folktales mention people who grew a sort of fur to protect themselves. That people who wore pieces of fur and skin could have been mistaken for "hairy"—or interpreted as being such when years later the stories became secondhand—is not out of the realm of possibility. Tales of hairy people, who, absurdly, were said to have developed a "swamp scent" that made wild animals less afraid, easily morphed into fictions of wild Africans.[69] The swamp was said to be inhabited by "whole tribes of negroes, strange black tribes wherein a descendant of African kings might again be the ruler of his kind and of blacks from every corner of Africa." The maroons had "relapsed into a primitive state," led "a lazy, semi-savage life, hunted, fished and slept, fought when elemental passions aroused themselves."[70] Caleb Winslow, a physician who grew up on a plantation in Perquimans County, claimed that the maroons "enacted a rude system of government, bound themselves together by the severest penalties and condemned the traitor and spy to inevitable Death."[71] What his sources were he did not say, and there is no documentation as to the kinds of social structures the maroons created.

The secrecy that surrounded the secluded maroons and the consequent fantastic tales about them persisted for decades. Writing in 1878, a newspaper correspondent informed his readers: "There is a legend to the effect that three or four years ago, a man from this colony made his way out, and astonished people by never having heard of the war."[72] He cautiously added that he could find no one to vouch for the accuracy of the story. But at least until the 1940s, some people living on the borders of the swamp believed that "savage" descendants of the maroons still wandered around.[73]

Tall tales reveal how successful the maroons were at preserving their isolation. Only bits and pieces of information about them filtered out, never enough to put them at risk. And a century and a half later, most of the mystery that surrounded them still has not been pierced.

A NOT-SO-SAFE HAVEN

In the eighteenth century, John F. Smyth Stuart let it be known that "At present I shall only just observe that these places are in a great degree inaccessible, and harbour . . . run-away Negroes, who in these horrible swamps are perfectly safe, and with the greatest facility elude the most diligent search of their pursuers."[74] Echoing him, an article in *The Daily Advertiser* in 1790 informed readers that the swamp was a haven for "run-away negroes, many of whom live here to be old, without the least danger of being discovered."[75] As late as the mid-nineteenth century, Edmund Jackson believed it was probably not in Virginia's power to capture or expel the maroons. "From this extensive swamp they are very seldom, if now at all, reclaimed," he asserted.[76] This assessment was shared by a former maroon, already cited, who had hidden there for fifty years: "De runaway ketchers cum in dar to look for me, but didn't get me. . . . I tell you, boss, when you git in de desart ef nobody ses nuffin, de runaway ketchers can't kotch you."[77] Many observers, then, felt that once maroons had made their way into the swamp, they were safe in the impregnability of the morass.

Although this opinion was not totally inaccurate, it applied only to specific areas and times. While some maroons were able to live in the hinterland for at least two generations, those at the periphery and the borderlands could be doggedly pursued, if not always caught. A deputy sheriff of Nansemond County spent several days searching for a man. He finally spotted him, neck deep in the water. Back in Suffolk, he scratched off the man's name and wrote: "Seeable but not comeatable."[78]

Going after the maroons was perilous and complicated; so much so that in 1822 the North Carolina legislature thought it necessary to pass "[a]n act to encourage the apprehension of runaway slaves in the Great Dismal Swamp." It provided exceptional compensations for the men who would retrieve them, because no one was eager to venture into the swamp for the small rewards owners routinely offered slave catchers. For example, Horatio Butt was willing to give a $50 bounty for the capture of Ned, who disappeared while working in the swamp; and Baker Wiggins offered $25 each for Henry and Zango, who had come all the way from Mars Bluff, South Carolina, 250 miles away.[79]

The state eventually intervened between avaricious slaveholders and reluctant slave catchers. The legislators acknowledged it was "dangerous and difficult to apprehend runaway slaves who have secreted themselves in the great dismal swamp, from whence they commit depredations, to the great injury of the citizens of the neighboring" areas. Thus, when someone was demonstrably seized in the swamp, he would be assessed by three slaveholders and his owner would have to pay 25 percent of his appraised value to the captor.[80] At the time, the average price of a man was $925, so a slave catcher was to receive about $230, close to ten times more than what some people offered. Perhaps because the proposed bounties proved too onerous, the law was repealed in December 1823.

Faced with the reality of slave catchers disinclined to enter the swamp, some slaveholders found another solution: in North Carolina, they offered a reward if a runaway was taken in the state and a higher one if s/he was apprehended out of state or within the Dismal Swamp or at its borders. Catching Abram anywhere in North Carolina would bring $75, but his owner was disposed to give $100 if he was taken "in or on the borders of the Dismal Swamp." The same went for Prince, "of Guinea blood," whose apprehension in the swamp would double the bounty.[81]

Twenty-five years after the 1822 law was repealed, it reappeared under a new, more palatable form. The January 1847 Act had two main objectives: to better control the population of canal and shingle workers in order to weed out the maroons, and to make the challenging hunt for them more appealing. Without going back to the generous 1822 text, the legislature imposed a $25 bonus above the reward slaveholders offered.[82]

It was at this time that a more systematic approach to chasing the maroons got under way. The abolitionist newspaper *The North Star* noted the trend: "Recently, parties of young men, with dogs, have hunted out these poor creatures; and, to use the expression of my informant, have 'shot them down like partridges.'"[83] The shingle industry was booming, an estimated twenty-five million pieces being extracted every year.[84] Policing and controlling the area and the workers, and especially removing maroons to ensure that enslaved workers would not emulate them, became a priority. According to an informant, so many were shot and wounded that others emerged and returned to the plantation world. Some were captured and sold to unsuspecting slaveholders. This raiding frenzy became so well-known that a foreign correspondent in Paris wrote in 1848 that the chasing of thieves in the French capital could have been no more eager and obdurate than a "negro hunt" in the Dismal Swamp.[85]

* * *

Beyond the legends, the people of the Great Dismal Swamp were a unique population.

Those in the hinterland evolved in a more secure environment than most hinterland maroons in the rest of the South. Their very isolation allowed them to farm on a scale that enabled them to limit or cut off their interaction with the outside world and raise children who had no firsthand knowledge of its ferocity. There were surely secluded maroons who lived in full or close-to-full self-sufficiency in other parts of the country whose stories may eventually be revealed, but for now the closest we are to getting a glimpse of this particular way of life is by studying those who settled in the Great Dismal Swamp.

As for the shingle-getters, they were not the only maroons who worked on the side, as other examples have shown; but they built it up into an effective system. They were free agents whose main connection with the world of slavery was the work they did for enslaved men. Although living at the margins, through that work they became part of the larger economy. They retained their freedom but by mingling with others and settling at the industrial borderlands, they were liable to being betrayed and hunted down.

For most maroons, the Great Dismal Swamp lived up to the reputation it had acquired among black men and women. In contrast to the widespread belief among whites in the purported abysmal living conditions of the swamp's exiles, a perceptive—albeit a bit overoptimistic—view was expressed by a commentator in 1890: "[T]he slaves who escaped to the Dismal Swamp in the old time must have lived happily in their absolute freedom," he stated. "The negro in the swamp is at home. He has helped to spread and exaggerate the terror of the place to keep it more securely for himself. If I were a slave, in slave time, and could get to the Dismal Swamp, I should ask no pity from any one."[86]

The raiding parties of the 1840s and 1850s took a toll on the men and women who lived in the most accessible areas. But, as mentioned earlier, no "hunt" in the interior was reported. The secluded families successfully established themselves and survived for decades; indeed some lived there until Emancipation and beyond. In 1851, as they burst onto the national scene, Edmund Jackson wrote with premonition of the maroons who

have established themselves, with entire security, in the largest slaveholding State of the South; that though subject, doubtless, to poverty and many privations, they obtain a living, are increasing, and that, through their efforts, and the ordinance of nature, they have established a city of refuge in the midst of Slavery, which has endured from generation to generation, and is likely to continue until Slavery is abolished throughout the land.[87]

9

THE MAROON BANDITS

F ROM the slave society's perspective
maroons were outlaws in more
senses than one. Since they were someone else's property, by absconding
they committed theft. Additionally, they were considered to be rebelling
against their enslavers, which was a crime, and by raiding plantations
and farms they engaged in yet another level of "banditry." In an effort
to demean the men and women who had freed themselves and criminal-
ize their aspirations the maroons' adversaries conspicuously and liberally
used the labels "bandits" and "banditti" to describe them all. The generalization was uncalled for but there were indeed some criminals among
the maroons.

One may argue that the injustice of slavery justified the bandits'
actions; but does that reality automatically make them something other
than common criminals? Social bandits, for example? The prototype of
late historian Eric Hobsbawn's social bandit as a peasant dispossessed by
the forces of commercial agriculture who becomes the outlaw champion
of the poor, does not fit the profile of the maroons. The return to an
idyllic past—the ultimate goal of the social bandit—was patently a non-
starter for enslaved people. However, some elements that characterize
social bandits do apply to the maroons. First is the backing of a community made up of active supporters who provide shelter, information and
food; and of sympathizers. A social bandit is also distinguished from an
ordinary criminal by his readiness to take from the rich (but only rarely
to give to the poor, as Hobsbawn stressed) and by the fact that he kills in

self-defense or "legitimate" retaliation. In addition, there is a certain flair to the social bandit. David P. Thelen notes that because they seem to strike at will and make their victims look ridiculous and incompetent, their supporters see them as heroes. Going beyond these particulars, William L. Van Deburg, writing about black villains and social bandits, defines them simply as people who engage in "the act of being bad for a good reason."[1]

Despite these descriptions and definitions, it is often difficult to distinguish between bandits and "ordinary" maroons because of subjective reports that painted all of them with the same brush, and a dearth of testimonies from the enslaved community that would help us understand its perception of the bandits. This last point has to be inferred from the manner in which the latter were able to operate and from white fear and denunciation of suspected bandit-slave complicity. While the analysis in this chapter of the types of criminal activities typical of the bandits and of the lives and actions of specific groups is not exhaustive, it helps delineate this subgroup of maroons and illustrates how they differentiated themselves from the larger maroon community.

HORSE THIEVES, HIGHWAY BANDITS, AND BURGLARS

Some runaways escaped on horseback but they generally got rid of the horses as soon as they could, because they stood a better chance of traveling undetected on their own. Horse stealing by maroons was different. For example, a link between horse stealing and marronage was suspected when Ephraim of Halifax County, North Carolina "absented himself" on September 23, 1796. The same night a sorrel horse disappeared from a neighbor's stable. The two were understood to be together. Ephraim was raised in Southampton County, Virginia, and his owner thought he may have been heading back home, but he also had reason to believe that he might "be in the company with a gang of runaways, in the neighbourhood of Gilmore's quarter, near Halifax."[2] Ephraim's horse may well have been his ticket for entry into the group, because to maroon bandits the animals were not only a means of transportation but also a form of currency.

In South Carolina, Caesar, a notorious horse thief, was the leader of a group of seven deemed "one of the most daring Gangs of Fellows that ever infested the Province."³ When Caesar had escaped from Daniel Drose's plantation in Dorchester, he had left with a forged pass written by "one of the half-breed people." Although one might assume that maroons did not need passes since their destination was the wilderness, passes were useful when they roamed the open roads as bandits or traded in town. Caesar and his partners lived in a camp at Beech Hill, only three miles from George Galphin's Silver Bluff Plantation, close to other horse thieves. One was "The noted Tilly, a Horse Thief [who] harboured about the same camp to the Southward." Jeremiah Tilly was a white outlaw whose band included black fugitives. In between raids, Caesar and the other bandits also spent time at Black Swamp, a noted maroon area on the Savannah River.⁴ Caesar and his band not only stole "many horses," as the leader acknowledged, but they were also involved in various kinds of thefts. Probing into one of their expeditions reveals how they used the horses they kept for themselves, what goods they were after, and to what extremes they were disposed to go to get them.

In late June 1773, after carefully choosing their night—it was the beginning of the new moon, when nights were at their darkest—Caesar and his men, armed with firearms, cutlasses, and other weapons, galloped on their stolen horses to a plantation to stock up. They selected Drayton Hall, an imposing rice estate located on the Ashley River near Charleston. It was the property of John Drayton, a member of the South Carolina Royal Council. Having inherited several dozen men, women, and children from his father, he had brought others from Africa and Barbados and established one of the major domains in the area.⁵

The men were neither intimidated by the Draytons' power nor by the mansion that looked like a small brick fortress. They burglarized the outbuildings and made it to the three-story Main House. While the Draytons slept, Caesar stood guard, gun in hand, ready to shoot. The men stole sugar, rum, bacon, soap, wine, a bale of cloth, and "other Articles to a very great Amount." Like other maroons, Caesar's men sought necessary items that were hard to obtain. As for the rum and wine, they may either have stolen it for their own consumption and/or intended to sell it to white storeowners. The group left Drayton Hall unheard and unseen, at least by the Draytons, and made it back to camp, their horses loaded with goods. Over several months, four of Caesar's men were caught and executed. One was "admitted as evidence,"and another was pardoned by the lieutenant governor. But these developments did not stop their companions.

In April 1774, Caesar and three men robbed and beat a Ms. Pender. After a reward was posted for his capture, Caesar was arrested and brought to Ashley Ferry on April 26. Whether willingly or under torture, he gave a great deal of information. He revealed that his partner Andrew was still in the woods and sometimes stayed at the camp near Silver Bluff. He also gave the names of four horse thieves who lived there. After he had betrayed his friends, Caesar, the "notorious rogue," was tried, convicted, and executed.

As Caesar's story illustrates, horses enabled maroon bandits to dash quickly to and fro as they burglarized stores, plantations, and farms. But the real value of stealing horses was to sell them to smuggling rings, individual speculators, or farmers. Native Americans and white men (and sometimes women) were all part of this underground industry.

Horse stealing continued in the nineteenth century. In Mississippi, a group of maroons made the news in Wilkinson County when two horses were discovered in their possession.[6] Around Piscataway in Maryland, maroon bandits "who had collected to a considerable number," burglarized meat houses, stole horses, and threatened travelers on the highway.[7] As if that were not bad enough, they were also accused of fomenting an uprising, the perpetual fear of Southerners who routinely perceived ordinary and bandit maroons as potential insurrectionists. Some of the bandits had gathered at a "negro quarter" where a white man overheard them. According to him, they declared that before August 1801 "a great deal of blood of the whites, must and would be spilt." A posse was formed to hunt them down and several were captured. Among them were three "desperate villains," one of whom attacked the intruders with an axe.

It is ironic that throughout slavery, horse stealing and "negro stealing" were linked in white people's mind. As Reverend Philo Tower, summed it up, "Horses and slaves are almost the only thing capable of transportation, which can be stolen."[8] Abolitionists and defenders of slavery alike used the analogy. The latter accused the former of being no better than the people who stole horses. Abolitionists routinely returned the compliment: "The same principle on which the buyer of a stolen horse, knowing him to have been stolen, is a horse-thief," remarked Reverend George Cheever, "makes the slave buyer and the slaveholder a man-stealer."[9]

* * *

Highway robbery along country roads was another common activity among maroon bandits. Here they lay in wait, launched their attacks, and took their loot back to their camp. Some areas were reputed to be teeming with such outlaws. Traveling through a deserted stretch of the Winyaw Bay, South Carolina, in 1773, naturalist William Bartram encountered a party of black men carrying axes, hoes, and clubs. He wrongly believed them to be "a predatory band of Negroes" because he had heard that travelers were frequently attacked, robbed, and at times murdered in this neighborhood.[10] Four years later, Elkanah Watson, passing through the same area, noted, "We had been cautioned to be on our guard against the attacks of runaway negroes, in the passage of swamps near Wingan Bay. As we entered the second swamp, fourteen naked negroes armed with poles, presented themselves in the attitude of hostility, across the road."[11] As there was no attack, it is not clear whether these men were outgunned bandits or simply maroons who did not want to be disturbed. What is clear is that the bandits' reputation had remained unchanged

Highway robberies committed by groups of maroons were so numerous that in April 1779 the *sindico procurador general* of Louisiana held a meeting devoted to the issue. He announced that there were not enough funds to protect the most frequented roads. To alleviate the problem, eighty inhabitants of Pointe Coupée agreed to pay four *reales* for each captured maroon to meet the expenses for a policing force.[12] In South Carolina, "a gang of outlying negroes, headed by a notorious fellow named Primus," operated in the 1780s between Dorchester and Charleston. They robbed travelers and the wagoners who encamped in the area. The planters hired Catawbas to hunt the bandits down and Primus was hanged.[13]

Robbers were after money and valuables, but they took whatever else they could from passersby. In Virginia, Sutton was willing to take anything he could get when he jumped behind Henry Sadler, Jr., who was riding a horse. He grabbed a bag hanging from the saddle. The sack, containing three bushels of meal, went down along with a sheepskin. Sadler galloped to his father's house and they both went, together with a pack of dogs, back to the place of the incident. As they followed Sutton's tracks, the dogs, spotting a fox or hare, got distracted and the hunt for the highway robber had to be called off. But the next day the Sadlers, accompanied by fourteen neighbors, resumed the search and discovered four maroons and the sheepskin in one cave. In the second, they recovered Sadler's bag with half a barrel of meal. One of the maroon bandits' caves also hid various items stolen from a neighbor.[14]

Burglary was a more common crime than highway robbery. As already noted, maroons routinely raided farms and plantations to get food and other necessities; but the bandits did not limit themselves to granaries and smokehouses. They entered homes and rummaged through drawers and closets for cash and valuables. In Louisiana, a group of twelve—including several women—who lived close to a plantation in St. Charles Parish, stole tools, money, and several other items from plantations and broke into a New Orleans house, from which they took 1,500 piastres.[15]

Some bandits chose a more professional method than breaking and entering. This was the case with a man originally from Alabama who, in the summer of 1852, had a conversation with a Mr. Core, planter of Fayette County, Tennessee. He accosted Core in a field, exhibited "a splendid brace of pistols and a bowie knife," and told him he had been living in the woods for five years. He showed Core a stack of bills and told him he wanted to pay him because "your negroes have been feeding me for several months." The money, he said, came from the burglary of several houses in Memphis. He named names and showed Core a set of false keys to back up his claim.[16] Entering without breaking was also the modus operandi of a group of five—including two women—who lived in Cabarrus Pocosin in North Carolina. The small group was found in possession of "a vast deal of plunder."[17] They had a "great number of keys" with which they let themselves into their victims' dwellings. They had either stolen them or relied on a network of accomplices: the trusted people who had access to the original keys and the blacksmith who made the copies. These kinds of far-reaching networks were crucial to the success of the bandits' activities.

THE GENERAL OF THE SWAMPS

In May and June 1795, Brunswick and New Hanover counties, North Carolina, witnessed a spate of "depredations" committed by "outlying runaway negroes [who] had collected themselves together."[18] Their exact number is not known, but based on advertisements and reports of arrests, they must have been at least nine. Augustus, Robert, and Hannah–the only woman mentioned—had run away from William Howe's near New Bern. Pickle made his way to the camp from the plantation of Alexander Duncan Moore, a trustee of the University of North Carolina. Matthews had escaped from Benjamin Smith, representative of Brunswick County to the General Assembly, benefactor of the university, and future governor. Will had fled from the farm of a Mr. Brice. Of Bacchus and Christmas, nothing is known. Although the name and particulars of their leader have remained obscure, he was known as the General of the Swamps.

Under his leadership, the bandits slaughtered cattle and robbed white inhabitants. These were common maroon activities, but they also killed or attempted to kill a number of individuals. Their first known victim was William (or John) Steely. When he came upon their camp, they tried to kill him, missed, but succeeded in wounding him. They wisely left that location and turned their attention to Jacob Lewis, the overseer of Alexander Duncan Moore, who was active in tracking maroons. They came up with a simple but efficient ruse. Led by Pickle, they knocked on his door in the middle of the night, telling him they had caught a runaway. When he opened the door, they shot him, and as Will held him down they beat him to death.[19] The murder was as much an act of revenge as it was preventive: Lewis was paying for his assaults against the maroons, who made sure he would not be a threat again.

Eager to put an end to their "predatory excursions," "enormities," and "continued outrages," several men from New Hanover and Brunswick decided to capture the men or break up their camp. As happened a number of times when citizens took matters into their own hands, there was some confusion. A group took position near Green's Mill where the maroons were expected to go by, and one volunteer accidentally shot another in the shoulder.[20] The overseer's execution, following the wounding of Steely, prompted the justices of the peace to outlaw the maroons. On July 2, they informed the population that $60 would "be paid upon the production of the heads of any of the Negroes concerned" in the murder. A few days earlier Hannah had been arrested.[21]

Things happened so fast that on the same day, the General of the Swamps was killed. Will was tried, found guilty of having held Jacob Lewis while he was being killed, confessed, and was hung at Gallows Green. Matthews, Will, and Pickle were caught.[22] Matthews was so severely wounded when he tried to flee, "it was apprehended he would have eluded the vengeance of the law." But to the satisfaction of the populace, it later appeared he would "live long enough to make a public exit." Augustus and Robert were arrested sometime after July 10 and by mid-month it was believed that "one only of their leaders" was still at large. Pickle, charged with acting as a guide to Lewis's was hung on August 22. Robert, also condemned to die, watched his companion being put to death but just before his turn came, the sheriff brought in the governor's pardon.

This particular case exposes one of the main differences between ordinary maroons and bandits. When the General of the Swamps and his men shot and tried to kill William Steely as he came upon their camp it was an act of self-preservation undertaken on the spur of the moment. Not premeditated, it was the kind of response one could expect from most maroons. Jacob Lewis's murder, on the contrary, was a deliberate assassination. It was planned, complete with an elaborate scheme, and brutally accomplished by several men against one defenseless individual. Ordinary maroons, as far as can be ascertained through the cases detailed in this study, did not indulge in this type of action. Instead, they avoided confrontation and did not go out of their way to execute white men. But the killing that can be seen as part "legitimate revenge" part "preemptive strike" was emblematic of social banditry. As an overseer and an active pursuer of maroons, Lewis was a threat not only to the General of the Swamps and his group, but also to other maroons, runaways, and most likely to the men, women, and children placed under his direct control. Many must have thus rejoiced at his death, turning the bandits into avenging heroes.

BILLY JAMES AND HIS "MAROON BANDITTI OF NEGROES"

On October 10, 1817 three individuals ran away from three plantations in North Carolina.[23] One was Jacob, eighteen. Another was a woman enslaved by former governor David Stone, the Princeton-educated lawyer and trustee of the University of North Carolina, landlord of eight thousand acres, two plantations, and 138 people in Bertie and Rowan counties.[24] The woman's body mapped her defiance as a habitual runaway: her right ear was cropped and her back was scarred by whippings. The third, named Billy James, was about twenty-four years of age. Over the following two years, he made a name for himself as the leader of a "maroon banditti of Negroes."

Throughout 1818, James's band of "daring runaway Negroes" performed "considerable mischief."[25] One night in early November, they went to Robert Young's store, about ten miles from Louisburg. According to sources, they set fire to the store, shot Young while he tried to put out the flames; and as he sought help from a neighbor, they plundered his store. The scenario seems odd since it describes the men plundering a room in flames; it is more plausible that they first robbed Young, shot him when he surprised them, and then torched the place. They left the store with their loot and entered the nearby house of the widow Fox. Breaking open a desk, they took all the money they found: two gold half eagles.[26] Shortly thereafter, one maroon was captured with some articles from Young's store and was jailed in Raleigh. Young eventually died from his wounds. At that moment, Billy James, also called Andey, was outlawed. He could be killed on sight, no questions asked.

Less than two weeks later, on November 24, the bandits executed another audacious assault. They selected a store at Stone's Mills, eight miles east of Raleigh. Four of them entered the shop pretending to buy something from the owner, a Mr. Jones, but they promptly revealed their intentions as they snatched a gun. Jones attacked them with a dirk (a long straight-bladed dagger), and they ran out, but one man was not fast enough and Jones threw him to the ground. After locking the door he started to tie him up. The man's three companions, demanding his release, tried to break the door down. Jones shot at them from a window and the men returned fire. A neighbor and his son ran to the rescue and came upon the group from behind. The three maroons retreated.[27]

Determined to put a definitive stop to Billy James's activities and to avenge Young's death, Governor John Branch issued a proclamation on November 26, offering a reward of $250 for the "lawless Negroes of the number of 7." Whoever brought James to jail would receive $100; $150 would be given for the other six.[28] In late December 1818 or early January 1819, a group of white men went searching for the band. In another episode of friendly fire, Robert Tapley, who had lagged behind, mistook his colleagues for the maroons and shot at them. They in turn, believing that the "banditti" were shooting, returned fire and killed Tapley.[29] In late February, James was located on the plantation of Colonel William Hinton; but when Hinton tried to catch him, he discovered that James, having heard "no doubt, from some of the negroes of the plantation, what was going on, escaped."[30] James had black friends and he likely had some white connections too. When he and his men stole two gold coins word went out that "If they should attempt to pass these pieces of gold, it may lead to a discovery. It behooves the public to keep a strict look out for these daring marauders."[31] However, several months later the money had still not reappeared in black hands. It is doubtful that James was saving his money. More likely the compromising coins had since passed on to trusted white men in exchange for the guns and ammunition that would enable the bandits to continue their activities.

Billy James attained a certain degree of notoriety among the white population. He was known as Abaelino from *Abaelino the Great Bandit,* a play that had great success in the United States.[32] It was a singular "honor" for a black man to be compared to the Venetian outlaw, a white literary figure. The nickname was a measure of James's recognized—and dreaded—skills and of his larger-than-life image. In Governor Branch's words the "old offender" Billy James, then about twenty-six, was "a stout well made Negro with full face and well dressed."[33] The last remark was odd, especially concerning someone who lived in the woods. But Branch had reason to emphasize that James was an elegant man. Indeed, he did not look like a woodsman, not even like an "ordinary Negro." The man had panache; he was stylish and appropriated the type of finery that was out of reach for most free men, white or black. He was said to regularly steal clothes, including the fine shirts of some members of the General Assembly.[34] These thefts were audacious, particularly as they were superfluous.

James made fools of the gentry, which must have gained him some admiration in other quarters. His success illustrates the extent of the community's support of the bandits. It is clear that without a network of informants and friends, the "outlawed outlaw" would never have been able to survive as a bandit, let alone in such a brazen manner.

BOB'S BAND

A group of maroons who lived in the woods of Gates County, North Carolina, but whose activities extended to several counties of that state as well as Virginia became notorious in the 1820s; by one vague account they were "a considerable gang."[35] Only a handful of them are known by name. Jim, Elisha, Willis, and Jack had escaped from the notoriously cruel Miles Parker of Gates County; and the group's leader Bob, alias Sam, from a Mr. Ricks of Southampton, Virginia.[36] One of the last to join was another Sam, owned like sixty-four other people by Colonel Josiah Riddick, vice president of the Nansemond County American Colonization Society.[37] This Sam had absconded in December 1823.

The band attracted attention in 1822 but its notoriety increased the following year. Around midnight on March 1, 1823 Jim robbed John B. Baker of twenty pounds of beef and twenty pounds of bacon. On March

10, with Elisha and Jack, he took another twenty pounds of bacon from Elisha H. Bond. Since no specific burglary was attributed to them in the following weeks, it is possible that they took their activities elsewhere. But on September 10, Willis, Elisha, Jim, and Jack were captured and thrown into jail. Ten days later, perhaps with the help of their companions still on the outside, they managed to break out.[38]

One man who was active in trying to bring "these wretches" to justice was Elisha Cross, "a respectable man and a good citizen," a father of seven, and a small slaveholder.[39] Sometime in January 1824, he shot Jim in the thighs after he broke open a smokehouse and stole bacon. On the 23rd, as Cross was coming back from a sale at 1:00 a.m., he was ambushed close to home. According to newspaper reports, he screamed for help and when his family came running they found him shot twice (once in the back), his throat slit, and both corners of his mouth cut down to the jawbone. One thumb was almost severed and he had several stab wounds. If this was the case, the objective of the men who assaulted him was not merely to kill him, but to make him suffer. However, the official indictment was much less gory than the press reports. It simply stated that Jim shot Cross in the right side of his belly and the man died instantly.[40] The murder was preemptive: Cross would never again hunt them or any other maroon down, and it was revenge as well for his past activities. The maroons were outlawed and a reward of $600 was offered for their arrest.

Bob and his men were not heard from for several months, but they reappeared with fanfare on April 22, the day they ambushed Whitfield and Tompkins, two slave dealers from Warren, Georgia. The speculators had left Elizabeth City with a coffle of seventeen people and were en route to sell them to the Deep South. Among the captives were six men Whitfield and Tompkins had taken out of the Gates Court House jail. One was condemned to banishment. Habitual runaways, "bad characters," rebels, and thieves were routinely sold away and lodged in jail before their deportation. As the coffle of heavily shackled men approached Mrs. Cross's house—Elisha's widow—six men rushed out of the woods. Pointing their guns at the speculators, they demanded the release of the prisoners. The slave dealers ran off, leaving their wagon, their luggage, and the seventeen prisoners. The maroons took the shackles off two of the men and gave them guns, then they all disappeared.[41] The general sentiment among the white population was that the rest of the captives refused to follow. This may have been the case, but it is more likely that they were not part of the rescue mission to begin with because the attack was not random. The banished man who followed the maroons was the brother of one of them. The other was named Willis. He may have been the Willis who was already a member of Bob's band. If so, he would have been caught again after his escape from jail in September 1823, and condemned to deportation. In any event, the release of these two men was premeditated and it is possible that Sam and his men had no intention of freeing anyone else.

The bandits left a trail of thefts in Virginia. In May, six were seen together about fifteen miles from Halifax. Despite their success at staying clear of the militias and slave hunters who tracked them all the more closely after they had killed a white man, four of them concluded that the woods were no longer safe enough. They decided to exchange their life as "banditti" in the South for that of runaways posing as free men in the North. Like other fugitives who left the region, they had to face the prospect of parting from their loved ones and friends and, as maroons who had lived far from white control and scrutiny, a life once again spent under white authority.

The men who opted for the North knew the Southern land like no one else. Their survival skills were optimal. They could have made their way through the woods crossing the Mason-Dixon Line, but they chose another path, one that was faster but more perilous. In June, Jim, Jack, Willis, and Sam boldly walked with their weapons into Petersburg, Virginia. They went to the docks, asked Captain Collins where his ship was sailing, and told him they wanted to go to New York. The captain suspected he was talking to runaways and asked for their documents. They produced papers that identified them as free men but Collins had little doubt they were forged. He took the men to the ship's hold as if to accommodate them and locked them up.

The four men were promptly jailed and questioned. Jack confessed that Jim had killed Elisha Cross.[42] The weapons they carried on board Collins's ship were examined. They offer valuable insights into the maroons' endless search for and dependence on arms and ammunition. They had two guns, one was very large and its barrel was broken in two. Interestingly, "it was loaded with shot, slugs, old buttons, &c." The makeshift ammunition is proof that Bob's group was going through difficult times in terms of supply, which may have contributed to the four men's attempt to go North.[43] The other weapon was a "most dangerous knife, evidently intended for the purpose of a dirk, having been ground to a very sharp point."[44]

The men were transferred from Petersburg to Gates County, where they had killed Cross and freed two men from the speculators' coffle. The reward for their apprehension, that now amounted to $1,200, was divided among several people.[45] In November, Jim was hung for Cross's murder and confessed at the gallows.[46] What happened to his companions is not clear, but their leader Bob remained at large.

The group committed a long list of what were considered crimes and felonies: they marooned, robbed in two states, procured or wrote counterfeit free papers, broke out of jail, freed slaves, killed a white man, and tried to escape North. The variety of their illegal undertakings is a good illustration of the range of activities in which bandits engaged.

FROM JOE TO FOREST

Between May 1821 and October 1823, a large area around Georgetown was plagued and truly transfixed by the activities of a band of bandits who caught the local imagination like no others. For over two years their saga appeared in newspapers not only in South Carolina but also across the Northeast. The alluring personality of their leader was part of the fascination, as was the group's ability to strike in broad daylight, disappear without a trace, and reemerge far away for another hit.

The story started with maroons gathering around a charismatic leader, who according to aggrieved citizens "had the art and the address to inspire his followers with the most wild and dangerous enthusiasm."[47]

His name was Joe, and he escaped at an unknown date from Mr. Carroll in Richland District about 140 miles north of the site of the first incident for which he became a wanted man. One of his close associates was Jack. Born in Virginia and a victim of the domestic slave trade, Jack was owned by a Mr. Fonberg in Lancaster District close to North Carolina.[48] He had walked about 200 miles before joining the group. Another man, also named Jack, had run away from Mrs. Horry from Cat Island, a few miles south of Georgetown. Seventeen people, including five women and one child, appear in a variety of records.

On May 27, 1821 Joe and the two Jacks left their camp on South Island, jumped into their canoe, paddled down the North Santee River, took a turn on a small creek, and went cattle killing on George Ford's plantation. Ford, a wealthy planter who owned forty-nine people, learned from some of them that his livestock was in danger, and went with them and a white carpenter in search of the thieves.[49] The three maroons, anticipating their arrival, walked up one and a half miles, choosing a convenient place to ambush the group. Jack the Virginian shot and killed Ford while a slave took the other Jack prisoner.

Jack, willingly or under duress, implicated Joe in another violent incident. He said he had shot at a Mr. McClenan of Santee who had narrowly escaped with his life when his horse had veered and taken flight. Following this revelation and "[t]he unprovoked and dreadful murder of [a] worthy fellow-citizen," Governor Thomas Bennett issued a proclamation offering $200 for the apprehension and conviction of Joe and Jack.[50] This money was in addition to the $300 the citizens of Georgetown and vicinity had already raised.

No doubt through Jack's confession, it was leaned that the maroons would go back to their camp on South Island to get their clothes and then take refuge in a swamp created by the confluence of the Wateree River and Thomas's Creek. Its location was judiciously chosen: the camp was hidden behind canebrakes and offered an excellent view of the river and everyone who traveled on it. To get there, the maroons had to go up the Santee River, cross the Congaree, and pass through several counties. It was a long and risky trip. Armed with this information, in the heat and the pouring rain, day and night, the militias scoured the woods and the swamps up to thirty miles from Georgetown. Their dedication paid off because on May 30, three days after Ford's murder, one of their detachments came across Joe, Jack, and a woman. When the trio refused to stop, the militia fired. Once again, Joe was able to escape but the woman was wounded, and Jack was caught.[51] Charged with Ford's murder, he was tried the very next day.

Using the words and the perspective of a black man and a friend, Jack (Horry) had described Jack the Virginian simply as being short and thick, but white citizens reinterpreted this as the physical characteristics of the stereotypical "black brute" akin to an ape that loomed large in the white imagination. Of medium height, 5 feet 7 inches, he was "athletic, black, [with] projecting forehead,[and] dark, heavy and lowering eyebrows." As if his physique were not frightening enough, his demeanor was also characterized as scary and nasty: Jack had "a terrible expression of countenance." During his trial, he was true to his reputation. He "exhibited no[t] one mark of penitence or sorrow, but preserved the utmost stubbornness of features and of manner."[52] Seen from another perspective, his defiance and his refusal to participate in his own trial revealed a man who declined to abide by the rules of a system he knew was heavily stacked against him. By not repenting, he refused to admit he had done anything wrong. The court found the evidence "very conclusive that he was either the actual perpetrator of the deed, or so far an accomplice, as to have been at the elbow of him that shot the fatal gun." Condemned to be hanged, Jack was executed a week later on June 8, and his body was given to surgeons for dissection.[53]

Volunteers, ordinary citizens, and the militia continued to search for the rest of the group and especially for its leader. They were looking for a man whom Jack (Horry) had described as being "yellow" but not a mulatto. Out of the corpus of color and race terminology established to describe "others," Governor Bennett chose "Indian complexion."[54] In other words, according to that particular color scheme, he was light-skinned and of copper hue. Another white man described him as "not very yellow."[55] Joe's color evidently varied according to who was describing it: he appeared lighter to blacks than to whites. However, all agreed that he was not "black." They also concurred that he was tall: "about," "at least," "over" six feet. Tall, slim—he weighed about two hundred pounds—and light-skinned, Joe was not the conventional black brute of racist lore. But if he did not look the part, he too was a "bad Negro." His body—described by the governor—mapped many battles. He had a scar the size of a half dollar on one of his cheeks, occasioned by the bite of a black man during a fight. One of his arms had been scarred by a saber, perhaps the vestige of an attack by a white man. He had been shot at, maybe as he ran away, and bore the marks on both legs.

According to a Charleston paper he was "an artful and bold fellow, and approaches in hardihood to the character of 'Three Fingered Jack,' the celebrated bandit of Jamaica."[56] It is interesting to note the similarities between Joe and Three Fingered Jack, the leader of a group of about sixty maroons who lived in the Blue Mountains. Both men acquired almost mythical stature while alive, their audacious raids and killings duly covered by the press. Jack—an African whose ethnic identity has been debated—became so legendary that novels, a pantomime, and a play inspired by his life started the very year he was killed, in 1780.[57] He was presented as a fallen aristocrat, intrepid, astute, artful, and a born leader; but also as vengeful and violent against both whites and blacks. Likewise, Joe, the tall, slim, and light-skinned man could also capture white people's imagination. He was charismatic, they conceded with dread; he had that élan often found in social bandits. Joe was also absolutely determined to stay free at all costs. Information relayed to the governor stressed that he threatened to sell his life dearly, and had declared he would not be taken alive.

Soon Joe's skill at remaining well hidden earned him a nickname. He was called Forest (and will be referred to as such in this book from here on). Forest was, indeed, well adapted to life in the woods. A white man who ran into him reported that the tall athlete walked with long strides that quickly covered much land. He also had a peculiar appearance. The few descriptions of maroons' dress that have surfaced generally depict the piteous appearance of those who came out of the woods with not much on. But Forest's garb was different in two respects. First, his clothes were brown. Newspaper notices reveal that the dominant color of the runaways' garments was white, followed by blue, and less frequently brown. Because Forest was a careful, skillful maroon his clothes may well have been a camouflage for a hidden life in the swampy, woodsy environment that was his home. Maroons had difficulty getting clothes and they took what was available, but it is conceivable and indeed logical that if they could put their hands on dark cloth or clothes, that would be their first choice. It is not possible to know for sure if Forest's dark dress was typical of the maroons, but basic survival dictated that the men and women who lived in the wilderness concealed their bodies by taking on the color of the trees and bushes that surrounded them. It was easy to dye light-colored garments in the woods. The various barks that people on the plantations used to change the color of their own clothes came from the forests around them.[58]

The second striking element in Forest's appearance is that it involved a garment that can only be called a bulletproof vest. He had fabricated a large pack "which no ball can well penetrate."[59] There is no description of this device and what it was made of, but a depiction of a protective garment manufactured and worn by a maroon who lived in the Great Dismal Swamp does exist. When captured, the man "had on a coat that was impervious to shot, it being thickly wadded with turkey feathers."[60] Whether they were efficient or not, these contraptions are of major interest. They showcase the men's ingenuity and their determination to stay alive and free as well as how they constantly felt at risk. There was hardly a moment or a place when and where maroons could consider themselves safe. The bandits were even more exposed as they confronted white men on their own turf: plantations, stores, or open roads. Was similar gear common among maroons? There are too few descriptions of their way of life to make a positive determination, but the existence of protective garments, reported in two states at different times, suggests that they were probably not exceptional.

Forest and his followers continued to elude capture. They were adept at moving undetected through several districts. How many there were in the band was never established, but a newspaper deemed them "very inconsiderable."[61] When one adds up the names of all the individuals who were recorded as having been killed, captured, or sighted, they seem to have been fewer than twenty. It was rather large on the maroon scale for the United States, especially for a mobile group whose territory stretched over South Island, Richland, Orangeburg, Beaufort, Georgetown, Williamsburg, and Sumter districts (counties). The maroons' "neighborhood" was thus close to 5,500 square miles; the logistics needed to move men, women, and children undetected—even if they did not all travel at the same time—from one area to another were not simple. The journey itself was uncertain, and once they reached their destination they had to procure enough food and other necessities for the whole group. Their peregrinations covered the entire maroon landscape. They sometimes disappeared in "the deep recesses of the swamps and cane-brakes," the "dark and impervious swamps," but they also stayed close to plantations.[62] Forest's "own range" was Mrs. Horry's plantation on Cat Island. The group thus practiced both borderland and hinterland marronage, and each type of site it stayed at required the mastery of different skills.

An efficient network of allies enabled the band to move around undetected. Forest was on the verge of being arrested several times; but thanks to "intelligence and support furnished him from some of the neighboring plantations," he escaped even when closely monitored. In early June he tried to go up the Santee but had to abandon his canoe, provisions, and some clothes and hide again in the swamps when he was—as he had been so many other times—informed of the militias' moves.[63]

But Forest was soon to make a mistake that almost cost him his life. On June 21, he daringly camped out half a mile from Captain William S. Harvey's plantation on the Sampit River, thirteen miles from Georgetown.[64] Around 6:00 p.m., Harvey noticed some smoke in the distance and accompanied by one of his men, he approached the area, where Forest was quietly cooking. When discovered, he seized his gun and fled to the bush. There was another armed "stout black fellow" with him, so Harvey thought prudent not to engage the duo. He retreated. Forest and his companion did not attempt to shoot and the incident was closed.

Or so it seemed. The near fatal episode did not deter the men, who had unfinished business. At midnight Harvey heard his cattle rumble, twenty yards from his door. He did not get out to check but the next morning, he noticed the tracks of three individuals coming from the area where Forest and his companion had been eating the night before. He also found that about six pounds of lead had been unfastened from a large seine and that a small canoe and a flat were missing. The maroons had taken off with a provision of lead for their guns, a boat to navigate the creeks and the rivers, and a flatboat to transport whatever goods they could get. Two detachments of the militia traced the maroons to a swamp but were unable to find them. Forest, true to his name, had melted back into the woods.

He reappeared on July 1, a Sunday morning, when an elderly dark-skinned man and a "stout mulatto" named Joe, armed with a gun and what seemed like plenty of ammunition, entered a house on Turkey Creek in Williamsburg District. To the girl who threatened to call her owner, Joe responded that he would kill him if she did. When she tried to escape, he warned her he would shoot her if she ever gave the alarm. The men left with two pounds of shot and some powder. A manhunt came up empty-handed.[65] Even though they came with ammunition, Forest and his companion wanted more. A large mobile group constantly on the run and with no other source of food than what they hunted and stole needed a constant supply. Still in July, Jack was tried "as an accomplice or associate" in the murder of George Ford. He must have acted in a manner quite different from Jack the Virginian, his late companion, and perhaps provided useful information, because even though he was sentenced to be executed the court unanimously asked the governor to pardon him, provided he was banished from the state.

Banditry along with his community's support allowed Forest and his group to continue their exploits into the summer of 1822. A newspaper lamented:

Indeed, by threats and persuasion, his communication through that means, with different parts of the country, had become very extensive;

and his intimacy and influence over the negroes in the neighborhood of his encampment, rendered every attempt which had been made to take him, abortive. The various channels through which he received information of every movement made or plan devise, to effect that object, enabled him to act with impunity in many instance, under circumstances and in places, which the most daring villainy would scarcely have conceived.[66]

The connection that bandits maintained with the men and women on the plantations was key to their continued existence, and domestics and other trusted people were undoubtedly the most critical link in their information networks. They were the ones in a position to overhear search plans and even to be integrated into the parties put together to purge the wild areas surrounding farms and plantations of maroons. Forest was undoubtedly quite adept at winning them over.

But at last some good news for white South Carolinians came in November 1822 when the news broke that Forest had been wounded in Clarendon District and was "quite lame." Two of his men were captured and stated that their companions were on their way to Mrs. Horry's plantation.[67] Winter was approaching and they may have opted for the lives of plantation maroons, close to friends and relatives. With that kind of precise information, hopes began to rise that the group could be got rid of once and for all. Yet nothing more was heard about it until nine months later. By then the maroons had retreated to one of their hinterland camps in the swamps.

In September 1823, the press was eager to publish the account of another fatal episode that added to Forest's infamous reputation as a murderer.[68] On August 29, he and four armed men left their secluded swamp camp and walked up to the plantation of former Governor James Burchill Richardson in Sumter District. In front of everyone in the field, Forest shot the driver dead and also fired at the overseer several times, but missed. The killing of the driver is noteworthy for three reasons. First, the manner in which it was executed in plain daylight, in the presence of the field hands and the overseer, bespeaks an immense bravado and disregard for Forest's own safety and that of his men. Their status in the community must have been greatly enhanced by this latest audacious action. Second, that the driver was a black man, a member of the community, did not necessarily temper their enthusiasm, because many drivers were perceived as traitors and mere instruments of white domination. Third, the killing was retribution. Forest had threatened the man's life several times, it was reported, and finally acted upon his menace, which may be the most significant part of the episode.

Forest had a wife, Dinah or Diannah of St. Matthews Parish in Orangeburg (now Calhoun) District.[69] He was also reputed to have in the camp with him a young mistress.[70] He also supposedly held a third woman (from Belleville, the plantation of French doctor Jean-Louis Raoul of St. Matthew's Parish) against her will for several months in his various camps and forced her to be his wife. The story went that Richardson's driver was instrumental in freeing her and had therefore incurred Forest's wrath, which led to his murder.

If the driver had rescued the woman once, then she was kidnapped again because she was with Forest until the end. The sequence of events and the reality of the kidnapping are not clear, but the official version from her owner was that she had been "forced from [his] Employment."[71] He had good reason for wanting to present her as a hostage because he thought he had a case for compensation. The driver's murder—he was "a valuable slave"—and his firing at the overseer together signed Forest's death warrant. If the boldness of a man hunted down through several districts knew so few limits, it was legitimate to wonder what dreadful action he could engage in next. So on October 2, the citizens of Pineville settled on a new tactic. They decided to offer rewards "to certain negroes" to get their assistance.[72] The plan did not have time to come to fruition.

For several days, a party from Clarendon District had been searching the Santee River Swamp in oppressive heat. They were discouraged and dispirited as they realized that the maroons had numerous places of refuge at their disposal, all difficult to find and access. They were ready to give up when on October 4, Royal led them close to the maroons' camp on the Santee near the canal.[73] This Royal "with considerable judgement [*sic*] and address managed to decoy those whom he had long sought towards the boat, where were stationed a party expressly detailed for this duty." When Forest and his men realized they had been ambushed, they charged with their muskets. The militia returned fire and Forest and three men were killed on the spot.[74]

Another version, given by one of the militiamen, stated that it was the four maroons, muskets in hand, who had ordered the boat to land. When it did, the white men fired at them. Three maroons fell dead into the canal and the fourth jumped overboard but was shot and drowned.[75] However the incident unfurled, true to his word, Forest was not caught alive but, contrary to his desire, was unable to sell his life dearly. He was defiled in death, his body mutilated. The severed head of the young man was "stuck on a pole at the mouth of the creek, as a solemn warning to vicious slaves."[76]

Three days later, a raiding party irrupted into the survivors' camp. In the melee, a three-year-old child was shot through the head and died. One maroon was captured, one escaped, and a white man was wounded with duck shot. The next day, the militia came across more of the group in the woods: two males and three females. One man escaped after slightly wounding a pursuer. The other was caught, as were the women. One, described as a girl, was said to be Forest's mistress. Another was the widow of Anderson, a maroon who had recently been killed. The third, who was wearing a man's coat, was shot and seriously wounded. She was Forest's "kidnapped" wife.[77] The fact that she had remained with her companions even after his death and had been shot during the raid raises serious questions about the reality of her status as an unwilling maroon.

Forest's group survived for at least three years. It was relentlessly pursued and in the end, decimated. Jack and Stephon were hung, four men and a child were shot dead, two men and four women were captured, and Jack was banished. The death ratio was high: close to half the maroons were killed. Two men and a woman eluded capture but one man, Isham, was finally arrested almost a year later, in the summer of 1824.

The role a handful of enslaved men played in the capture and killing of Forest and his companions had been crucial, but the people they helped were not eager to compensate them. The rewards they expected and were promised were a long time coming, if they came at all. Jack and Tom, who arrested one of the maroons, collected $50 ($1,200 today) each in 1834, twelve years after the event. Billy, the man who had made a deal with the citizens of Pineville and "had endangered his Life" in an unsuccessful attempt to capture Forest, was told he would receive $47 (about $1,000 today.) In 1824, a group of citizens petitioned the legislature on behalf of Royal, the man who took the militia to Forest's camp. They asked for "such compensation as may be fully adequate." Finally the decision was reached in December 1825 that his owner would be paid $700 ($15,000 today) if she freed him within three years, but no documentation has surfaced as to the effective payment. It is therefore possible that Royal remained enslaved.[78]

When Joe became Forest, he turned into a quasi-mythical figure. To enslaved men and women the forest was the place of freedom; by bestowing such a name on him, they acknowledged his preeminence as a skilled maroon, a man who merged with the woods, the perimeter of autonomy and liberty. Forest was a hero who enjoyed the admiration and support of his community even as he was branded a dangerous criminal by whites. This esteem was precisely what made him feared the most. Forest's life

> was marked by crimes, by mischiefs and by the dissemination of notions the most dangerous among the blacks in our sections of the country. Such as were calculated in the end to produce insubordination and insurrections with all the hideous train of evils that usually follow. Such at length began as we believed to be the danger arising from the power and influence of this example and such we believed were the indications given of approaching insurrection, that we deemed expedient to call on the proper military department to send an adequate force either to capture or destroy a species of enemy that kept our families and neighbourhoods in a constant state of uneasiness and alarm.[79]

This petition, signed by eighty citizens of five districts, vastly overstates the case. If Forest ever encouraged others to settle in the swamps they did so without joining his ranks, and nowhere on the plantations or in town did any insurrection take place, nor was one even in the making. All the same, Forest the daring bandit, the charismatic leader, the woodsman with the bulletproof vest, inspired much admiration among his people; they in turn offered him crucial assistance.

* * *

As the cases studied here show, banditry was one of the means that allowed a minority of maroons to support themselves as they sought to maintain their freedom and improve their living conditions. Paradoxically, given their lives of crimes, the bandits enjoyed widespread complicity. Enslaved and free blacks acted as intermediaries, purchasing with stolen money what the bandits could have difficulty buying on the open market. And while bandits robbed white men and women, they also relied on networks of white traders, fencers, and small farmers. Sooner or later the horses, the silver, and the gold found their way back into white hands. White dispossession and white complicity were thus intrinsically linked to the point of forming one of the cornerstones of many bandits' very existence. In the end they reinjected some of what they had taken into the larger economy, but there is no indication from the sources as to what they did with the rest.

From a social point of view the bandits were a tangible threat. In contrast to ordinary maroons who killed mostly in self-defense, the bandits' attacks were cold-blooded retaliations, the taking out of someone they considered a nuisance. The hate and fear they inspired were symbolized by some of the terminology used to describe them: monsters in human shape, wretches, lurking assassins, lawless predators, desperadoes, daring villains. Moreover, they aroused alarm not only because of their assault on property and life but also because they were viewed—even more than ordinary maroons—as potential initiators of widespread trouble. It was feared that such audacious men who, instead of avoiding contact with whites, dared to menace and kill them, could inspire sympathetic enslaved men and women to revolt.

However, bandits were not revolutionaries whose intention was to overthrow slavery. But criminality itself was a means of resistance, epitomizing their rejection of the social and moral order. To people on the plantation, bandits offered a counterimage as daring outlaws, avenging champions overtly challenging white authority, living on their wits, and attacking and sometimes killing in cold blood those who benefited from an oppressive system. As long as they did not turn against their own people, which would have put them in a precarious situation, enslaved men and women lent them the support crucial to their very existence.

[10]

MAROONS, CONSPIRACIES,
AND UPRISINGS

THE Alleghenies "are the basis of my plan. God has given the strength of the hills to freedom, they were placed here for the emancipation of the negro race; they are full of natural forts, where one man for defense will be equal to a hundred for attack; they are full also of good hiding places, where large numbers of brave men could be concealed, and baffle and elude pursuit for a long time." This was John Brown's vision of guerillas as liberators of the enslaved, as he confided in a skeptical Frederick Douglass in 1847.[1] He believed he could gather a hundred hardy men whose main occupation would be to "run off the slaves in large numbers," thereby destroying the monetary value of slavery. This in turn would cause slavery to collapse, as it would no longer make economic sense. From this perspective, runaways like Douglass were only chipping at the system on a small scale and Brown had only contempt for them. In his plan, the men of the mountains would "send the weak and timid to the North by the Underground Railroad." Guerilla ranks would increase only with "the brave and strong ones."

More than a hundred years after they were first touted as a potential Jamaica-like source of dangerous conflicts because of a hypothetical maroon expansion, Brown was putting the Alleghenies back on the map of black freedom and maroon guerillas at the heart of his grand plan to end slavery. His friend, journalist and activist James Redpath, was also convinced of the revolutionary potential of the maroons, the prospective leaders of a "servile revolution."[2]

We know what happened to these plans and predictions. But did the maroons organize conspiracies, did they launch or participate en masse in insurrections? Did they attack the slave system, guerilla-style as some scholars continue to assert? The analysis of major conspiracies and uprisings in South and North Carolina and Virginia allows us to bring some responses to these questions.

THE 1765 SOUTH CAROLINA CHRISTMAS CONSPIRACY

Sometime in December 1765 Isaac Huger informed Lieutenant Governor William Bull that his wife had overheard two black men talking about a general insurrection "to massacre the white people." The slaughter was scheduled for Christmas Eve. Confirmation of the plot came from two black men from Johns Island who revealed it "through friendship to the white people." Bull, noting that eight thousand Africans had been introduced that year despite a three-year ban on the international slave trade, wondered if "this sudden Addition to a number already beyond a prudent proportion will be productive of unhappy consequences." The rumored insurrection, he believed, was one of them. To thwart it, a party of one hundred militias was ordered to guard Charleston; in addition the numerous sailors already in town were requisitioned.[3]

Bull later learned that 107 individuals left their plantations soon after the conspiracy was discovered and joined "a large number of Runaways in Colleton County, which might increase to a formidable Body." Several slaves suspected of taking part in the plot were apprehended and endured "a very long examination." Bull told the Council to be on its guard and not to let itself be lulled into complacency by the apparent tranquility. "The cause of our Danger is domestic," he stressed, "and interwoven with almost all the employments of our Lives, so ought to be our attention to the Remedy."[4]

To dislodge the maroons and the new runaways, Bull ordered the recruitment of Catawbas as Indians struck "terrour into the Negroes and the Indians manner of hunting render them more sagacious in tracking and expert in finding out the hidden recesses where the Runaways conceal themselves" than the English could ever be. "To spirit them on in their hunting out the negro camps," in addition to a blanket and ammunition, they were to receive 30 pounds for each maroon taken alive and fifteen if dead; while the owner was to be paid 200 pounds maximum.[5] The search lasted several weeks, at the end of which the Catawbas brought in five individuals while the militia seized another two to four. It was a meager result given that the group of new runaways alone was said to be over a hundred.

Perhaps they were not that numerous to begin with. But what is more important is that maroons and runaways were quite adept at eluding capture. Even the expert Catawba trackers were not able to discover what Bull called "these dangerous knots of runaways." When, three years after the event, Governor Charles Montagu described it to Wills Hill, then Secretary of State for the Colonies, he may have overstated the Catawbas' prowess:

The year 1766 afforded a very strong proof of their utility on such services for about the Christmas of 1765, many negroes having fled into large swamps and other circumstances concurring there was great room to apprehend that some dangerous Conspiracy and Insurrection was intended and though the Militia was ordered on duty and were very alert on this occasion the Governor thought it proper also to invite a number of the Catawba Indians to come down and hunt the negroes in their different recesses almost impervious to White Men at that season of the year. The Indians immediately came and partly by the Terror of their name and diligence and singular sagacity in pursuing enemies thro' such Thickets soon dispersed the runaway negroes apprehended several and most of the rest of them chose to surrender themselves to their Masters and return to their duty rather than expose themselves to the attacks of an enemy so dreaded and so difficult to be resisted or evaded for which good service the Indians were amply rewarded.[6]

That a number of refugees left the swamps and returned to slavery is doubtless true, but at the same time desertions continued. As late as April botanist John Bartram complained, "plantation negroes . . . is daily running away." He added, "ye people was forced to hire ye Catawba Indians to hunt them & if thay can take them alive to do it for double price of those thay killed which made several to come home again but yet many lurketh about in ye swamps amongst ye inhabitants."[7]

The Christmas 1765 episode raises a number of questions. One concerns the difference between maroons, conspirators, and runaways; especially because maroons were referred to as runaways. Did the maroons take part in the plot? Bull believed that the large numbers of "negroes, said to be run'd away" who lived in the swamps near Horse's Shoe and Spoons Savanna, "may give some kind of encouragement" to others to think of a general insurrection.[8] In other words, these runaways were indeed maroons since they *lived* in the swamp. But they were neither the instigators of the conspiracy nor did they play any part in it. It was only suspected that they could *encourage* the plan. Was their mere presence an incitement to revolt because the conspirators knew they could fall back on the maroons if their movement failed? The 107 people said to have fled to the swamps after the plot's discovery could indicate as much. But was there a plot to begin with? The Christmas revolt was a recurrent theme throughout Southern history, and the reality of this one is as doubtful as most others.

TOM COPPER AND THE 1802 NORTH CAROLINA CONSPIRACY

Coming on the heels of Gabriel's conspiracy that gripped Virginia in 1800, fear of a widespread insurrection swept through seventeen of its southern counties at the beginning of 1802. Copies of subversive letters, allegedly written by the conspirators, were sent to the governor in January. They enumerated the number of men involved, the types of weapons in their possession—muskets, scythe blades, swords, clubs—and their objectives, which consisted of killing the whites, destroying Richmond, and taking the state.[9] Fear engulfed eleven counties in northeastern North Carolina in the spring. "We are all under arms—a negro plot was discovered ten days past, which had been very serious," an anxious citizen of Elizabeth City lamented, "and we find that there is a chain of those horrid savages running through this state and Virginia."[10] Searches, arrests, interrogations, whippings, ear cropping, and hangings followed. Through questioning it emerged that an uprising had been planned for June 10 during a religious meeting. The objective was to kill the whites, take their weapons, and burn down their houses. Witnesses and defendants made several mentions of help anticipated from Virginia.

What happened in Pasquotank County is of special interest because the presumed head of the conspiracy, Tom Copper, was said to live in the swamps. He has been presented by historians as a maroon leader from the Great Dismal Swamp, even though contemporary court documents clearly show that his supposed sanctuary was located miles away from there.[11] People in North Carolina were full of dread as a result of news received through word of mouth and documents. One of these was a letter from Enoch Sawyer who relayed on May 10 what he had heard earlier that day at the Court House in Camden County. Sawyer was the owner of thousands of acres and twenty-one people, operated a ferry, had been a member of the House of Commons, and the host of President James Monroe at his Fairfield residence.[12]

According to Sawyer's letter, the conspirators' plan in Camden was to march to the River Bridge, gathering all those who would join. They would then massacre the whites and continue on to Elizabeth City where they expected to receive reinforcements. A number of poor whites, they hoped, would join them. Joe (owned by Mr. Jarvis) of Pasquotank County was to command the cavalry they planned to raise there. The conspiracy was far more extensive than previously thought, stressed Sawyer, with blacks from Edenton and Norfolk in on the plot.[13]

Although the letter did not mention him, it was quickly asserted that the leader in Pasquotank was Thomas, alias Tom, alias Tom Copper. The name Tom appears in various documents, but refers to more than one man. Evidence for the fact that they were different individuals lies in the name of their owners. Two court documents state that Tom Copper was the property of "Andrew Knox, practioner [*sic*] of Physick [*sic*] & surgery of the County of Pasquotank."[14] Knox owned a plantation in Nixonton worked by more than thirty individuals—including the carpenter Elijah

Knox, Harriet Jacobs's father.[15] Following his escape from Knox's plantation, Copper was reported to be living in a camp in the swamps.

After the plot was revealed the Elizabeth City jail was soon "full of negroes." At least thirty-two men were locked up in May. Within two days, two men said to be Tom's lieutenants were caught and sent to Hertford, Perquimans County.[16] The circumstances of Copper's own arrest are not known, but he was detained and managed to break away. He was already gone by May 12 and was consequently outlawed.[17] Two Toms appear on the list of prisoners compiled by the jailer at Elizabeth City for the month of May, but they were not Tom Copper. Their owners were William Mosley and the estate of John Swan.[18] Because Copper was not on that roll, which recorded the number of days each man spent in jail (from two days to thirty-two), he must have escaped perhaps no more than a few hours after his arrest. This was no small accomplishment given the high alert, with militia and ordinary people on the lookout for anything and anybody suspicious.

Copper's getaway was bold in these circumstances and what followed at the jail a few days later displayed similar fearlessness: a group of "six stout negroes, mounted on horseback" tried to free the prisoners.[19] The rescue effort was dangerous; the men who launched it put not only their freedom but also their lives on the line in order to save their companions. This degree of determination and self-sacrifice speaks of strong discipline and cohesiveness. Four men were arrested.

On May 12, a number of men implicated Copper when questioned. Moses declared that Caesar told him there would be "a warm Winter, a dry Spring and a bloody Summer and that he expected the Negroes to rise." He testified that Minar brought him the news and that Gilbert told him "Tom had letters." Apparently, Moses did not say anything further and there was a pause in the interrogations, following which Malachi Sawyer (kin of Enoch Sawyer) testified. He stated under oath that Moses refused to work, "saying he wanted [to] be no mans slave much longer and seeing W. [Wilson] Emersons daughter, had repeatedly said there goes my wife." It seems improbable that a black man could repeatedly tell his owner that he had views on a white woman and that he would not be a slave for too long without such outlandish declarations eliciting a reaction. After Sawyer's testimony, Moses was brought back—perhaps following torture—and said he was now willing to tell all he knew. According to this second testimony, Tom Copper was to be the captain and Samuel Overton—a free man—Minar, and Caesar, his officers. Gilbert had told him that Joe (called Dr. Joe) preached "with a pistol in his pocket & that the plot was for the Negroes to rise at reaping time and kill all the White folks, young Likely Women excepted and all the Black Women."

Another witness, Bob, declared that Minar had told him that Tom Copper and Toney Harvey were to write to Virginia to get arms and ammunition and that the rising would start at Newbegun, eight miles south of Elizabeth City. To the question of who was going to bear arms, Bob responded, "all that was big enough was to have guns given them." As for the property seized, its division among blacks "was to be decided."[20] A week later, on May 22, the trials of six "certain slaves charged with conspiracy, in promoting insurrection among the slaves or people of colour" were held in Elizabeth City. The six accused were Peter Cobb, Jarvis's Joe, Luke, Aaron, Jacob, and Doctor Joe, a preacher.[21] Each of the six men was charged with having "feloniously consulted, advised and conspired together to rebel and make insurrection . . . with a certain negro Slave called Tom alias Tom Copper . . . to kill and murder the good citizens" of the county.[22]

The main prosecution witness was Mingo.[23] He testified that around April 11, while he was at Johnstone's quarters, he heard Tom say he was the general in charge of killing the whites in Pasquotank. That day, Copper asked the men who agreed to follow him to sign a paper. According to Mingo, fifteen did so.[24] He went on to say that along with David, he visited Copper in his swamp camp "last Thursday night." That was on May 13.

The court immediately ordered John McDonald, captain of the cavalry, to take a sufficiently large force and accompany Mingo to Newbegun, "where it is said there is a camp[,] to examine whether there is any such camp to be found."[25] It would have been unrealistic for anybody to think that after the arrests and the trials the camp would still be in operation. But evidently, as the phrasing suggests, the court was skeptical about Mingo's revelations, and on Monday it convicted its star witness of perjury. Did Mingo lead McDonald on a wild goose chase across swamps and marshes, unable to locate the camp? Or did he spare everybody the journey and admit he had lied? In any event, the prosecution's cases had already started to crumble.

In the end, the court completely absolved Peter Cobb, Aaron, and Jacob. It also found Joe and Doctor Joe not guilty. However, it was still suspicious and forbade them both from assembling or holding "any Meeting, Congregation or other Assembly of Slaves or other people of colour upon or under pretense of Preaching praying or exhorting or upon any other pretense whatsoever." Their owners had to post 500 pounds as security and if Joe and Doctor Joe breached the deal they would be deported from the state. Luke was found guilty of having threatened the life of his former owner, Noah Grandy, and of others as well. He was sentenced to forty lashes and had to stay in jail until his current owner posted a guaranty. Luke had to be on his "good behavior towards the good citizens" of the state for more than a year. If not, he too would be deported.

Ironically, the most severe punishment was reserved for Mingo. Convicted of perjury, he was punished according to the law of 1741. He was taken to the public pillory and stood for an hour with one ear nailed to a post. It was then cut off, after which the torture went on for another hour with his second ear. Following his mutilation, Mingo received thirty-nine lashes "well laid on his bare back."[26]

The trials and the verdicts raise some questions. That Mingo had fallaciously accused the six defendants seemed clear to the court, but what exactly did he lie about? Was Copper even involved in the conspiracy? Did the fact that Mingo could not locate his camp mean that it did not exist or simply that he had never been there? These questions are difficult to answer in part because Tom Copper proves quite an elusive figure. Nothing specific is known about him apart from the fact that, like several of the principal coconspirators, he could read and write. This was not exceptional, however; in North Carolina about 10 percent of the men advertised as runaways were said to be literate.[27] Copper's literacy does not in and of itself shed light on his personality and life because of the unknown circumstances in which he acquired that skill. He could have learned in secret as a rebel or been taught by an owner or preacher as a trusted servant. Nothing has transpired about Copper's life in the swamp. At no point in the various depositions was a group of maroons mentioned; Copper always appears in the records by himself and nothing is known as to his whereabouts after these events.

Still, maroons may indeed have been part of the 1802 conspiracy, but only a few clues show that some were involved. The clearest evidence comes from Bertie County. During his examination a man named Fed admitted that a certain Frank gave him a letter for Captain King Brown, adding that on June 10 they were going to rise and enjoining him, on that day, to break open Mr. Hunter's store to get powder. On June 2, during a search of slave cabins that letter was found in a barrel of cotton at Miles Raynor's in Colerain County.[28] The document, much washed out, is kept at the North Carolina State Archives. It is hardly legible but a transcription was made on June 6, 1802 by Captain Willis Riddick of Gates County in a letter to Colonel John Harvey. The words that can still be deciphered on the original match Riddick's transcription. Frank's letter went thus:

> Frank Sumner Capt. Will Command Merica Sumner, Ned Sumner, Cormmell Sumner, Harry, Bob Moore, Ned Moore, Jink Wateridge, Tom Simon, David Fitt, Peter Hassell, Buck Scul, Simon Hunter, Peter Hunter, Ganse Larry and we will rise at tent of June. Men wont join us we will kill them and all make to Colerain and get together and kill all, this is the line let you to Capt King Brown as you may get men in order, my guns is hid.[29]

The principals, Frank Sumner and King Brown, were jailed, tried, and hung. Scores of people were locked up and after a quick trial were branded and had their ears cropped, while others were whipped, as nothing could be found against them other than their names on the letter.[30]

Some of the men lived in Martin County where about thirty people were arrested, eight stood trial and two were hung. One witness testified that Tom (not Copper) "could get gun, powder, and shot at any time." Another stated that this Tom "expected to get arms as they would slay the country. That the runaways from the other side of the sound had brought over a case of Guns and 2 kegs of powder which were [hid?] in the swamp."[31] Evidence gathered in Bertie indicated that the conspiracy extended into Washington County, indeed on the other side of the Albemarle Sound. According to one witness, the conspirators could find a magazine containing about fifteen guns and were to get more from the neighborhood. He added, "Five or six negroes were in the swamp to guard the Magazine and ammunition."[32]

Thus, the examinations in Bertie and Washington counties revealed—among many other details about the plot and dozens of names—that men in the swamps were in charge of hiding and safeguarding guns and ammunition and perhaps also of getting more, as additional items were to be gathered "from the neighborhood." For sheer survival, maroons needed networks of ammunition providers; they could hide stockpiles of arms in their camps. Their participation in the plot as guardians and suppliers of weapons is thus plausible. In sum, what can be concluded from the evidence is that there was a maroon element in the 1802 conspiracy. Its scope is hard to assess but other than Tom Copper's activities in Pasquotank, which remain to some extent mysterious, a few maroons in other counties may have played roles in stockpiling and distributing weapons and ammunition. However, the conspiracy was not a maroon-driven movement; the people who still labored on the farms and plantations and in the towns and cities organized it and they paid dearly for it.

THE 1821 NORTH CAROLINA MAROON "INSURRECTION"

In the summer of 1821 Onslow, Bladen, Carteret, Jones, and Craven counties in southern North Carolina were gripped by a "universal panic" over an anticipated insurrection by "a number of outlawed and runaway slaves and free negroes."[33] Such panics were recurrent throughout the history of American slavery and were largely unfounded, but according to some scholars this one was based in reality.[34] They made their case on three petitions—as well as the response of the Committees of Claims to those petition—filed by Colonel William Hill of Onslow County; Captain Rhem of Craven County; and Terrence Pelletier of Carteret.[35] Hill petitioned in 1822 and 1824 on behalf of the two hundred men who, under his command, had scoured the swamps in the heat for twenty-six days in search of the maroons. A year later, they still had not been paid. Rhem and three other officers who were wounded, "probably disabled for life," during the events sought restitution in 1823 for medical bills to the total of $224, as well as financial help.

In his petition, Colonel William L. Hill—a planter who owned thirty-nine people—claimed, "an insurrection broke out."[36] There was "daily and nightly" plunder and rapine in "every corner of the county," and violence against "defenseless and unprotected families." The insurgents' ranks, he asserted, "were filled with many of the most daring cunning and desperate slaves" who were "well armed and accoutered." Not only had they "ravaged farms, [and] burnt houses," but they had also "ravished a number of females." Though the militiamen's testimonies are extremely valuable, they all had reason to magnify the "outrages of these villains" so as to better showcase the risks they took to protect their communities and thus maximize their chances of getting redress. However, when official letters and reports written at the time of the events, not merely self-serving petitions (as these documents often are), are examined, a different picture emerges.

The 1821 episode was set in motion on August 7 when six justices of the peace of Onslow County contacted William Hill in his capacity as commandant of the militia. They asked him to gather at least two hundred volunteers because they were informed that "a number of Negroes [were] lurking in our county, committing many outrageous acts sutch [*sic*] as shooting persons, breaking open Houses & burning Houses." Even more distressing, continued the magistrates, "from the length of their connection (being as far south as Wilmington and as far north as Washington [North Carolina] they intend an insurrection."[37] The upcoming uprising was thus believed to involve a large number of maroons living along an axis of about a hundred and thirty miles.

The following day, Hill forwarded a copy of the magistrates' letter to Governor Jesse Franklin and added that the "runaway and outlaying negroes" would be difficult to capture because they stayed in the swamps and dismals and could move easily to adjoining counties. Hill also reported that they increased their numbers daily "by seduction, threats and force." That maroons would recruit through "seduction" was a recurrent theme throughout the South, but accusations of coercion and kidnappings were nonexistent and these claims may have been based on nothing more than rumors. Interestingly, Hill noted that "a number" of people came from Alabama, Tennessee, Georgia, and South Carolina.[38] He probably failed to realize that some were most likely originally from North Carolina. During the 1820s, the state was an "exporter" of enslaved labor to the Deep South. There is little doubt that some of them escaped to return to their families in Onslow and were now living in the swamps.

On the afternoon of August 8, Hill sent another missive to the governor, stressing that the maroons were armed with rifles and double-barrel guns, whereas the citizens of Onslow neither had sufficient weapons, ammunition, and provisions, nor enough funds to buy them. In short order, given the alleged reach of the conspiracy, militias from other counties were called into action. In Craven, Captain John Rehm was ordered to patrol the district between Batchelor Creek and Powell's Branch. One hundred men were dispatched under the command of Lieutenant Colonel Lewis Foscue to search for the maroons in Jones County where, it was reported, one white man had been killed, several shot, and some stores and private residences robbed. In Bladen, where the maroons were accused of burglarizing houses and killing livestock, more than a hundred men volunteered to serve under the authority of Samuel B. Andres. In that county, in a daring attack similar to the one that occurred in Elizabeth City in 1802, the maroons had broken into a jail to free one of their companions, a brazen act that could have signified that the prisoner was someone of particular importance. Furthermore, it was said that the maroons made "repeated threats" to a number of citizens including

Andres himself. In Carteret, "slaves and free People of Colour had collected in arms and [went] about the County Committing thefts and alarming the inhabitants." The man in charge of putting an end to their ravages was Colonel John W. Hill.[39]

How many maroons were involved was notably difficult to ascertain. The justices of the peace in Onslow mentioned only "a number of Negroes lurking," but according to several newspapers, they were eighty in White Oak Swamp on Trent River.[40] Samuel Andres heard that there could be twenty-five to forty in Bladen, but warned that there might have been twice as many. Officials in Jones County did not go further than to say, "A number of Negroes are collected together." Exact figures were hard to come by because the maroons were mobile. In Jones, they were "going about the County," whereas in Bladen they were "ranging through the county" and "continually passing from one place to an other." Colonel Andres heard of groups of fifteen or twenty but admitted that "seldom more than 6 or 7 [were] seen together."[41]

From all indications, the maroons were well armed. Andres was informed that they had swords and guns, Onslow's justices of the peace stressed that they were "shooting persons," and William Hill had already asked the governor for arms because whites were outgunned, another of his numerous embellishments. In Jones County two white merchants, William Waters and Hardy Collins, were suspected of receiving stolen goods from the maroons in exchange for guns. The suspicion was based on the fact (or impression) that about that time Collins bought and disposed of "more guns than one private man could use."[42]

With armed maroons lurking all over the territory and hundreds of militiamen at their heels, a shootout was inevitable. It happened on August 21 in Craven County. A mailboy came to town saying he had seen three runaways near Street's Bridge on the Neuse River and one had pointed a gun at him. Based on this information, to make sure the maroons would not attack the Washington Mail Stage, Rhem's men escorted its driver across the bridge. Once on the north side, the mail driver informed the population that the runaways were near. Ten men volunteered to stop them. At night, they moved across the bridge until they came about twenty-five paces from shadows. They fired and shots were returned. Both parties retreated. Five men were injured but were able to leave the scene. After the dust had settled and day broke, the truth was revealed: the militia and the volunteers had shot at one another.[43] Among the wounded was Captain Rhem.[44] This was the only violent encounter of the entire 1821 episode.

Regardless of the silly incident, the hunt for the "insurrectionists" continued and in Bladen one hundred men in four companies—two on each side of the Cape Fear River—searched for eight days in all the places where maroons were the most likely to hide. They had orders to arrest and jail blacks caught without a pass and to confiscate weapons and ammunition. But even with this deployment of force, Andres reported that only one man, found with "an elegant Gun" in his possession, was arrested. The militia did, however, discover "considerable sign [*sic*] . . . such as camps." He attributed his failure to capture the maroons to widespread leaks: "If my intention could have been kept a secret, I have but little doubt, but that we would have been more successfull [*sic*], but they were not." Andres was blaming the people who relayed intelligence to the maroons about the militias' movements. "Consequently," he lamented, "most of the Negroes sliped [*sic*] over into other countys [*sic*] or hid themselves in some of our large swamps."[45]

In Jones County, Lewis Foscue was told that a party of white men had attacked some maroons, who in turn ran them out of the woods. The maroons pursued them through Collins's house. The accused "Negro trader" let the black men in and out and "manifested a hostile disposition toward his white neighbors." In that county, one hundred men patrolled in three groups. Forty-two went down White Oak to "skirmish up and down the river swamps and pocosins for four days." They did not see any sign of "encampment or retreat." Another group searched "all suspected places practicable in the lower end of the County and down Trent" and made "no discovery worth naming." The third group scoured the river Trent for three or four days and also searched a free blacks' settlement where the hunt proved the most fruitful: the men caught one maroon or runaway while others ran off.[46] The fifty men who scoured Carteret

County for twenty-one days under the command of Colonel Hill "submitted to many privations to the body and mind," but only arrested "some" people and drove others off. However, Hill was certain they had suppressed "the spirit of insurrection, so that peace and order was [*sic*] restored to the County."[47]

In all more than six hundred militiamen combed the woods, the swamps, the creeks, the pocosins, and the dismals of five North Carolina counties with close to nothing to show for their efforts except for a few arrests. It is significant that the patrols could not find any inhabited camps, a failure that was attributed to the maroons' mobility and efficient espionage networks. Except in Bladen, the landscape did not reveal any evidence of their presence, such as cabins, fields, stock, or tools. Even small groups should have left marks on the ground: vestiges of campfires or traces of the food and other items they were accused of stealing. Does their lack of footprints mean that their existence was simply a figment of the imagination of white citizens? There is enough evidence to the contrary. The vain efforts at finding the maroons mean rather that they had settled farther away than where they were believed to be and/or were hiding in areas that the various militias had overlooked.

In the end, only two men were detained for the 1821 "insurrection." One was Harry Black, a free black man. He was indicted for conspiracy and rebellion and was accused of having shot at whites and at their house when in the company of four or five runaways. After an appeal and a second trial Black was acquitted as these actions, in the absence "of any general or comprehensive design against legal establishments" did not amount to rebellion and treason.[48] In other words, there was no insurrection.

The second prisoner was Isom, said to call himself General Jackson, a returnee from South Carolina. In the cautious words of Lewis Foscue he was "the supposed leader." He was not hung or deported. The unusual leniency shown to him indicates that when the panic had abated, it became evident that the "peril" had been grossly exaggerated. Three years after the 1821 scare Isom was tried for larceny and condemned to receive thirty-nine lashes but he died in jail the day before the sentence was to be carried out.[49] He had cost the state "some hundreds of dollars, both for civil and military expenses," stressed a local newspaper that did not question the purportedly leading role he had played in the events of 1821.

The episode is significant for what it reveals about the maroons' activities, strategies, and the threats they could pose. There was a "universal panic" not because of what they did, but rather because of what people feared they could do if left unchecked. But why did the citizens of North Carolina think their worst nightmare might materialize that summer? What in the maroons' actions had made them think that the scenario described by the Committee on Claims in February 1825—four years after the events—was about to unfurl? According to the Committee:

> in a few fleeting hours, the houses of our citizens might be wrapt [*sic*] in flames, their throats cut, and their wives and daughters might become prey to the brutal lusts of wretches, who once let loose upon society, would stop at nothing to satiate their diabolical passions.[50]

The general reason for the panic may be found in the response in 1823 of the Committee to William Hill. It stated that the "Negroes . . . collected in unusual large Numbers, were well armed and instead of lurking about for the purpose of Concealment as had been the Custom of runaway Negroes; they had assumed a menacing attitude, had made use of threats and appeared to have [illegible] their operations to something like a system."[51] The maroons had adopted a new approach: rather than remaining well hidden and avoiding any contact, they had become assertive. In addition, they were believed to instill a spirit of confidence among the people still enslaved. Colonel Andres duly noted "[t]he insolence of those who have not left their owners."[52]

The most reasonable explanation for the maroons' increased activity, based on other cases, is the regrouping of small units in one area, particularly well chosen since it was not discovered. A large community in a transitional phase needed more food than was readily available, especially in the summer when vital crops like corn, rice, and potatoes were not ready for harvest but could be found in the plantations' storehouses. When groups coalesced, their raids focused on fewer areas—hence the sentiment that the maroon population had suddenly increased and become more predatory. Within the community itself, there would be new strength in numbers, which could explain the recent brazenness whites noted. Moreover, the maroons' ranks were filled with seasoned men from the Deep South who had proved their mettle by successfully crossing several states and avoiding slave hunters and packs of dogs. The accessibility of firearms, thanks to white traders, could only bolster the maroons' feeling of force. To the people on the plantations, this assertiveness must have been seductive and the sight of hundreds of white men vainly plodding through the swamps a satisfying one, hence their "insolence."

In Jones County, Colonel Foscue noticed there was "little annoyance" on the part of the maroons after the searches. Some, he learned, went back to their owners; "others has [*sic*] been taken," and he was sure the rest "dispersed immediately."[53] In Bladen, Colonel Andres claimed that several maroons went back to the plantations and he hoped the searches "occasioned some of the South Carolina & Georgia Negroes to hunt other quarters."[54] If he believed they had returned to the Deep South his optimism was most likely unfounded, but dispersing was the best strategy the maroons could follow given the intensity of the searches. However, as no camps or traces of camps were found in most counties, it is also quite possible that some stayed put in their well-hidden refuges.

When all was said and done, despite the white population's fears there was no 1821 conspiracy, no uprising, and, contrary to some scholars' assertions, no maroon rebellion either.

THE 1830 CHRISTMAS CONSPIRACY

On August 7, 1830 James McRea, magistrate of the Wilmington Police, sent an alarming letter to Governor John Owen of North Carolina. A "well-disposed" free black man had given him a copy of a pamphlet

> treating in most inflammatory terms of the condition of the slaves in the Southern States exaggerating their sufferings, magnifying their physical strength and underrating the power of the whites; containing

also an open appeal to their natural love of liberty; and throughout expressing sentiments totally subversive of all subordination in our slaves.[55]

The booklet, *Walker's Appeal in Four Articles*, was published in September 1829 by David Walker of Wilmington, a free man who settled in Boston. The 76-page soon-to-be-famous pamphlet unequivocally advocated violence by blacks for the overthrow of slavery: "[I]f there is an *attempt* made by us, kill or be killed. Now, I ask you, had you not rather be killed than to be a slave to a tyrant, who takes the life of your mother, wife, and dear little children?"[56]

The white population was all the more alarmed because, as McRea highlighted to Owen, enslaved and free blacks had "for the few months past frequently discussed the subject of a conspiracy to effect the emancipation of the slaves of this place." From what had been pieced together, it appeared that an uprising was to take place at Christmas. Governor Owen alerted police officials on August 19 and sent a copy of the *Appeal* to the General Assembly in November. He informed its members that the pamphlet was also circulating in Virginia, South Carolina, Georgia, and Louisiana.[57] Earlier that month Owen had received two letters that only confirmed the seriousness of the matter. One missive was sent by John Burgwyn, a New Bern merchant and slaveholder; the other by John Iredell Pasteur, major general of the militia, onetime editor of the *Carolina Centinel*, and owner and editor of the *Newbern Spectator*. Burgwyn's communication recounted how the conspiracy was actually organized, and how Walker's *Appeal* was connected to it. It also established the role maroons were believed to play in the overall plan.

At the center of Burgwyn's story was Moses. A maroon for years, "lurking" in Jones and Onslow counties, he was "well acquainted with all the haunts of the neighborhood of the runaways."[58] Moses was accused, falsely Burgwyn claimed, of killing a slave by mistake. He was actually trying to kill an overseer who was pursuing him. To avoid capture, he ran away to South Carolina where he was caught, and returned to North Carolina, where he was tried and condemned to death. While he was in prison in Newbern, the jailer's wife overheard him one night talking with two inmates: Abner, a maroon for eight or nine years, and Tom Whitfield, a "notorious bad character." A house painter in Newbern, Whitfield was advertised in December 1821. He was suspected of staying close to where his wife lived, in other words, he was a borderland maroon. Caught, he was sold in Johnston County and ran away again in 1823 before being captured in Craven County. In January 1829, after having changed owners twice, Whitfield took to the woods once more. He had "connexions" at several places, and his new owner let it be known that if Whitfield were to be killed he would not hold anyone responsible.[59]

According to the jailer's wife, Whitfield told Moses "they" had eight or nine captains and Abner said "they" had captains too and he was one of them. She could not hear anything else, but the next day she confronted Moses, asking him who those captains were and what they were going to do. Initially shocked, the prisoner proceeded to share what he knew. Whitfield told him "the negroes had determined to rise. . . . [T]hey had appointed captains . . . they had arms and ammunition secreted . . . . [T] hey had runners or messengers to go between Wilmington, Newbern and Elizabeth City to 'carry word' and to report to them." He added that they had a camp of thirty to forty people in Dover Swamp (Jones County), another about Gaston Island, Price's Creek—by Cape Fear River near Wilmington—or Brice's Creek [the original is hard to decipher], several by the Newport River (Carteret), and many others near Wilmington. Thus, according to Moses, the network of camps extended the whole length of North Carolina, from as far south as New Hanover County near South Carolina to the Virginia border in the North, and they were all connected through messengers.

Moses went on to confide to the woman "[t]hat a fellow named Derry, belonging to J. R. London [president of the Bank of Cape Fear] had come on from Wilmington [and] brought some of those pamphlets." According to what Moses had learned, "because of an alarm in the summer"—the discovery of the *Appeal*—the insurrection had been postponed until after the Christmas holiday. The plan was to rise at night; the "different gangs were to come down on the whites, fire their houses,

& kill all they met with. That the other negroes would then rise and help them." Based on Moses's confession, it appears that runaways and maroons were the prime movers of the planned insurrection, along with some people still enslaved. He gave the names of men who, according to Burgwyn, were known in town as "suspicious characters." The "other negroes" were expected to join the maroons once the movement started. The parties, Moses continued, met at different rendezvous. Some were in charge of the guns and kept them in good order. He indicated a few caches. Arms were indeed found in one of them, located in a remote area, and the white woman who had them in her possession could not give a satisfactory explanation as to what they were doing there. She also had meat, hidden somewhere in her place, and was not able to account for that either. Her young son revealed that his mother "dressed victuals" for four or five maroons every day.

A posse of neighbors were said to have located the camp in Dover and burned down its eleven houses "and made such discoveries as convinced them it was a place of rendezvous for numbers (it is supposed they killed several of the negroes)," stated Burgwyn. A camp with eleven houses could easily be home to thirty to forty people, as Moses had indicated. By American standards, it would have been a major settlement. Burgwyn was not sure if anybody was there when it was destroyed; he only supposed that several people were killed. This lack of crucial information concerning a key development is one more reason to be skeptical of the whole "discovery."

Indeed, Moses's entire testimony raises serious questions. Just transferred from South Carolina, his knowledge of the conspiracy was second hand, having supposedly been given to him a day earlier by Whitfield and Abner. Both men were in jail and thus available for questioning—including with "vigorous" methods—but there is no indication that they were interrogated. Burgwyn's case rested entirely on Moses's declarations. What may have happened is that once confronted with a conversation about "captains," he saw a chance to ingratiate himself with the authorities in the hope that this might lead to the commutation of his death sentence. He was able to point out the Dover Swamp camp and the white woman's small operation because as a maroon himself, "well acquainted with all the haunts of the neighborhood of the runaways," he doubtless knew about them long before he went to jail.

Burgwyn and the few people who were in on the explosive information wanted to keep it a secret "lest it should give those implicated time to remove all proof." They wanted time to make further inquiries and asked for a respite for Moses. John Pasteur, more pointedly, assured the governor that they needed "to ascertain the truth of his statement." Owen granted the respite, but Moses's story does not seem to have checked out: even after he had revealed that connected camps of insurrectionary maroons dotted the landscape from south to north, pointed toward their locations, and warned that the uprising was imminent, no major operation was launched to immediately annihilate the maroons. No massive arrests were made. Whitfield, one of the alleged prime movers, was later returned to his owner and escaped again in April 1831 in the company of two men as they were passing through Rockingham County.[60]

On December 1, the Joint Committee on Slaves and Free Persons of Color released its report affirming its conviction that a vast conspiracy was indeed in the works. What most worried the legislature was the possibility of an insurrection inspired by radical writings from the North and organized by literate men in the South. As a consequence, the General Assembly, meeting secretly, passed the most repressive bill in its history to further subjugate enslaved and free blacks. Evidence of the anxiety caused by *Walker's Appeal*, "An Act to Prevent the Circulation of Seditious Publications" stipulated that violators would be whipped and jailed for the first offense and would be put to death without the benefit of clergy for the second. Additional confirmation of the white population's apprehension was the passage of "An Act to Prevent All Persons from Teaching Slaves to Read and Write, the Use of Figures Excepted." It asserted that literacy excited dissatisfaction and produced insurrection or rebellion. White violators were to be fined from $100 to $200 or be jailed; the penalty for free blacks was a fine, plus jail time or whipping, and enslaved people were to receive thirty-nine lashes.[61]

In late December, the inhabitants of New Bern, Tarborough, and Hillsborough believed the uprising was still scheduled for Christmas. In Hillsborough, panic arose when a black woman allegedly told white children that she would soon be freed from them, that "the negroes were to rise & kill all the white men—some of the handsomest of the white women would be spared for wives for the leaders." In Edenton and Washington, citizens gathered weapons. In Pittsboro they received arms, and an "extraordinary insubordination" was denounced from Scotland Neck country. An unnamed "intelligent black free man" in Bladen was said to have demanded that blacks be freed and given the rights of citizens to "amalgamate with the whites without distinction." State senator Joseph Hinton was alarmed: "We are on a mine, it would appear—the match I hope will be snatched from the destructive hand."[62] In Newbern, rumors relayed by the press stated that the army had surrounded "an assemblage of sixty armed slaves in a swamp" and killed them all.[63]

Christmas night came and went. In January, a short notice from Wilmington appeared in several Northern newspapers with the information that there was "much shooting of negroes" recently in consequence of "symptoms of liberty having been discovered among them."[64] The federal troops brought on December 19 "to be prepared to meet any insurrectionary movement which may take place in Wilmington or its vicinity about the period of the Christmas holidays" remained posted until May 14.[65]

Despite widespread fears, the revelations by Moses, and the torture of numerous blacks to elicit confessions, no evidence of a conspiracy initiated by the people of the swamps was found.[66] As Hiram White, who refused to participate in the searches of slaves' cabins organized to seize written materials, concluded:

> Chatham jail was filled with slaves who were said to have been concerned in the plot. Without the least evidence of it, they were punished in divers ways; some were whipped, some had their *thumbs screwed in a vice* to make them confess, but no proof satisfactory was ever obtained that

the negroes had ever thought of an insurrection, nor did any so far as I could learn, acknowledge that an insurrection had ever been projected.[67]

NAT TURNER AND THE GREAT DISMAL SWAMP

On Sunday August 21, 1831 Nat Turner, Henry, Hark, Nelson, and Sam met at Cabin Pond, about a fifteen-minute walk from the farm of Joseph Travis, the man who had hired Nat. Two men who had not been invited also joined the group: Jack Reese (Hark's brother-in-law) and Will (a friend of Sam). They shared a dinner of barbecued pork and brandy before walking in the wee hours of Monday morning to Travis's house. Armed with hatchets and axes, they killed him, his wife, and their three children, took four guns, several old muskets, and some powder. Recruiting along the way, the group attacked three plantations, killed six other people, and took money and weapons. Turner's troop was now fifteen men strong, nine of them on horseback. By the end of the day, about fifty-five white men, women and children had been killed and reinforcements had crushed the uprising. The repression was vicious. John Hampden Pleasants, editor of the Virginia newspaper the *Whig*, stressed that some of the attacks on blacks were "hardly inferior in barbarity to the atrocities of the insurgents."[68]

Five days after General Nat, as he was known among blacks, launched what has remained the most famous slave uprising in the United States, and four days after it was defeated, some people still believed the movement had been organized and carried out by maroons. "It is now well ascertained," claimed the *Norfolk Herald*, "that the band of negroes who committed the horrid murders in Southampton, were composed chiefly or entirely of runaways, who have long infested the swamps of that county. Their object was probably to raise an insurrection among the slaves."[69] The Dismal Swamp and its maroon inhabitants figured prominently in various accounts of the events—and in some scholars' narratives.[70] A letter from a resident of Norfolk published in several newspapers asserted that "the number of insurgents had reached fourteen hundred; including six hundred and fifty who had organized themselves in the Dismal Swamp, but had not yet formed a junction with the others."[71]

The *Free Inquirer*, an abolitionist paper, informed its readers on September 17, "[S]ome fugitives who had taken refuge in the Dismal Swamp, had killed a number of persons in their pursuit of plunder."[72]

The swamp was also depicted as the intended destination of the rebels following victory. A widely shared hypothesis was that "[t]he great object of the negroes, after the rallying of the militia appeared to be to reach the Dismal Swamp, but such was the vigilance of the former that nearly every one was either shot down or captured."[73] Thomas W. Higginson, writing in *The Atlantic Monthly* in 1861, claimed, "Nat Turner intended to conquer Southampton County as the white men did in the Revolution, and then retreat, if necessary, to the Dismal Swamp."[74]

In the first scenario, the maroons became insurrectionists; in the second, the insurrectionists planned from the start on becoming maroons. In the third, the swamp was a place of refuge after the uprising had failed. According to newspaper accounts, the insurgents "are said to be on their way to South Quay, probably making their way to the Dismal Swamp, in which they will be able to remain for a short time in security."[75] The *Norfolk Herald* stated, "If any have escaped, they will be too anxious to bury themselves in the recesses of the Dismal Swamp. . . . It is believed that their gang consisted principally of runaways who have been for years collecting in the Swamp, and who are supposed to have amounted to a formidable number."[76] Although it is only logical that some people involved in the insurrection would have sought to reach the Great Dismal Swamp and other areas where they could hide—and indeed a few did—there was no massive exodus of defeated insurgents.

What about Turner? Did he, as some scholars have stated, personally retreat to the swamp? An account of his weeks on the run comes from Thomas Ruffin Gray's *The Confessions of Nat Turner*, a document whose reliability has been questioned for several decades.[77] There is no question that Gray did indeed talk with him; but the so-called verbatim quality of his text and some assertions are suspicious. However, there is little reason to doubt what Turner said about his hiding places, particularly as it has been corroborated by other sources. According to *The Confessions*, the day after the uprising Jacob, Nat, and Nat Turner concealed themselves in the woods and Turner sent both men in search of his coconspirators with instructions to meet, along with all those they could rally, at Cabin Pond, the place where they had had dinner just two days before. Turner made his way there and waited.[78]

On Wednesday he saw white men looking around the place and concluded that Jacob and Nat had been taken and "compelled to betray" him. The next day, he walked at night to the late Travis's place and gathered provisions. He then made himself a place to stay: "I scratched a hole under a pile of fence rails in a field, where I concealed myself for six weeks." Turner did not explain why he did so, but his decision was rational. The woods and swamps were teeming with militias since people believed the affair had been conducted by maroons. If he ever had plans of going to the Great Dismal Swamp, twenty miles away, they must have looked unworkable at that point. Rather than following the expected script, Turner dug himself a cave in plain view. It was a smart and bold move for a man who had $1,100 on his head.

Turner stated that in the beginning he only ventured out a few minutes at night to get water nearby. As he grew more confident, he left for hours on end, going around the neighborhood, eavesdropping in hope of gathering intelligence. Afraid of betrayal, he said he did not dare speak to anyone. This assertion is contradicted by Allen Crawford, a man born in 1835 three miles from Travis's place. He provided another version in 1937 learned from his family—his uncle Henry had taken part in the uprising and been hung—and others. "He built a cave and made shoes in this cave," he declared. "He came out a night fur food dat slaves would give him from his own mistress' plantation."[79] The reference to the shoes is unexpected, but what is important here is that in folk memory—and most likely in reality—Turner was known to have received help. If that was indeed the case, it is perfectly understandable that he would not betray his friends. For the second time since 1825 when he first ran away, he lived successfully as a self-reliant maroon, according to his own version; or he survived in hiding with the trustworthy assistance of neighbors who did not deceive him even when doing so would have been financially profitable.

The cave was a good refuge and Turner might have stayed there for a while longer. "I know not how long I might have led this life," he mused in *The Confessions*. Perhaps he envisioned remaining hidden in the open field until he could leave the area once the search subsided, but an unpredictable incident forced him to adjust his plans. The event itself was independently recorded but the details of what happened next come from *The Confessions*. One night a dog passed by the cave, and smelling meat, got in and emerged from the hole just as Turner was arriving. A few nights later, the same dog reappeared, this time with Red Nelson—who had protected his owner's wife during the revolt—and one of his friends. The men were out hunting. Nelson's dog went to the pile of fence rails and started to bark. Turner, who was close to the cave, thought he had been discovered and, stepping out in the open, begged the men not to reveal his whereabouts. They betrayed him, but before he could be caught—he may have been tipped off—he left his shelter. That Turner was deceived is not in doubt. His cave was searched and, according to newspaper reports, a pistol, a stick with notches marking the days—five weeks and six days—and a piece of bacon were recovered.[80]

Turner chose another unexpected location for his next refuge. For a while he hid in the fodder stacks of Nathaniel Francis, who saw him on October 27 and shot at him—piercing his hat, as reported in newspapers.[81] Turner probably thought that search parties would now concentrate on farmland and he changed his strategy accordingly. His next move was to conceal himself in the woods. He did not go far because the forests were still being heavily patrolled. He dug himself a cave on Dr. Musgrave's wooded land. He only had his sword, and perforce his cave was of the most rudimentary type. Nevertheless, digging a hole deep and wide enough for a man to hide in with only a sword as a tool is no small feat. Well apprised of the tricks of cave secreting, he hid the opening under the crown of a fallen tree and covered it with pine brush. His cover was obviously good as patrollers did not find him when they searched this very area on October 30.

Three versions of what happened next were recorded and their variations are minute. According to the *Norfolk Herald*, as the men moved away, Turner stuck his head cautiously out of the cave to assess the situation. The surreptitious movement caught the attention of a small farmer, Benjamin Phipps, who was dragging behind.[82] For his part, Colonel Thomas Trezevant (postmaster of Jerusalem) stated, "in a *Cave* [emphasis in the original] that he had just finished and gotton into; and while in the very act of fixing the bushes and bows to cover him, a gentleman by the name of Benjamin Phipps . . . discovered" him. Phipps pointed his gun at him, and Turner exclaimed, "[D]on't shoot and I will give up."[83] He threw down his old sword and surrendered. The *Norfolk Herald*'s version of Turner's last moments of freedom was more dramatic: Phipps asked the man whose head was protruding from a den, "'Who are you?' and was answered, '*I am Nat Turner.*'"[84] Turner's own account in *The Confessions* corroborated Trezevant:

> [I] was pursued almost incessantly until I was taken a fortnight afterwards by Mr. Benjamin Phipps, in a little hole I had dug out with my sword, for the purpose of concealment, under the top of a fallen tree. On Mr. Phipps' discovering the place of my concealment, he cocked his gun and aimed at me. I requested him not to shoot and I would give up, upon which he demanded my sword. I delivered it to him, and he brought me to prison.[85]

Knowing the woods were full of men he decided it was useless to resist and gave himself up, hoping he could still engineer an escape at a later time.

* * *

Interestingly, a significant part of the folk memory of the revolt centered on the borderland maroons' caves. William S. Drewry stated in 1900 that the second cave was about two miles from the first and "may still be seen on the farm of Mr. J. S. Musgrave, marked by the remains of a large pine, which stood at its entrance and which bears three gashes, cut by Mr. Phipps with Nat's sword."[86] Elderly African Americans from the Southampton area interviewed in the 1960s recalled stories passed on through three or four generations within a hundred and thirty years.[87] In

1969, Percy Claud could point out the location of the cave because "we worked the farm over there and my father carried us there and showed us the old cave round there."

However, the cave was not the end of the story, but the beginning:

> He [Claud's father] told me that was his cave and that was where he left from his home up there, he left his mistress and master's home, and come to build him a cave there to hisself, and while he was up there to hisself, he begin to get in union with many of his friends. And said then they began to come over here and have my table, and began to discuss the problems, what they want to do.[88]

In this version the conspirators' meeting place was not just a discreet spot, it was the cave—large enough to accommodate five men—dug by Nat, a den where he stayed before the revolt and where he took refuge after it failed. Other informants turned the revolt into a maroon guerilla war, "Old Nat's War," echoing the sentiment that prevailed at the outset of the events. According to them, Turner and his followers lived in caves in the far-reaching woods of St. Luke's Parish, Southampton County, and at night they raided the smokehouses, the cellars, and the "brandy houses." They supposedly murdered numerous whites with homemade swords over a long period of time. The basic truths of the story were multiplied and amplified. Turner's two small caves on plantation lands turned into several caves in remote locations inhabited by numerous maroons. His sword became swords, and the one-day killings turned into months of assassinations.

Although it is plausible that some of Nat Turner's followers found refuge in the Great Dismal Swamp, substantiation is scarce. A runaway who spent six weeks there in 1840 before reaching Canada met an isolated, famished man who told him he had been involved in the insurrection. He had lived in the swamp for nine years.[89] He may not have been alone from the start, but he was on his own then. Others made their way further north. In 1834, it was revealed—or believed—that a group had been living in caves near Petersburg—about fifty miles from Southampton—since the uprising.[90] On the North Carolina side, Juniper

Swamp was searched as early as September 6. A company spent several days combing the area and came back with twelve individuals, though there is no indication that they were insurgents.[91] There is no question that Turner lived as a borderland maroon for two months; but if he ever planned to create a maroon community in the Great Dismal Swamp, he never said so and none of his followers mentioned it either. Finally, although one can speculate that he might have envisioned hiding there later on, the reality is that he did not.

* * *

Evidence of American maroons engaged in guerilla warfare to destroy slavery is hard to find as the study of several events indicates even though, just as was the case with the maroons of Belleisle and Bear Creek, they have been touted as revolutionaries carrying on armed struggles for freedom. Maroons did raid plantations and sometimes killed white people but it is a mistake to see an incursion on a planter's territory as proof of war. To invade a plantation for food and supplies cannot be equated with guerilla warfare against the system.

That some maroons provided logistical support by getting and stockpiling firearms and ammunition during the 1802 conspiracy in North Carolina seems established and one cannot exclude the possibility that it happened elsewhere as well. While there is no reason to doubt that some people participated in plots and actual uprisings on an individual basis, the argument that maroons, collectively, were antislavery insurrectionists is a difficult one to make. This was the white population's fear, for sure, and when conspiracies were discovered and actual uprisings erupted, maroons were often suspected. But in the end all that remained was the suspicion that they might have encouraged the conspirators.

There is no indication that maroons inspired, led, or participated in large numbers in uprisings against slavery, either in North America or in the rest of the Western hemisphere.[92] They did not attack the military, the arsenals, the police, or the seats of political power. As historian Alvin Thompson notes for South America and the Caribbean, "Few, if any Maroon communities were in a position to wage a general anti-slavery or anti-colonial struggle."[93] But beyond mere capacity, from an ideological perspective one must question why they would have launched or triggered uprisings and revolutionary movements. They were separatists; they opted out and exiled themselves. Although they wanted to see an end to slavery, their primary goal was to obtain the kind of freedom and self-rule that could not be found within the framework of a nonslaveholding but still white-dominated society. In addition, the task of protecting their precariously free communities was demanding enough to make them weary of engaging in conspiracies and armed struggles that could result in their own annihilation.

[11]

OUT OF THE WILDS

MAROONS may have envisioned a long life of freedom in the wilderness, but most did not achieve that dream. For many, what pushed them out of the woods prematurely were militia attacks, slave hunters' assaults, sickness, and lack of prudence. The maroons who made it out alive emerged from the borderlands and the hinterlands profoundly changed both mentally and physically. The psychological repercussions of their reentry into the world of slavery were severe. Their anguish can only be guessed at, as they knew what to expect when they stepped back unto white-controlled territory and under the planters' ruthless power.

But for a number of people, the end of marronage was the end of their lives. "Some would run away en go in de woods en perish to death dere fore dey would come out en take a whipping," recalled Sylvia Cannon.[1] Men, women, infants, and children died in the wilds, their bodies never found, or discovered by chance. Charles Grandy of Virginia remembered how John Sally "[s]tayed right 'roun' de plantation. Use to come in at night an' steal hawgs an' chickens fer food. Dat ole man died in de woods. Never did come out."[2] Several men and women who went to the woods after a beating, weighed down by shackles that marked them as recent runaways, never recovered from the brutality they had endured. They died in their fetters, their bodies found by hunters. "White men come in sometimes with collars and chains and bells," said a former maroon who stated that he knew of a great many cases, "which they had taken from

[*286*]

dead slaves. They just take off their irons and then leave them, and think no more about them."[3] In the Great Dismal Swamp, "graves of people who had lived there in olden times" could still be seen in the twentieth century.[4]

When known, news of a maroon's demise could travel long distances, carried from farm to plantation by relatives and friends. As Jacob Stroyer pointed out:

> In general someone from the plantation from which they ran away, or confidential friends on some other plantation, had communications with them, so that if anything happened to them the slaves at home would find out through such parties. And sometimes the masters and overseers would find out about their death, but indirectly, however, because if it was known that anyone on the plantation had dealings with the runaway he would be punished, even though the information was gladly received by the master and overseer.[5]

Owners and overseers could rejoice because the maroon's death meant that he or she was no longer participating in the stealing, or contributing to the planter's suspicion that everyone on the plantation was flaunting his authority. But there was more to it: owners cared about their lost investment and asked to be reimbursed for their property "found dead in the woods."[6] They also petitioned to be paid the value of the maroons killed by patrols out of special funds reserved for that purpose.

Some maroons were the victims of accidents, as in the case of an out-lawed woman of Buckingham County, Virginia, who was trapped by a tree that fell on her as she was hiding. The woods were on fire, and unable to free herself she burned to death.[7] Others fell gravely ill and did not look for help, a determined stance that led twenty-three inhabitants from Christ Church Parish to complain in 1829 to the South Carolina House of Representatives that many of their slaves had died in the woods of "diseases occasioned by running away."[8]

For the vast majority of maroons, however, the end of free life did not entail death. Instead it came in one of two ways: either they were captured or they left the borderlands and the hinterland voluntarily.

RAIDING PARTIES

Professional slave hunters, like future General Cornelius Gilliam, were the maroons' scourge. His daughter Martha Collins recalled, "When my father was in his 'teens he was a man grown and a good shot and was good at tracking game, so he naturally took up tracking runaway slaves. They used to send for him all 'round the country, for a heap of slaves used to take to the swamps. He made good money at the business."[9] But going after the maroons, even isolated individuals, led a number of pursuers to lose their lives. With the help of his well-trained dog, Reuben Nash searched for a man who was "robbing and plundering in Mobile and had secreted himself in the vicinity." Nash located the maroon in the woods but as he approached, the man discharged his double barrel gun twice, killing him.[10] Joseph Stallings of Beach Island, South Carolina, was shot in the head by "one of his negroes," who had been "lurking about for a considerable time."[11] When he came upon the camp of a maroon in the Swamp of the Warrior near Demopolis, Alabama, an eighteen-year-old man was killed on the spot.[12] Several other cases of maroons killing or wounding their pursuers have come to light. But it is still safe to say that most maroons were captured without having fired a shot, even when they had a gun, perhaps for lack of ammunition. As we have seen, time and again the maroons' favorite strategy was to try to escape.

Hunting maroons down was not reserved to slave hunters. It could also be a community enterprise, as exemplified in an 1816 advertisement in an Edenton, North Carolina newspaper that invited gentlemen with dogs and guns to scour the pocosin between Nixon's Bridge in Perquimans County and Bear Swamp in Chowan "for the purpose of destroying the wild Vermin that infest them; and breaking up, if possible, the numerous camps of runaway Negroes, who outrage the peace and quiet of the neighborhood, and destroy the stock of the industrious Yeoman." This notice is particularly valuable as it reveals the existence of several camps as well as the trouble people had in locating them. The three-day expedition was expected to reinforce the social cohesion of the various strata of white society: the hunt, it was emphasized, would involve "old and young, rich and poor."[13]

Some hunting outings could be turned into pleasurable events, replete with fine food and merriment. Edward Thomas remembered vividly a particular expedition to dislodge the maroons who lived at the edges of his father's plantation:

> A well known man from Savannah, with his trail hounds, was engaged. I well remember the big eight-oared boat towed to the landing, the buffalo robes and blankets, and champagne baskets filled with hams and chickens and goodies of all kinds, the demijohns of good whiskey, in case of snake bite, the guns and ammunition, besides a sail to hoist if the weather permitted.

Everything was loaded into a boat and the blissful day proceeded quite well; the neighborhood men hopped on their horses and proceeded to search the mainland. Nobody expected what happened next:

> Scarcely had the party gotten to the woods, about a mile distant, when a large party of these runaways came running up from another quarter, and in the happiest mood, bid mother, who happened at the back door, "Good morning, Misses," and walked towards the well furnished boat at the landing. They all shook hands with me, and with a hurrah pushed off the boat and were gone. . . . I remember father's remark: "Well, they have the best boat in the county, and nothing more can be done now."[14]

Dogs were an integral part of the hunt and are as omnipresent in slave narratives as in freed people's interviews. "When you went to bed at night you could hear the blood hounds, and in the morning when you would wake up, you could hear them running colored people," remembered Scott Bond. "The white folks said the music they made was the sweetest music in the world."[15] The hounds, bred from birth to be "nigger dogs," could mangle, maim, and kill if not restrained. A hunt for maroons, described by freedman Isaac Throgmorton, shows the kind of damage dogs could inflict. Several people had been living in the canebrakes and were hunted down "with the hounds of Bullen, a great negro-hunter. The dogs pushed [one man] so that he and two others ran out, and they ran them right across a bayou, right across our road, and they catched one right at the edge of the water, and hamstrung him and tore him all to pieces."[16] Even worse, a slave hunter in South Carolina acknowledged to have killed several of the people he hunted down. He had fed at least one to his dogs.[17]

However, maroons and slaves fought back. "In general the slaves hated bloodhounds, and would kill them at any time they got a chance," Stroyer explained, "but especially . . . to keep them from capturing their fellow negroes, the runaways."[18] In abolitionist iconography and literature the fugitive was clearly the bloodhounds' victim, which buttressed the movement's propaganda that highlighted brutality against the enslaved; with few exceptions, such accounts avoided any representation of blacks as using violence. However, stories published after Emancipation and interviews of formerly enslaved men and women paint quite a different picture.

In the 1930s, Essex Henry of North Carolina, offered his insight into how bloodhounds were dealt with: "Pat Norwood took a long grass sythe when he runned away, an' as de fust dog come he clipped off its tail, de second one he clipped off its year an' dem dawgs ain't run him no more."[19] Both dogs escaped with their lives, but numerous others died at the hands of men armed with scythes fitted with a short, straight handle, the weapon of choice against bloodhounds.[20] Another freedman, William Robinson, explained how maroons made their own scythes:

> When men ran away, if in the day, they returned at night and secured a mowing scythe and took the crooked handle off and put a straight handle on it. Then they made a scabbard of bark, and would swing their saber to their side. This was to fight blood hounds with, and if the negro hunters got too close, many times they were hewn down.[21]

Octave Johnson and his group took their stand against the twenty hounds of Eugene Jardeau:

with clubs in their hands they waited at the point of junction for the attack. All day they stood together and fought the hounds, slowly retreating farther and farther into the swamp. They succeeded in killing eight of them. Towards sun-down, becoming thoroughly exhausted, with their arms and legs torn by the fangs of the dogs, and having lost much blood, the word was given to scatter and run.[22]

Unexpected allies came to their rescue. As they jumped into a bayou, "The hounds followed, and the alligators, not touching the negroes, attacked the dogs with great fury, killing six of them." Asked what he thought about the episode, Johnson replied, "Some ob 'em said dey tought t' was God; but, for my part, I tink de alligators loved dog's flesh better' n personal flesh."

With nothing more than a makeshift weapon, Isaac Williams had to get rid of two dogs as he was walking alone away from his cave. "I had rigged up a sort of weapon out of an old carving knife blade and tied it on the end of a stout pole. This knife was sharpened so that it would cut most anything," he recounted. "I slashed at the foremost [dog] and swung the heavy pole around as he sprang at my throat, cutting off his fore legs and laying him writhing and moaning on the ground." The other hound came right at him and he killed it with a stone before finishing off the first. So as not to attract attention to their presence and their dugout, Williams and his companion Henry Banks buried them.[23]

People who were the most adept at deceiving slave hunters and their dogs became folk heroes. In the woods of Richland County, South Carolina, for example, a man was celebrated and renamed in honor of his accomplishments as a maroon. He lived in the woods for seven years. "While in the woods he assumed the name of Champion, for his success in keeping slave hunters from capturing him." His last, heroic stand against dogs and their handler deserves to be recounted at length:

Champion had a gun and pistol; as the first dog ran up and opened his mouth to take hold of him, he discharged the contents of the pistol in his mouth which killed him instantly. The rest of the dogs did not take hold of him, but surrounded him and held him at bay until the hunter reached the spot. When Mr. Black rode up within gunshot, Champion aimed at him with a loaded double barrel gun, but the caps of both barrels snapped from being wet by running through the bushes. Mr. Black had a gun and pistol too; he attempted to shoot the negro, but Wm. Turner, Col. Singleton's overseer . . . would not let him do it. Mr. Black then attempted to strike Champion with the breech of his gun, but Champion kicked him down, and as he drew his knife to stab Mr. Black, Mr. Turner, the overseer, struck him on the back of his head with the butt of a loaded whip. This stunned him for a few moments, and by the time he regained his senses, they handcuffed him.[24]

Champion was sent back to his owner, who was also his father.

Men and women who did not want to engage in physical battles with the dogs concocted another kind of weapon, discreet and efficient, as described by John Hill Aughey:

> From a noxious plant indigenous to southern swamps, [the maroons] manufacture a subtle poison in which they saturate meat and place it near the kennels of hounds. The poison is nearly inodorous and insipid. . . . The maroons call it "stagger pizen," because the poisoned animal staggers as if intoxicated till almost the last moment of its existence. When pursued by hounds, pieces of meat saturated with this poisonous decoction are thrown on his tracks by the fugitive as he flies; the hounds devour it with avidity. It is a very active poison. Its fatal effects are speedily developed, and as there is no known antidote the hounds soon die in convulsive agony.[25]

Essex, a former driver and maroon in South Carolina, had still another strategy, "Firearms and poison he could not get; but, finding a bottle, he crushed it into small fragments, baked it in some bread, and fed it to the dogs, when their owners little dreamed that he was near. That meant sure death to the dogs."[26]

NEGLIGENCE AND LACK OF PRUDENCE

Some maroons were "found," which denotes a lack of caution on their part. A group of young Mississippians hunting in the forest between Bovina and Big Black River in Warren County, for example, happened upon a well-stocked camp. It was empty at the time, but they soon found and arrested two men, armed with horse pistols.[27] Likewise, nobody was intentionally looking for a family who had been successfully living in the Georgia woods for several years. Originally, a young couple had escaped and settled close to a plantation. Years later, white youngsters playing in the woods climbed up a tree and saw, in the distance, two black children. A party went looking for the latter, believing they were lost. Their search brought them to a cave where they found the couple and their two children, born in the woods.[28]

Lack of prudence was sometimes the maroons' downfall. In such cases they were not pursued or found, but they put themselves in a precarious situation. Such was the case with a woman who lived alone with her three children in the Alabama woods for a number of years. Pushed by hunger, she went out once in broad daylight to pluck corn from a plantation field. The overseer saw her and sent the dogs on her tracks. Her cave was discovered and the family brought back to their owner. Fortunately, they were caught just before the end of the Civil War and they were soon free again.[29] Hunger was also the catalyst that led to the capture of Martha Dickson of Tennessee. Hidden in the mountains, she lived on berries and the small game she trapped. When winter came and she could no longer find enough food on her own she went foraging near a village and was arrested.[30] Two men who lived in a camp made of bushes and trees in a swamp near Charleston went hunting for plums. "It was very hot, and we were tired," recalled one of them, "and towards the middle of the day we went to the brook to drink, and laid down by a log and fell asleep. Master's overseer and another man were out to hunt for niggers, and they came upon us before we knew it."[31]

These examples and others suggest that the search for food, one of the maroons' main and most dangerous occupations, may have been among the chief reasons why some were captured in the absence of specific searches for them.

Some people who were neither found nor tracked left the woods of their own volition, going back to a life of servitude, humiliation, and punishment because of their inability to continue to care for themselves. When parents died, children had little choice but to give themselves up if they could not find a maroon community to harbor them. This happened to three siblings who lived in the South Carolina woods for four years. One of them was born there. After their parents were killed, the children surrendered.[32]

Some maroons had to relinquish their freedom because they were wounded as they were being tracked down. After his owner, Mr. Thomas, shot at Emmanuel one night when he returned to Peru plantation to get food, he still managed to get back to his camp. He was seriously wounded, though, and unable to tend to his injuries he had a difficult decision to make: he could either die alone a mile from his family and friends or return to slavery. Emmanuel left the woods and told the planter's wife he had come back to die. Thomas' s son callous epilogue to Emmanuel's story was, "This man belonged to us, was worth before the shooting some $2,000; afterwards, perhaps, only $500; that shot from father's gun cost him $1,500, but it was necessary."[33]

Serious sickness often meant the end of the maroons' independence. Although they lived in the South, winter still could ruin their chances of survival. To have their toes crippled by frostbite was common. Frank had "by running away before, and getting frost bitten, lost two of the little toes of his left foot, and part of the third one."[34] Maroons suffered more serious afflictions as well: a young woman who took refuge in a hollow tree came back to the plantation because her legs had frozen. As a result, they were both cut off.[35]

Even people whose loved ones assisted them could encounter major problems in the woods. Jack Savage lived in swamps near the Savannah River for eighteen months and was helped by a network of relatives and friends. But he finally gave up and returned to Manigault's plantation, looking, according to the overseer, "half starved and wretched in the extreme."[36] Temporary or long-term disabilities could push people to abandon the wilds: a man who stayed in the woods for a year rather than leave his wife behind led such a hard existence that he temporarily lost the use of his hands.[37] Because many maroons resisted for a long time before seeking the help that would put an end to their independent lives, a number of them died prematurely. Harry Smith, a freedman born in Kentucky recalled, "Many of them often remained there [in the woods] so long exposed to cold and nearly starved that when they did return they often died from hunger and exposure."[38] A combination of unbearable stress and eating disorders was believed to have caused the demise of an Arkansan maroon. He returned to slavery emaciated and sick due to exposure and the fact that he went through periods of hunger followed by excessive eating when he finally got food. He was also extremely anxious as he tried to preserve his freedom and feed himself in the woods, and he died a few weeks later.[39]

The physical toll that maroon life took on some people was so well known that buyers sued sellers when their newly acquired property died or got sick after returning from the woods. For example, Peter's new owner learned "that some years ago, the negro ran away from his then master, in very cold weather, and that by sleeping out got both his feet frost bitten, so badly that he has never recovered."[40] In New Orleans, a buyer complained in 1855 that Dick was, unbeknownst to him, a habitual runaway. He escaped in March and was brought back in July "from the woods, where he had concealed himself in a dying condition." For three or four weeks, Dick lay in a makeshift hut, sick. Three days after his forced return, he had died of inflammation of the bowels, which, according to a physician, was "caused from exposure to dampness, cold, eating indigestible food, and various other causes."[41]

While some maroons lived quite well, they were all vulnerable to incapacitating health-related problems. The difficulty of life in the wilds was vividly demonstrated by the returnees' condition. But seen from another perspective, what their debilitated state demonstrated most clearly was their valiant effort to remain free for as long as they could.

TRANSFORMATIONS

Even when in good health, the people who emerged from the woods, the marshes, and the swamps were hard to recognize. The metamorphosis started with their clothes. They were often described as "half-clad," they "ain't wored much clothes," "de chilun didn't wear no clothes, 'cept a piece tied 'round deir waists," "'thout no clothes on," "entirely naked," "a wild, naked, little figure."[42] Such maroons, unlike some African newcomers, escaped with their clothes. Their state of half or full nakedness on their return attests to the great difficulty all maroons encountered when trying to get clothes. It also signals their marked degree of isolation.

The second thing people noticed about the maroons who returned or were brought back to the plantations was how "hairy" they were. "[H]airy as a cow," is how one woman described them. "[A] hairy ape," said another. "[H]airy as wild people," "look like wild men," stated others. The men had thick beards that hid their features. Adults and children alike had long hair.[43] They looked as wild as Cuban maroon Esteban Montejo who confided that when he came out of the woods he was "so hairy [his] whiskers hung in ringlets. It was a sight to inspire fear."[44] Green Cumby went beyond mere appearance, noting, "Sometimes dey cotched dem runaway niggers and dey be like wild animals and have to be tamed over 'gain."[45] His comment should not be dismissed as simply crude. It should come as no surprise that maroons—especially the long-term ones—who were used to being free, to taking care of themselves, to managing their time and activities, to making their own decisions, and to answering to no one, either could not or would not abide by slavery's rules. Cumby's remark illuminates the profound transformations, beyond the physical, induced by marronage.

The deep imprint of maroon life was also visible on children who had spent all or most of their existence in caves. They were noticeably different; their demeanor, posture, and attitudes were strongly marked by their unusual circumstances. "When dey come out of dat cave dey would run everytime dey seed a pusson," recalled Leah Garret.[46] Similarly, two boys, described by a man who observed them, bore the physical and psychological marks of their many years of confinement:

> After they had remained in town for more than a month, in the company of children who were noisy and clamorous, they were not known in a single instance to raise their voices higher than a soft whisper. At first, it was with great difficulty that they could stand or walk erect, and when they did attempt to walk, it was with low stoop, the bust inclining forward and with a hasty step like a partridge.[47]

Other children were said to have been "wild" and "ungovernable," only responding to their mother. They clung to her and could not be taken away.[48] Some had vision problems. One Georgia family reappeared after the war and, according to freedman George Womble, when the children got out of the cave where they had lived for several years, they almost went blind.[49] Paul Smith asserted that other children "went plumb blind when dey tried to live out in de sunlight. Dey had done lived under ground too long, and it warn't long 'fore bofe of dem chillun was daid."[50] These testimonies suggest that perhaps, for safety reasons, children were kept in caves during the day, going out only at night or maybe never at all.

For the children who got out of the woods before Emancipation, the shock of first contact was followed by the trauma of finding themselves deprived of freedom. In addition, they were thrust in the midst of strangers in a noisy environment, subject to unknown routines and rules. They witnessed the brutal punishments meted out to their parents and had to contemplate a lifetime of servitude after years of freedom, even if a restrictive one. The psychological repercussions of this vicious reality are hard to imagine.

PUNISHMENTS

Captured or returned, all maroons faced retribution. Laws that listed the punishments reserved to maroons and runaways varied in time and from one state to the other, as seen in chapter 1, but branding on the face, cutting of the ears, castration, and cutting of the Achilles tendon were all legal at one point or another. However, severe whippings were the most common penalty. They were designed to cause pain, humiliate, break the spirit, and terrorize. Even the terminology was degrading: "When they whipped us they often cut through our skin. They did not call it skin, but 'hide,'" recalled a former maroon.[51] Above all, punishments were brutally sadistic. Those who inflicted them reasoned that "There's no feeling in a nigger's hide," so one "must cut through his hide to make him feel!"[52] Elizabeth Sparks witnessed her owner "[b]eat women naked an' wash 'em down in brine."[53] On backs that were so lacerated that they looked like raw meat, owners, drivers, or overseers poured salt, red pepper, vinegar, or turpentine to increase the pain, stop the bleeding, and to act as an antiseptic.[54] William Moore, a former maroon, gave the most detailed description of the ordeal of being "whipped and pickled." His owner used to

> stake a nigger on the ground and make 'nother nigger hold his head down with his mouth in the dirt and whip the nigger till the blood run out and red up the ground. We li'l niggers stand round and see it done. Then he tell us, 'Run to the kitchen and git me some salt from Jane.' . . . He'd sprinkle salt in the cut, open places and the skin jerk and quiver and the man slobber and puke.[55]

Besides salt, brine was thickened and rubbed on the wounds with cornhusks.[56] After the lashing, people endured the additional pain of having their clothes stick to their bloody backs. Some took off their shirts and spent their workdays with the sun or the rain beating on their wounds. To keep flies and bugs away, others fixed boughs on their head and shoulders.[57] For runaways and maroons, the stocks routinely followed floggings. Locked in a cellar or a barn, they were chained by the neck to a beam, and had their feet and hands placed in holes between two pieces of wood; others had their neck and hands in the holes. They could languish in this position for several weeks, interrupted only by whippings, and for some, work in the fields during the day.[58]

The beatings were as much revenge as they were intended as a deterrent, but they did not always have the desired effect, as numerous cases of recidivism attest. Dora Franks's uncle, Ralf, got one hundred lashes and was sent immediately to the fields with blood running down his back. He worked hard until the overseer left. Then as he got to the end of the cotton row, closest to the swamp, he ran away again and was never caught.[59] Tom came back after being promised he would not be whipped, but his owner said he had changed his mind. He told the driver to give him "250 licks this time," while he watched, smoking a cigar and drinking whisky. Tom was then locked up and his neighbors were warned that they would be skinned alive if they dared give him something to eat. The elders took the risk and brought Tom bread and meat. When he finally got out of confinement, he ran straight to the woods.[60] A terrible whipping was often the very reason why some men and women had run away in the first place. A second beating, or even more in some cases, had exactly the same result. The most determined left time and again.

If sadistic whippings loomed large, other means of torture were also reserved to the captured maroons and runaways. "Granny" of Alabama, saw a boy fitted with "a piece o' iron in his mouth dat run back o' his head. He couldn't eat or speak or spit. Den dey works him in de field till he mo's dead."[61] Harry Grimes recounted that Richmond received a hundred lashes when caught, "and then they split both feet to the bone, and split both his insteps, and then master took his knife and stuck it into him in many places. After he had done him in that way, he put him in the barn to shucking corn."[62]

Some maroons never recovered. In Louisiana, "Old Lady Oater," who lived in a cave with her six children, was tied to a tree and whipped to death with a "platted rawhide whip." The driver "beat her until her skin fell off," said a witness, "an she died." The driver buried her in front of the quarters as a warning to her companions.[63] A degree lower in abjection was the fate of a young Louisiana boy who was caught by the blood-hounds, dragged behind a horse all the way back, and buried alive.[64]

It is hardly surprising, given these atrocities that a number of maroons refused to be taken alive. Suicide was their ultimate act as free people. London in 1766 and Cudgo in 1768, both outlawed in North Carolina, chose to end their lives the same way: cornered, they jumped into a river and drowned.[65] Luke, betrayed by a woman, was surrounded by three men with rifles; but he refused to surrender, telling them he knew they would kill him anyway and he was going to "sell his life as dear as he could." He kept his gun pointed to one man then another before being shot through the head.[66] In December 1836, a man in his late thirties with a long beard and "a stern countenance," who had been a maroon for a long time in a swamp near South Edisto, Georgia, continued running until he was shot so many times he had to stop. As the coroner explained, "He came to his death by his own recklessness. He refused to be taken alive—and said that other attempts to take him had been made, and he was determined that he would not be taken."[67]

Some men who deliberately chose death over slavery were ready to endure, by their own free will, torments worse than what they would have suffered if caught. Three men ran away from a plantation in Maryland and lived in the woods for several months before going back to their owner, Mr. Bris, who whipped them mercilessly until he was exhausted. He then had the first overseer whip them too. The second overseer refused to obey. The men escaped once more. Bris chased them on horseback and one gave himself up. The other two, seeing they were going to be taken, jumped into a furnace.[68] A man in Canton, Mississippi, related a similar case of ghastly suicide. A maroon who was chased on and off for four years was finally cornered by dogs: "At last, finding he could not escape, he ran deliberately into a blazing furnace and was burned to death rather than be caught and suffer the tortures that awaited him."[69]

It was not the fear of punishment that motivated these men to end their lives but the loss of their independence and their refusal to return to the degradation of servitude. They rejected compromise; their horrific suicides were an affirmation of their freedom, a challenge to the right of others to "own" them.

MAROONS AS FOLK HEROES

While the majority of maroons were captured, there were enough successes to inspire hope in those who strove to emulate them. One successful maroon (that is, until he was caught and hung) was "[t]he celebrated runaway negro Stepney" who lived free in the woods of South Carolina for twenty years, "committing depredations and violence." According to the *Charleston Patriot*, "[h]e was sagacious, active, and brave almost to desperation."[70] Some people were never found and others were able to remain in the woods until the Union troops arrived. There were quite a few of them, according to Ben from Alabama, and they were in poor shape, having survived in the worst conditions. But they had held up to the end. "Some men done run away an' don't git caught. When the Yankees come lots o' men walk out o' the woods. They'd wore iron so long that when they was cut off they dropped like they was dead. They was wore to the bone."[71] Thompson West, who escaped on the day he was sold, made a grand return to society. When the Yankees arrived in Plaquemine, Louisiana, he walked out of the woods and exclaimed, "I'm a free man!"[72] Hector Godbold of South Carolina saw John receive seventy-five lashes. When he was let go, John ran to the woods "an never come back no more till freedom come here. I telling you when he come back, he come back wid de Yankees."[73] Two men who swore they would no longer work for free lived in the woods for several years, escaping the dogs sent after them. They stayed there "until freedom, when they came out and worked for pay."[74] As for Jesse of Penfield, Georgia, once slavery ended he went straight to his former owner and told him he had lived for seven years just a stone's throw away. Colonel Calloway lent him a horse and a wagon to move his belongings from his cave to his former cabin. Not only did Jesse remain well hidden close to the plantation but he also accumulated quite a few assets.[75]

A number of people managed to live in the wilds without the help of their companions in the quarters. Consequently, they were not aware that slavery was over. Caesar stayed hidden even after the war was over, while

William Heard and his family were so secluded in their Georgia cave that it was only after Emancipation that they were "found."[76]

Former maroons readily acknowledged that they often went hungry and led a difficult life. James Williams, an expert on the topic since he lived on a tree and in a cave, offered a good summary of life as a maroon: "When I was in the woods I lived on nothing, you may say and yet something too. I had bread and roasting ears, and potatoes. I suffered mighty bad with the cold, and for the want of something to eat. One time a snake came and poked its head in the hollow and was coming in, and I took my axe and chopped him in two."[77]

But this reality did not alter the picture that freed people presented of the maroons decades after Emancipation. Some remembered them as leading a quasi-idyllic existence: "Yes, chile, I reckon that they got 'long all right in the caves," affirmed Julia Brown. "They had babies in thar and raised 'em too."[78] According to Liza Brown of Virginia, they "got plenty good somep'n to eat; better den we all did whar I belongst, 'cause dey steal hogs an' kill em."[79] Ishrael Massie said of his half-brother Bob, "Yas, yas, I don' et many er good meal of vituals in Bob's den."[80] Martha Showvely from Virginia stated that her uncle, who lived in a cave, had it good too: "When dey found him, he had plenty food an' a nice place back up under dere."[81] For people worked to their limits, the maroons seemed to have had as much leisure as they wanted. Eliza Robinson remarked, "My fathering-law say he ain't never hit a lick of work during slavery time. Says he live in de groun. He come up and git foods of all kinds and take hit back down dar."[82]

People also recalled the maroons' dexterity at eluding capture. Elizabeth Sparks was certain that "If yer git in the woods, they couldn't git yer."[83] "De Patterrollers couldn't find [Marthy] or nobody, and he ain't never showed hiss'f in daylight," derided Martha Jackson of Alabama, showing much contempt for the patrollers' ineptness.[84] Sis Shackelford of Virginia concurred: "Dey hid in Dismal Swamp in holes in de groun' so hidden dey stay dere years an' white folks, dogs, or nothin' else could fine 'em."[85]

* * *

It is fair to say that the majority of maroons died in the woods, were captured, or returned to the plantations. Even so, despite their ultimate failure they exposed to public view the fact that the dangers and uncertainties of their self-imposed exile were preferable, in their eyes, to enslavement and life away from their relatives. To white Southerners, their aspirations were criminal and the maroons were banditti to be destroyed, but they could also elicit curiosity and a certain amount of fear-based admiration. In the mid-1800s, Calvin H. Wiley, a novelist and legislator, was well aware of this when he wrote, "From the earliest times there have been, in eastern Carolina, remarkable runaway slaves, who lived in caves in the sand, and in swamps; and the exploits and crimes and stratagems of these black heroes have been, and are still, topics of wondering, and sometimes fearful interest, at the family fireside."[86]

To blacks, the maroons' very existence exposed the limitations of the slave regime of terror and repression. It attacked at its core the myth of whites' superiority. As Cornelia Carny, whose father, cousin Gabriel, and their friend Charlie were maroons, summed it up: "Niggers was too smart fo' white folks to git ketched. . . . De meanin' I git is dat niggers could always outsmart de white folks."[87] They were a daily reminder that slavers could not exercise absolute control on either the people in the woods or those in bondage who aided and abetted them. Cunning and smart, one step ahead of the men and women who set the dogs after them, the maroons were Brer' Rabbit who outsmarted the strong and the powerful. Their feats ridiculed slaveholders—and the institution of slavery—because they had been "had" right under their noses. They had proved incapable of finding a man, a mother with children, or a family of ten living two miles from their own bedrooms. Even more, they fed them their hogs, their chickens, and their corn. And because it was largely based on the active help and silent support of the enslaved community, the maroons' success, even when limited, was everyone's accomplishment.

The slaveholders' panoply of pickled whippings, brandings, and cropped ears was effective only to a point. Everyone either saw it or heard of it, and while it certainly discouraged many, it did not deter the most resolute from leaving and the most tenacious from staying away: independence, won the hard way, was worth the suffering. By exemplifying courage, fearlessness, and resilience, maroons became folk heroes and more than half a century after Emancipation, their exploits and successes continued to loom large in the black popular imagination.

CONCLUSION

WHEN American marronage is mapped from the borderlands to the hinterland it becomes evident that it was more widespread and more multifaceted than previously thought. Maroons did not constitute a monolithic population: they made the decision to settle in the wilds for varied reasons, they established a range of social and economic strategies, maintained different degrees of relations with the plantation world, traded with and worked for enslaved as well as white men or cut off all their links with the outside world, and farmed in one place or moved about.

Their very existence is a particularly strong indictment of slavery, as they were willing to take the most drastic measures to stay out of it. But marronage is even more significant for what it reveals about the people who defied slave society, enforced their own definition of freedom, and dared invent their specific alternative to what the country had delineated as being blacks' proper place. Maroons possessed a number of essential qualities without which they could not have made the decision to spend their lives in the wilderness and to fruitfully function there once confronted with its harsh reality. They had to be intrepid, dynamic, adaptable, self-reliant, and self-confident risk takers. They may have been pushed to the woods by despair but what dominated their lives thereafter was their confidence in their own capacity to endure a tough existence, their creativity, and their grit. These qualities enabled them to surmount the innumerable man-made and environmental obstacles they faced. Those who time and again fled to the woods, the African newcomers, the long-term exiles, and the cave dwellers in particular exhibited a fierce spirit of independence and reserves of physical and mental bravery.

* * *

"Things in the margins, including humans who wander there, are often on the brink of becoming something else, or someone else," essayist Barbara Hurd has observed.[1] And maroons were no exception. They reinvented themselves, creating their own alternative lives. In some cases, especially for the people in the borderlands, this alternative was a hybrid. With one spouse on the plantation and the other at its periphery, couples (and relatives) straddled both worlds and blurred the line between freedom and enslavement. The husband who built and furnished a home for his maroon wife and helped her deliver and raise their children assumed the role of a free man in the wilds, yet chose to remain enslaved because what he got from the plantation helped his family to survive. Relatives, friends, and neighbors fed, entertained, and hid borderland maroons in the quarters, but also visited them in the landscapes of freedom where they lived. Life, love, and friendship evolved on a fluid terrain at the confluence of freedom and bondage.

But whether in the borderlands or in the hinterland, almost all maroons had to function in a dichotomous world. They lived alternatively within their own free sphere and another, dangerous one that they still had to inhabit on a regular basis. As shown throughout this book, to safeguard their freedom they generally had to maintain or establish contact with free blacks, enslaved relatives, friends, and acquaintances; and poor whites, white traders, and sometimes farmers and planters. Paradoxically, then, to minimize the negative impact of this contact with the larger society they had to create a web of connections to it in order to better protect their own interests, be they physical, mental, sentimental, familial, communal, or commercial. It was a complex, difficult balancing act.

These connections, primarily with men and women still enslaved, reveal a high level of cooperation that is not apparent when only truants and runaways are taken into account, because for both these groups the

assistance was temporary. With the maroons it was a long-term investment, and they could not have persevered without this tacit and active
solidarity that expressed itself night after night. Were maroons a burden
on enslaved people? Or to put it another way, what did they have to
offer in return for assistance, food sharing, and occasional harboring?
Asking and answering this rhetorical question, historian Eugene Genovese claimed that the American maroons, contrary to their counterparts
elsewhere, failed their enslaved companions because they could not offer
them protection.[2] Yet some of the most powerful maroon communities
in Jamaica and Suriname were far from being protectors, as they turned
over runaways to the authorities as specified in their treaties. Nothing of
that sort happened with American maroons, although had they found
themselves in the same situation they might have responded in a similar
manner.

But maroons were not simply "taking." They bartered their surplus,
they traded, they entrusted people in the quarters with their crafts and
products to sell likely for a commission. Some, as exemplified by St.
Malo's community in Louisiana and the shingle-getters in the Dismal
Swamp, worked for their enslaved companions. To see the maroons as
parasites or as having had nothing to offer is to miss the close connections—personal, familial, and commercial—they had or established with
the people in the quarters. Besides, enslaved people obtained intangible
but important benefits as a result of the maroons' presence and activities.
The latter were an inspiration to them and a subtle threat to slaveholders.
Charles Manigault wrote to another planter who wanted to buy one of
his former maroons: "I never sold a corrupt Negro to reside . . . even on
the same river with my Plantation, to avoid the corruption that such a
Negro would effect on his former companions on my Plantation."[3] Walter Rimm could not agree more. His friend John had been a "run-awayer"
for four years and was badly wanted "'cause it 'spire other slaves to run
away if he stays a-loose."[4] Slaveholders noted "insolence" coming from
the quarters when maroons were known to be around making "depredations." The nonverbal warning that further desertions could ensue gave
enslaved men and women a little bit of breathing space.

To the larger society, maroons were bandits to be annihilated and they inspired the most barbaric laws, suffered sadistic torture, and along with insurrectionists, gruesome executions. Nonetheless, in spite of the apprehension they provoked, they did not inflict much bodily harm on the white population. But neither did the insurrectionists, for that matter: within close to two hundred and fifty years, probably less than a hundred and fifty whites were slain during revolts, while the number of blacks—whether actively involved in them and not—executed or killed was far in excess of this. Slave hunters and other pursuers were slain during small-scale raids; but large antimaroon operations were noticeably one-sided when it came to the loss of human life. As we saw in chapter 7, the "King of England's Soldiers," who fought twice against a combined force of militias and Catawbas in South Carolina and Georgia, killed one black driver. St. Malo's group in Louisiana murdered five (or nine, depending on the source) white and two black men in four separate incidents, but did not fire a shot when attacked. Yet any traces, sightings, and discoveries of the "banditti" and "brigands" provoked hysteria. Acts, petitions, personal and official correspondence, and military operations evidence the fear they inspired and the determination to obliterate them. More than the actual damage they inflicted, it was their potential to do so that made the maroons objects of dread. This projected harm was calculated in terms of the numbers of possible recruits, their negative influence, and the anticipated transformation of small armed bands into large armed groups no longer interested in staying in the wilderness but determined to "kill the whites."

But the significance of marronage cannot be measured only by the dominant society's anxiety about indiscriminate slaughter and bloody insurrections. It also exacted an economic and societal cost. The South as a whole did not lose workers when runaways hid in Southern cities and towns and continued to be involved in the local economy, but it did when there were flights to the North and across international borders. However, with the maroons the South not only lost workers, but it also lost food, supplies, security, and a sense of control over the people still held in bondage. The social and economic price of marronage per capita—not in the aggregate, because of the smaller number of maroons as compared to runaways—was high. But whereas the maroons remained under the national radar, runaways to the North (as opposed to the most numerous staying in the South) loomed large in the American slavery and antislavery narrative because they exacerbated the sectional tensions between North and South. It got to the point that the Fugitive Law of 1850 turned the North into an auxiliary of the Southern slave hunters, patrollers, and militias. Marronage, however, was a purely Southern issue and there was no reason for maroons to gain national attention. On the contrary, it was a problem the South had little incentive to advertise. It was easy to claim that runaways made it North only because they were helped by malevolent whites, but quite another to publicize the fact that slaveholders and militias were incapable of locating and seizing black men and women who had managed to live free just a short distance away.

Within the larger narrative of slave resistance, maroons offered a unique experiment. They created and exposed to whites and blacks an alternative to life in bondage, an alternative to free life in a slave society, and an alternative to free life in a free state. Whatever the immediate cause of their marronage, they opted to exile themselves from a despotic, discriminatory society. Their removal to the wilds was not only a denunciation of the social and political order of the land but more profoundly a radical ideological and very concrete rupture that left no place for compromise. The people who continued to live in seclusion in the Great Dismal Swamp after Emancipation—and it is not possible to affirm that they were the only ones in the country—are the best example of this rupture. The end of slavery was not to them the watershed event it represented for runaways and the people still enslaved. They wanted freedom on their own terms, not those of the larger society, and there was therefore no reason for them to leave their communities after the abolition of slavery.

* * *

In the end, did the maroons "achieve" anything? And what exactly did they want to achieve? Their diversity precludes any generalization, but their actions show that self-determination, self-reliance, and self-rule were their key objectives. In the aggregate they did achieve these goals, but only on a temporary basis. The vast majority did not have the time necessary to develop and consolidate their communities, as was also the case in South America and the Caribbean. However, caveats must be made in each of these geographical regions for the individuals and groups who escaped detection.

American maroons have often been unflatteringly compared with those in South America and the Caribbean, but their study shows many points of convergence. As was the case in the American South, large communities were the exception elsewhere as well. So were the fortified, militaristic settlements that have so permeated the general understanding of marronage and made American maroons invisible or not "maroon enough." Many groups in the Caribbean and South America too were known to have flourished close to inhabited areas and there too many if not most maroon communities, as historian Michael Craton has noted, "faded out in a few months or years or in at most a generation."[5] Agriculture, trade, and raids were all activities the maroons engaged in, from South Carolina to Brazil. In spite of these many commonalities, though, notable differences existed, particularly in the extent of the farming American maroons did when compared to their counterparts. And even though most communities in the rest of the Americas did not use breastworks and other types of strategic defenses, their quasi absence from the records in the United States is notable. In-depth research in comparative marronage integrating American maroons as genuine, not "ersatz" maroons, will bring additional insights and answer some still-unresolved questions.

American maroons complicate the neat categories established by historians and the popular concept of what maroon life was about. Those living in caves established permanent residency, although maroons at the margins were supposed to be "roaming bands." Mobile groups exploited the borderlands and the hinterland. Small farming operations could be found just a few miles from inhabited areas. Large groups went back and forth between borderlands and hinterlands. Maroon life in the United

States was fluid, complex, and dynamic, and much more remains to be unearthed to get a better sense of its specificities. Written records can only yield so much; the kind of archeological work done in the Great Dismal Swamp needs to be extended to other areas. In particular, the excavation of caves, which must still exist, would add considerably to our comprehension of that particular phenomenon. Only the conjunction and critical analysis of written records, archeological digs, oral history, and folklore can provide us with a sharper image of American marronage.

* * *

Few of the men and women whose stories fill these pages cut a dashing figure like Zumbi of Palmares, Alabi of the Saramacca, or Yanga of San Lorenzo de los Negros. There is little to be found here of the flamboyant, seductive heroism of the famous maroon leaders of the rest of the Americas. But the people who cultivated corn, fished, hunted, and made baskets for trade were as central to the survival of their families, groups, and communities as those who knew how to fight. Their vital contribution expressed itself daily; there is a quiet heroism in the mother who raises young children underground; in the African two days off the slave ship who dares confront an entirely unfamiliar environment; in the husband who follows his wife and children hundreds of miles; in the men who night after night put their lives at risk to carry back barrels of corn and a butchered ox.

For centuries maroons peopled the Southern swamps, the woods, and the mountains, determined to safeguard their unique way of life. Inevitably, they made mistakes, some of which cost them their freedom and their lives. They misjudged situations and people; miscalculated the potential danger to themselves of the raids they conducted on plantations, stores, and farms; did not always protect their settlements as they should have; were weakened by leadership quarrels; and sometimes betrayed their companions.

Maroons celebrated successes and also faced disappointments and disasters, but in their pursuit of freedom and autonomy they created and developed new forms of life as they retreated from but still measured themselves against a terrorist system and took advantage of a challenging environment. They knew it was a rewarding but complicated enterprise; they put their lives on the line, every day, to be free. Overall, their forgotten story is one of courage and resourcefulness, hardships endured and freedoms won.

To a planter who could not understand why a maroon did not return even when he was hungry, had frostbite, and suffered hard times, the latter simply replied, "I taste how it is to be free, en I didn' come back."[6]

NOTES

NOTES TO THE INTRODUCTION

1. Charles L. Perdue, Jr., et al., eds., *Weevils in the Wheat: Interviews with Virginia Ex-Slaves* (Charlottesville: University of Virginia Press, 1976), 125.

2. "Georgetown (S.C.), Dec. 21," *Carolina Gazette,* December 21, 1824.

3. This study is restricted to African and African American maroons and does not include Native American maroons.

4. Steven Hahn, *The Political Worlds of Slavery and Freedom* (Cambridge: Harvard University Press, 2009), 22–53.

5. Herbert Aptheker, "Maroons within the Present Limits of the United States," *Journal of Negro History*, 24, 2 (April 1939): 167–184; Herbert Aptheker, "Additional Data on American Maroons," ibid., 32, 4 (October 1947): 452–460.

6. Eugene D. Genovese, *From Rebellion to Revolution: Afro-American Slave Revolts in the Making of the Modern World* (Baton Rouge: Louisiana State University Press, 1979), 77; Michael Mullin, *Africa in America: Slave Acculturation and Resistance in the American South and the British Caribbean, 1736–1831* (Champaign: University of Illinois Press, 1995), 61; Peter Kolchin, *Unfree Labor: American Slavery and Russian Serfdom* (Cambridge: Belknap Press of Harvard University, 1987), 291.

7. Whites naming or knowing the names of maroon communities elsewhere stands in stark contrast with what happened in the colonies and states that inform this study. To name a settlement or to relay its name meant acknowledging its existence. It was an act of recognition that Southerners refused to commit. In their perspective maroons did not form communities, only ad hoc gangs of banditti "skulking" around. By denying their very existence, public opinion could thus be satisfied that there were no maroon communities in the country resembling those in Jamaica and Suriname.

8. Gwendolyn Midlo Hall, *Africans in Colonial Louisiana: The Development of Afro-Creole Culture in the Eighteenth Century* (Baton Rouge: Louisiana State University Press, 1992); Gilbert C. Din, *Spaniards, Planters, and Slaves: The Spanish Regulation of Slavery in Louisiana, 1763–1803* (College Station: Texas A&M University Press, 1999). In Hugo P. Learning's *Hidden Americans: Maroons of Virginia and the Carolinas* (New York: Routledge, 1995) one chapter focuses on African Americans. John Hope Franklin and Loren Schweninger, *Runaway Slaves: Rebels on the Plantation* (New York: Oxford University Press, 1999), 86–89; Timothy Lockley, *Maroon Communities in South Carolina: A Documentary Record* (Columbia: University of South Carolina Press, 2009). For swamp and environmental studies see, in particular, Jack Temple Kirby, *Poquosin: A Study of Rural Landscape and Society* (Chapel Hill:

University of North Carolina Press, 1995); Megan Kate Nelson, *Trembling Earth: A Cultural History of the Okefenokee Swamp* (Athens: University of Georgia Press, 2005); William Tynes Cowan, *The Slave in the Swamp: Disrupting the Plantation Narrative* (New York: Routledge, 2005); Anthony Wilson, *Shadow and Shelter: The Swamp in Southern Culture* (Jackson: University Press of Mississippi, 2006). Alvin O. Thompson, *Flight to Freedom: African Runaways and Maroons in the Americas* (Kingston: University of the West Indies Press, 2006).

9. See, in particular, Jane Landers, *Black Society in Spanish Florida* (Urbana: University of Illinois Press, 1999); Jane Landers, *Atlantic Creoles in the Age of Revolution* (Cambridge: Harvard University Press, 2010); Kevin Mulroy, *Freedom on the Border: The Seminole Maroons in Florida, the Indian Territory, Coahuila, and Texas* (Lubbock: Texas Tech University Press, 1993); Kevin Mulroy, *The Seminole Freedmen: A History* (Norman: University of Oklahoma Press, 2007); Nathaniel Millett, "Defining Freedom in the Atlantic Borderlands of the Revolutionary Southeast," *Early American Studies* (Fall 2007): 367–394; Patrick Riordan, "Finding Freedom in Florida: Native Peoples, African Americans, and Colonists, 1670–1816," *Florida Historical Quarterly*, 75, 1 (Summer 1996): 24–43.

10. Gabriel Debien, "Le marronage aux Antilles françaises au XVIIIe siècle," *Caribbean Studies*, 6, 3 (October 1966): 3, 7.

11. Richard Price, ed., *Maroon Societies: Rebel Slave Communities in the Americas* (Baltimore: Johns Hopkins University Press, 1979), 1.

12. Thompson, *Flight to Freedom*, 58–67.

13. There is an abundant literature on these landscapes. See in particular, Clifton Ellis and Rebecca Ginsburg, *Cabin, Quarter, Plantation: Architecture and Landscapes of North American Slavery* (New Haven: Yale University Press, 2010); John Michael Vlach, *Back of the Big House: The Architecture of Plantation Slavery* (Chapel Hill: University of North Carolina Press, 1993); S. Max Edelson, "The Nature of Slavery: Environmental Disorder and Slave Agency in Colonial South Carolina," in Robert Olwell and Alan Tully, eds., *Cultures and Identities in Colonial British America* (Baltimore: Johns Hopkins University, 2006): 21–44; Dell Upton, "White and Black Landscapes in Eighteenth-Century Virginia," in Robert Blair St. George, ed., *Material Life in America, 1600–1860* (Boston: Northeastern University Press, 1988): 357–369; James D. Kornwolf, *Architecture and Town Planning in Colonial North America* (Baltimore: Johns Hopkins University Press, 2002), 1: 469–499; Grey Gundaker, ed., assisted by Tyles Cowan, *Keep Your Head to the Sky: Interpreting African American Home Ground* (Charlottesville: University of Virginia Press, 1998).

14. Vlach, *Back of the Big House*, 14, 191.

15. Vlach, *By the Work of Their Hands: Studies in Afro-American Folklife* (Charlottesville: University Press of Virginia, 1991), 222.

16. *Report of the Special Committee of the House of Representatives of South Carolina* (Columbia: Steam Power Press Carolina Times, 1857), 30.

17. "Charles Town, August 19," *Farmer's Repository*, August 19, 1808.

18. For testimonies of freed people on hunting, see George P. Rawick, ed., *The American Slave: A Composite Autobiography* (Westport, Conn: Greenwood, 1972), 16, Pt. 3, 50. Hunting was also restricted. See ibid., 11, Pt. 2, 277-278; for blowguns, see 13, Pt. 3, 130. See also Herbert C. Covey and Dwight Eisnach, *What the Slaves Ate: Recollections of African American Foods and Foodways from the Slave Narratives* (Santa Barbara: Greenwood Press, 2009), 113–133.

19. Mart A. Stewart, "Slavery and the Origins of African American Environmentalism," in Dianne D. Glave and Mark Stoll, eds., *"To Love the Wind and the Rain": African*

Americans and Environmental History (Pittsburgh: University of Pittsburgh Press, 2006), 12; Scott Giltner, "Slave Hunting and Fishing in the Antebellum South," in Glave et al., *"To Love the Wind,"* 21–36.

20. Charles Ball, *Slavery in the United States* (New York: John S. Taylor, 1837), 167; Dylan C. Penningroth, *The Claims of Kinfolk: African American Property and Community in the Nineteenth-Century South* (Chapel Hill: University of North Carolina Press, 2003), 48–49, 60.

21. Charles Ball, *Fifty Years in Chains* (NewYork: H. Dayton, 1859), 246–247.

22. Edelson, "The Nature of Slavery," 27.

23. H. Roy Merrens, ed., *The Colonial South Carolina Scene: Contemporary Views, 1697–1774* (Columbia: University of South Carolina Press, 1977), 264.

24. H. Cowles Atwater, *Incidents of a Southern Tour: or, The South, as Seen with Northern Eyes* (Boston: J. P. Magee, 1857), 49.

25. Stewart, "Slavery," 12; Lewis W. Paine, *Narrative of Lewis W. Paine* (Boston: Bela Marsh, Publisher, 1852), 28–29.

26. Rhys L. Isaac, *The Transformation of Virginia, 1740–1790* (Chapel Hill: University of North Carolina Press, 1982), 52–53. See also Rebecca Ginsburg, "Freedom and the Slave Landscape," *Landscape Journal*, 26, 1 (2007): 36–44.

27. Gabino La Rosa Corzo, *Runaway Slave Settlements in Cuba: Resistance and Repression* (Chapel Hill: University of North Carolina Press, 2003); Gabriel Stedman, *Narrative of a Five Years' Expedition against the Revolted Negroes of Surinam* (London: J. Johnson, 1806); Wim Hoogbergen, *Out of Slavery: A Surinamese Roots History* (Berlin: Lit Verlag, 2008).

28. For example of maps and plans, see Stedman; *Narrative*, 2:128–129; R. K. Kent, "Palmares: An African State in Brazil," *Journal of African History*, 6, 2 (1965): following 168; Stuart B. Schwarz, "The 'Mocambo': Slave Resistance in Colonial Bahia," *Journal of Social History*, 3, 4 (Summer 1970): 330; La Roza Corzo, *Settlements*, 236–237; Judith A. Carney and Richard Nicholas Rosomoff, *In the Shadow of Slavery: Africa's Botanical Legacy in the Atlantic World* (Berkeley: University of California Press, 2009), 85, 86, 95, 96; Thompson, *Flight to Freedom*, 116,134,182, 183, 189.

29. Throughout this book the term African(s) refers exclusively to persons born in Africa. I do not adhere to the convention of referring to everyone as "enslaved Africans." At some point people were "African Americans" with a particular culture. In addition, the blanket terminology is not applicable when describing and analyzing experiences that were different according to place of origin. Africans had been free, uprooted from their lands, suffered the Middle Passage, arrived in a new country, and did not speak the dominant language. People born in the colonies and the United States did not go through the same experience.

NOTES TO CHAPTER 1:
THE DEVELOPMENT OF MARRONAGE IN THE SOUTH

1. Henry R. McIlwaine, ed., *Minutes of the Council and General Court of Colonial Virginia, 1622–1632, 1670–1676* (Richmond, 1924), 468.

2. Ibid., 466.

3. William W. Hening, ed., *Statutes at Large, Being a Collection of all the Laws of Virginia From the First Session of the Legislature, in the Year 1619* (New York: For the Author by R. W. & G Bartow, 1823), 1:226.

4. Ibid.,, 2:26.

5. Ibid., 2: 299–300.

6. Ibid., 2:481–482.

7. See, for example, Mississippi 1822 in A. Hutchinson, ed., *Code of Mississippi* (Jackson, 1848), 518; Florida 1835 in John P. Duval, ed., *Compilation of the Public Acts of the Legislative Council of the Territory of Florida* (Tallahassee: Samuel S. Simley, 1839), 222; Alabama 1852 in John J. Ormond et al., ed., *The Code of Alabama* (Montgomery: Britain and De wolf, 1852), 239–240.

8. Hening, ed., *Statutes*, 3: 86–88.

9. *Old Rappahannock County Order Book 1686–1692*, 240; *Middlesex County Order Book 1680–1694*, 526–527, 535, Library of Virginia. Also in Ruth Sparacio and Sam Sparacio, *Order Book Abstracts of Old Rappahannock, 1689–1692* (McLean, Va.: Antient Press, 1990), 88; *Order Book Abstracts Middlesex County, 1690–1694* (McLean, Va.: Antient Press, 1994), 31, 35.

10. Darrett B. Rutman and Anita H. Rutman, *A Place in Time: Middlesex County, Virginia, 1650–1750* (New York: W. W. Norton, 1984), 166.

11. Hening, ed., *Statutes*, 3: 210–211.

12. Ibid., 3: 456.

13. For the entire Act, see ibid., 447–461.

14. McIlwaine, ed., *Executive Journals of the Council of Colonial Virginia, June 11, 1680–June 22, 1699* (Richmond: Davis Bottom, 1925), 234–235.

15. Warrant for apprehending Negros in Bruton Parish, March 20; March 24, 1709, Colonial Papers, Virginia State Library.

16. McIlwaine, ed., *Executive Journals*, 3:236.

17. Ibid., 3: 242–243.

18. H. R. McIlwaine, ed., *Journals of the House of Burgesses of Virginia, 1702/03, 1705–06, 1710–1712* (Richmond, 1911), 270; Hening, *Statutes*, 3:537–538.

19. Ibid., 3:336–337.

20. Ibid., 3:549–553. Already in a letter dated October 5, 1712, during the Tuscarora War that convulsed North Carolina, Spotswood warned the Board of Trade that Native Americans and blacks were major threats. He deplored the laissez-faire attitude of the colonists, noting that "the insurrection of our own Negroes, and the Invasions of the Indians are no less to be dreaded [than European incursions] while the people are so stupidly adverse to the only means they have left to protect themselves against either of these events." In William L. Sanders, ed., *The State Records of North Carolina, 1775–1776* (Raleigh: J. Daniels, Printer to the State, 1886–1890), 1:886.

21. Peter H. Wood, *Strange New Land: Africans in Colonial America 1526–1776* (New York: Oxford University Press, 2003), 39.

22. *The Trans-Atlantic Slave Trade Database*, www.slavevoyages.org (accessed 11/1/2010).

23. Philip D. Morgan, *Slave Counterpoint: Black Culture in the Eighteenth-Century Chesapeake and Lowcountry* (Chapel Hill: University of North Carolina Press, 1998), 61, table 10.

24. E. B. O'Callaghan, ed., *Documents Relative to the Colonial History of the State of New York* (Albany, N.Y.: Weed, Parsons, and Co., 1855), 5: 674.

25. Ibid., 5: 676.

26. William H. Browne, ed., Archives of Maryland, *Proceedings of the Council of Maryland, 1698–1731* (Baltimore: Maryland Historical Society, 1905), 25: 394–395.

27. Bernard C. Steiner, ed., Archives of Maryland, *Proceedings and Acts of the General Assembly, 1724–1726* (Baltimore: Maryland Historical Society, 1916), 37:211. On July 28, 1731, the Upper House sent the following letter to the Lower House:

> The Commissioners Appointed to receive runaway Slaves taken up beyond Monococy, & pay the takers up of such Slaves the Sume of five pounds Current Money directed by Act of Assembly, being gone off with what money has been advanced for that purpose And Whereas Flayl Pain an Inhabitant of those parts hath now brought a runaway Slave from beyond Monococy, We propose that the sd Person be immediately paid out of the publick Stock the sume of five pounds Current Money, and also that a further Sume be ordered into such Commissioners hands as shall hereafter be Appointed for the purposes in the said Act mentioned[.]"

The Lower Court concurred. See Steiner, ed., Archives of Maryland, 37: 211–212.

28. Prince George's County Court Records, 1696–1770, 414–415. Her information was deemed "groundless." There is no precision as to what part was unsubstantiated, but there is no refuting the fact that "many Negroes" lived among the Indians, and maroons' visits to families and friends were relentlessly denounced. What perhaps appeared to the court as specious was the information, three months old, about the Indians' planned massacre.

29. "The Humble Representation of William Byrd Esq of Virginia," Letter to Mr. Ochs, 1735, in John Spencer Bassett, ed., *The Writings of "Colonel William Byrd, of Westover in Virginia, Esqr."* (New York: Doubleday, Page & Co., 1901), 392.

30. Byrd continued: "All these matters duly consider[e]d, I wonder the Legislature will Indulge a few ravenous Traders to the danger of the Publick safety, and such Traders as woud freely sell their Fathers, their Elder Brothers, and even the Wives of their bosoms, if they coud black their faces and get anything by them." See "Documents," *American Historical Review*, 1 (October 1895–July 1896): 89.

31. Mattie Erma Edwards Parker, ed., *North Carolina Higher-Court Records, 1697–1701* (Raleigh: State Department of Archives and History, 1971), 241.

32. John Brickell, *The Natural History of North Carolina* (Dublin: James Carson, 1737), 357.

33. Ibid., 263, 273, 357.

34. Walter Clark, ed., *The State Records of North Carolina, 1715–1776.* (Goldsboro: Nash Brothers, 1904), 23:62–66; Evarts B. Greene and Virginia D. Harrington, *American Population before the Federal Census of 1790* (New York: Columbia University Press, 1932), 4.

35. Clark, ed., *State Records*, 23: 201.

36. "Craven County," *North Carolina Gazette*, September 2, 1774.

37. Thomas Cooper, ed., *The Statutes at Large of South Carolina, 1682–1716* (Columbia: A. S. Johnson, 1837), 2:13; David J. McCord, ed., *The Statutes at Large of South Carolina* (Columbia: A. S. Johnson, 1840), 7: 343–347.

38. Thomas J. Little, "The South Carolina Slave Laws Reconsidered, 1670–1700," *South Carolina Historical Magazine*, 94, 2 (April 1993): 88–89.

39. An Act for the Better Ordering of Slaves, Records of the General Assembly, March 2–16, 1696, South Carolina Department of Archives and History. See also William M. Wiecek, "The Statutory Law of Slavery and Race in the Thirteen Mainland Colonies of British America," *William and Mary Quarterly*, Third Series, 34, 2 (April 1977): 270; Christopher Tomlins, *Freedom Bound: Law, Labor, and Civic Identity in Colonizing English America 1580–1865* (Cambridge: Cambridge University Press, 2010), 439–440.

40. *Journal of the Commons House of Assembly, 1710–1712*, South Carolina Department of Archives and History. By 1715 the colony counted 10,500 blacks and 6,250 whites. See Greene et al., *American Population*, 173.

41. Edwin C. Holland, *Refutation of Calumnies against the Southern and Western States* (Charleston: A. M. Miller, 1822), 64–65.

42. *South Carolina Council Journal*, May 29, 1735.

43. "By a Letter from South-Carolina," *Boston News-Letter*, March 4, 1736.

44. The request for two ears was made because Native Americans had become masters at manufacturing two or more scalps out of one.

45. McCord, ed., *Statutes*, 7: 413–414.

46. Alexander Hewatt, *An Historical Account of the Rise and Progress of the Colonies of South Carolina and Georgia* (London: Alexander Donaldson, 1779), 2: 86.

47. Greene et al., *American Population*, 174.

48. McCord, ed., *Statutes*, 7: 424–425.

49. Alan Gallay, *The Indian Slave Trade: The Rise of the English Empire in the American South, 1670–1717* (New Haven: Yale University Press, 2002), 345–352; Peter H. Wood, *Black Majority: Negroes in Colonial South Carolina from 1670 through the Stono Rebellion* (New York: Alfred A. Knopf, 1974), 116; David H. Corkran, *The Creek Frontier, 1540–1783* (Norman: University of Oklahoma Press, 1967), 68. For the 1736 agreement on returned runaways, see J. H. Easterby, *Colonial Records of South Carolina* (Columbia: South Carolina Archives Department, 1958), 1: 108–110.

50. J. H. Easterby, ed., *Journal of the Commons House of Assembly November 10, 1736–June 7, 1739* (Columbia, S.C.: Historical Commission of South Carolina, 1951), 1:108–110.

51. "Oglethorpe's Treaty with the Lower Creek Indians," *Georgia Historical Quarterly*, 4, 1 (March 1920): 1–16.

52. Edmund Gray to John Fallowfield, May 15, 1751, and Deposition of Richard Smith, July 12, 1752, in William L. McDowell, *Documents relating to Indian Affairs* (Columbia: University of South Carolina Press, 1982): 1:83, 103.

53. Lt. Governor Bull to Board of Trade, May 8, 1760, in Tom Hatley, *The Dividing Paths: Cherokees and South Carolinians through the Revolutionary Era* (New York: Oxford University Press, 1995), 74.

54. Dr. George Milligen-Johnson, *A Short Description of the Province of South Carolina*, in B. R. Carroll, ed., *Historical Collections of South Carolina* (New York: Harper and Brothers, 1836), 2: 480.

55. Ibid., April 4, 1769, 32:145–146.

56. See full Code in Charles Gayarré, *Histoire de la Louisiane*, vol. 1 & 2 (Nouvelle-Orleans: Magne & Weisse, 1846), 203–215.

57. Cuban Papers, leg. 134A, in Din, *Spaniards, Planters, and Slaves*, 201.

58. Dunbar Rowland, ed., *Official Letter Books of W. C. C. Claiborne, 1801–1816* (Jackson, Miss.: State Department of Archives and History, 1917), 380.

59. For official orders to prevent flight to the British, see Lathan A. Windley, *A Profile of Runaway Slaves in Virginia and South Carolina from 1730 to 1790* (New York: Garland Publishing, 1995), 12–13; for a detailed analysis, see Jim Piecuch, *Three Peoples, One King: Loyalists, Indians, and Slaves in the Revolutionary South, 1775–1782* (Columbia: University of South Carolina Press, 2008).

60. For the runaways on Tybee and Sullivan's as maroons, see William S. Willis, "Divide and Rule: Red, White and Black in the Southeast," *Journal of Negro History*, 48, 3 (July

1963): 157–176; Cynthia M. Kennedy, *Braided Relations, Entwined Lives: The Women of Charleston's Urban Slave Society* (Bloomington: Indiana University Press, 2005), 33; Ray Raphael, *Founders: The People Who Brought You a Nation* (New York: New Press, 2009), 225; William R. Ryan, *The World of Thomas Jeremiah: Charles Town on the Eve of the American Revolution* (New York: Oxford University Press, 2012), 112, 143.

61. Henry Laurens to Capt. Thornborough, December 18, 1775, in *Collections of the South Carolina Historical Society* (Charleston South Carolina Historical Society, 1859), 3:94.

62. Ibid., 3:102.

63. Stephen Bull to Henry Laurens, March 14, 1776, in David R. Chesnutt, ed., *Papers of Henry Laurens: Jan. 5, 1776–Nov. 1, 1777* (Columbia: University of South Carolina Press, 1988), 163.

64. Culled from notices in these newspapers.

65. For details, see Piecuch, *Three Peoples*, 296.

66. Sanders, ed., *State Records*, 10:569.

67. Petition of Joseph Locke to the Senate and affidavit, April 30, 1784, and 1780 declaration of outlawry, *General Assembly State Records*, Senate Joint Resolutions, 1784, North Carolina State Archives.

68. Runaways from Virginia and North Carolina "organized themselves into bands and fled into the Dismal Swamp." Sylvia R. Frey, *Water from the Rock: Black Resistance in a Revolutionary Age* (Princeton: Princeton University Press, 1991), 226.

69. Johann David Schoepf, *Travels in the Confederation 1783–1784*, translated and edited by Alfred J. Morrison (Philadelphia: William Campbell, 1911), 2: 100; John Ferdinand Smyth Stuart, *A Tour in the United States of America* (London: G. Robinson, 1784), 2:102.

70. Winslow C. Watson, ed., *Men and Times of the Revolution or Memoirs of Elkanah Watson* (New York: Dana & Co., 1856), 36.

71. Robert Reid Howison, *A History of Virginia* (Richmond: Drinker & Morris, 1848), 2: 225–226.

72. Jeffrey J. Crow, *The Black Experience in Revolutionary North Carolina* (Raleigh: Division of Archives and History, 1983).

73. James W. Walker, *The Black Loyalists: The Search for a Promised Land in Nova Scotia and Sierra Leone, 1783–1870* (New York: Africana Publishing Co., 1976), 17 n. 35; Ellen Gibson Wilson, *The Loyal Blacks* (New York: Putnam's Sons, 1976), 69.

74. Philip D. Morgan, "Lowcountry Georgia and the Early Modern Atlantic World, 1733–ca.1820," in Philip D. Morgan, ed., *African American Life in the Georgia: The Atlantic World and the Gullah Geechee* (Athens: University of Georgia Press, 2010), 25.

75. Patrick Riordan, "Finding Freedom in Florida: Native People, African Americans, and Colonists, 1670–1816," *Florida Historical Quarterly*, 75, 1 (Summer, 1996): 41.

NOTES TO CHAPTER 2: AFRICAN MAROONS

1. Rawick, ed., *American Slave*, 16, Pt. 3, 2.

2. Ibid., 7, 427.

3. Philip D. Morgan, "Colonial South Carolina Runaways: Their Significance for Slave Culture," in Gad Heuman, *Out of the House of Bondage: Runaways, Resistance and Marronage in Africa and the New World* (London: Frank Cass, 1986), 59.

4. For a detailed summary of the numbers computed by various historians, see Marvin L. Michael Kay and Lorin Lee Cary, *Slavery in North Carolina, 1748–1775* (Chapel Hill: University of North Carolina Press, 1995), 127, 263–265.

5. Betty Wood, *Slavery in Colonial Georgia 1730–1775* (Athens: University of Georgia Press, 1984), 173–187.

6. Ministre secrétaire d'état de la marine et des colonies, *Exposé général des résultants du patronage des esclaves dans les colonies françaises* (Paris: Imprimerie royale, 1844), 347.

7. See, in particular, Gerald W. Mullin, *Flight and Rebellion: Slave Resistance in Eighteenth-Century Virginia* (New York: Oxford University Press, 1972), 39, 42; Michael Mullin, ed., *American Negro Slavery: A Documentary History* (Columbia: University of South Carolina Press, 1976), 11; Alex Bontemps, *The Punished Self: Surviving Slavery in the Colonial South* (Ithaca: Cornell University Press, 2001), 92–93.

8. See *Virginia Gazette*, February 9, 1738; *Virginia Gazette* (Purdie & Dixon), August 16, 1770, August 1, 1771, and March 12, 1772; ibid. (Purdie), September 19, 1777, October 10, 1777, and November 28, 1777; ibid. (Pinkney), January 16, 1776; ibid. (Dixon & Hunter), June 27, 1777; *Virginia Gazette and General Advertiser* (Davis), September 28, 1791; *Virginia Gazette or Weekly Advertiser* (Nicolson & Prentis), August 24, 1782; *Virginia Gazette or American Advertiser* (Hayes), January 11, 1783; *Virginia Gazette and Weekly Advertiser* (Nicolson & Prentis), September 20, 1783; *Virginia Independent Chronicle* (Davis), February 28, 1787; *South-Carolina Weekly Gazette*, November 19, 1785.

9. "Strayed or Stolen," *Charleston Morning Post*, July 13, 1787.

10. "Ranaway," *City Gazette*, August 5, 1807; "Five Dollars Reward," ibid., July 4, 1807.

11. Steiner, ed., *Archives of Maryland,* 585–586.

12. See "Left at the Subscriber's Plantation," *South-Carolina Weekly Gazette*, April 5, 1783; "Forty Dollars Reward," *Maryland Journal*, May 2, 1786; "Notice," *State Gazette of South-Carolina*, December 6, 1787; "Advertisement," *Columbian Museum and Savannah Advertiser*, August 9, 1796.

13. "Ran Away," *Maryland Gazette*, September 6, 1770; ibid., October 4, 1770. *The Trans-Atlantic Slave Trade Database,* VIN 77170 www.slavevoyages.org (accessed 9/9/2011).

14. See, for example, *Moniteur de la Louisiane*, October 6 and December 10, 1806; March 11, April 1; and May 13 (Supplement), 1807.

15. "Nègres marrons," *Moniteur de la Louisiane*, supplément, April 7, 1807.

16. *South-Carolina Gazette*, January 9, 1742; July 15, 1751; June 6, 1761; April 10–17, 1755.

17. "Ran Away," *Royal Georgia Gazette*, March 8, 1781.

18. "Recollections of Slavery by a Runaway Slave," *Emancipator*, August 23, 1838.

19. "Brought to the Work-House," *Georgia Gazette*, June 29, 1768; "Brought to the Work-House," *State Gazette of South-Carolina*, July 28, 1785; *South Carolina Gazette*, June 14, 1735; quoted in Wood, *Black Majority*, 251; "Run Away," *Georgia Gazette*, July 14, 1763.

20. "The Slave in the Swamp," *Frederick Douglass' Paper*, January 27, 1854.

21. Wood, *Slavery*, 180.

22. John Spencer Bassett, *Slavery and Servitude in the State of North Carolina*, (Baltimore: Johns Hopkins University Press, 1896), 32.

23. Major Steve Power, *The Memento of Old Natchez, 1700–1897* (Natchez: S. Power, 1897), vol. 1, 13.

24. "New Negroes," *Emancipator and Free American*, March 30, 1843.

25. "Lately Run Away," *South-Carolina Gazette*, October 24–31, 1761.

26. "From the Boston News Letter, October 4, 1759," in Elizabeth Donnan, ed., *Documents Illustrative of the Slave Trade* (Washington, D.C.: Carnegie Institution of Washington, 1930), 4: 34. "Ran Away or Stolen," *Maryland Gazette*, September 13, 1759; *Slave Trade Database, Upton,* VIN 90772 (accessed 1/5/2009).

27. "Run Away about a Month Ago," *South-Carolina Gazette*, June 9, 1757.

28. "Run Away," *South Carolina Gazette*, July 21, 1733; *Slave Trade Database, Speaker*, VIN 76714 (accessed 05/03/2010).

29. "Run Away from a Waggon," *South-Carolina Gazette*, November 7–14, 1761; Duke of York, slavevoyages.org, voyage 75369. See also "St. Matthew's Parish, July 25, 1772," *South-Carolina Gazette Extraordinary*, August 10, 1772, and "Run Away," *South Carolina Gazette*, August 8, 1772; "Gone Away from Mitton Plantation," *South-Carolina Gazette*, September 4–11, 1736, and October 23–30, 1736; "Run Away from Cow Savannah," *South-Carolina Gazette*, May 25, 1769.

30. Carter Diary, July 12, 17, 25, 1727, in Lorena S. Walsh, *From Calabar to Carter's Grove: The History of a Virginia Slave Community* (Charlottesville: University Press of Virginia, 1997), 82.

31. Daniel C. Littlefield, *Rice and Slaves: Ethnicity and the Slave Trade in Colonial South Carolina* (Urbana: University of Illinois Press, 1991), 162; Crow, *The Black Experience in Revolutionary North Carolina*, 43, 44.

32. "Run Away," *Virginia Gazette*, June 23, 1768.

33. See *Georgia Gazette*, September 28, 1774; November 9, 1774; October 4, 1775; June 25, 1789; "Twenty Pounds Reward," *Virginia Gazette* (Purdie & Dixon), September 12, 1771.

34. "Run Away," *South-Carolina Gazette*, November 21, 1754. "Run Away from Mr. Boone's Plantation," ibid., October 2, 1758.

35. "Run Away," *Georgia Gazette*, September 28, 1774; "Run Away," ibid., October 4, 1775.

36. "Hanover Town, August 5, 1773," *Virginia Gazette* (Purdie & Dixon), August 19, 1773; "Hanover Town, October 20, 1773," ibid., October 28, 1773; William Ronald Cocke, *Hanover County Chancery Wills and Notes* (Baltimore: Clearfield Co., 1992), 24–25.

37. Ball, *A Narrative*, 326–337.

38. Morgan, *Counterpoint*, 467.

39. Michael P. Johnson, "Runaway Slaves and the Slave Communities in South Carolina, 1799 to 1830," *William and Mary Quarterly*, Third Series, 38, 3 (July 1981), 437.

40. "Twenty Dollars Reward," *Gazette of the State of Georgia*, October 20, 1785. Betty absconded with two native-born men. She had lived in the "Indian nation" with her former owner.

41. "Fairfax County (Virginia) August 11, 1761," *Maryland Gazette* (Annapolis), August 20, 1761.

42. *The Papers of George Washington*, Alderman Library, University of Virginia, http://gwpapers.virginia.edu/documents/slavery/aug1761.html (accessed August 5, 2011).

43. See *Slave Trade Database, Molly*, VIN 17441(accessed 05/03/2010).

44. Worthington Chauncey Ford, ed., *The Writings of George Washington* (New York: Putnam's Sons, 1889), 2:145–146.

45. See University of Virginia, *The Papers of George Washington*, http://gwpapers.virginia.edu/documents/slavery/aug1761.html (accessed 3/5/2011).

46. Wood, *Slavery*, 185, 178.

47. See, for example, "Brought to the Work-House," *State Gazette of South-Carolina*, June 16, 1785; "Brought to the Work-House," ibid., April 20, 1786; "Brought to the Work-House," ibid., September 10, 1787; "Brought to the Work-House," ibid., April 24, 1786; "Brought to the Work-House," ibid., July 23, 1787; "A New Negro Fellow," ibid., June 12, 1786; "Run Away," *Gazette of the State of Georgia*, September 8, 1785.

48. "Nègres marrons," *Moniteur de la Louisiane*, Supplément, May 13, 1807. "Notice," *City Gazette and Daily Advertiser*, July 11, 1797. See also "Brought to the Work-House," *South Carolina Gazette*, February 3, 1759; "Run Away," *Georgia Gazette*, August 4, 1763.

49. "Run Away from the Subscriber about Ten Days Ago," *South-Carolina Gazette*, June 25–July 2, 1763.

50. "100 Dollars Reward," *Columbian Museum*, December 23, 1796.

51. "Run Away about Ten Days Ago," *Georgia Gazette*, November 9, 1774.

52. "Runaway Negroes," *Columbian Herald*, May 23, 1785. See also "Rock-Creek, October 9, 1761," *Maryland Gazette*, October 22, 1761; "Ran Away from the Subscriber, on Sunday," *South-Carolina Gazette*, August 26, 1765; "Ran Away," *South-Carolina Gazette*, August 26, 1765; "Run Away from My Plantation," *Georgia Gazette*, November 1, 1769.

53. "Twenty Pounds Reward," *Georgia Gazette*, January 25, 1775.

54. James Walvin, *Questioning Slavery* (New York: Routledge, 1996), 127.

55. "Run Away," *Virginia Gazette* (Purdie & Dixon), October 20, 1768.

56. "Ran Away," *Maryland Gazette*, August 25, 1780.

57. "50 Dollars Reward," *Carolina Federal Republican*, September 6, 1817, ibid., November 8, 1817.

58. "Committed to *Isle of Wight* Jail," *Virginia Gazette* (Purdie & Dixon), November 25, 1773.

59. "Brought to the Work-House," *South Carolina Gazette and Country Journal*, October 30, 1770.

60. "Run Away," *South-Carolina Gazette*, June 5, 1736; "Eloped," *The Times*, July 27, 1804.

61. "Brought to the Work-House," *Georgia Gazette*, June 29, 1768; "Newbern," *North Carolina Gazette*, April 10, 1778.

62. "Run Away from the Subscribers," *South-Carolina Gazette*, November 28–December 5, 1761. "Ran Away from Mrs. Croll's Plantation," *South-Carolina Gazette*, September 14, 1765.

63. Sylviane A. Diouf, *Dreams of Africa in Alabama: The Slave Ship Clotilda and the Story of the Last Africans Brought to America* (New York: Oxford University Press, 2007), 75, 84.

64. See for example, "Run Away Saturday," *South-Carolina Gazette*, May 3, 1735; "Run Away from Ja: Bulloch's Plantation," *South Carolina Gazette*, December 7, 1738; "Run Away," *Georgia Gazette*, November 1, 1775; "Ran Away from Mr. M'Gillivray's plantation," *Georgia Gazette*, November 22, 1769; "Run Away from the Subscriber," *Georgia Gazette*, October 15, 1766.

65. "Run Away," *Georgia Gazette*, November 12, 1766.

66. "20 Dollars Reward," *South Carolina State Gazette and Columbian Advertiser*, November 29, 1806.

67. "Run Away from the Subscriber's Plantation True-Blue," *South-Carolina Gazette*, November 28–December 1761. See also *Georgia Gazette*, September 3, 1766, December 24, 1766, May 13, 1767; *South Carolina Gazette*, June 14, 1760.

68. "Taken Up," *North Carolina Gazette*, February 24, 1775.

69. Based on the study of the 4,000 ads of *The Geography of Slavery in Virginia*, http://www2.vcdh.virginia.edu/gos/index.html (accessed 05/03/2010).

70. "Run Away," *South-Carolina Gazette*, June 7, 1773.

71. "Run Away from My Plantation," *South-Carolina Gazette,* October 17, 1761.

72. "Run Away from Mr. Paine's Plantation," *South Carolina Gazette*, February 9, 1734.

73. "Run Away from One of the Subscriber's Plantations," *South-Carolina Gazette*, October 31, 1761. "Run-Away Some Time in February Last," *State Gazette of South Carolina*, April 3, 1786.

74. Numerous ads mention tools in the hands of artisans. See, for example, *Virginia Gazette* (Purdie & Co), May 2, 1766; *Maryland Journal*, January 27, 1778; *Wilmington Centinel and General Advertiser*, June 18, 1788; *Virginia Gazette* (Purdie & Dixon), September 14, 1769; *Gazette of the State of Georgia*, December 11, 1783; *Gazette of the State of Georgia*, December 9, 1783; Thomas Jefferson advertised for his shoemaker, Sandy, who took his tools and a horse, *Virginia Gazette* (Purdie & Dixon), Williamsburg, September 14, 1769.

75. Gooch to the Lords of Trade, Williamsburg, June 29, 1729, *Colonial Office Papers*. Reproduced in Michael Mullin, ed., *American Negro Slavery: A Documentary History* (Columbia: University of South Carolina Press, 1976), 83. See, for example, Mullin, *Flight and Rebellion*, 43; Allan Kulikoff, *Tobacco and Slaves: The Development of Southern Cultures in the Chesapeake, 1680–1800* (Chapel Hill: University of North Carolina Press, 1986), 328; James Sidbury, *Ploughshares into Swords: Race, Rebellion, and Identity in Gabriel's Virginia, 1730–1810* (New York: Cambridge University Press, 1997), 22, n25; Mechal Sobel, *Trabelin'on: The Slave Journey to an Afro-Baptist Faith* (Princeton: Princeton University Press, 1988), 258, n25.

76. T. E. Campbell, *Colonial Caroline: A History of Caroline County*, Virginia (Richmond: Dietz Press, Inc., 1954), 72.

77. John Pendleton Kennedy, ed., *Calendar of Transcripts: Including the Annual Report of the Department of Archives and History* (Richmond: Davis Bottom, Superintendent Public Printing, 1905), 373.

78. "Hanover Town," *Virginia Gazette* (Purdie & Dixon), August 19 and October 28, 1773.

79. *Slave Trade Database* (accessed 11/1/2010).

80. "Taken Up," *Cape Fear Mercury*, November 24, 1769; "Brought to the Work-House," *State Gazette of South-Carolina*, August, 11, 1785; "Notice," ibid., December 6, 1787; "Brought to the Work-House," ibid., January 23, 1786; "Notice," *Columbian Herald*, August 10, 1785.

81. Declarations regarding runaway slaves in St. Charles Parish, in Albert Thrasher, *On to New Orleans! Louisiana's Heroic 1811 Slave Revolt* (New Orleans: Cypress Press, 1995), 228.

82. "Run Away from Mr. George Sommer's," *South-Carolina Gazette*, February 16–23, 1738; "Run Away from the Subscriber," *South-Carolina Gazette and the Public Advertiser*, November 26, 1785; Declarations regarding Runaway Slaves in St. Charles Parish, in Thrasher, *On to New Orleans!* 228; "Strayed," *Charleston Morning Post and Daily Advertiser*, April 28, 1786; "Ten Dollars Reward," *Georgia Gazette*, January 1, 1790.

83. "Just arrived from Africa," *Virginia Gazette* (Purdie & Dixon), Williamsburg, August 16, 1770; "RUN Away," *Virginia Gazette* (Rind), Williamsburg, February 7, 1771; "Now in the Gaol of Alexandria," *Virginia Gazette* (Rind), Williamsburg, August 1, 1771.

84. "Run Away from the Plantation of Isaac Porcher," *South-Carolina Gazette*, August 6–13, 1737.

85. "One Hundred and Ten Pounds Reward," "Newbern, December 20, 1774," *North-Carolina Gazette*, February 4, 1775.

86. "Runaways," *North-Carolina Gazette*, May 5, 1775.

87. "Taken Up," *South Carolina Gazette*, February 25, 1734.

88. "Runaway Negroes," *Telegraph and Texas Register*, April 6, 1839.

89. "Williamsburg, Jan. 14, 1766," *Virginia Gazette* (Purdie & Dixon), January 15, 1767.
90. "Run Away," *North Carolina Gazette*, July 18, 1777.
91. "Run-Away," *South-Carolina Gazette and Country Journal*, January 15, 1771. Also "Run Away Last July," *South-Carolina Gazette*, March 1, 1773.
92. "Run Away," *Gazette of the State of Georgia*, July 17, 1788; "Run Away," *Georgia Gazette,* December 4, 1788; "Ran Away the Week before Last," *Georgia Gazette*, July 23, 1789; "Run Away," *Georgia Gazette*, July 22, 1790. A woman named Patty left at the same time, but there is no indication that they stayed together.
93. "Run Away from Tho: Wright," *South Carolina Gazette*, April 27, 1738.
94. "Surry County, June 25, 1754," *Virginia Gazette* (Hunter), July 19, 1754.
95. "Committed," *North Carolina Gazette*, February 24, 1775.
96. "Run Away from My Plantation at Ashepoo," *South-Carolina Gazette*, December 19–26, 1761; "Run Away, the Beginning of September Last," ibid., January 22–29, 1763; "Run Away in November Last," ibid., January 14–28, 1764.
97. "200 Dollars Reward," *Moniteur de la Louisiane*, January 15, 1811.
98. *Slave Trade Database*, VIN 90734 (accessed 1/5/2009).
99. "Run Away from My Plantation at Ashepoo," *South-Carolina Gazette*, December 19–26, 1761. Parson stated that Arrow had left "about fourteen months" earlier.
100. "Run Away, the Beginning of September Last," *South-Carolina Gazette*, January 22–29, 1763; "Run Away in November Last," ibid., January 14–28, 1764.
101. "Taken Up," *Georgia Gazette*, April 19, 1769.
102. "William Walker," *South-Carolina Gazette*, November 29, 1760.
103. "Negroes Taken Up," *Virginia Gazette and General Advertiser* (Davis), November 23, 1791.
104. "Committed," *Virginia Gazette* (Purdie), December 27, 1776.
105. "The Owner of a New Negro Man," *South Carolina Gazette*, September 3, 1772.
106. "Came into the Subscriber's Plantation," *Royal Georgia Gazette*, January 4, 1781. See also "A New Negro," *City Gazette*, July 4, 1805; "A New Negro Woman," *City Gazette and Daily Advertiser*, September 10, 1807.
107. "Came to My Plantation," *Royal Georgia Gazette*, March 8, 1781. This James Butler is not the South Carolina James Butler.
108. Le Page du Pratz, *The History of Louisiana or of the Western Parts of Virginia and Carolina* (London: T. Becket, 1774), 22, 27.
109. "Taken in Santee River Swamp," *South Carolina Gazette*, May 11, 1765.
110. "Taken Up," *South Carolina Gazette*, January 3, 1771.

1. Perdue, ed., *Weevils*, 117.
2. Frederick Law Olmsted, *A Journey in the Back Country* (New York: Mason Brothers,1860), 48.
3. Morgan, "Colonial South Carolina," 67.
4. Kulikoff, *Tobacco*, 344–345; Gerald W. Mullin, *Flight and Rebellion,*108–109.
5. Freddie L. Parker, *Running for Freedom: Slave Runaways in North Carolina 1775–1840* (New York: Garland Publishing, 1993), 175, 180.
6. Morgan, *Slave Counterpoint*, 525–526.
7. Meaders, *Advertisements,* 21, 35; Billy G. Smith and Richard Wojtowicz, eds., *Blacks Who Stole Themselves: Advertisements for Runaways in the Pennsylvania Gazette, 1728–1790*

(Philadelphia: University of Pennsylvania Press, 1989), 107, 122; "Run Away," *American Gazette and Norfolk and Portsmouth Public Advertiser*, March 4, 1796.

8. Drew, *A North-Side View*, 225.

9. *South Carolina Gazette and American General Gazette*, August 16, 1780.

10. *Columbian Museum & Savannah Advertiser*, March 23, 1798.

11. "Abroad marriages" were welcomed by females' owners, especially on small farms, because they resulted in the increase of their enslaved property.

12. Anonymous, "On the Management of Slaves," *Southern Agriculturist and Register of Rural Affairs*, 6, 6, (June 1833), 285.

13. "Singular Relation from the Petersburg Republican," *American Masonic Register and Ladies and Gentlemen's Magazine*, 1, 3 (November 1820), 196.

14. "The Subscriber Having Removed," *South-Carolina and American General Gazette*, April 17, 1777.

15. "Fifty Dollars Reward," *Reflector*, February 10, 1818; *Register*, February 10, 1818.

16. John Davis, *Travels of Four Years and a Half in the United States of America during 1798, 1799, 1800, 1801, and 1802* (London: T. Ostell, 1803), 92–93.

17. *Virginia Gazette* (Purdie), August 21, 1778.

18. *Norfolk Herald* (Willett and O'Connor), July 14, 1801.

19. "$10 Reward for Negro Sip," *Raleigh Register and North Carolina Weekly Advertiser*, July 24, 1818.

20. Vincent Colyer, *Report of the Services Rendered by the Freed People to the United States Army in North Carolina, in the Spring of 1862* (New York: V. Colyer, 1864), 22.

21. "Taken Up," *Raleigh Register*, February 17, 1826.

22. "Taken Up," *Carolina Sentinel*, April 8, 1826; "Twenty-Five Dollars Reward," *Alexandria Daily Advertiser*, September 15, 1814.

23. Moses Grandy, *Narrative of the Life of Moses Grandy, Late a Slave in the United States of America* (London: C. Gilpin, 1843), 53–54.

24. Colyer, *Report*, 18–19.

25. "Run Away on Monday," *Gazette of the State of South Carolina*, October 7, 1778.

26. "Twenty Dollars Reward," *Western Carolinian*, June 20, 1826.

27. "New Bern," *North Carolina Gazette*, June 23, 1777.

28. Drew, *A North-Side View*, 205.

29. *North Carolina Gazette*, July 31, 1778.

30. Colyer, *Report*, 19.

31. "Fifteen Dollars Reward," *Alexandria Daily Advertiser*, October 16, 1809.

32. William Henry Singleton, *Recollections of My Slavery Days* (Peekskill, N.Y.: Highland Democrat, 1922), 4.

33. Charles Thompson, *Biography of a Slave* (Dayton, Ohio: United Brethren Publishing House, 1875), 24.

34. Colyer, *Report*, 21.

35. Grandy, *Narrative*, 54; *Independent*, LXVIII (May 26, 1910), in Blassingame, ed., *Slave Testimony*, 536.

36. William Lynwood Montell, *The Saga of Coe Ridge: A Study in Oral History* (Knoxville: University of Tennessee Press, 1970), 55–56.

37. Singleton, *Recollections*, 4–5.

38. Joseph Kelly Turner, *History of Edgecombe County, North Carolina* (Raleigh: Edwards & Broughton, 1920), 177.

39. William Dusinberre, *Them Dark Days: Slavery in the American Rice Swamps* (New York: Oxford University Press, 1995), 145.

40. Rhys Isaac, *Landon Carter's Uneasy Kingdom: Revolution and Rebellion on a Virginia Plantation* (New York: Oxford University Press, 2004), 201.

41. *The State vs. Harriett.* Harboring a Fugitive Slave. Anderson District Court of Magistrates & Freeholders. L04190. Trial Papers #271. South Carolina Department of Archives and History. Bob was condemned to receive twenty-five lashes, to be jailed for two weeks, and to receive another twenty-five lashes when he got out. Harriett was condemned to forty lashes, and Dina, because she was quite old, was not punished.

42. McCord, ed., *The Statutes at Large of South Carolina*, 10: 280.

43. *The State vs. Harry.* Harboring a Fugitive Slave. Anderson District Court of Magistrates & Freeholders. L04190. Trial Papers #136. South Carolina Department of Archives and History.

44. *The State vs. Mary. Harboring a Fugitive Slave*, Anderson District Court of Magistrates & Freeholders. L04190. Trial Papers #139. South Carolina Department of Archives and History.

45. See, for example, "Forty Dollars Reward," *Alexandria Daily Advertiser*, January 24, 1804; "100 Dollars Reward," ibid., April 13, 1813; "Forty Dollars Reward," *Richmond Enquirer*, May 31, 1807; "Ranaway," ibid., December 3, 1813; "15 Dollars Reward," ibid., May 11, 1814.

46. For relations between free blacks and runaways, see in particular Morgan, *Counterpoint*, 493–496; Franklin and Schweninger, *Runaway Slaves*, 109–111.

47. Cooper, ed., *The Statutes at Large of South Carolina*, 7:402.

48. See George McDowell Stroud, *A Sketch of the Laws relating to Slavery in the Several States of the United States of America* (Philadelphia: Kinder & Sharpless, 1827), 16–18; North Carolina 1741 Act, *Laws of North Carolina*, 89; "An Act to Provide More Effectually against the Offense of Harbouring Negro or Other Slaves," *City Gazette*, January 5, 1822; McCord, ed. *Statutes,* 10: 280; Oliver H. Prince, *A Digest of the Laws of the State of Georgia* (Milledgeville: Grantland and Orme, 1822), 452; William Goodell, *The American Slave Code in Theory and Practice* (New York: American and Foreign Anti-Slavery Society, 1853), 232–233.

49. "Ran-Away," *Carolina Federal Republican*, March 18, 1818.

50. *Virginia Gazette* (Rind), March 24, 1768; *Virginia Gazette* (Purdie & Dixon), September 29, 1768, and May 11, 1769.

51. "Run Away from Roger Saunders," *South Carolina Gazette*, April 27, 1738.

52. "Two Guineas Reward," *Georgia State Gazette*, January 12, 1788.

53. *The Charleston Daily Courier*, May 28, 1825.

54. Ronnie W. Clayton, ed., *Mother Wit: The Ex-Slave Narratives of the Louisiana Writers' Project* (New York: Peter Lang, 1990), 194.

55. "Twenty Dollars Reward," *Alexandria Advertiser and Commercial Intelligencer*, May 4, 1803; "Ran-Away," *Richmond Enquirer*, June 13, 1807.

56. James Williams, *Life and Adventures of James Williams, a Fugitive Slave, with a Full Description of the Underground Railroad* (San Francisco: Women's Union Print, 1873), 75.

57. James McKaye, *The Mastership and Its Fruits: The Emancipated Slave Face to Face with His Old Master* (New York: W. C. Bryant & Co., 1864), 8–11.

58. Rawick, ed., *American Slave*, 4, pt. 1, 22–27.

59. 1870 United States Federal Census, Troup, Georgia, 438; 1880 United States Federal Census, La Grange, Troup, Georgia, 722.

60. William H. Heard, *From Slavery to the Bishopric in the A. M. E. Church: An Autobiography* (Philadelphia: A. M. E. Book Concern, 1928), 27.

61. Henry Clay Bruce, *The New Man: Twenty-Nine Years a Slave, Twenty-Nine Years a Free Man* (York, Pa.: P. Anstadt & Sons, 1895), 36.

62. Clayton, *Mother Wit*, 107.

63. Franklin and Schweninger, *Runaway Slaves*, 78. See also Philip J. Schwarz, *Twice Condemned: Slaves and the Criminal Laws of Virginia, 1705–1865* (Baton Rouge: Louisiana State University Press, 1988), 144.

64. Rawick, ed., *American Slave*, 14, pt. 1, 27.

65. William H. Robinson, *From Log Cabin to the Pulpit or Fifteen Years in Slavery* (Eau Claire, Wis.: James H. Tifft, 1913), 29–30.

66. John James Audubon, *Ornithological Biography* (Edinburgh: Adam Black, 1831–39), volume 2, 27–32.

67. *Arkansas Gazette*, February 1, 1832, in Orville W. Taylor, *Negro Slavery in Arkansas* (Durham: Duke University Press, 1958), 216.

68. *The Charleston Mercury*, March 26, 1828.

69. Perdue, ed., *Weevils*, 125.

70. *Charleston Daily Courier*, May 8, 1825.

71. "Singular Relation," *Petersburg Republican*, 196.

72. "Recollections of Slavery by a Runaway Slave," *Emancipator*, September 20, 1838; John Homes, who lived as a maroon before running away to Canada concurred. The overseer "whipped the women, but he did not whip the men, for fear they would run away." Drew, *A North-Side View*, 168.

73. See Franklin and Schweninger, *Runaway Slaves*, 211–212.

74. Anthony E. Kaye, *Joining Places: Slave Neighborhoods in the Old South* (Chapel Hill: University of North Carolina Press, 2007), 146–147; Stephanie M. H. Camp, *Closer to Freedom: Enslaved Women & Everyday Resistance in the Plantation South* (Chapel Hill: University of North Carolina Press, 2004), 38; Dunaway, 193.

75. "Narrative of James Curry," *Liberator*, January 10, 1840.

76. "Ten Dollars Reward," *Alexandria Daily Advertiser*, May 28, 1807.

77. Morgan, "Colonial South Carolina," 67.

78. Betty Wood, "Some Aspects of Female Resistance to Chattel Slavery in Low Cuntry Georgia, 1763–1815", *Historical Journal*, 30, 3 (September 1987), 614.

79. Timothy James Lockley, *Lines in the Sand: Race and Class in Lowcountry Georgia, 1750–1860* (Athens: University of Georgia Press, 2001), 119.

80. "To Be Sold for Ready Money," *Georgia Gazette*, April 19, 1764.

81. *Georgia Gazette*, May 17, 1764.

82. *New Bern Spectator*, August 30, 1838.

83. *Virginia Gazette* (Parks), October 26 to November 2, 1739.

84. *Georgia Gazette*, December 24, 1788.

85. "Singular Relation," 196.

86. Grandy, *Narrative*, 54.

87. Petition of R. L. T. Beall to the County Court of Westmoreland, Virginia, February 1856, Library of Virginia, in *Digital Library on American Slavery*, PAR 21685603.

88. "Records of the Superior Council of Louisiana," *Louisiana Historical Quarterly*, 8, 3 (July 1925), 527–528.

89. Glenn R. Conrad, *The German Coast: Abstracts of the Civil Records of St. Charles and St. John the Baptist Parishes, 1804–1812* (Lafayette: University of Louisiana at Lafayette Press, 1981), 21. For the slave trade to Louisiana, see Thomas N. Ingersoll, "The Slave Trade and the Ethnic Diversity of Louisiana's Slave Community," *Louisiana History* 37, 2 (Spring 1996): 133–161.

90. Conrad, *German Coast*, 65–66.

91. Rawick, ed., *American Slave*, 16, Pt. 3, 248–249; John Hill Aughey, *Tupelo* (Lincoln, Nebr.: State Journal Company, 1888), 250; James W. C. Pennington, *A Narrative of Events in the Life of J. H. Banks, an Escaped Slave from the Cotton State, Alabama, in America* (Liverpool: M. Rourke, 1861), 65; Rawick, ed., *American Slave*, 12, Pt. 3, 94; F. D. Srygley, *Seventy Years in Dixie: Recollections and Sayings of T. W. Caskey and Others* (Nashville: Gospel Advocate Publishing, 1893), 278.

92. Clayton, *Mother Wit*, 179; Thompson, *Biography*, 97; Rawick, ed., *American Slave*, 11, Pt. 1, 163; Octavia V. Rogers Albert, *The House of Bondage* (New York: Hunt & Eaton, 1890), 22; McKaye, *The Mastership*, 11.

93. "Recollections," *The Emancipator*, September 13, 1838.

94. John George Clinkscales, *On the Old Plantation: Reminiscences of His Childhood* (Spartanburg, S. C., Band & White, 1916), 12.

95. William Still, *The Underground Railroad* (Philadelphia: Porter & Coates, 1872), 242.

96. Audubon, *Ornithological Biography*, 2:29.

97. Still, *Underground Railroad*, 381.

98. Liverpool *Albion*, February 20, 1858, in Blassingame, ed., *Slave Testimony*, 340.

NOTES TO CHAPTER 4: DAILY LIFE AT THE BORDERLANDS

1. Williams, *Life and Adventures*, 74.

2. "On Sunday the 21st," *Edenton Gazette and North Carolina General Advertiser*, March 2, 1819.

3. Rawick, ed., *American Slave*, 2, Pt. 6, 82; Emily P. Burke, *Reminiscences of Georgia* (Oberlin: O. J. M. Fitch, 1850), 167.

4. Rawick, ed., *American Slave*, 1:264.

5. McKaye, *The Mastership*, 8.

6. Albert, *The House of Bondage*, 3:14.

7. Colyer, *Report*, 20.

8. Rawick, ed. *American Slave*, 4, Pt. 4, 301.

9. Ibid., 4, Pt. 4, 191.

10. Ibid., *American Slave*, 1:220.

11. Heard, *From Slavery*, 26–27.

12. Perdue, ed., *Weevils*, 25.

13. Rawick, ed., *American Slave*, 1:30.

14. William Webb, *The History of William Webb Composed by Himself* (Detroit: Egbert Hoekstra, Printer, 1873), 4–5.

15. David Dodge, "The Cave-Dwellers of the Confederacy," *Atlantic Monthly* 68, 1408 (October 1891): 514–521. Details about the construction of a cave come from this text, unless they are attributed to specific informants.

16. Perdue, ed., *Weevils*, 210.

17. Rawick, ed., *American Slave*, 1:30.

18. Perdue, ed., *Weevils*, 210.

19. Ibid., 125, 209.

20. Dodge, "The Cave-Dwellers," 517.

21. Col. J. C. Stribling, "'Goober Jack,' The Runaway Slave," in *Pendleton Farmer's Society* (Atlanta: Foote & Davies Co., 1908), 93–94.

22. Mary White Ovington, "Slaves' Reminiscences of Slavery," *Independent* 68 (May 26, 1910): 1134.

23. Perdue, ed., *Weevils*, 210.

24. *Macon Telegram*, November 27, 1838.

25. Rawick, ed., *American Slave*, 4, Pt. 2, 15.

26. Ibid., 14, Pt. 4, 113.

27. Ibid., 1: 265.

28. Purdue, ed., *Weevils*, 265.

29. "Banditti," *New-Hampshire Gazette*, December 12, 1828.

30. Perdue, ed., *Weevils*, 238.

31. Ibid., 210.

32. Rawick, ed., *American Slave*, 4, Pt. 2, 14.

33. Deposition of Octave Johnson, Corporal, military records, in John W. Blassingame, *Slave Testimony: Two Centuries of Letters, Speeches, Interviews, and Autobiographies* (Baton Rouge: Louisiana University Press, 1977), 395.

34. Isaac D. Williams, *Sunshine and Shadow of Slave Life: Reminiscences as Told by Isaac D. Williams to "Tege"* (East Saginaw, Mich.: Evening News Printing and Binding House, 1885), 11.

35. Robinson, *From Log Cabin*, 32; Perdue, ed., *Weevils*, 209.

36. Ovington, "Reminiscences," 1134.

37. *Macon Telegram*, November 27, 1838; Rawick, ed., *American Slave*, 4, Pt. 2, 14; Perdue, ed., *Weevils*, 209.

38. Williams, *Sunshine*, 11.

39. Perdue, ed., *Weevils*, 125.

40. Dodge, "The Cave-Dwellers," 516–517.

41. William Wells Brown, *Clotel, or the President's Daughter* (London: Partridge & Oakey, 1853), 212–213.

42. Clinkscales, *On the Old Plantation*, 18.

43. Francis Jackson, "Fugitive Slaves," *The Liberty Bell* (Boston: Anti-Slavery Bazaar, 1858), 32.

44. Atwater, *Incidents*, 50; Helen Tunncliff Catterall, ed., *Judicial Cases concerning American Slavery and the Negro* (Washington, D.C.: Carnegie Institution, 1932), 3: 414.

45. Isaac Weld, *Travels through the States of North America* (London: John Stockdale, 1799), I, 179; Colyer, *Report*, 20.

46. Clayton, *Mother Wit*, 194.

47. Solomon Northup, *Twelve Years A Slave: Narrative of Solomon Northup* (Auburn, N.Y.: Derby and Miller, 1853), 247.

48. Rawick, ed., *American Slave*, 9, 51.

49. Ibid., 11, Pt. 1, 84.

50. Clinkscales, *On the Old Plantation*, 18; Rawick, ed., *American Slave*, 4, Pt. 1, 199.

51. Blassingame, ed., *Slave Testimony*, 652.

52. "Recollections of Slavery," *Emancipator*, September 13, 1838.

53. Drew, *A North-Side View*, 205.

54. Examples are too numerous to enumerate, but see Henry Clay Bruce, *The New Man: Twenty-Nine Years a Slave, Twenty-Nine Years a Free Man* (York, Pa.: P. Anstadt & Sons, 1895), 33; James S. G. Richardson, *Reports of Cases at Law Argued and Determined in the Court of Appeals and Court of Errors of South Carolina* (Charleston: McCarter & Co. McCarter, 1853), 6: 69–72; Still, *Underground Railroad*, 133.

55. "Records of the Superior Council of Louisiana," *Louisiana Historical Quarterly*, 19, 4 (October 1936): 1087–1088.

56. Thomas Jefferson, Edwin Morris Betts, ed., *Thomas Jefferson's Farm Book* (Chapel Hill: University of North Carolina Press, 1959), 46; Jack McLaughlin, *Jefferson and Monticello: The Biography of a Builder* (New York: MacMillan, 1990), 117.

57. Theodore Rosengarten, *Tombee Portrait of a Cotton Planter* (New York: Quill William Morrow, 1986), 638.

58. Perdue, ed., *Weevils*, 125.

59. Ibid.; Rawick, ed., *American Slave*, 14, Part 4, 113.

60. Northup, *Twelve Years a Slave*, 246.

61. Burke, *Reminiscences*, 168.

62. Williams, *Life and Adventures*, 74.

63. Rawick, ed., *American Slave*, 2, Pt. 3, 172.

64. Burke, *Reminiscences*, 168.

65. Clayton, *Mother Wit*, 88.

66. *Georgia Gazette*, September 22, 1763.

67. *The State vs. George*. Harboring a Fugitive Slave. Anderson District Court of Magistrates & Freeholders. L04190. Trial Papers #151. South Carolina Department of Archives and History.

68. Spanish Judicial Records, June 30, 1784. Louisiana State Museum.

69. Blassingame, ed., *Slave Testimony*, 321.

70. Thompson, *Biography*, 99.

71. Edward J. Thomas, *Memoirs of a Southerner 1840–1923* (Savannah, Ga., 1923), 14.

72. *Newbern North Carolina Gazette*, July 11, 1777.

73. Rawick, ed., *American Slave*, 4, Pt. 3, 96.

74. Ibid., 4, Pt. 1, 147.

75. Ibid., 4, Part 1, 147.

76. Perdue, ed., *Weevils*, 324.

77. Rawick, ed., *American Slave*, 4, Pt. 4, 301.

78. Ovington, "Reminiscences,"1133.

79. Jacob Stroyer, *My Life in the South* (Salem: Salem Observer Book and Job Print, 1885), 65; Northup, *Twelve Years a Slave*, 246.

80. Rawick, ed., *American Slave*, 4, Pt. 2, 14–15.

81. Blassingame, ed., *Slave Testimony*, 538.

82. Dusinberre, *Them Dark Days*, 164; Plantation Journal, September 20, 1862, in James M. Clifton, ed., *Life and Labor on Argyle Island: Letters and Documents of a Savannah River Rice Plantation, 1833–1867* (Savannah: Beehive Press, 1978), 342.

83. Perdue, ed., *Weevils*, 67.

84. Bruce, *The New Man*, 32.

85. Rawick, ed., *American Slave*, 4, Pt. 1, 144.

86. Russell Herman Conwell, *The Life and Public Services of James G. Blaine* (Boston: B. B. Russell, 1884), 142.

87. E. Ophelia Settle, "Social Attitudes during the Slave Regime," in August Meier and Elliott Rudwick, ed., *The Making of Black America: Essays in Negro Life and History* (New York: Atheneum, 1969), 150.

88. Rawick, ed., *American Slave*, 11, Pt. 1,163.

89. Ibid., 4, Pt. 1, 147.

90. Jeff Forret, *Race Relations at the Margins: Slave and Poor Whites in the Antebellum Southern Countryside* (Baton Rouge: Louisiana University Press, 2006), 136–138; Larry Gara, *The Liberty Line: The Legend of the Underground Railroad* (Lexington: University of Kentucky Press, 1961).

91. Allen Parker, *Recollections of Slavery Times*. Worcester, Mass.: Chas. W. Burbank & Co., 1895), 82.

92. Peter Bruner, *A Slave's Adventures toward Freedom* (Oxford, Ohio: 1919), 29.

93. Colyer, *Report*, 20.

94. Drew, *A North-Side View of Slavery*, 187. See also Northup, *Narrative*, 246.

95. N. C. Wentworth, "Slave Telegraphy," *Zion's Herald*, September 16, 1875.

96. Thompson, *Biography*, 22–23.

97. Rawick, ed., *American Slave*, 16, Pt. 1, 203; Kaye, *Joining Places*, 48.

98. Francis Fedric, *Slave Life in Virginia and Kentucky or Fifty Years of Slavery in the Southern United States* (London: Wertheim, MacIntosh and Hunt, 1863), 79.

99. Thompson, *Biography*, 98.

100. Charles F. Adams, ed., *The Works of John Adams, Second President of the United States* (Boston: Little, Brown, and Company, 1865), 2: 428.

101. W. J. Megginson, *African American Life in South Carolina's Upper Piedmont 1780–1900* (Columbia: University of South Carolina Press, 2006), 133.

102. Charles Manigault to Louis Manigault, Charleston, January 19, 1861, in Clifton, ed., *Life and Labor*, 313.

103. Leslie H. Owens, *This Species of Property* (New York: Oxford University Press, 1976), 88.

104. *South Carolina Gazette*, March 9, 1734.

105. Stroyer, *My Life*, 65.

106. Rawick, ed., *American Slave*, 4, Pt. 1, 199; Robinson, *From Log Cabin*, 32.

107. Spanish Judicial Records for May 26–27, 1781, Louisiana State Museum.

108. "State of North Carolina," *Newbern Spectator*, May 2, 1829. Tomahawks, along with guns, were also noted in the hands of a group of twelve runaways from Virginia traveling on a road at 3:00 a.m. "Runaway Slaves—Grand Battle," *Carolina Watchman*, June 14, 1845.

109. Thomas, *Memoirs*, 15. The planter shot at him. Although wounded, Emmanuel did not stop and disappeared into the woods

110. Orville W. Taylor, *Negro Slavery in Arkansas* (Durham: Duke University Press, 1958), 228; Morgan, *Slave Counterpoint*, 389–391.

111. Atwater, *Incidents*, 50.

112. "25 Dollars Reward," *Carolina Centinel*, May 30, 1818.

113. *Raleigh Register* and *North Carolina Gazette*, May 3, 1816, in Parker, *Stealing*, 259.

114. See among other such notices: *Memphis Enquirer*, May 17, 1839; *Ulster Plebeian*, May, 23, 1818; *Republican Star*, April 10, 1810; *New England Weekly Journal*, October 10, 1738, and December 9, 1728; *Pennsylvania Gazette*, May 4, 1749; *New-York Gazette*, November 5, 1770, and July 1, 1776; *Virginia Gazette* (Purdie and Dixon), May 28, 1767; *City Gazette* and *Daily Advertiser*, August 30, 1794; *South Carolina Gazette* and *Country Journal*, December 11, 1770; *South Carolina Gazette*, July 21, 1766.

115. Wood, *Slavery*, 185.

116. Morgan, *Slave Counterpoint*, 390–391.

117. *The Geography of Slavery*, http://www.vcdh.virginia.edu/gos/ (accessed 1/2/ 2010).

118. For a sample, see "Runaway Slaves Captured," *Arkansas Intelligencer*, July 16, 1858; "Liberty or Death," *Liberator*, December 31, 1859, and "Escape," June 11, 1831; "The Insurrection Excitement," *(Houston) Weekly Telegraph*, July 31, 1860, and "Texas Items," May 29, 1860; "Elopement of a Gang of Runaway Negroes," *Vermont Phoenix*, July 18, 1845; "Runaway Negroes," *North Star*, October 12, 1849; "More Troubles with Slaves," *Liberator*, June 21, 1861.

119. Stroyer, *My Life*, 65.

120. Conrad, *German Coast*, 65, 69.

121. Theodore Weld, *American Slavery as It Is: Testimony of a Thousand Witnesses* (New York: American Anti-Slavery Society, 1839), 14–15.

122. Bringier *Messenger*, April 28, 1854, in Taylor, *Negro Slavery*, 192.

123. "Records of the Superior Council of Louisiana," February 22, 1749, *Louisiana Historical Quarterly* 20, 2 (April, 1937): 493.

124. Colyer, *Report*, 20. For poor whites and guns and powder, see Forret, *Race Relations at the Margins*, 89, 100.

125. Stroyer, *My Life*, 66.

126. Melvin Grigsby, *The Smoked Yank* (Sioux Falls: Dakota Bell Pub. Co., 1888),155.

127. *Charleston Daily Courier*, May 28, 1825.

128. *Charleston Mercury*, March 26 and April 17, 1828.

129. Cutting firewood was also one of the activities of the maroons who lived near Lima, Peru. Enslaved and free women sold it in the streets. See Christine Hünefeldt, *Paying the Price of Freedom: Family and Labor among Lima's Slaves, 1800–1854* (Berkeley: University of California Press, 1994), 82.

130. "New Orleans, July 11," *Boston Daily Advertiser*, August 12, 1820.

131. "Runaway Negroes' Camp," *Daily Picayune*, March 30, 1848.

132. Morgan, *Slave Counterpoint*, 304.

133. *City Gazette* and *Daily Advertiser*, November 13, 1806.

134. Paquet had fed the men, although he knew they were maroons. Found guilty of harboring runaways on June 4, 1808, he was ordered to pay $124 in fines to two slave owners and to the parish. Conrad, *German Coast*, 65–66.

135. Singleton, *Recollections*, 5.

136. Robert G. McLean, ed., "A Yankee Tutor in the Old South," *North Carolina Historical Review*, 47 (1970): 62.

137. Ovington, "Reminiscences," 1133.

138. Perdue, ed., *Weevils*, 210.

139. Rawick, ed., *American Slave*, 16, Pt. 3, 248–249.

140. Singleton, *Recollections*, 4.

141. Thompson, *Biography*, 30.

142. Pickard, *The Kidnapped*, 188.

143. Rawick, ed., *American Slave*, 11, Pt. 1, 163.

144. Drew Gilpin Faust, "Culture, Conflict, and Community: The Meaning of Power on an Ante-Bellum Plantation." *Journal of Social History*, 14, 1 (Autumn 1980), 91; E. E. McCollam Plantation Diary, April 1847, and William Taylor Diary, August 2, 1840, in Taylor, *Slavery in Louisiana*, 191.

145. Rawick, ed., *American Slave*, 4, Pt. 2, 52; 1880 U. S. Federal Census, Penfield, Greene County, Georgia, 334.

146. Colyer, *Report*, 21.

147. Rawick, ed., *American Slave*, Supplement, Series 1, Pt. 4, 1500–1501.

148. American Freedmen's Inquiry Commission in Blassingame, ed., *Slave Testimony*, 434.

149. See Kaye, *Joining Places*, 132–135; Thomas C. Buchanan, *Black Life on the Mississippi: Slaves, Free Blacks, and the Western Steamboat World* (Chapel Hill: University of North Carolina Press, 2004), 114–115; Morgan, *Slave Counterpoint*, 467–468; Weld, *American Slavery*, 21.

150. William J. Anderson, *Life and Narrative of William J. Anderson, Twenty-Four Years a Slave* (Chicago: Daily Tribune Book and Job Printing Office, 1857), 29; Drew, *A North-Side View*, 211.

151. Drew, *A North-Side View*, 205.

152. Clinkscales, *On the Old Plantation*, 20.

153. Rawick, ed., *American Slave*, 14, Part 4, 113.

154. Ibid., 16, Pt. 1, 261.

155. Ibid., 4, Pt. 1, 147.

156. Stroyer, *My Life*, 66; Bruce, *The New Man*, 33–34.

157. Will T. Hale, *History of DeKalb County Tennessee* (Nashville: Paul Hunter Publisher, 1915), 101–103.

158. Fedric, *Slave Life*, 79–83.

159. "Negro Camp Discovered—High Living," *Jamestown Journal*, February 20, 1857.

160. "A Camp of Runaways Arrested," *Georgia Telegraph*, February 20, 1855.

NOTES TO CHAPTER 5: HINTERLAND MAROONS

1. For all these reasons, locating maroon sites is a difficult archeological endeavor. See, in particular, Holly K. Norton and Christopher T. Espenshade, "The Challenge in Locating Maroon Refuge Sites at Maroon Ridge, St. Croix," *Journal of Caribbean Archeology*, 7 (2007): 1–16; Charles E. Orser, Jr., and Pedro P. Funari, "Archeology and Slave Resistance and Rebellion," *World Archeology*, 33, 1 (June 2001): 61–72.

2. For men in the West Indies who fetched their wives and children once the crops had matured, see in particular Jean Baptiste Du Tertre, *Histoire générale des Antilles habitées par les François* (Paris: Chez Thomas Iolly, 1667), 2: 536.

3. Letter from Roderick McIntosh to Isaac Young, November 18, 1765, *Royal Council Journals*, November 25, 1765; "By the Mails New Orleans, Nov. 23," *Newport Mercury*, December 15, 1827; "Runaways," *Marion Star*, June 18, 1861.

4. "Eight Dollars Reward," *Gazette of the State of Georgia*, July 28, 1785; ibid., September 8, 1785; "Run Away," ibid., August 24, 1786; "Ran Away," *Georgia Gazette*, May 21, 1789; "Run Away," ibid.

5. "One Hundred Dollars Reward," *Georgia Gazette*, February 5, 1795.

6. *East Florida Papers*, February 28, March 5, March 12, April 26, April 27, April 30, May 1, 1795, reel 51.

7. Seagrove to Governor Henry White of East Florida, July 4, 1797, *East Florida Papers*, July 4, 1797, reel 42.

8. Robinson, *From Log Cabin*, 29.

9. Ibid., 31.

10. Allen D. Candler, ed., *The Colonial Records of the State of Georgia* (Atlanta: Franklin-Turner, 1907), 14:292–293.

11. In other maroon camps in the Americas, a probation period was customary for new—voluntary and involuntary—recruits. For example, in Jamaica the Leeward Maroons isolated the newcomers and the Windward Maroons made them take a drastic oath; in Cuba they were not allowed to leave their new settlement for two years. In French Guiana a captured fifteen-year-old who, with his parents, had been a maroon for "eighteen moons," revealed that new recruits were taken to the settlement—which counted seventy-two people—by numerous detours off the regular paths so that they could not find their way back. The people of Neti Jambon in Suriname were just as careful. They made a borderland maroon who wanted to join them wait for two months before they took him to their village. Price, ed., *Maroon Societies*, 17 ; Sylvie Mirot, "Un document inédit sur le marronage à la Guyane française au XVIIIe siècle," *Revue d'histoire des colonies*, 41(1954): 245–256; Wim Hoogbergen, *Out of Slavery: A Surinamese Roots History* (Berlin: Lit Verlag, 2008), 28.

12. *Royal Council Journal*, November 25, 1765.

13. Letter from Roderick McIntosh to Isaac Young, November 18, 1765, *Royal Council Journal*, November 25, 1765, South Carolina Department of Archives and History.

14. Ibid., McIntosh to Isaac Young, November 18, 1765.

15. Richard M. Brown, *The South Carolina Regulators* (Cambridge: Harvard University Press, 1963), 32; Ira Berlin, *Many Thousands Gone: The First Two Centuries of Slavery in North America* (Cambridge, Mass.: Belknap Press of Harvard University Press, 1998), 170.

16. "Extract of a Letter from South Carolina Dated October 2," *Gentleman's Magazine*, 10 (1740): 127–129.

17. David J. McCord, ed., *The Statutes at Large of South Carolina* (Columbia, 1840), 7: 410.

18. For the significance of the flags, see John Thornton, "African Dimensions of the Stono Rebellion," *American Historical Review*, 96 (October 1991): 111.

19. *Journal of the Commons House of Assembly, 1763–68*, 347 in Lockley, ed., *Maroon Communities*, 21.

20. "Wilmington, July 2," *Wilmington Centinel*, July 2, 1788.

21. Harriet Jacobs recounted that when she passed through Cabarus Pocosin, "Peter took a quantity of tobacco to burn to keep off the mosquitos. It produced the desired effect on them." Harriet Jacobs, in L. Maria Child, ed., *Incidents in the Life of a Slave Girl. Written by Herself Linda Brent* (Boston: 1861), 172.

22. Petition of Richard Lewis and twenty-one others, August 25, 1856, Governors Letter Book, 43, 514–515, North Carolina State Archives.

23. "Killed by Runaway Slaves," *Sun*, August 16, 1856.

24. See, for example, David Davidson, "Negro Slave Control and Resistance in Colonial Mexico, 1519–1650," *Hispanic American Historical Review*, 46, 3 (August 1966): 248; Thomas Atwood, *The History of the Island of Dominica* (London, Printed for J. Johnson, 1791), 237, 242.

25. "By the Mails New Orleans, Nov. 23," *Newport Mercury*, December 15, 1827.

26. "Georgetown S. C. June 14," *Rhode Island Republican*, July 6, 1826.

27. "Runaways," *Marion Star*, June 18, 1861, in Howell Meadoes Henry, "The Police Control of the Slave in South Carolina," Ph.D. dissertation, Vanderbilt University (Emory, Virginia, 1914), 120.

28. Judith A. Carney and Richard N. Rosomoff, *In the Shadow of Slavery: Africa's Botanical Legacy in the Atlantic World* (Berkeley: University of California Press, 2009), 91.

29. Northup, *Twelve Years a Slave*, 169.

30. Robinson, *From Log Cabin*, 32.

31. Henry Bibb, *Narrative of the Life and Adventures of Henry Bibb, An American Slave, Written by Himself* (New York: Published by the Author, 1849), 27; Herbert C. Covey, *African American Slave Medicine: Herbal and Non-Herbal Treatments* (Lanham: Lexington Books, 2007), 28, 69, 109–110, 140.

32. For cabbage leaves, see Rawick, ed., *American Slave*, 13: 35, 94, and 18: 112; S. J. Celestine Edwards, *From Slavery to a Bishopric* (London: John Kensit, 1891), 39; Austin Stewart, *Twenty-Two Years a Slave and Forty Years a Freeman* (Canandaigua, N.Y.: Published by the Author, 1867), 16.

33. Covey, *Slave Medicine*, 118, 143; Rawick, ed., *American Slave*, 11, Pt. 2, 135.

34. Rawick, ed., *American Slave*, 4, Pt. 4, 75.

35. Louis Dupre, *Fagots from the Camp Fire* (Washington, D. C.: Emily Thornton Charles & Co., Publishers, 1881), 52; Rebecca Latimer Felton, *Country Life in Georgia in the Days of My Youth* (Atlanta: Index Printing Company, 1919), 103.

36. Rawick, ed. *American Slave*, 16, Pt. 2, 99, 183; ibid., 4, Pt. 1, 302.

37. "A Party of Three Gentlemen," *City Gazette*, December 20, 1824; "Georgetown (S.C.), Dec. 21," *Carolina Gazette,* December 21, 1824.

38. "Negroes," *Liberator*, April 28, 1832.

39. Petition of Inhabitants of Craven County to the North Carolina General Assembly, December 19, 1831, Records of the General Assembly, Session Records, North Carolina State Archives.

40. "Index to the Spanish Judicial Records of Louisiana," *Louisiana Historical Quarterly*, 20, 3 (July 1937): 849.

41. "Remark," *South Carolina Gazette*, September 14, 1772.

42. Deposition of Octave Johnson, in Blassingame, ed., *Slave Testimony*, 395.

43. In 1816 the militia was sent after them, and their leaders Mowby and Dunmore, as well as other principals, were executed. Governor David Williams's annual message to the General Assembly, November 24, 1816, in *Charleston City Gazette*, December 6, 1816; undated petition to the General Assembly, no. 2849, South Carolina Archives.

44. This and subsequent paragraphs are based on "A Nest of Runaway Negroes," *Torch Light and Public Advertiser*, July 12, 1827; "Mobile, June 21st," *New-York Spectator*, July 17, 1827.

45. *The Annual Report of the Commissioner of Indian Affairs* (Washington, D.C.: Thomas Allen, 1841).

46. "The Tuscarora Expedition. Letters of Colonel John Barnwell," *South Carolina Historical and Genealogical Magazine*, 9, 1–3 (January 1908), 43.

NOTES TO CHAPTER 6: THE MAROONS OF BAS DU FLEUVE, LOUISIANA: FROM THE BORDERLANDS TO THE HINTERLAND

1. Several letters are part of the "Cuban Papers" or "Papeles Procedentes de Cuba" held in Sevilla, Spain. The "Actas" or *Acts and Deliberations of the New Orleans Cabildo* are held at the New Orleans Public Library. The original transcripts of several depositions, used in this study, are at the Louisiana State Museum. Summaries (in English) can be found in "Index to the Spanish Judicial Records of Louisiana," *Louisiana Historical Quarterly*, 16, 3 (July 1933), 517–520; ibid., 20, 3 (July 1937): 840–865.

2. The description of these events is based on the sixty-page interrogations (in Spanish) of Juan Bautista, Pedro St. Martin, Luis St. Martin, Santiago Lamothe, and Alexandro Dupont; and the maroons Juan Baptista, Pedro, Margarita, Nancy, Maria Juana,

and Zephir in *Spanish Judicial Records* for May 26–27, and June 20, 1781, Louisiana State Museum.

3. It was composed of Bienvenu and ten of his men, the widow Arnoult's overseer Santiago Lamothe, Pedro St. Martin, his son Luis, and the tutor Alexandro Dupont, as well as Mr. Girard and six of his slaves.

4. John H. Deiler, *The Settlement of the German Coast of Louisiana and the Creoles of German Descent* (Philadelphia: Americana Germanica Press, 1909), 136.

5. "Records of the Superior Council of Louisiana," *Louisiana Historical Quarterly,* 4 (January–October 1921): 224.

6. *Actas del Cabildo*, May 28, 1784.

7. On April 1, 1785, d'Arensbourg signed a document acknowledging having received one hundred piastres—out of two hundred—for his "Negre St Malo." The receipt is in the Heartman Manuscript Collection, Xavier University Library.

8. Unless specified, the following paragraphs are based on the interrogations of Goton, Theresa, Catiche, Maria, Juan Pedro, Carlos, Jasmin, and Alexandro in the *Spanish Judicial Records*, March 1, 1783.

9. Miro to de Galvez, July 31, 1784, *Cuban Papers*, leg. 3A, doc. 638.

10. *Actas del Cabildo*, May 28, 1784.

11. *An Account of Louisiana: Being an Abstract of Documents, in the Offices of the Department of State and the Treasury* (Philadelphia: William Duane, 1803), 45, 12.

12. The episode was described by Juan Pedro, pages 161–162 of the *Spanish Judicial Records* for March 1, 1781.

13. Interrogations of Patricio McNamara, Francisco Delery, and the free mulattoes Pedro Langlishe Luis, and Santiago called Belair. Continuation of the interrogations of Goton, Theresa, Catiche, Maria, Juan Pedro, Carlos, Jasmin, and Alexandro, in *Spanish Judicial Records*, March 1, 1783.

14. In 1786, Francisca Pugeol, the widow of St. Amant, was still asking for compensation for his death. *Actas del Cabildo*, August 10, 1786.

15. See *Spanish Judicial Records*, October 25, 1784, verso of 198. Juan Luis Chabert and Antonio Delery were pardoned because they had helped capture the rest of the fugitives.

16. Bouligny to Miro, June 14, 1784, *Cuban Papers*, leg. 10, 182–185.

17. *Spanish Judicial Records*, May 14, 1783, 172–182.

18. Ibid., 184–185 verso.

19. Ibid.,186–194.

20. Estevan Miro to Conde de Galvez, July 31, 1784, *Cuban Papers*, leg. 3A, doc. 638.

21. Miro to de Galvez, July 31, 1784, *Cuban Papers*, leg. 3A.

22. Lt. Col. Francisco Bouligny sent a long report to Governor Miro covering the events of May 18 to 21, 1784. Details were provided by captured maroons, *Cuban Papers,* leg. 10. The following paragraphs are based on this document, unless otherwise specified.

23. *Actas del Cabildo*, April 26, 30. See Caroline M. Burson, *The Stewardship of Don Esteban Miro, 1782–1792: A Study of Louisiana Based Largely on the Documents in New Orleans* (New Orleans: American Printing Company, 1940), 111–113 for translation.

24. *Cuban Papers*, leg. 2549, doc. 127, fol. 550–553; *Actas del Cabildo*, April 30, 1784.

25. *Cuban Papers,* leg. 10, May 18 to 21, 1784. The following paragraphs are based on this document, unless otherwise specified.

26. *Actas del Cabildo*, May 28, 1784; see also Burson, *Stewardship*, 113–114.

27. Miro to Bouligny, May 28, 1784, *Cuban Papers*, leg. 3A, doc. 609.

28. *Actas del Cabildo*, June 4, 1784.

29. Bouligny to Miro, June 3, 1784, *Cuban Papers*, leg. 10, 160–164. The following paragraphs are based on this document, unless otherwise specified.

30. Bouligny to Miro, June 9, 1784, *Cuban Papers*, leg. 10, 173–176.

31. Bouligny to Miro, June 3, 1784, *Cuban Papers*, leg. 10, 160–164

32. The fifteen women were Cecilia, Caton, Francisca, Theresa, Janneton, Meli (Nely), Naneta, Margarita, Charlota, Genoveva, Julie, "a black woman," Margarita, Venus, and Rosete.

33. *Spanish Judicial Records*, October 25, 1784.

34. Bouligny to Miro, June 14, 1784, *Cuban Papers*, leg. 10, 186–189.

35. Ibid.

36. When comparing the June 3rd list of maroons thought to be with St. Malo and the list of people who were condemned, it is possible to identify the seventeen men and women imprisoned after the raid.

37. Miro to de Galvez, July 31, 1784, *Cuban Papers*, leg. 3A, doc. 638.

38. *Actas del Cabildo*, June 25, 1784.

39. Bouligny to Miro, June 14, 1784, *Cuban Papers*, leg. 10, 182–185.

40. Bouligny to Miro, June 19, 1784, *Cuban Papers*, leg. 10, 192–195.

41. Because of the controversy over the arrest and condemnation of Bautista, the clergy refused to cooperate and to give the extreme unction to the condemned. *Actas del Cabildo*, June 25, July 2, 1784. For details about the polemic, see Din, *Spaniards*, 103–106, 114.

42. *Spanish Judicial Records*, October 25, 1784.

43. Bouligny to Miro, June 19, 1784, *Cuban Papers*, leg. 10,192–195.

44. Gwendolyn M. Hall dismisses the reality of the confession on the grounds that Juan Pedro did not mention Henri, Prince, and Bautista when he had described the Bay St. Louis incident during his interrogation a year earlier. However, this argument does not hold because Juan Pedro mentioned the men's presence more than once on this occasion as noted in the court records. Her second argument is that Bouligny wanted to prove to Miró that not only were the maroons guilty, but also that he acted correctly in letting de Reggio try them. See Hall, *Africans*, 231–232. For a rebuttal, see Din, *Spaniards*, 112–115.

45. *Spanish Judicial Records*, August 7, 1784. Juan (Guenard), because he was a notorious maroon, the murderer of Francisco (Mandeville's slave) and "a great thief"; Esteban, a maroon of two years, and associate of St. Malo and Juan Pedro; Colin (Gentilly), who had run away four times and had broken into several storehouses in Barataria; and Antonio, because he had run away twice in one year and had joined St. Malo in several robberies in New Orleans and Barataria.

46. Janeton (being a maroon two years with St. Malo), Venus (eighteen months a maroon with St. Malo), Nely (one year a maroon, no association with St. Malo was mentioned), Genevieve (one year), Magdalena (two years in Barataria), and Nancy (she had been involved in the events of 1781 and 1783).

47. Margarita, Louison, and Julia (Doriocourt), Francisca, Roseta, Ansa, Naneta, Felicite (Robin Delaugny), Roseta Belhumene, and Maria Luisa Leconte.

48. Telemaco Doriocourt, a maroon of five months, Francisco Veret (six) Cupidon Veret (four), Luis Larche (four), Henrique Conway (four— he became too ill to be whipped), Treme Veret (four), Lucito Leconte (four), Cesar Maxent (five), Telemaque Macarty (six), Francisco Prebot (four), Juan Luis Rieux (six), Luis Dupard (three), Maturin Dupard (three), Jacob Dupard (three), Juan Luis Dupard (five), Cesar Gentilly (four), Queto and

Jason Leconte (one month), and Remon Leconte, who had surrendered because he "feared the expedition."

49. *Spanish Judicial Records*, October 25, 1784.

50. *Actas del Cabildo*, July 30, 1784, January 28, 1785, February 9 and 16, 1785.

51. Bastien was indeed freed and Charles Honoré Olivier received one thousand pesos as compensation. *Actas del Cabildo*, February 16, 1785.

52. George Washington Cable, "Creole Slave Songs," *Century Magazine*, 31, 6 (April 1886): 814. Creole version:

> Ouarrà St. Malo
>
> Aie! zein zens, vini fé ouarrà
> Pou' pôv' St. Malo dans l'embas!
> Yé ç'assé li avec yé chien,
> Yé tiré li ein coup d'fizi,
> Yé halé li la cyprier,
> So bras yé 'tassé par derrier,
> Yé 'tassé so la main divant;
> Ye 'marré li ape queue choual,
> Yé trainein li zouqu'à la ville.
> Divant michés là dans Cabil'e
> Yé quisé li li fé complot
> Pou' coupé cou à tout ye blancs.
> Ye 'mandé li qui so compères;
> Pôv St. Malo pas di' a-rien!
> Zize la li lir' so la sentence,
> Et pis li fé dressé potence.
> Ye hale choual—ç'arette parti—
> Pôv St. Malo resté pendi!
> Eine hèr soleil deza levée
> Quand yé pend li si la levée.
> Ye laissé so corps balancé
> Pou' carancro gagnein manzé.

53. As Gilbert Din has convincingly shown, the song mixed two episodes: the actual events of 1784 and the 1795 conspiracy at Pointe Coupée. Din, *Spaniards*, 114, 167.

NOTES TO CHAPTER 7: THE MAROONS OF BELLEISLE AND BEAR CREEK

1. Herbert Aptheker, *American Negro Slave Revolts* (New York: International Publishers, 1970. Reprint 1943), 208; Frey, *Water from the Rock*, 226–227; Morgan, "'Lowcountry Georgia' and the Early Modern Atlantic World, 1733–ca. 1820," in Philip Morgan, ed., *African American Life in the Georgia Lowcountry: The Atlantic World and the Gullah Geechee* (Athens: University of Georgia Press, 2010), 36; Betty Wood, "'High Notions of Their Liberty': Women of Color and the American Revolution in Lowcountry Georgia and South Carolina, 1765–1783," ibid., 68; Ira Berlin, *Generations of Captivity: A History of African-American Slaves* (Cambridge: Belknap Press of Harvard University Press, 2003) 128; Julia F. Smith, *Slavery and Rice Culture in Low Country Georgia, 1750–1860* (Knoxville: University of Tennessee Press, 1985), 188.

2. Savannah Writers' Project, *Savannah River Plantations* (Savannah: Georgia Historical Society, 1947), 66–69, 115–117; Harold E. Davis, *The Fledgling Province: Social and Cultural*

Life in Colonial Georgia 1733–1776 (Chapel Hill: University of North Carolina Press, 1976), 40, 42, 135.

3. William J. Northern and John Temple Graves, *Men of Mark in Georgia*, (Atlanta: A. B. Caldwell, 1912), 17–18; Philip Thomas Tucker, *The Forgotten "Stonewall of the West": Major General John Stevens Bowen* (Macon: Mercer University Press, 1997), 18.

4. *Georgia Gazette*, November 27, 1788.

5. Savannah Writers, *River Plantations*, 118. His father, one of the wealthiest men in Georgia, owned eleven plantations on over 25,000 acres. See Davis, *The Fledgling Province*, 42; Robert S. Lambert, "The Confiscation of Loyalist Property in Georgia, 1782–1786," *William and Mary Quarterly*, Third Series, 20, 1 (January 1963): 93.

6. Both men placed several newspaper ads, as they were looking for a dozen runaways from their own plantations, some absent since 1783. "Augusta, February 10," *Columbian Herald*, February 26, 1787; "Run Away," *Gazette of the State of Georgia*, September 6, 1785; "Run Away," ibid., September 21, 1786; March 1787, September 25, 1783; April 28, 1785; January 19, 1786.

7. "John Nutt, Esq.," *Royal Georgia Gazette*, May 3, 1781. Fatima was more likely a Senegambian. Along with her, a mother of three, was sold: her name was Cumba, a common name in that region.

8. "The Memorial of Lieut. Col. Graham," in Wilbur Henry Siebert, *History of the Loyalists in East Florida 1774 to 1785 during the American Revolution When Florida Was Part of the English Colony* (Florida State Historical Society, 1929), 2: 76.

9. Ibid., 2: 76–83.

10. "Run Away," *Gazette of the State of Georgia*, May 12, 1785.

11. Part of one of Mahomedy/Mahomet's ears was cut off, proof that he had run away and been captured before. *Georgia Gazette*, September 7, 1774.

12. The Petition of Godin Guerard and Sworn Oath of Samuel Bostick, December 3, 1793, Records of the General Assembly, South Carolina Department of Archives and History.

13. The Petition of Godin Guerard.

14. Also among the maroons were Jimmy, Nancy, and Patience, who freed themselves from Philip Ulmer's plantation in Chatham County, Georgia. Joe made his way to the settlement after absconding from John Lewis Bourquin, Jr., a Huguenot merchant and planter in Purrysburg, South Carolina. Peter escaped from a "Mr. Heriatt," who was most likely Robert Heriott (also spelled Heriot), a Scottish immigrant and indigo planter on the Waccamaw in Georgetown County, South Carolina.

The maroon named Dick escaped from the plantation of a retired sea captain and merchant, Clement Martin, Sr., who had migrated from the Caribbean island of St. Kitts to Jekyll Island in 1767. It is possible that Dick had come all the way to the maroon settlement from Jekyll Island more than a hundred miles away. However, there is another possible explanation for his entry into the community. After the death of Clement Martin, Sr., his son John, a Loyalist, left Jekyll and fled to East Florida; he then returned and surrendered in July 1782 in Effingham County, Georgia. Dick may have been taken to East Florida and then to Effingham from where he escaped.

About the maroons Cupid and Fortune, nothing is known; but at least one man, whose name is not known, belonged to John Lowrman (Johannes Loarman, whose Americanized name was variously spelled Lowerman, Lohrman, Lourman), a blacksmith turned overseer in Purrysburg who became a planter in Abercorn. Phillis and a boy named Sharper escaped from the plantation of Elizabeth Wright. *Gazette of the State of Georgia*, May 17, 1787, and Lewis trial record; *Journal of the Council of Safety*, October 10, 1776, in Allen D. Candler, ed., *The Revolutionary Records of the State of Georgia* (Atlanta: Franklin-Turner Co, 1908), 1: 207–208; Petition of John Lourman, January 12, 1788, in *Georgia House Journals, 1788*, 285–287. Lourman asked for compensation "for a Negro killed among the Runaway Negroes."

15. *The State vs. Lewis.*

16. Chatham County Superior Court Minutes, in the *Gazette of the State of Georgia*, October 19, 1786.

17. "Savannah, October 19," *Charleston Morning Post and Daily Advertiser*, October 26, 1786.

18. Ibid.

19. Ibid.

20. Thomas A. Williams, *U. S. Department of Agriculture Bulletin no. 101: Millets* (Washington, D.C.: Government Printing Office, 1899), 11–19; Charles Joyner, *Down by the Riverside: A South Carolina Slave Community* (Urbana: University of Illinois Press, 1984), 45–50, 96–97; Morgan, *Slave Counterpoint*, 149–153.

21. Guion Griffis Johnson, *A Social History of the Sea Islands with Special Reference to St. Helena* (Chapel Hill: University of North Carolina Press, 1930), 85; Joyner, *Down by the Riverside*, 91.

22. *Charleston Morning Post*, October 26, 1786.

23. Gen. James Jackson to the Governor of South Carolina, 1787, *Joseph Vallence Bevan Papers*, 71, 86, Georgia Historical Society.

24. A rice planter, tax collector, commissioner of roads, and representative of St. Peter Parish in the South Carolina House (1785–86 and 1789–90), Joachim Hartstone owned forty-seven people in 1790, and 1,600 acres. Lawrence S. Rowland et al., *The History of Beaufort County, South Carolina 1514–1861* (Columbia: University of South Carolina Press, 1996), 299–300; Arlin C. Miggliazzo, *To Make This Land Our Own: Community, Identity, and Cultural Adaptation in Purrysburg Township, South Carolina, 1732–1865* (Columbia: University of South Carolina Press, 2007), 288.

25. Jackson to the Governor of South Carolina.

26. "Charleston, January 8," *State Gazette of South-Carolina*, January 8, 1787.

27. Gen. James Jackson to the Governor of Georgia, 1787, *Joseph Vallence Bevan Papers*, 71, 87, Georgia Historical Society.

28. J. L. Bourquin, Jr., to Joachim Hartstone, March 14, 1787, Governor's Messages, 1783–1830, no. 423-11, South Carolina Department of Archives and History.

29. Joachim Hartstone to Peter Porcher and W. Fenwick, Representatives for St. Peter's Parish, March 15, 1787, Governor's Messages, 1786–1788, no. 423-07, South Carolina Department of Archives and History.

30. Michael E. Stevens, ed., *Journals of the House of Representatives 1787–1788,* (Columbia: University of South Carolina Press, 1981), 236–241.

31. Ibid., 241.

32. Louise N. Bailey and Elizabeth Ivey Cooper, *Biographical Directory of the South Carolina House of Representatives, 1775-1790* (Columbia: University of South Carolina Press, 1981), 3: 366–367.

33. Adele Stanton Edwards, ed., *Journals of the Privy Council, 1783–1789* (Columbia: University of South Carolina Press, 1971), 186.

34. Thomas Pinckney to Col. Thomas Hutson, March 20, 1787, *Thomas Pinckney Letter Book, 1787–1789*, South Carolina Department of Archives and History.

35. Thomas Pinckney to Colonel Patton, March 26, 1787, ibid.

36. "Proclamation," *State Gazette of South Carolina*, March 26, 1787; Thomas Pinckney to George Matthews, April 2, 1787, *Pinckney Letter Book*.

37. Military Dispatch from Col. James Gunn to Brig. Gen. James Jackson, May 6, 1787, *Joseph Vallence Bevan Papers*, Georgia Historical Society.

38. *The State vs. Lewis*.

39. Ibid. All paragraphs until the end of this section of the chapter are from *The State vs. Lewis*.

40. Col. C. C. Harshman, *The Harshman, Hashman, Hershman, Hersman Family: A History and Genealogy* (Berkeley: Col. C. C. Harshman, 1976), I, xxii–xxiii; George F. Jones and Sheryl Exley, eds., *Ebenezer Record Book 1754–1781* (Baltimore: Genealogical Publishing Co., 1991), 69, 78, 91.

41. Thomas Pinckney to Col. Thomas Hutson, March 23, 1787; Governor's Messages, 1788, no. 459. South Carolina Department of Archives and History.

42. *Gazette of the State of Georgia*, April 26, 1787.

43. James Gunn to Genl. Jackson, May 6th 1787. *Joseph Vallence Bevan Papers*, 71, 84, Georgia Historical Society; *Charleston Morning Post*, May 8, 1787.

44. *The State vs. Lewis*.

45. Gunn to Jackson.

46. *Charleston Morning Post*, May 8, 1787; *Gazette of the State of Georgia*, May 17, 1787.

47. Jane Landers, *Atlantic Creoles in the Age of Revolutions* (Cambridge: Harvard University Press, 2010), 98.

48. "Brought to the Workhouse," *Gazette of the State of Georgia*, May 31, 1787.

49. "Savannah. May 10."

50. Candler, *Revolutionary Records*, 3: 560.

51. *Gazette of the State of Georgia*, May 24, 1787.

52. Governor's Messages, 1788, no. 459. As late as February 26, 1788, no payment had been made. Stevens, *Journals*, 509, 525.

53. *The State vs. Lewis*.

54. Gunn to Jackson.

55. The planters, having lost investments in the attack, wanted to be compensated. In January 1788, John Lowrman asked for the price of one individual. The committee who reviewed the case denied his petition. Godin Guerard asked, unsuccessfully, to be compensated for "sundry negroes." In 1793, he presented another petition explaining that among the numerous people he had acquired at St. Augustine in 1785, "four . . . negroes whose proportionable value was at least one hundred guineas each were killed by the militia of this State." He confided that he and his family were "bordering on Indigence." He was not exaggerating his sudden reversal of fortune: in February 1793, a marshal's notice announced that "twenty-five Negroes, prime fellows, wenches, boys, and girls" seized from Guerard would be put up for sale in Savannah on March 30. In May, more than a thousand acres Guerard had owned were also sold at auction and in July, he died. *Georgia House Journals, 1788*, 285–287, Georgia Archives in Lockley, ed., *Maroon Communities*, 68; The Petition of Godin Guerard and Sworn Oath of Samuel Bostick, December 3, 1793, Records of the General Assembly, 1793, #151, South Carolina Department of Archives and History; "Marshal's Sale," *Georgia Gazette*, February 28, 1793; "Sale at Auction," *Georgia Gazette*, May

16, 1793; Mary Bondurant Warren, *Marriages and Deaths Abstracted from Extant Georgia Newspapers* (Heritage Papers, 1968), 1: 44.

    56. "Savannah. May 10," *Columbian Herald*, May 28, 1787.

    57. Arnoldus Vanderhorst was the owner of most of Kiawah Island and more than one hundred and forty people. He was a former House representative and state senator and a future governor (1794–1796). He was also the father of a mixed family he emancipated. See Kennedy, *Braided*, 114.

    58. Edwards, ed., *Journals of the Privy Council*, 203.

    59. "New-York, June 15," *Massachusetts Centinel*, June 23, 1787.

    60. "Savannah. May 10."

    61. La Rosa Corzo, *Runaway Slave Settlements*, 106; Wim Hoogbergen, *The Boni Maroon Wars in Suriname* (New York: Brill, 1990), 15; ibid.,17; Mirot, "Un document inédit," 254; John Gabriel Stedman; *Narrative of a Five Years' Expedition against the Revolted Negroes of Surinam* (London: J. Johnson, 1806), 118.

    62. Frey, *Water from the Rock*, 227; Wood, "High Notions of Their Liberty," 68; Morgan, "Lowcountry Georgia," 36.

NOTES TO CHAPTER 8: THE GREAT DISMAL SWAMP

    1. Henry Latham, *Black and White: A Journal of a Three Month's Tour in the United States* (London: Macmillan and Co., 1867), 109.

    2. Henry Wadsworth Longfellow, *The Poetical Works of Henry Wadsworth Longfellow* (Boston: Ticknor and Fields, 1866), 1:174–175.

    3. Floyd J. Miller, ed., *Martin R. Delany Blake; or, The Huts of America (1859–1862)* (Boston: Beacon Press, 1970), 114.

    4. Published as "Slaves in the Dismal Swamp," *Non-Slaveholder*, 3, 1 (May 1848).

    5. Frederick Douglass, *My Bondage and My Freedom* (New York and Auburn: Miller, Orton & Mulligan, 1855), 436.

    6. Edmund Jackson, "The Virginia Maroons," *Liberty Bell*, January 1, 1852.

    7. Robert Williams Fogel and Stanley L. Engerman, *Time on the Cross: The Economics of American Negro Slavery* (Boston: Little, Brown, 1974), 73–74.

    8. "The South," *Niles' Register*, September 17, 1831; "Somewhat Alarming," *Norwich Courier* (September 21): 1831.

    9. "The Insurrection," *New Hampshire Gazette*, September 6, 1831.

    10. Aptheker, *American Negro Slave Revolts*, 308.

    11. Michael Gomez, *Reversing Sail: A History of the African Diaspora* (Cambridge: Cambridge University Press, 2004), 119; Adéléké Adéèkó, *The Slave's Rebellion* (Bloomington: Indiana University Press, 2005),164; Parker, *Running for Freedom*, 33.

    12. "Dismal Swamp Canal," *Virginia Chronicle*, September 8, 1792.

    13. Frederick Street, "In the Dismal Swamp," *Frank Leslie's Popular Monthly* (March 1903): 530; Edmund Ruffin, "Observations Made during an Excursion to the Dismal Swamp," *American Railroad Journal*, 6 (February 23, 1837), 125.

    14. The men were hired at about $100 a year paid to their owners. For details, see Olmsted, *A Journey*, 114–115. Robert C. McLean, ed., "A Yankee Tutor in the Old South," *North Carolina Historical Review*, 68, 1 (January 1970), 56–57.

    15. Grandy, *Narrative*, 11.

    16. He escaped from the South in 1833.

    17. "Fifty Dollars Reward," *Star*, August 21, 1812.

[342]

18. "50 Dollars Reward," *Edenton Gazette*, February 1, 1811.

19. James Redpath, *The Roving Editor, or Talks with Slaves in the Southern States* (New York: A. B. Burdick Publisher, 1859), 289–290.

20. "Slaves in the Dismal Swamp," *Non-Slaveholder*, 115; Street, "In the Dismal Swamp," 530.

21. *The New American Encyclopaedia: A Popular Dictionary of General Knowledge*, vol. 6 (New York: Appleton and Co., 1872), 505.

22. Olmsted, *A Journey*, 121.

23. Alexander Hunter, "The Great Dismal Swamp," *Outing*, 27, 1 (October 1895): 71.

24. "Ran Away from the Subscriber," *Herald of Freedom*, March 27, 1799.

25. Calvin Henderson Wiley, *Adventures of Old Dan Tucker, and His Son Walter: A Tale of North Carolina* (London: Willoughby, 1851), 94–95; Jackson, "Virginia Maroons"; Hunter, "The Great Dismal Swamp," 71.

26. Street, "Dismal Swamp," 530; Roy F. Johnson, *Tales from Old Carolina: Traditional and Historical Sketches of the Area between and about the Chowan River and Great Dismal Swamps* (Murfreesboro, N.C.: Johnson Pub. Co., 1965), 160.

27. William Byrd, *The Westover Manuscripts . . . Written from 1728 to 1736, and Now First Published* (Petersburg: Edmund and Julian C. Ruffin, 1841), 17.

28. "Historic Sullivan Pond," *Times Dispatch*, February 12, 1905.

29. "One Hundred Dollars Reward," *American Beacon*, June 22, 1816.

30. North Carolina General Assembly, *Laws of North Carolina 1846–1847* (Raleigh: Thomas J. Lemay, 1848), 109–113. "An Act to provide for the apprehension of runaway slaves in the great Dismal Swamp and for other purposes" (chapter 46).

31. Gates County, *Registration of Slaves to Work in the Great Dismal Swamp, 1847–1861*, North Carolina State Archives.

32. *Laws of North Carolina*, 110.

33. Redpath, *The Roving Editor*, 292.

34. Olmsted, *A Journey*, 179.

35. "The Great Dismal," *The Daily Advertiser*, August 13, 1790; Schoepf, *Travels*, 2:100; Stuart, *A Tour*, 2, 102; Redpath, *The Roving Editor*, 293; Olmsted, *A Journey*, 159.

36. McLean, ed., "Yankee Tutor," 62 .

37. "The Dismal Swamp," *Sun*, April 17, 1845.

38. Robert Arnold, *The Dismal Swamp and Lake Drummond: Early Recollections* (Norfolk: Green, Burke & Gregory, 1888), 38–41.

39. "Slaves in the Dismal Swamp," *The Non-Slaveholder*, 3, 1 (May 1848), 115.

40. Redpath, *The Roving Editor*, 293.

41. Henry Clay Roome, *Southward in Roamer: Being a Description of the Inside Route from New York to Florida* (New York: The Rudder Publishing Company, 1907), 36.

42. Hunter, "The Great Dismal Swamp," 71.

43. Porte Crayon [David Hunter Strother], "The Dismal Swamp." *Harper's New Monthly Magazine* (September 1856): 451.

44. Perdue, ed., *Weevils*, 252.

45. Porte Crayon, "The Dismal Swamp,"*Harper's New Monthly Magazine*, (September 1856): 441–455.

46. Marion Blackburn, "American Refugees," *Archeology* (September/October 2011): 49–58.

47. Frank H. Taylor, "Tide-Water Virginia," *Independent*, January 22, 1891.

48. *Godey's Magazine*, 133 (October 1896), 363–364; Blackburn, "American Refugees," 52.

49. Workers of the Writers' Program of the Works Projects Administration in the State of Virginia, *The Negro in Virginia* (New York: Hastings House, 1940), 126.

50. "Peat in the Dismal Swamp," *DeBow's Review*, 4, 4 (October1867): 371.

51. Street, "In the Dismal Swamp," 530.

52. Alexander Hunter, "Through the Dismal Swamp," *Potter's American Monthly*, 17, 115 (July 1881): 7. See also Hunter, "The Great Dismal Swamp," 70.

53. Burke, *Reminiscences*, 166–167.

54. Henry Clapp, Jr., *The Pioneer or Leaves from an Editor's Portfolio* (Lynn: J. B. Tolman, 1846), 77.

55. Johnson, *Tales*, 162–163.

56. Redpath, *The Roving Editor*, 291.

57. Street, "In the Dismal Swamp," 530.

58. Johnson, *Tales*, 162–163.

59. Hunter, "Dismal Swamp," 70.

60. Redpath, *The Roving Editor*, 292.

61. Weld, *Travels*, 1: 179; "The Game of the Dismal Swamp," *Forest and Stream*, 38, 21 (May 5, 1892): 420; "The Dismal Swamp and Its Occupants," *Natural Science News*, 1, 37 (October 12, 1895): 146.

62. H. B. Frissell and Isabel Bevier, *Dietary Studies of Negroes in East Virginia in 1897 and 1898* (Washington, D. C.: Government Printing Office, 1899), 10–11.

63. Stuart, *A Tour*, 2:102; Schoepf, *Travels*, 100; Jackson, *The Virginia Maroons*, 145; Alfred Trumble, "Through the Dismal Swamp," *Frank Leslie's Popular Monthly*, 11, 4 (April 1881), 409.

64. B. S. De Forest, *Random Sketches and Wandering Thoughts* (Albany, N.Y.: Avery Herrick, 1866), 109–110.

65. "The Dismal Swamp," *Child's Friend and Family Magazine* (January 1, 1855): 143-144.

66. "The Dismal Swamp," *Inter Ocean*, September 21, 1878.

67. Roome, *Southward*, 36.

68. Hunter, "Great Dismal," 71; Street, "In the Dismal Swamp," 530.

69. Johnson, *Tales*, 162–163.

70. "Dismal Swamp on Display," *Custer County Republican*, December 27, 1906.

71. *Caleb Winslow Family Papers*, Box 18, North Carolina State Archives.

72. "The Dismal Swamp," *Inter Ocean*, September 21, 1878.

73. WPA, *Negro in Virginia*, 127.

74. Stuart, *A Tour*, 2:101.

75. "The Great Dismal," *Daily Advertiser*, August 13, 1790.

76. Jackson, "The Virginia Maroons," 147.

77. Arnold, *Dismal Swamp*, 39.

78. WPA, *Negro in Virginia*, 127.

79. "Fifty Dollars Reward," *Star*, August 21, 1812; "$25 Reward," *New Bern Spectator*, March 7, 1829.

80. John L. Taylor, *A Revisal of the Laws of the State of North-Carolina: Passed from 1821–1825* (Raleigh: J. Gales & Sons, 1827), 82–83.

81. "Ranaway," *Phoenix*, December 31, 1838; "$100 Reward," ibid., March 9, 1839.

82. *Laws of North Carolina*, 112.

83. "Slaves in the Dismal Swamp," *North Star*, March 31, 1848.

84. Peter C. Stewart, "The Shingle and Lumber Industry in the Great Dismal Swamp," *Journal of Forest Industry*, 25, 2 (April 1981): 102.

85. "A North Carolinian," *Alexandria Gazette*, September 23, 1856; "Foreign Correspondence," *Littell's Living Age* (August 5, 1848): 3.

86. John Boyle O'Reilly, *Athletics and Manly Sport* (Boston: Pilot Publishing Company, 1890), 393.

87. Jackson, "Virginia Maroons," 150.

NOTES TO CHAPTER 9: THE MAROON BANDITS

1. Eric Hobsbawm, *Primitive Rebels: Studies in Archaic Forms of Social Movements in the 19th and 20th Centuries* (Manchester: Manchester University Press, 1959); Eric Hobsbawm, *Bandits* (London: Weidenfeld & Nicolson, 2000); Eric Hobsbawm, "Social Bandits: Reply," *Comparative Studies in Society and History*, 14, 4 (September 1972): 503–505; David P. Thelen, *Paths of Resistance: Tradition and Dignity in Industrializing Missouri* (New York: Oxford University Press, 1986), 70; William L. Van Deburg, *Hoodlums: Black Villains and Social Bandits in American Life* (Chicago: University of Chicago Press, 2004), 68.

2. *North Carolina Journal*, November 7, 1796.

3. *South Carolina and American General Gazette*, May 6, 1774, in Lockley, *Maroon Communities*, 36–38.

4. See *Georgia Gazette*, March 1, 1764; March 16, 1768.

5. By 1778, the plantation was worked by at least ninety-nine people. Drayton owned almost 14,000 acres. M. Eugene Sirmans, "The South Carolina Royal Council, 1720–1763," *William and Mary Quarterly*, Third Series, 18, 3 (July 1961): 37–392.

6. *Woodville Republican*, October 6, 1829.

7. "Georgetown, July 10," *American and Daily Advertiser*, July 14, 1801.

8. Philo Tower, *Slavery Unmasked* (Rochester: E. Darrow & Brothers, 1856), 408.

9. George Barrell Cheever, *The Guilt of Slavery and the Crime of Slaveholding: Demonstrated from the Hebrew and Greek Scriptures* (Boston: John P. Jewett, 1860), 223. See also William Dexter Wilson, *A Discourse on Slavery: Delivered before the Anti-Slavery Society in Littleton, N.H.* (Concord: Asa McFarland, 1839), 48.

10. William Bartram, *Travels through North and South Carolina, Georgia, East and West Florida* (London: J. Johnson, 1792), 469.

11. Watson, *Men and Time*, 43.

12. Derek N. Kerr, *Petty Felony, Slave Defiance, and Frontier Villainy: Crime and Criminal Justice in Spanish Louisiana, 1770–1803* (New York: Garland Publishing, 1993), 139.

13. Philemon Berry Waters, *A Genealogical History of the Waters and Kindred Families* (Atlanta: Foote & Davies Co., 1902), 41–42.

14. Executive Papers, Letters Received (Governor John Tyler), February 10, 1810, trial of Sutton. Library of Virginia. Tried on February 10, Sutton was sentenced to be hung on March 16, and valued at $400. He did not go to the gallows, though: he was transported out of the state on October 12. *Condemned Slaves, Transported Slaves*, Sutton, February 10, 1810, Box 1967, Library of Virginia.

15. Conrad, *German Coast*, 21.

16. "A Negro Harvey Birch," from *Memphis Eagle* of September 21, 1852, in *Liberator*, October 1, 1852. For false keys, see also "Remark," *South Carolina Gazette*, September 14, 1772.

17. "Domestic," *Star*, March 28, 1811.

18. The story is reconstructed from articles and one petition: "Advertisement," *Wilmington Chronicle*, July 3, 1795; "To the Public," ibid.; "Outlying Negroes," ibid., July 10,

1795; "Since Our Last," ibid., July 17, 1795; "Extract of a Letter from a Gentlemen [*sic*] in Wilmington," *Gazette of the United States*, July 18, 1795; Memorial of Henry Taylor of New Hanover County, November 1795, and Petition of Henry Taylor, 1796, General Assembly, Session Records, Miscellaneous Petitions, November–December 1796, North Carolina State Archives.

19. Memorial of Henry Taylor, and Petition of Henry Taylor; "Wilmington, July 3," *Wilmington Chronicle*, July 3, 1795. Steely's first name is given as John by Taylor and William by the newspaper.

20. Taylor, a blacksmith, became disabled and unable to care for his family and pay the physician's bills. He asked compensation from the General Assembly in November 1795 and again in 1796. His requests were denied.

21. "Advertisement."

22. "Since Our Last," ibid., July 17, 1795.

23. *Star and North-Carolina State Gazette*, November 14, 1817.

24. Harry L. Watson, "The Culture of the Republic," in Joe A. Mobley, ed., *The Way We Lived in North Carolina* (Chapel Hill: University of North Carolina Press, 2003), 211–212. One of his plantations was the famous Hope, four miles west of Windsor in Bertie County.

25. "Raleigh [N.C], Nov. 27," from *Raleigh Star*, in *American Beacon and Norfolk and Portsmouth Daily Advertiser,* December 12, 1818.

26. "Daring Negroes," *Raleigh Register and North Carolina Gazette*, November 13, 1818.

27. "On Tuesday Night."

28. "A Proclamation: $250 Reward," *Raleigh Register*, December 18, 1818.

29. "Accidents, Crimes," *Hamden Patriot*, January 7, 1819.

30. *Louisiana Gazette*, February 24, 1819.

31. "Daring Negroes."

32. "On Tuesday Night." Other "bandits" were nicknamed Abaelino. See "Abalino Again," *American Beacon and Commercial Diary*, February 4, 1817; "Another Abaelin," *New-York Gazette and General Advertiser*, April 6, 1819.

33. "A Proclamation," *Raleigh Register*, December 18, 1818.

34. R. H. Taylor, "Slave Conspiracies in North Carolina," *North Carolina Historical Review*, 5, 1–4 (January–October 1928): 24.

35. "Banditti Apprehended," *Free Press*, June 11, 1824.

36. It is not clear which Ricks owned Bob. Of all the Ricks in Southampton County, Ned had two bondpeople; so did Oswin; William had twenty-four; and Robert Ricks, Jr., had fifteen. 1820 Federal Census, Virginia, Southampton County.

37. American Colonization Society, *The Tenth Annual Report of the American Society for Colonizing Free People of Colour of the United States* (Washington: Way & Gideon, 1827), 86; 1820 Federal Census, Virginia, Nansemond County.

38. Gates County, *Slave Records, Criminal Actions against Slaves 1803–1860*, Superior Court of Law Spring Term 1824, North Carolina State Archives; "Murder," *American Mercury*, February 17, 1824; "Gates County (N. C.), Jan. 31, 1824," *Newburyport Herald*, February 13, 1824; "Horrid Murder!" *Middlesex Gazette*, February 18, 1824; "Alarming Occurrence," *Star and North Carolina State Gazette*, May 14, 1824;"Banditti Apprehended," *Free Press*, June 11, 1824.

39. He had six slaves in 1790. Walter Clark, ed., *The State Records of North Carolina* (Goldsboro: Nash Brothers, 1905), 26: 558.

40. Gates County, *Slave Records, Criminal Actions against Slaves 1803–1860*, Superior Court of Law Spring Term 1824, North Carolina State Archives.

41. "Alarming Occurrence," *Elizabeth City Star*, May 1, 1824. The version of these events related by Thomas C. Parramore in *Southampton County Virginia* (Charlottesville: University Press of Virginia, 1978) and reprised by several scholars, is inaccurate. According to Parramore, Ricks recruited the seventeen men from the coffle, then killed Cross. The rescue of two men only, not seventeen, happened three months after Cross's murder.

42. "Banditti Apprehended"; "Murderers Apprehended," *Hampden Journal*, June 23, 1824.

43. The stratagem they used is reminiscent of the maroons of Suriname and French Guiana who were reduced to using small stones and pieces of iron. Hoggbergen, *The Boni Maroon Wars*, 17; Mirot, "Un document inédit," 245–256.

44. "Banditti Apprehended."

45. "The Runaways," *Free Press*, June 25, 1824.

46. *Times and Hartford Advertiser*, November 30, 1824.

47. Petition of the inhabitants of Claremont, Clarendon, St. Johns, St. Stevens, and Richland Districts, General Assembly, 1824, Petition ND 1874, South Carolina Department of Archives and History.

48. There is no Fonberg in the various South Carolina censuses of 1810, 1820, or 1830. Fonberg may be a corruption of Fortenbery or Funderburgh. Both names appear several times in the 1820 census of Lancaster District.

49. U.S. Federal Census 1820, South Island, Georgetown, South Carolina.

50. Gov. Thomas Bennett Proclamation, South Carolina Historical Society.

51. "Charleston, Thursday Morning, May, 31," *City Gazette and Commercial Daily Advertiser*, June 1, 1821.

52. Unfortunately, all records pertaining to the trials of enslaved and free people have been destroyed. Only newspapers accounts are extant.

53. *Charleston Courier*, June 15, 1821.

54. Proclamation of Governor Thomas Bennett, in Lockley, ed., *Maroon Communities*, 98.

55. "Georgetown June 13," *City Gazette*, June 25, 1821.

56. "Militia," *Boston Commercial Gazette*, June 21, 1821.

57. William Earle, *Obi, or the History of Three-Fingered Jack* (London: Earle and Hemet, 1800); William Burdett, *The Life and Exploits of Three-Finger'd Jack, the Terror of Jamaica* (Sommers Town: A. Neil, 1801).

58. For dyeing with bark on plantations, see Elizabeth Fox-Genovese, *Within the Plantation Household: Black and White Women of the Old South* (Chapel Hill: University of North Carolina Press, 1988), 182; Morgan, *Slave Counterpoint*, 128.

59. "Joe," *City Gazette*, June 25, 1821.

60. Robert Arnold, *The Dismal Swamp and Lake Drummond: Early Recollections* (Norfolk: Green, Burke & Gregory, 1888), 8.

61. "Pineville (S.C.), 5th Oct. 1823," *Milledgeville Recorder*, October 21, 1823, in Lockley, ed., *Maroon Communities*, 112.

62. "Extract of a Letter, dated Manchester, September 1, 1823," *Southern Chronicle*, September 17, 1823; *Charleston Courier*, June 11, 1823.

63. "Georgetown, June 9," *Charleston Courier*, June 11, 1821.

64. "Joe," *Charleston City Gazette*, June 25, 1821. Harvey had thirty-three slaves in 1820; 1820 Federal Census, Sampit, Georgetown, South Carolina.

65. "Turkey Creek," *City Gazette and Daily Advertiser*, July 2, 1821.

66. "Pineville."

67. *City Gazette*, November 22, 1822.

68. *Southern Chronicle*, September 17, 1823, and *Savannah Georgian*, September 13, 1823, in Lockley, ed., *Maroon Communities*, 107–108.

69. Her owner was a Mr. McCord. It is not clear exactly which McCord it was. In 1820, John McCord owned 49 slaves; Joseph 17; and Russell 35. 1820 Census, Orangeburg, South Carolina.

70. She had escaped from a Mr. Ballard. There was a William S. Ballard in Richland District in 1820, the owner of twenty slaves; and a William Ballard in Sumter, who owned eleven. 1820 Census, South Carolina.

71. Petition of Jean Lewis Raoul, in Lockley, ed., *Maroon Communities,* 114–115.

72. Proceedings of the Standing Committee, October 2nd, 1823, in Lockley, ed., *Maroon Communities*, 108–109.

73. There was a Christian Perrin in Richland in 1820. He owned sixteen slaves. Royal may have been the personal property of Perrin's wife. However, in 1830 only one elderly white female was enumerated under the name Christian Perrin. It is therefore possible that he was already dead in 1823 and the entire workforce was thus his widow's property. 1820 Census and 1830 Census, South Carolina.

74. "Petition of the Inhabitants."

75. "Nelson's Ferry, October 6, 1823," *Baltimore Patriot*, October 17, 1823; "The Murderer Joe Destroyed," *American Repertory*, October 30, 1823.

76. *Southern Chronicle*, October 8, 1823, in Lockley, ed., *Maroon Communities*, 112.

77. *Southern Chronicle*, October 22, 1823.

78. See details in Lockley, ed., *Maroon Communities*, 118–120.

79. "Petition of the Inhabitants."

NOTES TO CHAPTER 10: MAROONS, CONSPIRACIES, AND UPRISINGS

1. Douglass, *Life and Times*, 280–281.

2. Redpath, *The Roving Editor,* 302–306.

3. Lt. Governor Bull to the Council, December 17, 1765, *South Carolina Council Journal*, 680–681, South Carolina Department of Archives and History.

4. Lt. Governor Bull, January 14, 1766, *Journals of the Common House of Assembly*, 34–35, SCDAH.

5. For a variety of official correspondence, see Lockley, ed., *Maroon Communities*, 23–33.

6. *South Carolina Council Journal,* April 4, 1769, 32:14–146, South Carolina Archives; See also at http://docsouth.unc.edu/csr/index.html/document/csr08-0212 (accessed 5/5/2012).

7. John Bartram to William Bartram, April 9, 1766, in Edmund Berkeley and Dorothy Smith Berkeley, eds., *The Correspondence of John Bartram, 1734–1777* (Gainesville: University Press of Florida, 1992), 665.

8. Bull to Col. Jackson, December 30, 1765, in Lockley, ed., *Maroon Communities*, 25–26.

9. For copies of these letters, see James Hugo Johnston, *Race Relations in Virginia & Miscegenation in the South 1776–1860* (Amherst: University of Massachusetts Press, 1970), 34–36.

10. "Extract from a Letter from Elizabeth City, North Carolina, dated May 12th, 1802," *Eastern Herald*, June 7, 1802.

11. Aptheker, *Slave Revolts*, 231; David S. Cecelski, *The Waterman's Song: Slavery and Freedom in Maritime North Carolina* (Chapel Hill: University of North Carolina Press, 2001), 129.

12. 1800 Federal Census, North Carolina, Camden; William A. Griffin, *Elizabeth-City: The History of a Canal Town* (Elizabeth City, N.C.: Roanoke Press, 1970), 38. For a time, he hired future runaway Moses Grandy. Sawyer sold Grandy's wife to a slave trader when he needed money and Grandy recalled his three years of starvation and bad treatment under Sawyer's rule as "cruel living." Grandy, *Narrative*, 10–11.

13. Letter from Enoch Sawyer, Camden, May 10th 1802, Perquimans County Slave Records 1759–1864, Insurrection among Slaves 1802–1803, North Carolina State Archives.

14. Pasquotank County, Minutes of Pleas and Quarters, 1785–1806 (sentencing of Jarvis Joe), North Carolina State Archives.

15. 1810 Federal Census, North Carolina, Pasquotank County. Knox placed an ad in the *Edenton Gazette*, on February 26, 1806 announcing the opening of his practice in Edenton: "Lately removed from Nixonton to this place, intends practicing Physic, Surgery, and Midwifery." He moved back to Nixonton in 1808.

16. "Extract of a Letter from Elizabeth-City, North Carolina, dated May 12th 1802," *Eastern Herald*, June 7, 1802.

17. Ibid.

18. County of Pasquotank, Prison Fees, Records of Slave and Free Persons of Color, 1733–1866, 1892, Court-Travel, North Carolina State Archives.

19. "From a Norfolk Paper of May 23. More about the Negroes," *New-York Herald*, June 2, 1802.

20. Perquimans County Slave Records 1759–1864, Insurrection among Slaves 1802–1803, North Carolina State Archives.

21. 1790 Federal Census, North Carolina, Pasquotank County. All the accused were owned by small farmers.

22. Auditions of Joe, Peter Cobb, Jarvis's Joe, Luke, Aaron, Jacob, and Mingo, Elizabeth City, May 22 and 25, 1802, Pasquotank County, Minutes of Pleas and Quarters, 1785–1806, North Carolina State Archives.

23. Mingo was enslaved, like twenty other individuals, by Jesse Redding. 1800 Federal Census, North Carolina, Pasquotank County.

24. Deposition taken by Charles Grice, in "From a Norfolk Paper of May 23," *New-York Herald*, June 2, 1802.

25. Pasquotank County, Minutes of Pleas and Quarters, 1785–1806, North Carolina State Archives.

26. Ibid.; Records of Slave and Free Persons of Color, North Carolina State Archives.

27. Compiled from Parker, ed., *Stealing a Little Freedom*.

28. Examination of Fed and examination of Jude, Bertie County, Slave Collection 1748–1856, North Carolina State Archives.

29. Letter dated Gates June 6 1802, Perquimans County Slave Records 1759–1864, Insurrection among Slaves 1802–1803.

30. *Raleigh Register*, June 6, 1802. "Extract of a Letter from a Gentleman in North Carolina," *New-York Evening Post*, June 23, 1802; "Halifax (N.C.), June 28," *Connecticut Journal*, July 15, 1802.

31. Slave Collection, 1748–1856, Bertie County, North Carolina State Archives.

32. The original examinations were conducted at Plymouth, a copy was made at Windsor, Bertie County, on June 20, and was sent to General Carney in Halifax County. Bertie County, Slave Collection 1748–1856, North Carolina State Archives.

33. Petition of William L. Hill, General Assembly Session Records, Miscellaneous Petitions, November 1823–January 1824, North Carolina State Archives.

34. Herbert Aptheker asserted, "[T]he activities of considerable groups of these black Robin Hoods in North Carolina, aided by some free Negroes, assumed the proportions of rebellion in the summer of 1821." Peter P. Hinks described it as "a serious uprising of some eighty armed outliers." John Hope Franklin and Loren Schweninger stated that it took two hundred men "to subdue" the North Carolina group. Joan R. Sherman called it "a month-long dangerous rebellion of maroons." Aptheker, *Slave Revolts*, 267; Peter P. Hinks, *To Awaken My Afflicted Brenthren: David Walker and the Problem of Antebellum Slave Resistance* (University Park: Pennsylvania State University Press, 1997), 44; Franklin and Schweninger, *Runaway Slaves*, 87.

35. Petition of William Hill to the General Assembly, 1823; Petition of John Rehm, November 1823; Petition of Terrence Pelletier and Others, November 1822; Committee of Claims on Petition of John Rehm, December 17, 1822; Committee of Claims on Petition of Terrence Pelletier, October 12, 1822 and December 12, 1822, Committee of Claims on Petition of W. Hill, December 1823; Committee of Claims on Petition of John H. Hill, December 20,1825; Committee of Claims on Petition of W. Hill, February 1825; GASR, North Carolina State Archives.

36. Petition of William Hill to the General Assembly, 1823. *1820 Federal Census*, Onslow County, Stump Sound. He put his three plantations up for sale in 1823, "Notice," *Carolina Centinel*, February 1, 1823.

37. Justices of the Peace to William L. Hill, August 7, 1821, North Carolina State Archives.

38. Col. William Hill to Jesse Franklin, August 8, 1821.

39. Justices of the Peace, Onslow County to William Hill, August 7, 1821; Justices to Lewis Foscue, August 13, 1821; Lewis Foscue to Governor Franklin, August 17; Governor Franklin to Samuel B. Andres, August 28; Petition of J. Hill and Others, December 1825, North Carolina State Archives.

40. "Communication," *Hillsborough Recorder*, September 5, 1821. This number found its way into other newspapers such as "Fayetteville, N.C. Aug. 30," *Evening Post*, September 6, 1821, and *New Hampshire Sentinel*, September 29, 1821; "New Bern," *American Mercury*, September 11, 1821.

41. Andres to Franklin, September 18, 1821.

42. L. Foscue to Franklin, October 10, 1821.

43. "Newbern," *Carolina Centinel*, August 25, 1821.

44. Petition of J. Hill and Others, December 1825; Committee of Claims on Petition of John Rehm, December 17, 1822.

45. Andres to Franklin, September 18, 1821.

46. L. Foscue to Franklin, October 10, 1821.

47. Petition of J. Hill and Others, December 1825.

48. "Craven Court of Oyer and Terminer," *Carolina Centinel*, February 9, 1822.

49. "Wilmington, May 1," *Free Press*, May 21, 1824. Citing an erroneous report from the *New York Evening Post* of May 11, 1824, Herbert Aptheker states that Isom died "from lashes publicly inflicted at Cape Fear." *Slave Revolts*, 267.

50. Senate Committee of Claims 1824–1825.

51. Committee of Claims on Petition of W. Hill, December 1823.

52. Andres to Franklin, September 18, 1821.

53. Foscue to Franklin, October 10, 1821.

54. Andres to Franklin, September 18, 1821.

55. James F. McRee to Governor John Owen, August 7, 1830, *GLB, 1828–1830*, 218–219, North Carolina State Archives.

56. David Walker, *Walker's Appeal, in Four Articles* (Boston: David Walker, 1830), 30.

57. *Journals of the Senate and House of Commons of the General Assembly of the State of North Carolina, 1830–1831* (Raleigh, 1831), 161.

58. J. Burgwyn to Governor Owen, November 15, 1830, GLB; J. I. Pasteur to Governor Owen, Governors Papers, 60, North Carolina State Archives.

59. "Ten Dollars Reward," *Carolina Centinel*, December 8, 1821; "Fifty Dollars Reward," ibid., December 3, 1825; "$25 Reward," ibid., October 10, 1829.

60. "$30 Reward," *Newbern Spectator and Literary Journal*, May 7, 1831.

61. *Acts Passed by the General Assembly of the State of North Carolina at the Session of 1830–1831* (Raleigh, 1831), 11. North Carolina was one of only four states—Georgia, South Carolina, and Virginia were the others—that maintained an official ban on slave literacy until 1865.

62. John Gray Blount to Joseph B. Hinton, December 13, 1830; Hinton to Blount, December 14, 20, and 23, in David T. Morgan, ed., *John Gray Blount Papers* (Raleigh: North Carolina Department of Cultural Resources, 1982): 4:542–547.

63. "Milton, (N.C.)," *Liberator*, January 15, 1831 (from *Roanoke Advertiser*).

64. "Wilmington, [N.C.] January 7," *Genius of Universal Emancipation*, 12, 1 (March 1831): 192.

65. Robert Arthur, *History of Fort Monroe* (Fort Monroe: Printing Plant of the Coast Artillery School, 1930), 69.

66. But maroons continued to be a problem and those in neighboring counties were denounced at the end of the year for being assertive and using the same bold strategy as the people who evoked so much fear during the scare of 1821. Their approach was based on targeted reprisals against the men who went after them. Their activities led "sundry inhabitants of Sampson, Bladen, New Hanover and Duplin" to send a petition to the General Assembly lamenting that their slaves were almost uncontrollable, coming and going as they pleased. When one attempted to correct them, they went to the woods where they stayed for months and years, committing depredations on their hogs, cattle, and sheep, "and many other things." They acknowledged that they could not raise patrols to suppress the maroons because patrollers feared for their lives and property. Two men who had gone after them had seen their houses and outbuildings burned down, while a third had lost his fodder stacks to arson.

The seventy-eight petitioners asked for a coercive system of patrols that would search all the suspected "places houses or thicks." The men would be given the "privilege of shooting and destroying" the recalcitrant individuals who refused to surrender. As compensation for their service, they would receive the reward advertised by owners; but for the runaways who did not come with a bounty, the patrollers would get $15 if the individual had been away less than six months, $25 if absent up to one year, and $50 for someone in hiding for more than one year. The owners would pay those fees, but if one could not be found, all the possessions confiscated from the maroons would go to the company. This last point is significant; it confirms that some could accumulate property. As seen earlier, the most flourishing settlements had various quantities of money, rice, corn, bacon, meat, vegetables, cattle, canoes, tools, firearms, and ammunition.

Senate Committee Report, General Assembly, Session Records, Petitions Miscellaneous, 1830–1831, North Carolina State Archives.

67. Weld, *American Slavery*, 51.

68. Eric Foner, *Nat Turner* (Englewood Cliffs, N.J.: Prentice-Hall, 1971), 14.

69. "Southampton, Jerusalem, Aug. 24," "Richmond, Aug. 28th, 1831," *Columbian Register*, September 3, 1831.

70. Eugene Genovese admits that Turner's plans have remained obscure, but "he may have expected to form a large maroon colony in the Dismal Swamp." Henry Louis Gates and Evelyn Brookes Higginbotham agreed: "He may have planned to establish a maroon colony within the nearby Dismal Swamp." According to William H. Freehling, "He may have anticipated marching back south and hiding gunmen in the dismal swamp." For Megan K. Nelson, "Nat Turner . . . had planned to establish a black community in the Great Swamp." Genovese, *From Rebellion*, 49; Henry Louis Gates and Evelyn Brookes Higginbotham, *African American Lives* (New York: Oxford University Press, 2004), 828; William H. Freehling, *The Road to Disunion: Volume I: Secessionists at Bay, 1776–1854* (1990), 180; Megan K. Nelson, *Trembling Earth: A Cultural History of the Okefenokee Swamp* (Athens: University of Georgia Press, 2005), 37. Others stated that he personally retreated to the swamp: William S. McFeely, *Frederick Douglass*, (New York: Norton, 1991), 175; Ann Vileisis, *Discovering the Unknown Landscape: A History of America's Wetlands* (Washington, D.C.: Island Press, 1997), 104; David A. Copeland, *The Antebellum Era: Primary Documents on Events from 1820 to 1860* (Westport: Greenwood Publishing, 2003), 123. In contrast, Anthony E. Kaye firmly inscribed the uprising and Turner's hideout in the neighborhood. Anthony E. Kay, "Neighborhoods and Nat Turner: The Making of a Slave Rebel and the Unmaking of a Slave Rebellion," *Journal of the Early Republic*, 27 (Winter 2007): 705–720.

71. "The Insurrection and Massacre in Virginia," *Rhode-Island American*, September 2, 1831.

72. "Insurrections," *Free Inquirer*, September 17, 1831.

73. "Insurrection of the Blacks," *Niles' Register*, September 8, 1831.

74. Thomas W. Higginson, "Nat Turner's Insurrection," *Atlantic Monthly* (August 1861): 175.

75. "Insurrection of the Blacks," *National Gazette and Literary Register*, August 27, 1831; *Edenton Gazette*, August 31, 1831.

76. "The Insurrection," *New-Hampshire Gazette*, September 6, 1831.

77. McFeely, *Frederick Douglass,* 175; Vileisis, *Discovering*, 104; David A. Copeland, *The Antebellum Era: Primary Documents on Events from 1820 to 1860* (Westport: Greenwood Publishing, 2003), 123. Thomas R. Gray, *The Confessions of Nat Turner, The Leader of the Late Insurrection in South Hampton, VA.* (Baltimore: Thomas R. Gray, 1831).

78. Turner's account of his life after the insurrection and until his capture is on page 17.

79. Perdue, ed., *Weevils*, 76.

80. "Richmond Compiler," *Salem Gazette*, November 4, 1831; Letter from Elliot Whitehead, Esq., in *Richmond Enquirer*, November 15, 1831.

81. Ibid., "Nat Turner Certainly Taken," *Norfolk Herald*, November 4, 1831.

82. Ibid.

83. "Post Office, Jerusalem," *American Beacon*, November 2, 1831.

84. "Nat Turner Certainly Taken," *Norfolk Herald*, November 4, 1831.

85. Gray, *The Confessions*, 17.

86. William S. Drewry, *Slave Insurrections (1830–1865)* (Washington: Neale Company, 1900), 91.

87. See F. Roy Johnson, *The Nat Turner Slave Insurrection* (Murfreesboro, N.C.: Johnson Publishing Co., 1966), 167–168, 179; Tragle, *The Southampton Slave Revolt*, 13; Foner, *Nat Turner*, 173.

88. Foner, *Nat Turner*, 173. Foner transcribed part of the tape recorded by Tragle. The original tape is held at the Virginia Historical Society, Henry Irving Tragle Papers.

89. General Anti-Slavery Convention, *Proceedings of the General Anti-Slavery Convention* (London, 1843), 78.

90. "Negro Banditti," *Portsmouth Journal*, November 28, 1834.

91. Charles E. Morris, "Panic and Reprisal: Reaction in North Carolina to the Nat Turner Insurrection, 1831," *North Carolina Historical Review*, 72, 1 (January 1985): 37.

92. For Suriname, Wim Hoogbergen remarks that maroons' raids failed when they did not contact people in the quarters to obtain permission to attack "their" plantation to get food, women, and tools; and revolts faltered when rebels did not make arrangements for their escape with the maroons. In the greater Caribbean, they were a powerful symbol to insurrectionists and were perceived as prospective allies, but no leadership was expected from them. Even the *marrons* of St. Domingue have come under scrutiny. Revisionist historians argue that although they were presented in the past as having played a key role in the launch of the revolution, they actually did not. Wim Hoogbergen, "Marronage and Slave Rebellions in Surinam," in Wolfgang Binder, ed., *Slavery in the Americas* (Wurzburg: Konigshausen & Neumann, 1993), 165–196; Michael Craton, *Testing the Chains: Resistance to Slavery in the British West Indies* (Ithaca: Cornell University Press, 2009), 224; Laurent Dubois, *Avengers of the New World: The Story of the Haitian Revolution* (Cambridge: Harvard University Press, 2005), 54–55; David Patrick Geggus, "Slavery, War, and Revolution in the Greater Caribbean," in David Barry Gaspar and David Geggus, eds., *A Turbulent Time: The French Revolution and the Greater Caribbean* (Bloomington: Indiana University Press, 1997), 20.

93. Thompson, *Flight to Freedom,* 315.

NOTES TO CHAPTER 11: OUT OF THE WILDS

1. Rawick, ed., *American Slave*, 14, Pt. 1, 184.

2. Perdue, ed., *Weevils*, 117.

3. "Recollections," September 13, 1838.

4. WPA, *The Negro in Virginia*, 127; Olmsted, *A Journey*, 159; Johnson, *Tales,* 163.

5. Stoyer, *My Life*, 64.

6. See, for example, H. R. McIlwaine, ed., *Journals of the House of Burgesses of Virginia, 1758–1761* (Richmond, 1908), 19, 80.

7. The circumstances of the fire were not explained; see Petition of John Beafley in John Pendleton Kennedy, ed., *Journals of the House of Burgesses of Virginia 1766–1769* (Richmond: The Colonial Press, E. Waddey Co., 1906), 211.

8. Petition of John Jonah Murrell et al., in Schweninger, ed., *The Southern Debate,* 105–109.

9. Fred Lockley, "Reminiscences of Mrs. Frank Collins nee Martha Elizabeth Gilliam," *Quarterly of the Oregon Historical Society* 17, (1916): 358. Ms. Collins went on, "He was so

good at tracking them and bringing them back to their owners that when he ran for sheriff the people said, 'He is so successful catching runaway niggers, he will be good at catching criminals,' so he was voted in as sheriff."

10. "A Negro Outrage," *Texas State Gazette*, August 29, 1857.

11. *New Hampshire Gazette*, September 6, 1836.

12. See, for example, "Murder by a Negro Slave," *Emancipator and Weekly Chronicle*, February 12, 1845; "Murder!!" *City Gazette and Daily Advertiser*, February 10, 1820, *Charleston Courier, February 14, 1820,* "The Murderer Taken," *City Gazette*, February 14, 1820; "Conviction and Sentence," ibid., February 17, 1820; "Shadow of Southern Life," *Ohio State Journal*, September 25, 1860.

13. "Scouring the Pocosin," *Albany Advertiser*, December 11, 1816.

14. Thomas, *Memoirs*, 19–20.

15. Dan A. Rudd and Theo Bond, *From Slavery to Wealth: The Life of Scott Bond* (Madison, Ark.: Journal Printing Co., 1917),142.

16. American Freedmen's Inquiry Commission Interviews, 1863, in Blassingame, ed., *Slave Testimony*, 433. The dogs got their practice on the plantations. "They used to make me run off a good ways," recalled a former maroon, "when I was very small, and then send the pups on my tracks. I thought it was fine sport. Sometimes they called the hands from the field and made them run round the house and climb trees, with the dogs after them." In "Recollections," September 13, 1838. According to America Morgan from Kentucky, the dogs were raised to identify "nigger blood." "When the overseer lashed a slave to death, they would turn the bloodhounds out to smell the blood, so they would know 'nigger blood,' that would help trace runaway slaves." In Rawick, ed., *American Slave*, 5:143.

17. Stoyer, *My Life,*75–78.

18. Ibid., 72.

19. Rawick, ed., *American Slave*, 11, pt.1, 397.

20. Ibid., 4, pt.1, 199; see also Robinson, *From Log Cabin*, 35; Heard, *From Slavery*, 27; Colyer, *Report*, 20; Stoyer, *My Life,* 50.

21. Robinson, *From Log Cabin*, 32.

22. McKaye, *The Mastership*, 11.

23. Williams, *Sunshine and Shadow*, 16–17. Dogs' shallow graves could be found on plantations too. In a single episode field hands killed six dogs out of a pack of twenty-five as they were chasing eight of their companions who had made their way to the woods. They buried them in the cotton rows. Stroyer, *My Life,* 72.

24. Ibid., 73–74.

25. Aughey, *Tupelo*, 394–395.

26. Clinckscales, *On the Old Plantation*, 19.

27. "Encampment of Runaway Slaves Broken Up," *National Era*, December 25, 1856.

28. Rawick, ed., *American Slave,* 1, Pt. 3, 332.

29. Ovington, "Reminiscences," 1134.

30. *Philadelphia Sunday Item*, July 24, 1892, cited in Blassingame, ed., *Slave Testimony*, 507.

31. "Recollections," September 13, 1838.

32. Petition of John Jonah Murrell et al. to the speaker and members of the South Carolina House of Representatives, 1829, Records of the General Assembly, in Schweninger, ed., *The Southern Debate*, 1:105–109.

33. Thomas, *Memoirs*, 16.

34. "Five Pounds Reward," *North-Carolina Chronicle*, November 1, 1790. See also Clink-scales, *Old Plantation*, 20; Burke, *Reminiscences, 172.*

35. Rawick, ed., *American Slave*, 2, Pt. 6, 82; see also ibid., 16, Pt. 1, 282.

36. Dusinberre, *Them Dark Days*, 165.

37. Atwater, *Incidents*, 50.

38. Smith, *Fifty Years of Slavery*, 67.

39. Taylor*, Negro Slavery*, 228–229.

40. Petition of Thomas Jones, November 2, 1824, Bourbon County Courthouse, Paris, Kentucky, *Digital Library of American Slavery*, case # 20782407, http://library.uncg.edu/slavery/ (accessed 4/5/2011).

41. A. N. Ogden, reporter, *Reports of Cases Argued and Determined in the Supreme Court of Louisiana* (New Orleans, 1858), 12:451–455.

42. Bruce, *The New Man*, 33; Rawick, ed., *American Slave*, 11, Pt. 1, 84; ibid., 4, Pt.2, 14; 9, 51; *South Carolina Gazette*, August 5, 1776; Ovington, "Reminiscences," 1134.

43. Perdue, ed., *Weevils*, 55; Rawick, ed., *American Slave*, 9:51; 16, Pt. 4, 38; 4, Pt. 2, 14.

44. Miguel Barnet, ed., *The Autobiography of a Runaway Slave, Esteban Montejo* (New York: Pantheon Books, 1968), 59.

45. Rawick, ed., *American Slave*, 16, Pt. 1, 261.

46. Ibid., 4, Pt. 2, 14.

47. "Singular Relation," 195–196.

48. Ovington, "Reminiscences," 1134.

49. Rawick, ed., *American Slave*, 4, Pt. 4, 191.

50. Ibid., 4, Pt. 3, 332.

51. "Recollections," August 23, 1838.

52. "Recollections," September 13,1838. See the third installment of this article, September 20, 1838, for a detailed description of the various types of flogging.

53. Perdue, ed., *Weevils,* 274.

54. Rawick, ed., *American Slave*, 11, Pt. 1, 164; ibid., 3:111; Brown, *Slave Life in Georgia*; Webb, *The History of William Webb*, 105.

55. Rawick, *American Slave*, 16, Pt. 3, 133–34.

56. "Recollections," August 23, 1838.

57. "Recollections," September13, 1838.

58. For personal descriptions, see "Recollections," September 13, 1838; Watson, *Narrative*, 14; Rawick, ed., *American Slave*, 2, Pt. 1, 32; ibid., 13, 153, among others.

59. Rawick, ed., *American Slave*, 9:51.

60. Ibid., 16, Pt. 4, 38.

61. Ovington, "Reminiscences," 1134.

62. Williams, *Life and Adventures,* 74.

63. Clayton, *Mother Wit*, 102–103.

64. Ibid., 191.

65. Alexander McDonald Walker, ed., *New Hanover County Court Minutes* (Bethesda, Md.: A. M. Walker, 1958), 69, 92.

66. Weld, *American Slavery*, 15.

67. From *Georgia Constitutionalist*, quoted in Charles Alexander, *Battles and Victories of Allen Allensworth* (Boston: Sherman, French & Co., 1914), 82.

68. Edward Everett Brown, ed., *Sketch of the Life of Mr. Lewis Charlton and Reminiscences of Slavery* (Portland, Maine: Daily Press Print, n.d.), 5.

69. Rudd and Bond, *From Slavery to Wealth*, 142.

70. "From the Charleston Patriot," *Evening Post*, November 25, 1816. Stepney was captured and executed on November 4, 1816.

71. Ovington "Reminiscences," 1132.

72. Clayton, *Mother Wit*, 191.

73. Rawick, ed., *American Slave*, 14, Pt. 2, 145.

74. Ibid., 3:15.

75. Ibid., 4, Pt. 2, 52.

76. Ibid., 1:36; 4, pt.1, 24.

77. Williams, *Life and Adventures*, 75.

78. Rawick,ed., *American Slave*, 4, Pt. 1, 147.

79. Perdue, ed., *Weevils*, 63.

80. Ibid., 210.

81. Ibid., 265.

82. Ibid., 238.

83. Ibid., 274.

84. Rawick, ed., *American Slave*, 1:220.

85. Perdue, ed., *Weevils*, 252.

86. Wiley, *Adventures of Old Dan Tucker*, 107.

87. Ibid., 67.

NOTES TO THE CONCLUSION

1. Barbara Hurd, *Stirring the Mud: On Swamps, Bogs, and Human Imagination* (New York: Mariner Books, 2003), 7.

2. Genovese, *From Rebellion*, 80.

3. Cited in Dusinberre, *Them Dark Days*, 165.

4. Rawick, ed., *American Slave,* 16, Pt. 3, 248–249.

5. Craton, *Testing the Chains,* 62–63.

6. Clinkscales, *The Old Plantation*, 20.

SELECT BIBLIOGRAPHY

PRIMARY SOURCES

Archival Documents

GEORGIA

East Florida Papers, 1795–1797. Microfilm, New York Public Library.

From the Govn. of South Carolina to the Govn. of Georgia, 2nd April 1787. Joseph Vallence Bevan Papers, 71, 83, Georgia Historical Society.

James Gunn to Genl. Jackson, May 6th 1787. Joseph Vallence Bevan Papers, 71, 84, Georgia Historical Society.

James Jackson to the Governor of South Carolina, 1787. Joseph Vallence Bevan Papers, 71, 86. Georgia Historical Society.

James Jackson to the Governor of Georgia, 1787. Joseph Vallence Bevan Papers, 71, 87, Georgia Historical Society.

Lucian Lamar Knight, *Georgia's Roster of the Revolution*. Georgia Dept. of Archives and History.

The State vs. Lewis a Negroe. May 21, 1787. Telamon Cuyler Collection, MS 1170, box 71, folder 12. Hargrett Library, University of Georgia.

LOUISIANA

Actas del Cabildo, 1783–1784. New Orleans Public Library.

Cuban Papers. Center for Louisiana Studies, University of Louisiana at Lafayette.

John Merriman to F. E. Richardson, November 11, 1840, David Weeks Family Papers, Hill Memorial Library, Louisiana State University.

Spanish Judicial Records, 1781, 1783. Louisiana State Museum.

NORTH CAROLINA

Assembly, Session Records, Miscellaneous Petitions, November 1823–January 1824. North Carolina State Archives.

Col. John Hill's Petition (attached militia records) 1825, Session of 1825–26, General Assembly Session Records. NCSA.

Col. William Hill to Jesse Franklin, n.d. 1821, Governor's Address Session 1821–22, GASR. NCSA.

Col. William Hill to Jesse Franklin, August 7, 1821, Governors Letter Books. NCSA.

Col. William Hill to Jesse Franklin, August 8, 1821, Governors Letter Books. NCSA.

Committee of Claims Report on the Carteret Militia's Petition, 1825, House Committee Reports, Session of 1825–26. NCSA.

Committee of Claims Report on the Claim of Col. William Hill, December 1824, Session of 1824–25, GASR. NCSA.

Committee Report on the Claims of the Onslow, Bladen, and Carteret Militia, 1824, Session of 1824–25, GASR. NCSA.

Committee Reports, Session of 1822–23, GASR. NCSA.

Gates County, Registration of Slaves to Work in the Great Dismal Swamp, 1847–1861. NCSA.

Gates County, Slave Records, Criminal Actions against Slaves 1803–1860, Superior Court of Law Spring Term 1824. NCSA.

Insurrection among Slaves 1802–1803. Perquimans County Slave Records 1759–1864. NCSA.

James F. McRee to Governor John Owen, August 7, 1830. Governors Letter Books, 1828–1830. NCSA.

Josiah Smith, Jr. to George Austin, July 22, 1774 in Josiah Smith, Jr., Letterbook, Southern Historical Collection. University of North Carolina Archives.

Letter dated Gates June 6 1802, Perquimans County Slave Records 1759–1864, Insurrection Among Slaves 1802–1803. NCSA.

Letter from Enoch Sawyer, Camden May 10th 1802, Perquimans County Slave Records 1759–1864, Insurrection Among Slaves 1802–1803. NCSA.

Lt. Colonel Samuel Andres to Jesse Franklin, August 28, 1821, Governors Letter Books. NCSA.

Memorial of Henry Taylor of New Hanover County, November 1795, and Petition of Henry Taylor, 1796, General Assembly, Session Records, Miscellaneous Petitions, November–December 1796. NCSA.

Minutes of Pleas and Quarters. Pasquotank County 1785–1806. NCSA.

Petition from Carteret County Militia, November 1822, Miscellaneous Petitions, Session of 1822, GASR. NCSA.

Petition of Inhabitants of Craven County to the North Carolina General Assembly, December 19, 1831, GASR. NCSA.

Petition of Richard Lewis and twenty-one others, August 25, 1856, Governors Letter Book, 43, 514–515. NCSA.

Petition of William L. Hill to the Assembly of the State of North Carolina. General Records of Slave and Free Persons, 1733-1866, 1892. Pasquotank County, Court Travel. NCSA.

Report of the Committee of Claims on the Petition of Ferrence Pelletier, 1822. NCSA.

SOUTH CAROLINA

Indian Book 1750–1752, 11, 221, South Carolina Archives.

J. L. Bourquin, Jr. to Joachim Hartstone, March 14, 1787, Governor's Messages, 1783–1830, no. 423–11, South Carolina Department of Archives and History.

Joachim Hartstone to Peter Porcher and W. Fenwick, Representatives for St. Peter's Parish, March 15, 1787, Governor's Messages, 1786–1788, 423–07, SCDAH.

Lt. Governor Bull to the Council, December 17, 1765, South Carolina Council Journal, 680–681, SCDAH.

Lt. Governor Bull, January 14, 1766, Journals of the Common House of Assembly, 34–35, SCDAH.

Lord Charles Greville Montagu to the Earl of Hillsborough, Charles Town, 19th April 1769, South Carolina Council, 8: 554–560, SCDAH.

Petition of Edward Brailsford. Records of the General Assembly, Petition November 16, 1816, #100; 1821, ND, #1838. SCDAH.

[Petition to free Royal]. Records of the General Assembly, Petition, ND, 1874. SCDAH.

Petition of Godin Guerard and Sworn Oath of Samuel Bostick, December 3, 1793. SCDAH.

Petition of Jean Raoul. Records of the General Assembly, Petition December 1823, #142. SCDAH.

Records of the General Assembly, 1793, #151. SCDAH.

Robert Heriot to Polly Heriot, June 9, 1781. Robert Heriot Correspondence, South Carolina Historical Society.

Roderick McIntosh to Isaac Young, November 18, 1765. *Royal Council Journals*, November 25, 1765, 674–675, SCDAH.

Royal Council Journal, November 25, 1765. SCDAH.

The State vs. George. Harboring a Fugitive Slave. Anderson District Court of Magistrates & Freeholders. L04190. Trial Papers #151. SCDAH.

The State vs. Harriett. Harboring a Fugitive Slave. Anderson District Court of Magistrates & Freeholders. L04190. Trial Papers #271. SCDAH.

The State vs. Harry. Harboring a Fugitive Slave. Anderson District Court of Magistrates & Freeholders. L04190. Trial Papers #136. SCDAH.

The State vs. Mary. Harboring a Fugitive Slave. Anderson District Court of Magistrates & Freeholders. L04190. Trial Papers #139. SCDAH.

The State vs. Mattison & Stephen. Insurrection with intent to kill. Anderson District Court of Magistrates & Freeholders. L04190. Trial Papers #252. SCDAH.

The State vs. Tim, George & Ben. Harboring a Fugitive Slave. Anderson District Court of Magistrates & Freeholders. L04190. Trial Papers #128. SCDAH.

Thomas Pinckney to Col. Thomas Hutson, March 20, 1787, Thomas Pinckney Letter Book, 1787–1789. SCDAH.

VIRGINIA

Condemned Slaves. Transported Slaves, Sutton. February 10, 1810. Box 1967. Library of Virginia (LVA).

Condemned Slaves. Trial of Mingo. November 4, 1819. Box 1968. LVA

Deposition of John Wilson. Executive Papers Letters Received, Governor James Patton Preston, February 19, 1819. LVA.

The Geography of Slavery in Virginia. http://www2.vcdh.virginia.edu/gos/

Middlesex County Orders Book 1680–1691. LVA.

Old Rappahannock County Orders Book, 1686–1692. LVA.

Silas Summer to Governor James Pleasants. Executive Papers Letters Received, Governor James Pleasants, April 6, 1825, LVA.

Trial of Cooper. Executive Papers Letters Received, Governor James Patton Preston, August 23, 1819. LVA.

Trial of Nelson. Executive Papers Letters Received, Governor James Patton Preston, August 23, 1819. LVA.

Trial of Sutton. Executive Papers Letters Received, Governor John Tyler, February 10, 1810. LVA.

Miscellaneous

Digital Library on American Slavery. http://library.uncg.edu/slavery/

The Papers of George Washington. http://gwpapers.virginia.edu/documents/slavery/aug1761.html

The Trans-Atlantic Slave Trade Database. http://www.slavevoyages.org

Books

Albert, Octavia V. Rogers. *The House of Bondage*. New York: Hunt & Eaton, 1890.

American Colonization Society. *The Tenth Annual Report of the American Society for Colonizing Free People of Colour of the United States*. Washington, D.C.: Way & Gideon, 1827.

An Account of Louisiana: Being an Abstract of Documents, in the Offices of the Department of State and the Treasury. Philadelphia: William Duane, 1803.

Anderson, William J. *Life and Narrative of William J. Anderson, Twenty-Four Years a Slave*. Chicago: Daily Tribune Book and Job Printing Office, 1857.

Arnold, Robert. *The Dismal Swamp and Lake Drummond: Early Recollections; Vivid Portrayal of Amusing Scenes*. Green, Norfolk: Green, Burke & Gregory, 1888.

Atwater, H. Cowles. *Incidents of a Southern Tour: or The South, as Seen with Northern Eyes*. Boston: J. P. Magee, 1857.

Audubon, John James. *Ornithological Biography*. Edinburgh: Adam Black, 1831–1839.

Aughey, John Hill. *Tupelo*. Lincoln, Neb.: State Journal Co., 1888.

Ball, Charles. *Slavery in the United States: A Narrative of the Life and Adventures of Charles Ball*. New York: Published by John S. Taylor, 1837.

———. *Fifty Years in Chains or the Life of an American Slave*. New York: H. Dayton Publishers, 1859.

Barnet, Miguel, ed. *The Autobiography of a Runaway Slave Esteban Montejo*. New York: Pantheon Books, 1968.

Bartram, William. *Travels through North and South Carolina, Georgia, East and West Florida*. London: J. Johnson, 1792.

Bassett, John Spencer, ed. *The Writings of "Colonel William Byrd, of Westover in Virginia, Esqr."* New York: Doubleday, Page & Co., 1901.

Berkeley, Edmund, and Dorothy Smith Berkeley, eds. *The Correspondence of John Bartram, 1734–1777*. Gainesville: University Press of Florida, 1992.

Bibb, Henry. *Narrative of the Life and Adventures of Henry Bibb, an American Slave, Written by Himself*. New York: Published by the Author, 1849.

Blassingame, John, W., ed. *Slave Testimony: Two Centuries of Letters, Speeches, Interviews, and Autobiographies*. Baton Rouge: Louisiana University Press, 1977.

Bluett, Thomas. *Some Memoirs of the Life of Job, the Son of Solomon the High Priest of Boonda in Africa*. London: R. Ford, 1734.

Brickell, John. *The Natural History of North Carolina*. Dublin: James Carson, 1737.

Brown, Edward Everett, ed. *Sketch of the Life of Mr. Lewis Charlton and Reminiscences of Slavery*. Portland, Maine: Daily Press Print, n. d.

Brown, John. *Slave Life in Georgia: A Narrative of the Life, Sufferings, and Escape of John Brown, a Fugitive Slave, Now in England*. London,1855.

Browne, William H., ed. *Archives of Maryland, Proceedings of the Council of Maryland, 1698–1731*. Baltimore: Maryland Historical Society, 1905.

Bruce, Henry Clay. *The New Man: Twenty-Nine Years a Slave, Twenty-Nine Years a Free Man*. York, Pa.: P. Anstadt & Sons, 1895.

Bruce, Philip A. *Virginia in the Seventeenth Century: An Inquiry into the Material Condition of People, Based upon Original and Contemporaneous Records*. New York: MacMillan & Co., 1896.

Bruner, Peter. *A Slave's Adventures toward Freedom*. Oxford, Ohio: 1919.

Burke, Emily P. *Reminiscences of Georgia*. Oberlin: O. J. M. Fitch, 1850.

Byrd, William. *The Westover Manuscripts: Containing the History of the Dividing Line betwixt Virginia and North Carolina*. Petersburg: Edmund and Julian C. Ruffin, 1841.

Cable, George Washington. "Creole Slave Songs." *Century Magazine* 31, 6 (April 1886): 807–828.

Candler, Allen D., ed. *The Colonial Records of the State of Georgia*. Atlanta: Franklin-Turner Co., 1907.

———. *The Revolutionary Records of the State of Georgia*. Atlanta: Franklin-Turner Co., 1908.

Carroll, B. R., ed., *Historical Collections of South Carolina*. New York: Harper and Brothers, 1836.

Carter, Clarence E., ed. *The Territorial Papers of the United States*. Washington, D.C.: U.S. Government Printing Office, 1940.

Clapp, Henry, Jr. *The Pioneer or Leaves from an Editor's Portfolio*. Lynn: J. B. Tolaman, 1846.

Clark, Walter, ed. *The State Records of North Carolina*. Goldsboro: Nash Brothers, 1905.

Clayton, Ronnie W., ed. *Mother Wit: The Ex-Slave Narratives of the Louisiana Writers' Project*. New York: Peter Lang, 1990.

Clifton, James M., ed. *Life and Labor on Argyle Island: Letters and Documents of a Savannah River Rice Plantation, 1833–1867*. Savannah: Beehive Press, 1978.

Clinkscales, John George. *On the Old Plantation: Reminiscences of His Childhood*. Spartanburg, S. C.: Band & White, 1916.

Cobb, Howell. *A Compilation of the General and Public Statutes of the State of Georgia*. New York: Edward O. Jenkins, 1859.

Colyer, Vincent. *Report of the Services Rendered by the Freed People to the United States Army in North Carolina, in the Spring of 1862, after the Battle of Newbern*. New York: V. Colyer, 1864.

Commons, John R. et al., eds. *A Documentary History of American Industrial Society*. Cleveland: A. H. Clark Company, 1910–1911.

Conrad, Glenn R. *The German Coast: Abstracts of the Civil Records of St. Charles and St. John the Baptist Parishes, 1804–1812*. Lafayette: University of Louisiana at Lafayette Press, 1981.

Cooper, Thomas, ed. *The Statutes at Large of South Carolina*. Columbia: A. S. Johnston, 1840.

Davis, John. *Travels of Four Years and a Half in the United States of America during 1798, 1799, 1800, 1801, and 1802*. London: T. Ostell, 1803.

De Forest, B. S. *Random Sketches and Wandering Thoughts*. Albany: Avery Herrick, 1866.

Desaussure, Henry William, ed., *Reports of Cases Argued and Determined in the Court of Chancery of the State of South Carolina from the Revolution to December 1813 Inclusive*. Columbia: Cline & Hines, 1817.

Donnan, Elizabeth. *Documents Illustrative of the History of the Slave Trade to America*. 4 vols. Washington, D.C.: Carnegie Institution, 1930.

Douglass, Frederick. *My Bondage and My Freedom*. New York and Auburn: Miller, Orton & Mulligan, 1855.

———. *Life and Times of Frederick Douglass*. Hartford: Park Publishing Co., 1881.

Drew, Benjamin. *A North-Side View of Slavery*. Boston: John P. Jewett and Company, 1856.

Dupre, Louis. *Fagots from the Camp Fire*. Washington, D. C.: Emily Thornton Charles & Co. Publishers, 1881.

Dwight, Theodore. *Slavery and the Internal Slave Trade*. London: Thomas Ward, 1841.

Easterby, J. H., ed. *The Journal of the Commons House of Assembly November 10, 1736–June 7, 1739*. Columbia, S.C.: Historical Commission of South Carolina, 1951.

———. *Colonial Records of South Carolina*. Columbia: South Carolina Archives Department, 1958.

Edwards, Adele Stanton, ed. *Journals of the Privy Council, 1783–1789*. Columbia: University of South Carolina Press, 1971.

Edwards, S. J. Celestine. *From Slavery to a Bishopric, or, The Life of Bishop Walter Hawkins of the British Methodist Episcopal Church Canada*. London: John Kensit, 1891.

"Extracts from Diary of Col. Landon Carter." *William and Mary Quarterly* 13, 1 (July 1904): 45–53.

Fedric, Francis. *Slave Life in Virginia and Kentucky or Fifty Years of Slavery in the Southern United States*. London: Wertheim, MacIntosh and Hunt, 1863.

Felton, Rebecca Latimer. *Country Life in Georgia in the Days of My Youth*. Atlanta: Index Printing Company, 1919.

Frissell, H. B., and Isabel Bevier, *Dietary Studies of Negroes in East Virginia in 1897 and 1898*. Washington, D. C.: Government Printing Office, 1899.

General Anti-Slavery Convention. *Proceedings of the General Anti-Slavery Convention*. London: J. Snow,1843.

Grandy, Moses. *Narrative of the Life of Moses Grandy, Late a Slave in the United States of America*. London: C. Gilpin, 1843.

Gray, Thomas R. *The Confessions of Nat Turner, the Leader of the Late Insurrection in South Hampton, Va*. Baltimore: Thomas R. Gray, 1831.

Green, J. D. *Narrative of the Life of J. D. Green, a Runaway Slave, from Kentucky, Containing an Account of His Three Escapes, in 1839, 1846, and 1848*. Huddersfield: Printed by Henry Fielding, Pack Horse Yard, 1864.

Grigsby, Melvin. *The Smoked Yank*. Sioux Falls: Dakota Bell Publishing Co., 1888.

Grimes, John Bryan, ed. *North Carolina Wills and Inventories*. Raleigh: Edwards and Broughton Printing Company, 1912. Reprint: Westminster: Heritage Books, 2008.

Heard, William H. *From Slavery to the Bishopric in the A. M. E. Church: An Autobiography*. Philadelphia: A. M. E. Book Concern, 1928.

Hening, William Waller, ed. *The Statutes at Large, Being a Collection of All the Laws of Virginia, from the First Session of the Legislature, in the Year 1619*. 1810–1823. 13 volumes. http://vagenweb.org/hening/.

———. *Statutes at Large Being a Collection of all the Laws of Virginia From the First Session of the Legislature, in the Year 1619*. New York: For the Author by R. W. & G Bartow, 1823.

Hewatt, Alexander. *An Historical Account of the Rise and Progress of the Colonies of South Carolina and Georgia*. London: Alexander Donaldson, 1779.

Hughes, Louis. *Thirty Years a Slave: From Bondage to Freedom*. Milwaukee: South Side Printing Co., 1897.

Jefferson, Thomas. *Thomas Jefferson's Farm Book*, ed. Edwin Morris Betts. Chapel Hill: University of North Carolina Press, 1959.

Jones, George F., and Sheryl Exley, eds. *Ebenezer Record Book 1754–1781*. Baltimore: Genealogical Publishing Co., 1991.

Kennedy, John Pendleton, ed. *Calendar of Transcripts: Including the Annual Report of the Department of Archives and History*. Richmond: Davis Bottom, Superintendent Public Printing, 1905.

———. *Journals of the House of Burgesses of Virginia 1766–1769*. Richmond: Colonial Press, E. Waddey Co., 1906.

Latham, Henry. *Black and White: A Journal of a Three Month's Tour in the United States*. London: Macmillan and Co., 1867.

Lockley, Timothy James, ed. *Maroon Communities in South Carolina: A Documentary Record*. Columbia: University of South Carolina Press, 2009.

McCord, David J., ed. *The Statutes at Large of South Carolina*. Columbia: A. S. Johnston,1840.

McDowell, William L. *Documents relating to Indian Affairs*. Columbia: University of South Carolina Press, 1982.

McIlwaine, Henry R., ed. *Journals of the House of Burgesses of Virginia, 1702/03-1705, 1705–06, 1710–1712*. Vol. 4, Richmond, 1912.

——. *Minutes of the Council and General Court of Colonial Virginia, 1622–1632, 1670–1676*. Richmond, 1924.

——. *Executive Journals of the Council of Colonial Virginia, June 11, 1680–June 22, 1699*. Richmond: Davis Bottom, 1925.

McKaye, James. *The Mastership and Its Fruits: The Emancipated Slave Face to Face with His Old Master. A Supplemental Report to Hon. Edwin M. Stanton, Secretary of War*. New York: W. C. Bryant & Co., 1864.

McRae, Sherwin, ed. *Calendar of Virginia State Papers and Other Manuscripts, August 11, 1792 to December 31, 1793*. Richmond: A. B. Micou, Superintendant of Public Printing, 1886.

Meaders, Daniel. *Advertisements for Runaway Slaves in Virginia, 1801–1820*. New York, Garland Publishing, 1997.

Merrens, H. Roy, ed. *The Colonial South Carolina Scene: Contemporary Views, 1697–1774*. Columbia: University of South Carolina Press, 1977.

Milligen-Johnson, Dr. George. *A Short Description of the Province of South Carolina*. In B. R. Carroll, ed., *Historical Collections of South Carolina*. New York: Harper and Brothers, 1836.

Mirot, Sylvie. "Un document inédit sur le marronage à la Guyane française au XVIIIe siècle." *Revue d'histoire des colonies* 41 (1954): 245–256.

Mobley, Joe A., ed. *The Way We Lived in North Carolina*. Chapel Hill: University of North Carolina Press, 2003.

Morgan, David T., ed. *John Gray Blount Papers*. Raleigh: North Carolina Department of Cultural Resources, 1982.

Mullin, Michael, ed. *American Negro Slavery: A Documentary History*. Columbia: University of South Carolina Press, 1976.

North Carolina General Assembly. *Laws of North Carolina 1846–1847*. Raleigh: Thomas J. Lemay, 1848.

Northup, Solomon. *Twelve Years a Slave: Narrative of Solomon Northup*. Auburn, N.Y.: Derby and Miller, 1853.

O'Callaghan, E. B. ed., *Documents Relative to the Colonial History of the State of New York, Procured in Holland, England, and France*. Albany, N.Y.: Weed, Parsons, and Co., 1855.

Ogden, A. N., reporter. *Reports of Cases Argued and Determined in the Supreme Court of Louisiana*, XII. New Orleans, 1858.

Olmsted, Frederick Law. *A Journey in the Back Country*. New York: Mason Brothers, 1860.

Paine, Lewis W. *Narrative of Lewis W. Paine*. Boston: Bela Marsh, Publisher, 1852.

Parker, Allen. *Recollections of Slavery Times*. Worcester, Mass.: Chas. W. Burbank & Co., 1895.

Parker, Freddie L. *Running for Freedom: Slave Runaways in North Carolina 1775–1840*. New York: Garland Publishing, 1993.

————. ed. *Stealing a Little Freedom: Advertisements for Slave Runaways in North Carolina, 1791–1840*. New York: Garland Publishing, 1994.

Parker, Mattie Erma Edwards, ed. *North Carolina Higher-Court Records, 1697–1701*. Raleigh: State Department of Archives and History, 1971.

Parker, William B., ed. *Letters and Addresses of Thomas Jefferson*. New York: Unit Book Publishing Co., 1905.

Pennington, James W. C. *A Narrative of Events in the Life of J. H. Banks, an Escaped Slave from the Cotton State, Alabama, in America*. Liverpool: M. Rourke, 1861.

Perdue, Charles L., Jr., and Thomas E. Barden, eds. *Weevils in the Wheat: Interviews with Virginia Ex-Slaves*. Charlottesville: University of Virginia Press, 1976.

Phillips, Ulrich B., ed. *Plantation and Frontier Documents, 1649–1863*. Cleveland: Arthur H. Clark Co., 1909.

Pickard, Kate E. R. *The Kidnapped and the Ransomed*. Syracuse: William T. Hamilton, 1856.

Rawick, George P., ed. *The American Slave: A Composite Autobiography*. Westport, Conn.: Greenwood Pub. Co.,1972. 19 volumes.

————. *The American Slave*, Supplement, Series 1. Westport, Conn.: Greenwood Pub. Co., 1977. 12 volumes.

————. *The American Slave*, Supplement, Series 2. Westport, Conn.: Greenwood Pub. Co., 1979. 10 volumes.

Redpath, James. *The Roving Editor: Or, Talks with Slaves in the Southern States*. New York: A. B. Burdick Publisher, 1859.

Report of the Special Committee of the House of Representatives of South Carolina. Columbia.: Steam Power Press Carolina Times, 1857.

Richardson, James S. G. *Reports of Cases at Law Argued and Determined in the Court of Appeals and Court of Errors of South Carolina*. Charleston: McCarter & Co., 1853.

Robinson, William H. *From Log Cabin to the Pulpit or Fifteen Years in Slavery*. Eau Claire, Wis.: James H. Tifft, 1913.

Rogers, George. *Memoranda of the Experience, Labors, and Travels of a Universalist Preacher*. Cincinnati: John A. Gurley, 1845.

Rose, Willie Lee, ed. *A Documentary History of Slavery in North America*. New York: Oxford University Press, 1976.

Rowland, Dunbar, ed. *Official Letter Books of W. C. C. Claiborne, 1801–1816*. Jackson: State Department of Archives and History, 1917.

Rudd, Dan A., and Theophilus Bond. *From Slavery to Wealth: The Life of Scott Bond*. Madison, Ark.: Journal Printing Company, 1917.

Saunders, William, ed. *The Colonial Records of North Carolina*. Raleigh: P. M. Hale, Printer to the State, 1886.

————. *The State Records of North Carolina, 1775–1776*. Raleigh: J. Daniels, Printer to the State, 1886–1890.

Savannah Unit, Georgia Writers' Project. *Drums and Shadows: Survival Studies among the Georgia Coastal Negroes*. 1940. Reprint: Athens: University of Georgia Press, 1986.

Savannah Writers' Project, *Savannah River Plantations*. Savannah: Georgia Historical Society, 1947.

Schoepf, Johann David. *Travels in the Confederation 1783–1784*. Translated and edited by Alfred J. Morrison. Philadelphia: William Campbell, 1911.

Schweninger, Loren, ed. *The Southern Debate over Slavery: Volume 1: Petitions to Southern Legislatures, 1778–1864*. Urbana: University of Illinois Press, 2001.

Singleton, William Henry. *Recollections of My Slavery Days*. Peekskill, N.Y. : Highland Democrat Co. Print, 1922.

Smith, Billy G., and Richard Wojtowicz, eds. *Blacks Who Stole Themselves: Advertisements for Runaways in the Pennsylvania Gazette, 1728–1790*. Philadelphia: University of Pennsylvania Press, 1989.

Smith, Harry. *Fifty Years of Slavery in the United States of America*. Grand Rapids: West Michigan Printing Co., 1891.

Sparacio, Ruth, and Sam Sparacio, eds. *Order Book Abstracts of Old Rappahannock, 1689–1692*. McLean, Va: Antient Press, 1990.

———. *Order Book Abstracts Middlesex County, 1690–1694*. McLean, Va.: Antient Press, 1994.

Srygley, F. D. *Seventy Years in Dixie: Recollections and Sayings of T. W. Caskey and Others*. Nashville: Gospel Advocate Publishing, 1893.

Steiner, Bernard C., ed. *Archives of Maryland: Proceedings and Acts of the General Assembly of Maryland, July 1727–August 1729*. Baltimore: Maryland Historical Society, 1916.

———. *Archives of Maryland, Proceedings and Acts of the General Assembly, May, 1730–August, 1732*. Baltimore: Maryland Historical Society, 1917.

Stevens, Michael E., ed. *Journals of the House of Representatives 1787–1788*. Columbia: University of South Carolina Press, 1981.

Stewart, Austin. *Twenty-Two Years a Slave and Forty Years a Freeman*. Canandaigua, N.Y.: Published by the Author, 1867.

Stroud, George McDowell. *A Sketch of the Laws Relating to Slavery in the Several States of the United States of America*. Philadelphia: Kinder & Sharpless, 1827.

Stroyer, Jacob. *My Life in the South*. Salem: Salem Observer Book and Job Print, 1885.

Stuart, John Ferdinand Smyth. *A Tour in the United States of America*. London: G. Robinson, J. Robson, and J. Sewel, 1784.

Taylor, John L. *A Revisal of the Laws of the State of North-Carolina: Passed from 1821–1825*. Raleigh: J. Gales & Sons, 1827.

Thomas, Edward J. *Memoirs of a Southerner 1840–1923*. Savannah, Georgia: 1923.

Thompson, Charles. *Biography of a Slave; Being the Experiences of Rev. Charles Thompson*. Dayton: United Brethren Publishing House, 1875.

Walker, Alexander McDonald, ed. *New Hanover County Court Minutes 1738–1769*. Bethesda, Md.: A. M. Walker, 1958.

Warren, Mary Bondurant. *Marriages and Deaths Abstracted from Extant Georgia Newspapers*. Heritage Papers, 1968.

Watson, Henry. *Narrative of Henry Watson, a Fugitive Slave*. Boston: Bella March, 1848.

Watson, Winslow C., ed. *Men and Times of the Revolution or Memoirs of Elkanah Watson*. New York: Dana & Co., 1856.

Webb, William. *The History of William Webb Composed by Himself*. Detroit: Egbert Hoekstra, Printer, 1873.

Weld, Isaac. *Travels through the States of North America*. London: John Stockdale, 1799.

Weld, Theodore. *American Slavery as It Is: Testimony of a Thousand Witnesses*. New York: American Anti-Slavery Society, 1839.

White, George. *Historical Collections of Georgia*. New York: Pudney and Russell, 1855.

Wiley, Calvin Henderson. *Adventures of Old Dan Tucker, and His Son Walter: A Tale of North Carolina*. London: Willoughby & Co., 1851.

Williams, Isaac D. *Sunshine and Shadow of Slave Life: Reminiscences as Told by Isaac D. Williams to "Tege."* East Saginaw, Mich.: Evening News Printing and Binding House, 1885.

Williams, James. *Life and Adventures of James Williams, a Fugitive Slave, with a Full Description of the Underground Railroad.* San Francisco: Women's Union Print, 1873.

Windley, Lathan A. *Runaway Slave Advertisements: A Documentary History from the 1730s to 1790.* 4 volumes. Westport, Conn.: Greenwood Press, 1983.

For runaway notices and newspapers articles, see Notes.

SECONDARY SOURCES

Books

Aptheker, Herbert. *American Negro Slave Revolts.* New York: Columbia University Press, 1943. Reprint: New York: International Publishers, 1970.

Bassett, John Spencer. *Slavery and Servitude in the Colony of North Carolina.* Baltimore: Johns Hopkins University Series in Historical and Political Science, Series 14 (April–May 1896).

Bogger, Tommy. "Maroons and Laborers in the Great Dismal Swamp." In *Readings in Black and White: Lower Tidewater Virginia,* ed. Jane H. Kobelski, 1–8. Portsmouth: Portsmouth Public Library, 1982.

Borick, Carl P. *A Gallant Defense: The Siege of Charleston.* Columbia: University of South Carolina Press, 2003.

Braisted, Todd W. "The Black Pioneers and Others: The Military Role of Black Loyalists in the American War for Independence." In *Moving On: Black Loyalists in the Afro-Atlantic World*, ed. John W. Pulis, 3–38. New York: Garland Publishing, 1999.

Burson, Caroline M. *The Stewardship of Don Esteban Miro 1782–1792; A Study of Louisiana Based Largely on the Documents in New Orleans.* New Orleans: American Printing Company, 1940.

Campbell, T. E. *Colonial Caroline: A History of Caroline County, Virginia.* Richmond: Dietz Press, 1954.

Carney, Judith A. *Black Rice: The African Origins of Rice Cultivation in the Americas.* Cambridge: Harvard University Press, 2001.

Carney, Judith A., and Richard Nicholas Rosomoff. *In the Shadow of Slavery: Africa's Botanical Legacy in the Atlantic World.* Berkeley: University of California Press, 2009.

Cecelski, David S. *The Waterman's Song: Slaves and Freedom in Maritime North Carolina.* Chapel Hill: University of North Carolina Press, 2001.

Corkran, David H. *The Creek Frontier, 1540–1783.* Norman: University of Oklahoma Press, 1967.

Covey, Herbert C. *African American Slave Medicine: Herbal and Non-Herbal Treatments.* Lanham: Lexington Books, 2008.

Covey, Herbert C., and Dwight Eisnach, *What the Slaves Ate: Recollections of African American Foods and Foodways from the Slave Narratives.* Santa Barbara: Greenwood Press, 2009.

Cowan, William Tynes. *The Slave in the Swamp: Disrupting the Plantation Narrative.* New York: Routledge, 2005.

Craton, Michael. *Testing the Chains: Resistance to Slavery in the British West Indies.* Ithaca: Cornell University Press, 2009.

Davis, Harold E. *The Fledgling Province: Social and Cultural Life in Colonial Georgia 1733–1776*. Chapel Hill: University of North Carolina Press, 1976.

Din, Gilbert C. *Spaniards, Planters, and Slaves: The Spanish Regulation of Slavery in Louisiana, 1763–1803*. College Station: Texas A&M University Press, 1999.

Diouf, Sylviane A. *Dreams of Africa in Alabama: The Slave Ship Clotilda and the Story of the Last Africans Brought to America*. New York: Oxford University Press, 2007.

Drewry, William S. *Slave Insurrections (1830–1865)*. Washington, D.C.: Neale Company, 1900.

Dusinberre, William. *Them Dark Days: Slavery in the American Rice Swamps*. New York: Oxford University Press, 1995.

Edelson, S. Max. "The Nature of Slavery: Environmental Disorder and Slave Agency in Colonial South Carolina." In *Cultures and Identities in Colonial British America*, eds. Robert Olwell and Alan Tully, 21–44. Baltimore: Johns Hopkins University Press, 2006.

Edgar, Walter B. *South Carolina: A History*. Columbia: University of South Carolina Press, 1998.

Egerton, Douglas R. *Rebels, Reformers, & Revolutionaries: Collected Essays and Second Thoughts*. New York: Routledge, 2002.

———. *Death or Liberty: African Americans and Revolutionary America*. New York: Oxford University Press, 2009.

Escott, Paul D. *Slavery Remembered: A Record of Twentieth-Century Slave Narratives*. Chapel Hill: University of North Carolina Press, 1979.

Fehrenbacher, Don Edward. *The Slaveholding Republic: An Account of the United States Government's Relations with Slavery*. New York: Oxford University Press, 2002.

Fett, Sharla. *Working Cures: Healing, Health, and Power on Southern Slave Plantations*. Chapel Hill: University of North Carolina Press, 2002.

Foner, Eric. *Nat Turner*. Englewood Cliffs, N.J.: Prentice-Hall, 1971.

Forret, Jeff. *Race Relations at the Margins: Slave and Poor Whites in the Antebellum Southern Countryside*. Baton Rouge: Louisiana University Press, 2006.

Fortier, Alcée. *Louisiana, Comprising Sketches of Parishes*. Madison: Century Historical Association, 1914.

Franklin, John Hope, and Loren Schweninger. *Runaway Slaves: Rebels on the Plantation*. New York: Oxford University Press, 1999.

Fraser, Walter J. *Charleston! Charleston! The History of a Southern City*. Columbia: University of South Carolina Press, 1992.

Frey, Sylvia. *Water from the Rock: Black Resistance in a Revolutionary Age*. Princeton: Princeton University Press, 1991.

Gallay, Allan. *The Indian Slave trade: The Rise of the English Empire in the American South, 1670–1717*. New Haven: Yale University Press, 2002.

Gayarré, Charles. *Histoire de la Louisiane*. Nouvelle-Orléans: Magne & Weisse, 1846.

Genovese, Eugene. *From Rebellion to Revolution: Afro-American Slave Revolts in the Making of the Modern World*. Baton Rouge: Louisiana State University Press, 1979.

Giltner, Scott. "Slave Hunting and Fishing in the Antebellum South." In *"To Love the Wind and the Rain": African Americans and Environmental History*, eds. Dianne D. Glave and Markl Stoll, 21–35. Pittsburgh: University of Pittsburgh Press, 2006.

Greene, Evarts B. and Virginia D. Harrington. *American Population before the Federal Census of 1790*. New York: Columbia University Press, 1932.

Griffin, William A. *Ante-Bellum Elizabeth City: The History of a Canal Town.* Elizabeth City: Roanoke Press, 1970.

Hadden, Sally E. *Slave Patrols: Law and Violence in Virginia and the Carolinas.* Cambridge: Harvard University Press, 2001.

Hale, Will T. *History of DeKalb County Tennessee.* Nashville: Paul Hunter Publisher, 1915.

Hall, Gwendolyn Middlo. *Africans in Colonial Louisiana: The Development of Afro-Creole Culture in the Eighteenth Century.* Baton Rouge: Louisiana State University Press, 1992.

Hall, Leslie. *Land and Allegiance in Revolutionary Georgia.* Athens: University of Georgia Press, 2001.

Higginbotham, A. Leon, Jr., *In the Matter of Color: Race and the American Legal Process: The Colonial Period.* New York: Oxford University Press, 1978.

Hinks, Peter P. *To Awaken My Afflicted Brethren: David Walker and the Problem of Antebellum Slave Resistance.* University Park: Pennsylvania State University Press, 1997.

Hobsbawm, Eric. *Primitive Rebels: Studies in Archaic Forms of Social Movements in the 19th and 20th Centuries.* Manchester: Manchester University Press, 1959.

———. *Bandits.* London: Weidenfeld & Nicolson, 2000.

Holland, Edwin C. *Refutation of Calumnies against the Southern and Western States.* Charleston: A. M. Miller, 1822.

Hoogbergen, Wim. *The Boni Maroon Wars in Suriname.* New York: Brill, 1990.

———. *Out of Slavery: A Surinamese Roots History.* Berlin: Lit Verlag, 2008.

Hough, Franklin Benjamin, ed. *The Siege of Savannah: By the Combined American and French Forces under the Command of Gen. Lincoln and Count d'Estaing in the Autumn of 1779.* Albany: J. Munsell, 1866.

Howard, John Hamilton. *In the Shadow of the Pines: A Tale of Tidewater Virginia.* New York: Eaton & Mains, 1906.

Hudson, Charles M. *The Catawba Nation.* Athens: University of Georgia Press, 2007.

Isaac, Rhys. *The Transformation of Virginia, 1740–1790.* Chapel Hill: University of North Carolina Press, 1982.

———. *Landon Carter's Uneasy Kingdom: Revolution and Rebellion on a Virginia Plantation.* New York: Oxford University Press, 2004.

Jones, Charles Colcock. *The History of Georgia.* Boston: Houghton, Mifflin and Co., 1883.

Johnson, Guion Griffis. *A Social History of the Sea Islands with Special Reference to St. Helena Island, South Carolina.* Chapel Hill: University of North Carolina Press, 1930.

Johnson, Roy F. *Tales from Old Carolina: Traditional and Historical Sketches of the Area between and about the Chowan River and Great Dismal Swamps.* Murfreesboro, N.C.: Johnson Pub. Co., 1965.

———. *The Nat Turner Slave Insurrection.* Murfreesboro, N.C.: Johnson Publishing Co., 1966.

Johnston, James Hugo. *Race Relations in Virginia & Miscegenation in the South 1776–1860.* Amherst: University of Massachusetts Press, 1970.

Joyner, Charles. *Down by the Riverside: A South Carolina Slave Community.* Urbana: University of Illinois Press, 1984.

Kay, Marvin L. Michael, and Lorin Lee Cary. *Slavery in North Carolina 1748–1775.* Chapel Hill: University of North Carolina Press, 1995.

Kerr, Derek N. *Petty Felony, Slave Defiance, and Frontier Villainy: Crime and Criminal Justice in Spanish Louisiana, 1770–1803.* New York: Garland Publishing, 1993.

Kirby, Jack Temple. *Poquosin: A Study of Rural Landscape and Society.* Chapel Hill: University of North Carolina Press, 1995.

Klein, Rachel N. *Unification of a Slave State: The Rise of the Planter Class in the South Carolina Backcountry, 1760–1808*. Chapel Hill: University of North Carolina Press, 1990.

Kulikoff, Allan. *Tobacco and Slaves: The Development of Southern Cultures in the Chesapeake, 1680–1800*. Chapel Hill: University of North Carolina Press, 1986.

Lamplugh, George R. *Politics on the Periphery: Factions and Parties in Georgia, 1783–1806*. Newark: University of Delaware Press, 1986.

Landers, Jane. *Atlantic Creoles in the Age of Revolutions*. Cambridge: Harvard University Press, 2010.

La Rosa Corzo, Gabino. *Runaway Slave Settlements in Cuba: Resistance and Repression*. Chapel Hill: University of North Carolina Press, 2003.

Littlefield, Daniel C. *Rice and Slaves: Ethnicity and the Slave Trade in Colonial South Carolina*. Urbana: University of Illinois Press, 1991.

Megginson, W. J. *African American Life in South Carolina's Upper Piedmont 1780–1900*. Columbia: University of South Carolina Press, 2006.

Miggliazzo, Arlin C. *To Make This Land Our Own: Community, Identity, and Cultural Adaptation in Purrysburg Township, South Carolina, 1732–1865*. Columbia: University of South Carolina Press, 2007.

Morgan, Philip D. "Colonial South Carolina Runaways: Their Significance for Slave Culture." In *Out of the House of Bondage: Runaways, Resistance and Marronage in Africa and the New World*, ed. Gad Heuman, 57–78. London: Frank Cass, 1986.

———. "Slave Life in Piedmont Virginia, 1720–1800." In *Colonial Chesapeake Society*, eds. Lois G. Carr, Philip D. Morgan, and Jean B. Russo, 433–484. Chapel Hill: University of North Carolina Press, 1988.

———. *Slave Counterpoint: Black Culture in the Eighteenth-Century Chesapeake and Lowcountry*. Chapel Hill: University of North Carolina Press, 1998.

———. "Lowcountry Georgia and the Early Modern Atlantic World, 1733–ca. 1820." In P. Morgan, ed., *African American Life in the Georgia Lowcountry: The Atlantic World and the Gullah Geechee*. Athens: University of Georgia Press, 2010.

Mullin, Gerald W. *Flight and Rebellion: Slave Resistance in Eighteenth-Century Virginia*. New York: Oxford University Press, 1972.

Mullin, Michael. *Africa in America: Slave Acculturation and Resistance in the American South and the British Caribbean, 1736–1831*. Urbana: University of Illinois Press, 1992.

Nelson, Megan Kate. *Trembling Earth: A Cultural History of the Okefenokee Swamp*. Athens: University of Georgia Press, 2005.

Nieves, Angel David and Leslie M. Alexander, eds. *"We Shall Independent Be": African American Place Making and the Struggle to Claim Space in the United States*. Boulder: University Press of Colorado, 2008.

Olwell, Robert. *Masters, Slaves, & Subjects: The Culture of Power in the South Carolina Low Country, 1740–1790*. Ithaca: Cornell University Press, 1998.

Owens, Leslie H. *This Species of Property*. New York: Oxford University Press, 1976.

Penningroth, Dylan C. *The Claims of Kinfolk: African American Property and Community in the Nineteenth-Century South*. Chapel Hill: University of North Carolina Press, 2003.

Phillips, Ulrich Bonnell. "Racial Problems, Adjustments and Disturbances." In *The South in the Building of the Nation*, eds. Julian Alvin, Carroll Chandler et al., 4: 194–241. Richmond: Southern Historical Publication Society, 1909.

———. *American Negro Slavery; A Survey of the Supply, Employment and Control of Negro Labor as Determined by the Plantation Regime*. New York: D. Appleton and Company, 1918. Reprint: Baton Rouge: Louisiana State University Press, 1969.

Pickett, Albert James. *History of Alabama, and Incidentally of Georgia and Mississippi from the Earliest Period*. Charleston: Walker & James, 1851.

Piecuch, Jim. *Three Peoples One King: Loyalists, Indians, and Slaves in the Revolutionary South, 1775–1782*. Columbia: University of South Carolina Press, 2008.

Power, Major Steve. *The Memento of Old Natchez, 1700–1897*. Natchez: S. Power, 1897.

Reiss, Oscar. *Blacks in Colonial America*. Jefferson, N.C.: McFarland & Company, 1997.

Rosengarten, Theodore, ed. *Tombee Portrait of a Cotton Planter*. New York: Quill William Morrow, 1986.

Rowland, Lawrence S., George C. Rogers, and Alexander Moore. *The History of Beaufort County, South Carolina 1514–1861*. Columbia: University of South Carolina Press, 1996.

Rutman, Darrett B., and Anita H. Rutman. *A Place in Time: Middlesex County, Virginia, 1650–1750*. New York: W. W. Norton & Co., 1984.

Savannah Writers' Project, Mary Granger, ed., *Savannah River Plantations*. Savannah: Georgia Historical Society, 1947.

Savitt, Todd L. *Medicine and Slavery: The Diseases and Health Care of Blacks in Antebellum Virginia*. Urbana: University of Illinois Press, 1978.

Schwarz, Philip J. *Twice Condemned: Slaves and the Criminal Laws of Virginia, 1705–1865*. Baton Rouge: Louisiana State University Press, 1998.

Sidbury, James. *Ploughshares into Swords: Race, Rebellion, and Identity in Gabriel's Virginia, 1730–1810*. New York: Cambridge University Press, 1997.

Siebert, Wilbur Henry. *History of the Loyalists in East Florida 1774 to 1785 during the American Revolution When Florida Was Part of the English Colony*. Deland, Fla.: Florida State Historical Society, 1929.

Smith Miles, Suzannah. *East Cooper Gazetteer: History of Mount Pleasant, Sullivan's Island and Isle of Palms*. Charleston: History Press, 2005.

Steckel, Richard H. "Women, Work, and Health under Plantation Slavery in the United States." In *More than Chattel: Black Women and Slavery in the Americas,* eds. David Barry Gaspar and Darlene Clark Hine, 43–60. Bloomington : Indiana University Press, 1996.

Stewart, Mart A. *"What Nature Suffers to Groe": Life, Labor, and Landscape on the Georgia Coast, 1680–1920*. Athens: University of Georgia Press, 1996.

———. "Slavery and the Origins of African American Environmentalism." In *"To Love the Wind and the Rain": African Americans and Environmental History*, eds. Dianne D. Glave and Markl Stoll, 9–20. Pittsburgh: University of Pittsburgh Press, 2006.

Taylor, Joe Gray. *Slavery in Louisiana*. Louisiana Historical Association, 1963.

Taylor, Orville W. *Negro Slavery in Arkansas*. Durham: Duke University Press, 1958.

Thompson, Alvin O. *Flight to Freedom: African Runaways and Maroons in the Americas*. Kingston: University of the West Indies Press, 2006.

Turner, Joseph Kelly. *History of Edgecombe County, North Carolina*. Raleigh: Edwards & Broughton, 1920.

Upton, Dell. "White and Black Landscapes in Eighteenth-Century Virginia." In *Material Life in America, 1600–1860*, ed. Robert Blair St. George, 357–369. Boston: Northeastern University Press, 1988.

Usner, Daniel H., Jr., *Indians, Settlers, & Slaves in a Frontier Exchange Economy: The Lower Mississippi Valley before 1783*. Chapel Hill: University of North Carolina Press, 1992.

Vernon, Amelia Wallace. *African Americans at Mars Bluff, South Carolina*. Baton Rouge: Louisiana State University Press, 1993.

Vlach, John Michael. *By the Work of Their Hands: Studies in Afro-American Folklife*. Charlottesville: University Press of Virginia, 1991.

———. *Back of the Big House*: *The Architecture of Plantation Slavery*. Chapel Hill: University of North Carolina Press, 1993.

Walsh, Lorena S. *From Calabar to Carter's Grove: The History of a Virginia Slave Community*. Charlottesville: University Press of Virginia, 1997.

Windley, Lathan A. *A Profile of Runaway Slaves in Virginia and South Carolina from 1730 to 1790*. New York: Garland Publishing, 1995.

Wood, Betty. *Slavery in Colonial Georgia 1730–1775*. Athens: University of Georgia Press, 1984.

Wood, Peter H. *Black Majority: Negroes in Colonial South Carolina from 1670 through the Stono Rebellion*. New York: Alfred A. Knopf, 1974.

———. *Strange New Land: Africans in Colonial America, 1526–1776*. New York: Oxford University Press, 2003.

Workers of the Writers' Program of the Works Projects Administration in the State of Virginia. *The Negro in Virginia*. New York: Hastings House, 1940.

Young, Jeffrey Robert. *Domesticating Slavery: The Master Class in Georgia and South Carolina, 1670–1837*. Chapel Hill: University of North Carolina Press, 1999.

Articles

Anderson, Robert Nelson. "The Quilombo of Palmares: A New Overview of a Maroon State in Seventeenth-Century Brazil." *Journal of Latin American Studies* 28, 3 (October 1996): 545–566.

Aptheker, Herbert. "Maroons within the Present Limits of the United States." *Journal of Negro History* 24, 2 (April 1939): 167–184.

———. "Additional Data on American Maroons." *Journal of Negro History* 32, 4 (October 1947): 452–460.

Blackburn, Marion. "American Refugees." *Archeology* (September/October 2011): 49–58.

Debien, Gabriel. "Le marronage aux Antilles francaises au XVIIIe siècle." *Caribbean Studies* 6, 3 (October 1966): 3–43.

Din, Gilbert C. "'Cimarrones' and the San Malo Band in Spanish Louisiana." *Louisiana History* 21, 3 (Summer 1980): 237–262.

Dodge, David. "The Cave-Dwellers of the Confederacy." *Atlantic Monthly* 68, 1408 (October 1891): 514–521.

Faust, Drew Gilpin. "Culture, Conflict, and Community: The Meaning of Power on an Ante-Bellum Plantation." *Journal of Social History* 14, 1 (Autumn 1980): 83–97.

Forret, Jeff. "Slaves, Poor Whites, and the Underground Economy of the Rural Carolinas." *Journal of Southern History* 70, 4 (November 2004): 783–824.

Higginson, Thomas W. "Nat Turner's Insurrection." *Atlantic Monthly* (August 1861): 173–187.

Ingersoll, Thomas N. "The Slave Trade and the Ethnic Diversity of Louisiana's Slave Community." *Louisiana History* 37, 2 (Spring 1996): 133–161.

Jameson, John F., ed. "Autobiography of Omar ibn Said, Slave in North Carolina, 1831." *American Historical Review* 30, 4 (July 1925): 787–795.

Johnson, Michael P. "Runaway Slaves and the Slave Communities in South Carolina, 1799 to 1830." *William and Mary Quarterly* 38, 3 (July 1981): 418–441.

Lambert, Robert S. "The Confiscation of Loyalist Property in Georgia, 1782–1786." *William and Mary Quarterly*, 3rd Series, 20, 1 (January 1963): 80–94.

Lichtenstein, Alex. "'That Disposition to Theft, with which They Have Been Branded': Moral Economy, Slave Management, and the Law." *Journal of Social History* 21, 3 (Spring 1988): 413–440.

McLaren, G. "The Virginia Clergy." *Virginia Magazine of History and Biography* 32, 4 (October 1924): 321–337.

McLean, Robert C., ed. "A Yankee Tutor in the Old South." *North Carolina Historical Review* 48, 1 (January 1970): 51–85.

Morris, Charles E. "Panic and Reprisal: Reaction in North Carolina to the Nat Turner Insurrection, 1831." *North Carolina Historical Review* 72, 1 (January 1985): 29–52.

Norton, Holly K., and Christopher T. Espenshade. "The Challenge in Locating Maroon Refuge Sites at Maroon Ridge, St. Croix." *Journal of Caribbean Archeology* 7 (2007): 1–16.

Orser, Charles E., Jr., and Pedro P. Funari. "Archeology and Slave Resistance and Rebellion." *World Archeology* 33, 1 (June 2001): 61–72.

Palmer, Vernon V. "The Customs of Slavery." *American Journal of Legal History* 48, 2 (April 2006): 177–218.

Price, Richard. "Subsistence on the Plantation Periphery: Crops, Cooking, and Labour among Eighteenth-Century Suriname Maroons." *Slavery and Abolition* 12, 1 (May 1991): 107–127.

Savannah Unit, Georgia Writers' Project, Works Projects Administration in Georgia, "Drakies Plantation." *Georgia Historical Quarterly* 24 (1940): 207–235.

Sayers, Daniel O. "Landscapes of Alienation: An Archaeological Report of Excursions in the Great Dismal Swamp." *Transforming Anthropology* 15, 2 (2007): 149–157.

Schweninger, Loren. "Slave Independence and Enterprise in South Carolina, 1780–1865." *South Carolina Historical Magazine* 93, 2 (April 1992): 101–125.

Seal, Graham. "The Robin Hood Principle: Folklore, History, and the Social Bandit." *Journal of Folklore Research* 46, 1 (January–April 2009): 67–89.

Sirmans, M. Eugene. "The South Carolina Royal Council, 1720–1763." *William and Mary Quarterly*, 3rd Series, 18, 3 (July 1961): 373–392.

Smith, Henry A. M. "The Town of Dorchester, in South Carolina—A Sketch of Its History." *South Carolina Historical and Genealogical Magazine* 6, 2 (April 1905): 62–95.

———. "The Ashley River: Its Seats and Settlements." *South Carolina Historical and Genealogical Magazine* 20, 1 (January 1919): 1–51.

Stribling, Col. J. C. "'Goober Jack,' The Runaway Slave." *Pendleton Farmer's Society* (Atlanta: Foote & Davies Co., 1908): 90–97.

Taylor, R. H. "Slave Conspiracies in North Carolina." *North Carolina Historical Review* 5, 1–4 (January–October 1928): 20–34.

Troxler, Carole Watterson. "Loyalist Refugees and the British Evacuation of East Florida, 1783–1785." *Florida Historical Quarterly* 60 (1981): 1–28.

Usner, Daniel H., Jr. "The Frontier Exchange Economy of the Lower Mississippi Valley in the Eighteenth Century." *William and Mary Quarterly*, 3rd Series, 44, 2 (April 1987): 166–192.

Wax, Darold D. "Preferences for Slaves in Colonial America." *Journal of Negro History* 58, 4 (October 1973): 371–401.

Wiecek, William M. "The Statutory Law of Slavery and Race in the Thirteen Mainland Colonies of British America." *William and Mary Quarterly*, 3rd Series, 34, 2 (April 1977): 258–280.

Woodward, C. Vann. "History from Slave Sources." *American Historical Review* 79, 2 (April 1974): 470–481.

Dissertations

Kaiser, John James. "Masters Determined to Be Masters": The 1821 Insurrectionary Scare in Eastern North Carolina." Master's thesis, North Carolina State University, 2006.

Martin, Jacqueline A. "The Maroons of the Great Dismal Swamp, 1607–1865." Master's thesis, Western Washington University, 2004.

Sayers, Daniel O. "The Diasporic World of the Great Dismal Swamp, 1630–1860." Ph.D. dissertation, College of William and Mary, 2008.

INDEX

ABOUT THE AUTHOR

Sylviane A. Diouf is an award-winning historian who specializes in the history of the African Diaspora. She is the author of *Dreams of Africa in Alabama: The Slave Ship Clotilda and the Story of the Last Africans Brought to America* (2007) and *Servants of Allah: African Muslims Enslaved in the Americas* (NYU Press, 1998 and 2013); the editor of *In Motion: The African American Migration Experience* (2005) and *Fighting the Slave Trade: West African Strategies* (2003). Diouf—a curator at the Schomburg Center for Research in Black Culture of The New York Public Library—is a recipient of the Dr. Betty Shabazz Achievement Award, the Imam Warith Deen Mohammed Award, the Pen and Brush Achievement Award, and the Rosa Parks Award.